TOM CRUISE
– UNAUTHORISED

Wensley Clarkson

TOM CRUISE
– UNAUTHORISED

BLAKE

Published by Blake Publishing Ltd,
98-100 Great North Road, London N2 0NL, England.

First published in Great Britain in 1994

ISBN 1 85782 086 X

British Library Cataloguing-in-Publication Data:
A catalogue record for this book is available
from the British Library.

Typeset by Pearl Graphics, Hemel Hempstead

Printed in Finland by WSOY

3 5 7 9 10 8 6 4 2

To Toby, Polly, Rosie and Fergus

Notes of Gratitude

The idea of using a leaden, dispassionate word like 'acknowledgements' for this section cannot begin to express the depth of my feelings for the many individuals who have made this book possible. I owe them my deepest and most heartfelt gratitude.

First to my publisher John Blake, without whom this book would never have happened. His support and guidance have been very much appreciated.

Then there are: Mark Sandelson, Shaun Redmayne, Father Aldric Heidlage, Caroline Mapother, Father Hilarian Kistner, Roger Fristoe, Julie Borders, Jeff Bayers, Anthony Clarkson, Bill Ellison, Warder Harrison, Bill Schwatz, Kale Browne, Mario Marcelino, Graham Berry, Henry Darrow, Andre Tabayoyon, John Stockwell, Mrs John Shiels, Mrs William Vesterman, Angelo Corbo, John Voskian, Jonathan Margolis, Anthony Bowman, Louise Frogley, Joe Poalella, Peter Wilson, John Bell, Martin Dunn, John Glatt, Bill

Lewis, Sadie Mayne, Rosie Ries and every other person who agreed to be interviewed for this book, although a number of them requested that I do not reveal their identities either in the text or on this page. My eternal thanks to the reference libraries at Globe, Mirror Group Newspapers, Associated Newspapers, News International, The News in New York and the Academy of Motion Pictures in Los Angeles.

In addition, *Top Gun – The Films of Tom Cruise* by Edward Gross (Pioneer Books Inc., 1990) and *Tom Cruise* by Joelene M. Anthony (St Martin's Press, 1988) provided some invaluable information about Tom Cruise and I am extremely grateful to them. Other books that have been helpful include: *Coppola* by Peter Cowle, *Totally Uninhibited* by Lawrence J. Quirk, *Martin Scorsese: A Journey, Levinson on Levinson* and *Fade Out* by Peter Bart, *Paul Newman* by Elena Oumano, *Scorsese on Scorsese* and *Paul and Joanne* by Joe Morella and Edward Z. Epstein.

However, my biggest debt of gratitude must go to Dr Dillon Mapother who agreed to help me with invaluable background material on Tom Cruise's family history.

WENSLEY CLARKSON

*'A true believer and a half ... a guy with a
halo turned on at all times.'*
Tom Wolfe, describing John Glenn in *The Right Stuff*

*'Life itself is a very humbling experience.
So that keeps you honest.'*
Tom Cruise

*'Art is not a handicraft, it is the transmission
of feeling the artist has accumulated.'*
Leo Tolstoy

*'You gotta have a dream,
If you don't have a dream,
How you gonna have a
Dream come true?'*
Rodgers and Hammerstein

Prologue

He's bigger than Jack, bigger than Pacino, bigger even than Arnold or Kevin. Tom Cruise is the most successful movie star in the world. His last two films garnered an international gross of close to half a billion dollars. In fact, although some of Tom's movies could be termed disappointments, it would be a stretch to call any failures. The closest was the Irish epic, *Far and Away* – and that raked in more than $100 million worldwide.

For years, the public has seen Tom as a fresh-faced wonder boy, the all-American quarterback. 'The guy all women want to date and who doesn't threaten any guy,' says one Hollywood producer who has worked with Tom.

Like Schwarzenegger, Tom has been careful to maintain a public image of the quintessential innocent, the good-looking guy who's just enjoying the ride of a lifetime. And, as with Schwarzenegger, any hints of a deeper, more fearfully controlling ego have been blamed on overzealous publicists.

WENSLEY CLARKSON

Experience is the name everyone gives to their mistakes but in Tom Cruise's case there have been few errors in his entire career. Although the Hollywood producer who has just signed up last-year's has-been may tell you otherwise, there is only a handful of genuinely bankable box-office stars – names who can 'open' a film regardless of its quality.

That list tends to change virtually every year, but Tom Cruise's name is always present. Ever since his first surprise hit, this actor has guaranteed that he can eliminate all risks at the box office, just so long as you can afford fees that tend to start at around the $15–20 million mark.

Tom Cruise is the only person from his generation of actors who is equipped to step into the shoes of Gary Cooper, James Stewart, Tyrone Power and Clark Gable. Already considered a great movie star in the United States, Tom is the great American hero to the rest of the world. People stop him in the street to tell him how proud they are of him and he has been credited with the revival of true, old-style, movie-star ideals.

Usually, prologues stick to a very traditional format but in this case I am going to present this introduction to Tom Cruise in a way I think he would appreciate, by providing a highly focused, point-by-point guide to what lies behind the phenomenal success of an actor whose films have grossed a figure approaching $2 billion worldwide, an astounding achievement in a time when more and more people are staying away from the movies.

Family background
Tom's difficult childhood has provided him with inner strength and the will to succeed – qualities that a person from a happier home might never have been capable of matching.

The theme of fathers and sons appears regularly in Tom's movies and, indeed, the issue of manhood is a common thread. Tom's father was not around much and he grew up having to prove something on his own. It proved to be a kind of catalyst. It drove him further into new areas of life experience. He was constantly proving to himself that he could do it.

Workaholic tendencies

The one through-line in Tom's films is the way he fixates on his work. It's reminiscent of Robert De Niro, only without the tics. He doesn't just get into character, he plunges right into the shaping of the entire project.

Everyone who has ever worked with Tom concedes that he is completely and utterly work orientated. After completing *Rain Man*, his equally perfectionist co-star Dustin Hoffman proclaimed: 'He's a demon. He gets up early, he works out, he goes home early, he studies, he watches his diet like he's an old fart, he doesn't drink and he always wanted to rehearse. It affected me emotionally being in his presence during that time.'

Tom is obsessed by preliminary research. He's flown jets, mixed drinks, used a wheelchair, shot pool and raced cars, all in pursuit of the perfect performance.

Tom's co-star in *A Few Good Men*, Kevin Pollack, enthused: 'He has a work ethic the like of which I've never seen. I can't believe I'm saying this, but this guy really works for his $15 million.'

The winning formula

Somehow, Tom has found a diverse series of winning formulae that have stretched across all 15 movies he has made to date. Let's break them down for a moment: in three movies he plays a young man haunted by the shadow of his deceased father (no doubt enhanced by his own painful real-life experiences). In another four hit roles he plays a soldier. Then, in two films, he is a Harvard-educated lawyer. In five movies he even lip-synchs to golden oldies. In another five roles he has affairs with older women (again, his real-life first marriage was to a lady some years his senior). In two roles he plays a nerdy type who romances wealthy socialites. In two other parts he spends much of his time on a motorcyle. In virtually all of his movies to date, he wears Ray-Bans. Then there are five films' worth of the classic, cocky young Tom being put on an even keel by a mentor.

Sometimes one has to wonder if Tom, at just 32, is in danger of becoming too serious for his own good. The idea first surfaced when watching his 1987 blockbuster *The Color of Money*. There were 22 different kinds of grin, each a magical money-in-the-bank moment, suggesting that the actor knows precisely where his biggest strengths lie.

Undoubtably, Tom is sometimes very reluctant to break the mould. He rejected the lead in *Edward Scissorhands* (too weird?), the title role in *Bright Lights, Big City* (too much drug taking), *Rush* (similar reasons) and *Backdraft* (presumably because there were so many other stars in that film).

Tom's decision to take on the highly controversial and definitely androgynous role of the vampire Lestat in Neil Jordon's just released *Interview with the Vampire* is very brave indeed. Many Hollywood observers believe that this is yet another example of Tom's near obsession with not being predictable even though the author of the book upon which the film is based was outraged by the casting of so-called squeaky-clean Tom in the main role.

No one really knows what makes a movie work. The whole enterprise is make believe; a triumph of fantasy over fact. It's what makes the job exciting. A film out of nowhere, with a nobody star, can send people out happy – and make movie producers very rich men.

In Hollywood 50 years ago, the ceiling was lower and the floor more secure than in today's boom-or-bust industry, where there is no safety net – no majority of compulsive moviegoers – to catch the weaker films. Every star, every studio, stands like a colossus on a fault line. If a star like Tom Cruise wants $15 million a picture, he'll get it – and he'll earn it.

Cruise control on the set

Tom denies that he is a control freak, but there is a lot of evidence that points towards this being the case. His over-focused ideals of what each role actually represents often turn him into an incredible perfectionist.

Even on the set of *Born on the Fourth of July*, he regularly bugged megapowerful director Oliver Stone about shots he felt were not quite right and scenes that did not, in Tom's opinion, work properly. Tom, then 27, was never shy about exerting his Hollywood clout if it was required.

Later, on *Far and Away*, crew members were warned not to speak to Tom as it might affect his concentration. While on his biggest hit of all – *Top Gun* – he made the movie's scriptwriter go back and redraft the screenplay at least 50 times before agreeing to the role.

Years earlier, when Tom complained bitterly about Rebecca DeMornay, his co-star in *Risky Business*, he was told he would have to fire her himself. The star, then just 21, had a passionate affair with her instead!

Religion

When Tom was a 14 year old, he seriously considered becoming a priest and it became clear in later years that he desperately needed a church to attach himself to as a kind of security blanket after all the lonely years of his childhood.

That seems to be how he became involved in the highly controversial Church of Scientology.

Along with a handful of other Hollywood stars, Tom has probably spent hundreds of thousands of dollars on training courses inside the church, invented by an eccentric one-time philanthropist. He often spends days at the church's basecamp in the middle of the Californian desert.

For years, Tom would not admit he was a Scientologist until confronted about it during a US television interview. The actor later influenced some film-makers he worked with to use a sound system invented by the Scientologists.

Hollywood observers believe that Tom's association with Scientology has helped him to maintain his highly focused work ethic and greatly assisted him in dealing with stardom.

Others find it more difficult to accept. The fact that members of the church apparently believe in inter-galactic travel, reincarnation and the possiblity of a more fulfilled existence through mind control probably isn't a big deal. Who in California doesn't? Yet some reports have suggested that members of the church can also end up deprived of their free will.

When I began making inquiries into the dealings of the church and Tom's links with it, a flurry of legal threats were made to me personally as well as to a number of associates who have helped me with my research into Tom's member-ship of the Scientologists. At one stage, the church traced my home address and unlisted phone number. There was an overriding impression in the tone of the letters that I should not continue my inquiries under any circumstances.

The entourage

In many ways, Tom lives in his own, carefully structured world. Few people are privy to his personal habits. Much of his social life revolves around his wife Nicole Kidman. There is a splattering of showbiz friends like Sean Penn and Emilio Estevez, but these relationships are not exactly regular. Tom can go for a year without speaking to either but at least a bond of comradeship is apparently retained.

In Hollywood, CAA chief Mike Ovitz and billionaire David Geffen – the two most powerful players in all movie-dom – are very close to Tom and they have probably done more to help guide his career than anyone else.

Corporate Hollywood adores Tom because he is such a finely tuned work-track individual. Some who have met him describe him as having the work ethics of a 50-year-old managing director of a large company. He takes every job deadly seriously and he is surrounded by wall after wall of advisors who try to take many of the minor decisions for him.

It is a strange existence but although Tom sometimes tries to get back into the real world, there is no way that he can lead life like the majority of us. From the high walls and sophisticated alarm systems he has just had installed in his vast Los Angeles mansion to the pairs of bodyguards who tend to shadow his every move, he now has no choice but to grin and bear it.

Restricting the media

Over the years, Tom has evolved into the most powerful actor in Hollywood, thanks partly to his complete control over all information regarding himself. Journalists are regularly asked to sign contracts forbidding the use of his words outside certain areas. Furthermore, Tom virtually never gives interviews that last longer than one hour. 'It is almost as if he is trying to stop anyone from finding out exactly who the real Tom Cruise is,' says one experienced showbusiness journalist.

I first tried to contact Tom in November of 1993 to request his co-operation in the writing of this book. Three faxes were sent to his PR lady Pat Kingsley. There was no response to any of them.

Then, when Tom's representatives discovered I had been contacting people involved in the Church of Scientology, a letter arrived at my publisher's office from Mr Bertram Fields, a renowned Hollywood attorney who recently represented Michael Jackson during the flurry of childsex accusations made against the singer. Mr Fields wrote:

> 'I represent Tom Cruise. I have been advised that you intend to publish a biography of Mr. Cruise. I believe that your book may contain numerous false and defamatory statements about Mr. Cruise. I urge you to check your facts very carefully before publication, since it is certainly Mr. Cruise's intention to institute an appropriate action should your book contain such statements.'

The publishers of this book immediately responded to Mr Field's letter by urging him to ask his client to meet me in order to ensure that every statement in the book was entirely accurate. Neither Mr Fields nor his client agreed to the request.

However, such demands are right in character for Tom, an intensely private person who sculpts his public image as carefully as he does his biceps. For example, almost until the time of their separation in January 1990, Tom insisted that his marriage to Mimi Rogers was perfectly happy.

Tom sometimes fails to turn up at press junkets to promote his latest movies. On one occasion his no-show was accompanied by an ingenuous note, complete with photocopied signature, explaining how sorry Tom was not to be there.

When Tom did some TV interviews for *The Firm*, his list of conditions read like those of a dictator. He refused to let one reporter interview him until he had seen a video tape of that journalist. Just before the release of *Cocktail* in 1988, Tom learned that a particular writer had written something critical of his then wife Mimi Rogers. This writer was barred from the press junket for the movie after Tom allegedly told the film company that he would not talk to any journalist unless the offending writer was disinvited.

Occasionally, Tom has hinted that his mistrust of the press stems from early bad experiences at the hands of journalists, but it must be said that there is no evidence of that in anything I have uncovered. It seems far more likely that he simply does not enjoy the fact that he cannot control the media in the same way he seems to have tamed Hollywood.

The family man image

By all accounts, Tom's first marriage to attractive older woman Mimi Rogers was just a regrettable mistake, although the way he refers to it now, one might get the impression it was just a business deal that went wrong. After their divorce, Mimi Rogers hinted at some elements of marital discord centred around Tom's lack of interest in sex. It was a rare, behind-the-scenes glimpse of the real man as opposed to the screen hero we all know and adore.

Tom's second marriage, to Nicole Kidman, seems to have got that image back on track. The adoption of a baby has completed the perfect family scenario, one that Tom is ever anxious to present to the world.

There seems to be another, highly understandable, motive behind Tom's obsessive quest for family togetherness. He genuinely wants to bring up a family that stays in one piece as opposed to the fragmented version he grew up with.

Now Tom and Nicole are up there with the legendary couples of Hollywood like Gable and Lombard, Tracy and Hepburn. In fact, as a duo they are probably a more powerful force than any other couple in La La Land history.

Extreme generosity

It has to be said that there is another side to Tom Cruise which rarely gets hinted at in public. The sterotypical work driven, 1980s-ultimate, yuppy-style figure has a soft, generous side to him.

Kevin Pollack, his co-star in *A Few Good Men*, tells this story:

> 'One day I was admiring a pen that Tom was using. I mean, this was a gorgeous pen. Tom explained that you could only get it from one place and so on. On my birthday, Tom gave me one of these pens, which came in a beautiful wooden box. I had it on authority that it was a very expensive pen.
>
> 'So, a few days later, Tom sees me using a pen that's not the one that he bought for me. I told him that I was scared to use it because, I dunno, I might lose it or something. Again, a few days later, I am in my trailer and one of Tom's assistants knocks on the door. He has another wooden box with a second pen. He told me that Tom had wanted me to have it.'

Tom did not hesitate to fly the entire cast of *A Few Good Men* to Las Vegas in his private jet for dinner and an evening of gambling. A few years earlier, Tom splashed out $25,000 for his *Top Gun* producer to attend a racing car school with him.

*   *   *

So, with precious little stage experience and no workshop or acting class background, Tom Cruise has, indeed, grabbed Hollywood by the balls. Now he has Tinseltown in a vice-like grip.

The key to Tom Cruise is that he knows exactly how to read situations and people. The adaptability that comes with moving constantly as a child, always being the outsider, and the burning need to rectify the sins of an absentee father have served him well as a performer. He is skilled enough to know how to elicit certain responses; which buttons to push.

Some say he is reminiscent of the young John Glenn from Tom Wolfe's famous account of the packaging of the astronauts, *The Right Stuff*. Always smiling, courteous and ineffably self-confident, Cruise is, as his *Born on the Fourth of July* director Oliver Stone once put it, 'a kid off the Wheaties box'. However, he is also, as Wolfe described Glenn, 'a true believer and a half... a guy with a halo turned on at all times'.

Nicknamed Laserhead, his gaze is all focus – no irony, no sarcasm, no cynicism – total attention. With the help of Scientology, Tom Cruise believes wholeheartedly in the persona he has invented. I hope that this book will demonstrate why.

'It's a morally superior position, people think, this idea of being driven to be the best. Especially in America. The myth is that good people are driven, and bad people are lazy, and mediocre people are just swimming in the middle somewhere. As if it's all a matter of choice.'

Jeanne Marie Laskas

Louisville, a town born in war on the turbulent western frontier of the United States of America, became the ante-bellum 'Gateway to the South' in the 1800s. Its proud inhabitants came from diverse ethnic, cultural and economic backgrounds, carved their city from the rugged Kentucky wilderness and welded it into a dynamic metropolis of driving civic pride and fierce hometown loyalty.

Founder George Rogers Clark had no way of knowing what would mushroom from the tiny enclave he established in the Kentucky countryside in the summer of 1778 when he settled with 150 volunteer soldiers and 20 families on tiny Corn Island, a short distance upstream from the falls of the Ohio River.

The soldiers were seeking a base from which to launch an attack against forts in the British Northwest Territory, which were also suffering increasing Indian attacks along the Kentucky frontier. English, Scottish and Irish families, from the party that had floated down the river in flatboats with Clark, were looking for fresh land where they could make a new beginning.

However, these settlers were not the first white people to reach the non-navigable falls that surrounded that first settlement on Corn Island. Captain Thomas Bullett had surveyed land in the area in 1773; Daniel Boone had stood at the falls two years before that and the dashing French explorer, Rene Robert Cavalier Sieur de LaSalle, searching for what he thought was the Gulf of Mexico, had ported canoes around the rapids in 1669.

Despite these previous visitors, it remained for Clark and his party to establish the first permanent white settlement in 1778. Blockhouses were built on the island, crops were planted and Clark immediately began his campaign against the British forts.

Realising that the island was not suited to be anything more than a temporary stopping point, Clark sent soldiers to the mainland to establish a more defensible fort, which they constructed on the edge of the Ohio River. News of Clark's victories in the northwest rapidly lured settlers to the region the following summer. Three hundred arrived in the spring of 1780 alone and in May that year the Virginia Legislature passed an Act establishing the town of Louisville, named in honour of Louis XVI, King of France, in gratitude for his aid in the revolutionary war.

Soon the town assumed the character of a commercial transhipment point and the portage of cargoes around the rapids was a main activity. Boats filled with goods were unloaded, carted overland and then reloaded for their continued journey up or downstream.

By the mid-1800s, a canal had been constructed around the falls and soon 1,500 steamers and 500 flatboats and keelboats, bearing 300,000 tons of cargo, were entering the canal annually. Louisville's population was edging towards the 30,000 mark and the city's strategic location as a river-rail crossroads gave it a role in America's great push to the west. Railroads connected Louisville with the cotton states to the south, with St Louis to the west, Pittsburgh to the east and the Great Lakes to the north.

The city was bursting with civic pride by 1850, a pride that had been fuelled two years earlier when Zachary Taylor – who had come to Louisville as a baby and lived there for more than 40 years – was elected twelfth President of the United States.

That same year surveyor Dillon Henry Mapother arrived in Louisville from southeast Ireland, seeking a new life away from his famine-ravaged homeland. He was the younger of two sons and believed that there was little future for him in the Emerald Isle. He felt the need to escape and the new, promised land of America seemed the perfect place to head for.

According to family legend, back in Ireland, the name of Mapother had originated when a male child was born to Queen Elizabeth I of England and her lover the Earl of Essex, hundreds of years earlier. The infant was banished to Ireland with a handful of royal servants, among them a woman who brought the child up as her own. That woman's children referred to the infant as 'my brother', which, in Gaelic, sounded like 'mapother', or so the legend goes. Thus Tom Cruise's family name was born.

Within months of arriving in Louisville in 1850, Dillan met, fell in love with and married a lady named Mary Cruise.

The Mapothers became known in Louisville as a caring, happy family. Even the onset of the Civil War, with Louisville being officially established as the port of entry for all Union troops in the west, did not affect their happiness. After the war, the city soon recovered by diversifying the output from its manufacturing plants and the post Civil War period became yet another era of growth for the area. *The Louisville Courier-Journal*'s first edition was published on 8 November 1868. Its headlines that day referred to how race riots in Savannah, Georgia had resulted in 'radical negroes' 1w4,6,9taking control of the polls and driving away white men.

Dillon and Mary had two sons, Dillon E. and and Wible Lawrence, born in 1872. However, tragedy cruelly invaded the Mapother household in the mid-1870s when Dillon Henry was struck down by a severe case of food poisoning and died almost instantly. The family was shocked by this unexpected death. Overnight Mary Cruise Mapother became a single mother trying to survive in a tough, bustling town with virtually no social services to support the recently bereaved. For the first time – but by no means the last – a strong woman was in charge of the Mapother clan. Mary took on part-time jobs and held on to the family's house through pure determination and the will to survive. Her bravery and single-mindedness would be passed down through many future generations.

Then she met and married another Irishman, called O'Mara, and, on 29 December 1876, the couple had a son. For some reason, which has never been clearly explained by the family, that child was christened Thomas Cruise Mapother. It has been a matter of conjecture among many of the Mapothers of Louisville ever since, because some of them do not consider themselves to be directly related to Tom Cruise's side of the family.

Thomas Cruise Mapother's half brother Wible stole much of the family thunder by becoming the youngest ever president of the Louisville and Nashville Railroad. He lived in a lavish mansion in one of Louisville's most sought-after neighbourhoods.

Legendary stories about Wible's determination to

succeed in life provide a fascinating insight into what has driven the Mapothers to success. It is said that, as a gangly 15 year old in Louisville, after scoring a home run during a baseball game, he was asked by one of his admiring team mates: 'What are you going to do tomorrow, Wible?'

'Look for a railroad job.'

'This is a vacation. Why don't you play baseball instead of work?'

'Because I'm going to be a railroad man.'

'Gee, you're only fifteen. How do you know what you're going to be?'

'I've made up my mind. I'm going to be a railroad man, and I'm going to start learning this vacation. I'm going to hunt for some kind of job that'll help.'

'You have it all doped out, haven't you?'

The following day, Wible presented himself at the office of the president of the railroad and wasted no words. 'I want to be an office boy for you.'

'Why?'

'Because I want to learn to be a railroad man,' responded young Wible promptly.

'You know what you want. And you shall be,' replied the president.

The same attitude applied when Tom Cruise made up his mind to be a movie star more than 100 years later...

Wible died of a heart attack at the tragically young age of 54 during a trip to Panama City. His death and funeral were front page news in the *Louisville Courier-Journal* for months and the paper described him as 'one of the greatest rail executives in the United States'. Headlines like 'City poorer by Mapother's Death, says Mayor' were splashed everywhere. However, the most touching reference to his untimely death came in a small article tucked away inside the newspaper, with the headline: 'Elevator man is grieved by loss'.

Summing up the racial divisions that were rife in Kentucky, even in 1926, the piece stated:

> 'Charles Gaines, colored elevator operator at the L and N office building, Ninth and Broadway, is deeply affected by the death of President Wible L. Mapother, for whom he had worked for almost thirty years. Gaines had served on Mr Mapother's private car on frequent trips. "Mr Mapother's death hits me as hard a blow as if he were a member of my family," Gaines said. "We will all miss him."'

Thomas Cruise Mapother was, perhaps not surprisingly, the apple of his mother's eye. After surviving so much heartbreak, she could not help being especially loving to Thomas – after all, he was her youngest child. She showered him with books and gifts all deliberately fashioned towards encouraging him to study hard at school and then college. Thomas reacted well to his mother's encouragement and became one of Louisville's youngest lawyers by the time he had reached his mid-twenties.

Mary Cruise Mapother gracefully accepted Thomas's bride Anna Stewart Batman into her home when they married in 1907 and was delighted to become a grandmother when Anna gave birth to a bouncing baby boy called Paul. Their second child, Thomas Cruise Mapother II, was born a couple of years later in 1908. Caroline Mapother, who still lives in Louisville, was their first cousin by marriage and remembers them well. 'They were a good solid family. Pillars of Louisville society and very loyal and dependable,' she explained.

Thomas Cruise Mapother even became a Jefferson Circuit Court Judge. He was a highly repected member of the Louisville and Kentucky State Bar Associations. A

Republican, he served as judge in the Second Common Pleas Division from 1928 to 1934. Thomas Cruise Mapother I once said that the happiest moment of his life was the occasion when he was presented with a portrait of himself which has hung in Louisville's Second Commons Pleas Court ever since. Cruise was an inveterate walker and a student of Shakespeare as well as being a member of the Knights of Columbus. Most notably, however, he gained a reputation as being something of a loner within the Louisville legal fraternity, as he always worked in practices without a partner. He died unexpectedly of a heart attack in April 1939, as he walked with his son, Thomas Cruise II, and his wife near their home on Lakeside Drive, Louisville. He was 62.

In later life his widow Anna frequently made quilts for the Queen's Daughter annual bizarre in aid of a local orphanage. That was typical of a Mapother wife – always there, always dependable, always solid. She died in the early 1960s.

Thomas Cruise Mapother II had excelled at St Xavier's High School and then went on to St Mary's College, Marion County, followed by the University of Louisville and the Jefferson School of Law. He married Catherine (Tom Cruise's sister Cass is named after her) and became a highly respected Louisville lawyer known as Tom to all his friends and family. He also worked as local campaign chairman for the Republican Party in the city and, in 1951, led the backing of Judge Eugene Siler for Governor of Kentucky after telling prospective voters bluntly: 'If you don't want Harry S. Truman and his political cronies inflicted upon this country for the next four years, vote the Republican ticket on 6 November.'

Tom and his wife had two children, Thomas Cruise Mapother III, Tom Cruise's father, who was born in 1934, followed by his brother William, who was born in 1938.

William continued the family tradition of having at least one lawyer in each generation of Mapothers. He became a judge at the Louisville Juvenile Court at the age of 29 and showed an intriguing level of compassion when dealing with young offenders. One time, William turned to a girl facing criminal charges and told her: 'And you are going to go to school. You are going to have to do something too – not just your parents. You have to help make a happy, stable home. Girls don't run away from happy, stable homes.'

Interestingly, William later became police chief for the Louisville suburb of Windy Hills and was partly responsible for the introduction of radar scanners for the volunteer police force in 1973, after much encouragement from his brother Thomas III. William even became president of a local organisation called Planned Parenthood, an interesting choice considering Tom Cruise's later desperation to have children of his own.

Tom Cruise's father attended the University of Kentucky and excelled at his engineering studies. The Mapother tradition of hard work, leaving little time for play, was being kept up. Thomas III was, by all accounts, a bit of a boffin who was more interested in studying the latest lasar technology than in going to a college dance.

But then he met Mary Lee Pfeiffer who had been born and raised in the slightly poorer Highlands area of Louisville. It was love at first sight and the wedding in Louisville, in the mid-fifties, was attended by every relative from both sides, including Cousin Caroline Mapother.

The long-standing schism that had split the family all those generations earlier was made even more apparant when the happy couple decided to marry in a Roman Catholic church, even though many of Thomas Cruise Mapother III's relatives were actually Church of Scotland regulars. Cousin Caroline later recalled that 'despite the differences it was a nice wedding'. However, the underlying tensions still exist, even to this day. 'Tom Cruise and his side of the family are not really true Mapothers because Mary Cruise adopted that name for her son Thomas I and we have always been made well aware of that,' explained Caroline Mapother.

Shortly after his marriage to Mary Lee, an attractive brunette with a friendly smile and a warm disposition, Thomas Cruise Mapother III joined General Electric as an engineer and ended up working alongside Caroline's husband.

Working as an engineer for GE was a highly sought-after position. It was expected that Thomas III would move around the country to wherever research projects were being undertaken and that his wife would follow him and set up home. At this time Thomas III was immersed in the development of light-emitting, solid state lasers. During those first few years of marriage, he became somewhat of a workaholic but this was no surprise to the rest of the family as hard work, some say obsessive, was second nature to the Mapothers.

'He was fascinated by the technological developments of the day. He spent every waking moment working on new projects,' explained cousin Dillon Mapother, a former engineer, now in his seventies, who has been Professor of Physics at the University of Illinois since 1949.

Thomas Cruise Mapother III hardly looked up and noticed when Mary Lee gave birth to daughter Lee Anne in Louisville. Then, after moving to Syracuse, New York State, another daughter, Marian, was born, followed on 3 July 1962 by a boy, later christened Thomas Cruise Mapother IV. Life at General Electric had become one long round of research projects and Thomas III was starting to dream of

life beyond the restricting surroundings of a large corporation. He wanted to put his knowledge to the ultimate test
in a free market economy and start trying to develop his own
inventions. He believed that if his own, personally developed lasar could be properly marketed, it might make him a
millionaire many times over.

Tom Cruise later described his father as, 'complex,
extremely bright, artistic'. That sounds like shorthand for
'not an easy person', but then, it takes all sorts to make a
world.

And, of course, there was Mary Lee, an energetic,
gregarious woman with more than a passing interest in
acting and the theatre. She was already carrying the majority
of the responsibility for bringing up the Mapother family,
just like all the Mapother women before her.

Mary Lee also relied on her strong sense of religion,
which prevented her from getting too swept up in all her
husband's impressive talk of million-dollar deals and
luxurious lifestyles. Mary Lee put all thoughts of wealth and
success behind her and looked for other ways to channel her
energy.

Life was pretty quiet in Syracuse, one of those medium-
sized cities partially based around a state university. Its main
industries were farm equipment and typewriters. It is not a
hick town but it is hardly the cultural mecca of the western
world either.

Soon after Tom Cruise's birth, the family moved yet
again. Mary Lee became pregnant with daughter Cass three
years later. At around that time, Tom proved himself to be
a bit of handful when he put his mother's car in reverse after
she had left it with the engine running in the garage. The
car rolled backwards towards the street and Mary Lee only
just made it to the driver's seat in time. Tom never forgot
the look of sheer terror on his mother's face as she jerked

the gear stick out of reverse. His later obsession with cars, which eventually manifested itself in a love affair with the race track, had been born.

When Tom was about two and a half years old, he sneaked out of the house and disappeared for so long that his mother had to call the police to track him down. When he was found wandering nearby, Mary Lee asked her son where he had been and Tom replied: 'I went on an adventure.'

So Mary Lee said: 'Next time you want to go on an adventure, why don't you get me and we'll go together.'

A few days later, Tom's mother was scrubbing the floor when he came up to her and said: 'It's time.' His mother got up, gathered together Tom's three sisters and they all walked down the street, following Tom. He took them to a pond in the middle of some nearby woods and Mary Lee was shocked to discover that the place her tiny son had been going to alone might well have ended in him drowning in that pond.

Mary Lee asked Tom: 'What do you do here, Tom?'

'Oh, I just sit and think and throw rocks in the water.'

After the arrival of baby sister Cass, the family continued to find themselves growing up in and around ever-shifting influences and environments. However, throughout all this moving, one thing remained the same. Wherever they went, Mary Lee would sniff out the local playhouse. At one stage, she even founded her own amateur dramatic group. It was inevitable that her obsession with the theatre would rub off on her impressionable youngsters.

Many years later, Mary Lee recalled proudly that Tom had displayed promise in the acting field when he was still under ten years of age. He loved to play imaginary games featuring soldiers and policemen. Mary Lee was as impressed as any proud parent would be and encouraged her only son to continue his playacting.

Part of Tom's repertoire involved imitating two of the great icons of cartoon history: Woody Woodpecker and Donald Duck. He was also especially fond of W.C. Fields. Tom was already becoming someone who preferred to be in a world of his own. It was like a training schedule for his eventual success, with lots of difficult bridges to cross.

Tom moved so much from school to school that he was always trying to adjust. It was as if he was picking up a part; playing a role along the way. He later explained: 'If we went South, I'd pick up a little Southern accent, because having a Canadian accent wasn't cool.'

By all accounts, he was a bit of a dreamer at this stage in his life:

'I was always the kid who forgot to take the garbage out on Tuesdays. I would be in the back yard staring at the clouds, daydreaming. I was the kind of kid who wanted adventure. I craved it. I'd go around the backyard, dreaming up monsters and dragons. It was all about needing adventure. I had an active imagination. My mother thought, "If you have all this imagination, why can't you take out the garbage!"'

Two years after the birth of Cass, the Mapother family packed up again and headed for the even colder climate of Ottawa, Canada, a relatively sophisticated and populous region of the Great White North. Other temporary home-towns were in Missouri and New Jersey. During the first 11 years of Tom's life, the family moved a total of seven times.

Inevitably, sport provided an outlet for Tom's natural agressiveness, no doubt brought on by the continued frustration of never settling in one place. It lent him some self-esteem, esteem that he didn't usually find in the classroom because of reading difficulties brought on by dyslexia. He began to play baseball at an early age. By the time the family moved to Canada, even his father noticed that Tom could skate backwards just as well as Canadian boys who'd been doing it all their lives.

These days, Tom can look back on his hectic childhood and, in retrospect, accentuate the positive elements to be gained from non-stop moving. 'It gave me the range to play different types of characters. I have a lot to draw on,' he says. At the time, however, the family must have been desperate to stay in one place long enough to settle down.

The moves were punctuated by visits to Louisville, Kentucky, the only place the Mapothers could truly call home. A host of old friends and relatives resided in the area and this, combined with the slow and easy pace of the city, helped the Mapothers to catch their breath after all their hectic travelling.

However, beneath the surface of those apparently happy trips back to Louisville lay a long-standing problem between Thomas Cruise Mapother III and his wife Mary Lee. They were increasingly drifting apart. He was completely engrossed in his obsession with becoming a self-made millionaire. She just wanted a simple, contented life without all the frustrations and disappointments that so often dominate the professional life of talented people. Mary Lee was also fed up with having to carry the full weight of moving the family from town to town like gipsies. The children were undoubtably affected, especially the two older girls, who seemed to be forever saying goodbye to their school friends.

Young Tom was feeling it too. He became more withdrawn than most of the kids in his class, not bothering to make close friends because he knew that, sooner rather than later, he would have to say goodbye to them, most probably forever. It seemed easier to him to immerse himself in his own games at home and study quietly at school without any emotional entanglement. Inevitably, his best friends were his three sisters. The older two doted on him like stand-in mothers whenever Mary Lee was not around.

Lee Anne's girlfriends all adored and mollycoddled cute little Tom with the sticky out teeth. One time, she invited a couple of friends over and they proceeded to test out their kissing skills on eight-year-old Tom.

But those constant moves were having a serious long-term effect on young Tom. He'd spend all his time getting into the right clique at school, finally buy the right pair of sneakers, and then the family would move. He got into a lot of fights. The school bully would come over and kick the hell out of the new kid. Tom learnt that he either had to fight back or the next guy was going to come over and pound him as well. It was sink or swim time for Tom. He chose to swim.

'I went through a period of really wanting to be accepted; wanting love and affection.'

Tom Cruise

Any 12 year old who moved around as much as Thomas Cruise Mapother IV, would have developed a sixth sense about certain things. The house in the little town outside Ottawa must have been the sixth or seventh home he'd lived in. The town was just another spread of bricks and mortar to the youngster. Through it all, at least he had the love and support of his family: his mom to comfort him; his dad to stick up for him when things got especially rough. However, he had known that something was up for quite some time.

On that particular day, his parents sat their four children down and told them what Tom had suspected all along; that their marriage was breaking up. Around the room the flow of tears that followed the news was uncontrollable. It was, Tom later recalled, as if someone had died.

A few minutes later, Tom's father took him outside to hit a few baseballs but sport was the furthest thing from his mind that day. Tom cried so hard in the backyard that he virtually could not breathe. The knowledge that this time his father was leaving for good left young Tom with one great fear echoing in his mind: *'What's going to happen to us now? What next?*

*   *   *

Many theories have been advanced to suggest how movie stars are formed. It is frequently found that a large number of them had lost a parent in childhood and many were deprived of love in their early years. Accordingly, they demonstrate the most powerful drive for attention and affection and are often abnormally sensitive, reserved and isolated.

Some of these epithets may apply to Tom Cruise; he is his mother's son by nature if not name, although he has added the steel of ambition. He rarely mentions his father even today.

During Tom's early days he had been just a hard-working father of four trying to earn an honest living and provide for his large family. Tom has always regretted that they were not closer. He also had a feeling that his father was a little eccentric. But there was another aspect to his father which Tom Cruise might not want to talk about – his father was an alcoholic.

The problem was not that noticeable when Tom was a young boy but, by the time the family began to fall apart, it had become obvious. Thomas Mapother III would fly into irrational temper tantrums, mainly caused by alcohol. He would often drink secretly before arriving home from his work as an engineer.

After the family broke up, Tom tried to piece the whole sad scenario together and realised that he had first become aware of his father's problem some years earlier. Because the family was in a more stable state then, it did not seem so important. After the break-up, the Mapother kids grew up never actually able to agree on how much of a drink problem their father had.

Some of Tom's sisters did not accept that he had a real problem at all. As children, all of them had shut themselves off from the situation. Even now, Tom has great difficulty in even talking about his father, let alone conceding that there was an alcohol problem.

Thomas Mapother III's drinking became more of a problem after his divorce from Mary Lee. He would wander off to California for months – in one case years – at a time, hardly ever bothering to contact his ex-wife or children. 'He never really accepted that he had a problem. Instead, he just kept on the move. But back in Louisville there were a lot of worried family members,' explained one relative, too scared to be identified for fear of upsetting Tom's Hollywood image.

Today, Mary Lee will only refer to the split with her husband as 'a time of growing, a time of conflict'. It was also a time of great poverty. With precious little income, she did what Mapother women do best, she fought her damndest to keep the children fed and clothed. They returned to Louisville and tried to start their lives again.

'You know, women have dreams of having careers and being whatever,' Mary Lee says. 'I had a dream of raising children and enjoying them and having a good family life.'

Mary Lee worked at a series of jobs to keep them afloat: hosting electrical conventions, selling appliances at Stewart's department store, anything. One Christmas, there was no money to buy gifts, so the family wrote poems to one another and read them out loud.

At first, the family moved into a low-rent house just off Taylorsville Road, Louisville and Mary Lee's brother, Jack

Pfeiffer, and her mother, Comala Pfeiffer Kremer, helped the struggling family to stay in one place.

Tom was emotionally drained by the stress and strain of what had happened. He was in daze, unable to grasp the reality of the situation because no one outside his immediate family could be told what had happened. He felt especially vulnerable but he did not dare tell any of his classmates what he was going through. When he was older, he realised that he had missed all the love, motivation and sense of self that comes from having a father. At the time, however, he didn't stop and say, 'My dad's not around – I've got to learn how to handle it.' He just felt very, very insecure.

That first winter was one of the coldest to hit the area in more than 30 years but Tom got up every morning at dawn and slogged up and down the nearby streets delivering newspapers.

'Nothing could stop him. He'd go out in the snow bundled up like an Eskimo,' recalled Granny Pfeiffer years later.

He even used to sneak out and do his paper round in his mother's beaten-up car some mornings. Getting up at 4 a.m., his two elder sisters would help their pint-sized brother push the family car out of the drive so that their mother would not hear it being started up. She would have been furious if she knew he was using the car.

Thankfully, at least one aspect of Tom's life remained partially consistent – his involvement in athletics and sport. He played hockey over the Kentucky border in Indiana, with kids older and bigger than him.

'He was so fast they couldn't keep up with him,' recalls Mary Lee proudly. 'One guy finally got so exasperated that he picked Tom up by the scruff of the neck and the seat of his pants and moved him outside the boundary. I laughed.'

Tom not only pitched in financially by doing that paper

round, he also helped out in other ways too. Every night he'd come home from school, bathe his mother's tired feet and then massage them for half an hour. Mary Lee remembers: 'This went on for six weeks, then Easter came and went, and the Monday after Easter I came home from work expecting the same treatment and he said, "Hey, Mom, Lent's over."'

Tom Cruise has rarely talked publicly about his parents' divorce but he opened up with surprising frankness to *Rolling Stone* journalist Christopher Connelly, in an interview in June 1986.

> 'After a divorce, you feel so vulnerable. And travelling the way I did, you're closed off a lot from other people. I didn't express a lot to people where I moved. They didn't have the childhood I had, and I didn't feel like they'd understand me. I was always warming up, getting aquainted with everyone. I went through a period, after the divorce, of really wanting to be accepted, wanting love and attention from people. But I never really seemed to fit in anywhere.'

School in Louisville became a disturbing trail of problems featuring narrow-minded teachers and rigid rules and regulations. Tom acknowledged his dilemma and tried to help himself and his sisters to adapt to their new life. One day when he was walking to school with them during a particularly difficult time, he said: 'Let's just get *through* this. If we can just get through this somehow...'

He found it extremely lonely without his father around. Cruise Senior had moved away from Kentucky and did not even pay any child support. He was rarely, if ever, in contact with his children. Things got so tough for Tom and his sisters that they frequently wore their cousins' hand-me-down clothes. That meant running around in tennis shoes that were too big and sloppy and wearing baggy sweaters but no one minded just so long as Mary Lee kept her family together.

Tom was now the man of the house and he took to his role like a fish to water. He enjoyed the responsibility and played an increasingly active part in the household. His clear ability to adapt is typical of those born under the sign of Cancer. They have an innate ability to fit in under trying circumstances. Poised on the edge of adolescence, Tom was facing a daily barrage of the essential issues that confront all teenagers. Of course, he had his mother to turn to, but there were certain questions that only a father could answer.

In a way that was mature beyond his years, Tom reached out to his mother and sisters and returned their love in a warm and sensitive way. All five developed a truly remarkable kinship that went beyond the traditional confines of male/female roles.

'My mother is very giving, very open, and really loves being around people. She's a great listener. My sisters are very much like her – very strong women,' explained Tom years later.

The family knew it had to pull together because they were on the verge of abject poverty. Mary Lee was (and still is) a very proud woman. She did everything she could to hold the family together and keep it going, but even Mary Lee had to bow to the financial pressures that were making life so difficult to maintain.

Once, when she went to get food stamps, she took one look at all the people waiting in the social security office and couldn't cope with the shame, so she turned around and walked straight out, determined that she would make enough money to feed the family on her own.

All five family members worked. Lee Anne, Marian

and, later, Cass took their turns as waitresses in local restaurants. Tom doubled his paper round and mowed every lawn in sight. Unlike other children on his block, Tom's goal was to help his family to survive, not to fritter his earnings away on comics and footballs.

'It wasn't a bad time,' remembered Tom. 'There was a lot of love and laughter... We all supported each other, although it was tough on my mother because she wanted us to have the best and she couldn't always give it to us.'

Tom also learned another important lesson from watching his mother struggle through those lean years. He witnessed the raw deals women get in the business world. He saw his mother's trials and tribulations as classic examples of sexual harassment, job discrimination and the dozens of other smaller problems faced by women every time they take on a job. Those experiences undoubtably helped shape his attitude towards his co-stars when he later made it to Hollywood.

'Women to me are not a mystery. I get along easily with them,' is one of his favourite replies to anyone asking about the females in his family. To this day, it is even said that Tom prefers the company of women. 'I trust women easier than men.' However, life in the Mapother household was no bed of roses. There were fights between Tom and his sisters and he usually ended up the loser, but all of that was to be expected inside any big family.

Yet another school – this time St Raphael's, in Louisville – was notable only because Tom made probably his best friend ever in fellow 13 year old Jeff Bayers.

Jeff, who is still in touch with Tom and understandably nervous about upsetting his famous friend, admitted that Tom was 'kinda lonely' when the two first linked up at St Raphael's. 'He'd only been in town for a few days but we hit it off immediately and soon became best friends,' explained Jeff.

He has followed Tom's career very closely and cannot get over how similar so many of the roles have been to Tom's real-life experiences. 'It's funny how true to life those roles have been. I guess it must have helped him.'

Jeff, ever the loyal friend, would only concede that Tom was 'very complicated about his father'. The two friends still exchange Christmas cards each year and Jeff keeps in touch with Tom's sister, Lee Anne.

At St Raphael's, which had taught Mapothers for four generations, the principal Paul De Zarn refused even to comment on Tom Cruise's time at the school. 'I would have to have some sort of written authorisation from the Cruise family. The Mapothers have a long history with us...'

While at St Raphael's, Tom apparently enjoyed creating entire childhoods to tell the other students about. He would happily hide his true persona behind a mask of tall tales about adventures in the Rocky Mountains and a never-ending stream of other fiction. As the perennial new boy in town, it was easy to get away with such outrageous stories.

At the time, Mary Lee and her children lived in a comfortable, but relatively modest, house at number three, Cardwell Way, in a lower-middle-class suburb of Louisville. It was a rented property but at least it was a quiet street with other kids to play with, although Tom did not mix much with the local children.

Residents still living in the street today recall Tom as 'the one who would sit on the steps of his house playing the guitar. Real quiet. Seemed like a loner.'

Neighbour Bill Lewis remembers when Tom knocked on his front door on St Valentine's Day 1976 and asked if he could mow the lawn. Bill and the lonely, sad-faced boy from up the street soon formed a strong bond of friendship, no doubt influenced by young Tom's desperate search for a father figure following the departure of his own parent.

'No job was too dirty or difficult for Tommy, as long as it paid money to help his mom out. While most other kids were out raising hell, he had his nose to the grindstone and was working day and night. He was an unusual lad. I told Mary Lee she should be awfully proud of him,' recalled Bill fondly.

Tom soon began regarding Bill as a true father figure. He craved a man's help and advice. On the day of Tom's school graduation, he went over to Bill's home with his necktie in his hand and sheepishly explained that he didn't know how to tie it and neither did his mom and sisters.

Often Bill, then in his fifties, and young 'Tommy' would sit on the wall outside Bill's house and sup a bottle of non-alcoholic birch beer together. Often the talk centred around Bill's experiences as a Marine during World War Two.

Bill also remembered that Tom not once even mentioned the existence of his father throughout the time he knew him. 'It was as if his father had been wiped from the face of the earth. But I didn't want to pry so I never asked him what happened to him.'

For a few months during the middle of 1976, Bill became a father substitute to desperately lonely 'Tommy'. The teenager even called him 'Sir' in the way every well-brought-up kid in the south has done for generations.

'I was a fatherly figure to him. I was always very good to him and we really had something going, the two of us. He was one hell of a nice kid, hard to get to know at first, but full of warmth and energy once you got beneath the surface,' remembered Bill.

Tom's friendship with Bill came to a close in the same way as every relationship Tom ever had in those days. He turned up on Bill's doorstep one blisteringly hot summer's day and told his friend that his family were on the move once again and he wouldn't be able to do the lawn anymore.

It still brings tears to Bill Lewis's eyes when he thinks about his young friend. 'I have very fond memories of Tommy. I'd love to get ahold of Tommy now and tell him how proud I am of what he turned out to be.'

Years after his career skyrocketed him to movie stardom, Bill Lewis wrote a heartfelt letter to Tom. He never got a reply.

That summer of 1976 was significant to Thomas Cruise Mapother IV because, as he later admitted, he finally learned to be himself instead of hiding behind a false smile and a reluctance to get involved with friends because the family were always on the move.

However, that lesson in life nearly cost Tom dearly. It happened when a classmate asked him over to ride motorcycles in his backyard and Tom, trying to fit in as usual, lied and said he knew how to ride bikes.

When the youngster turned up, he was greeted by the sight of three or four very serious kids riding their minibikes up and down a basketball court separated from his friend's house by a gully and a row of bushes. For at least ten minutes, Tom stood and studied the other riders, desperately trying to gather enough clues as to how to ride a motorbike.

'Finally I had to take my turn. I let out the clutch without realising it was the clutch. Then I turned the hand grip, thinking it was the brake. Instead, I was revving the engine, and the bike just took off, sailed over the gully, through the bushes and – wham! – into the side of the house. The moral of that story is, "Don't say you can ride a motorcycle if you can't." I nearly killed myself trying to be one of the guys.'

Bill Lewis had another reason to remember Tom because the 13 year old astonished him by talking about his intention to become a priest, even admitting he had decided to join St Francis's Seminary, near Cincinnati, later that year. Bill was surprised to hear a young boy talking in such serious terms about being a priest. 'I found it especially hard to advise him because I was a protestant but I did tell him that he should do whatever would make him happy,' recalled Bill.

A few weeks later, Tom headed off to join St Francis's Seminary, almost one hundred miles north of Louisville. There was no entrance exam to get into the school and the priests who ran the seminary did not want to make it too strict in case it put any prospective members of the priesthood off joining. The notion of leaving his mother and sisters for boarding school scared young Tom at first but then it started to dawn on him that the seminary might be a way to forget the problems of the previous few years and just be a kid again. It could be the perfect escape for a teenager still reeling from the heartbreak of seeing his family split in two.

He was well aware that the main reason for the existence of St Francis's was to train would-be priests. Most of the funds used to run the school were collected through Catholic charities determined to try to reverse the ever-shrinking numbers of men entering the priesthood. School fees were only charged to those who could afford them. In fact, the seminary had a policy of never asking for more than $800 a year no matter who the pupil was. Surprisingly, there was no uniform.

The Franciscans are a religious order founded by Francis of Assisi in AD 1209. According to the legend, St Francis was the son of a wealthy Italian merchant, who turned from a frivolous, hedonistic life to become the God-fearing, devoted and selfless friend of the poor and sick. Francis went from town to town to preach, dressed in sackcloth and lived on the alms he could beg from passing people.

The young men who flocked to him and joined his way of life came to be called Franciscans and, today, there are many branches of their brotherhood. Some live in monasteries, devoted to a life of prayer, others run hospitals or parishes, still others teach. Many Franciscans wear sandals, as St Francis did; most of them also wear brown habits tied by a cord around the waist, not unlike the simple garb the saint chose to wear.

Many of the brothers at the seminary had Germanic names because a large number of Franciscans had come to North America in the 1840s from the Austrian Tyrol. The seminary was also strongly influenced by the large numbers of Germans and Austrians who had settled in nearby Cincinnati.

Each monk who entered the order had to adopt a completely new name until controversial changes in the Catholic church in the early 1960s.

When Tom turned up for his first term at St Francis's in the autumn of 1976, the school had been depleted to just 100 pupils. However, there were distinct advantages in small numbers. It meant that each student could receive extra individual attention, something that larger schools could never manage.

It was Tom's freshman year and headmaster Father Laurian Rausch welcomed the boys to the imposing gothic mansion set in acres of lush countryside about ten miles outside Cincinnati. Prefects from the older classes were appointed to each table in the refectory to keep the younger boys in order, and faculty members were allowed to punish the boys if they misbehaved. The most regular punishment at St Francis's was writing lines but sometimes physical punishments were handed out by certain priests. That year one of the boys was given a severe beating with a paddle after being caught drinking. No one in Tom's class dared step out of line after stories of the boy's injuries circulated in the seminary.

The hierarchy who ran St Francis's were proud that at least 25% of the boys who attended the school eventually entered the priesthood. By enrolling their sons, parents clearly implied that their children were seriously considering a life of celibacy. 'We did not expect a permanent commitment from them but we did expect them to contemplate the priesthood seriously,' explained Father Aldric Heidlage.

The seminary had also become an ideal place for children from broken homes. At least a third of the boys who were there the same year as Tom had just been through the heartache of seeing their parents split up.

The pupils tended to come from areas in the United States where the Franciscans had a strong presence: Upper Michigan, Louisiana, Kentucky, Illinois, Kansas, New Mexico, Arizona, Texas, Oklahoma.

Life at St Francis's was quite tough and regimented compared with many of the schools Tom had attended during his travels around North America. The boys would be woken by a clanging bell at 6.40 a.m. and then be expected to be in the refectory by 7.00 a.m. for breakfast. At 7.45 a.m. a study period was held to ensure that the previous day's homework was properly completed, followed by classes that started at 8.30 a.m. and finished at 11.00 a.m. so that everyone could attend mass. At noon, lunch was given, immediately followed by more classes then sport. At 4.30 p.m. there was a study period once again, then supper, with lights out at 9.00 p.m. sharp.

Tom found himself in a dormitory sleeping upwards of 20 boys. Each bed was set in a makeshift cubicle with boarded walls on three sides, plus a curtain for privacy. At night, the coughing and farting of some children would spark off a round of giggling and sometimes the boys would whisper to each other but much of the time there was complete silence until wake-up call the next day.

That first term at the seminary, Tom missed his sisters and mother terribly. With only three family visiting days from September until Thanksgiving at the end of November, he found it especially hard. The remarkable bond that existed between him and his family had been cruelly broken, if only temporarily.

Thanksgiving that year was not easy. Tom – allowed back to Louisville for just two days – must have wanted to stay longer with his family. For the moment, however, Mary Lee knew that St Francis's was a better environment for Tom than the streets of Louisville where a lonely teenager could get himself into some real trouble.

For the rest of that term, Tom longed to be back with his family and counted the days until the start of the Christmas break. St Francis's had its own bus which took the poorer children back to their homes in the Louisville area because many parents could not afford the trip to Cincinnati. The night before Tom's departure for the holidays, the youngster was so excited that he could not sleep until the early hours. Next morning, he almost missed the bus by oversleeping. The incident always stuck in Father Aldric's mind because most boys got up especially early to catch the bus home.

Father Hilarion Kistner remembers meeting Mary Lee when she delivered Tom back to the school at the start of the following term because the staff of the seminary were extremely concerned that she might not make it back to Louisville safely after a severe snowstorm gripped the area.

It is not clear how strong Tom really felt about his religious calling; he is reluctant to be drawn into any conversations about such subjects. 'For me, religion is a very personal thing,' he confessed. He has also said that although he was, and still is, a believer, he did have other motives for enrolling at the seminary: 'We didn't have any money for school... it was a free education. They even clothed you.'

Tom tried desperately to find some focus in his life during his time at St Francis's but, even there, he felt quite different from everyone else. 'I went through a period of really wanting to be accepted; wanting love and affection,' he later recalled.

Although Tom missed his mother and sisters, he also felt reasonably comfortable in the presence of the Franciscan brothers, even although life inside the seminary was pretty basic. At least he was getting a solid education, probably for the first time in his entire life. Certainly, young Tom was heavily influenced by the teachings of the brothers and, up until the end of his first term at St Francis's, he was definitely seriously considering a life in the priesthood.

Tom was also remembered as being the shortest basketball player in the freshman year. Father Aldric recalls him well, despite the fact that he dropped out of St Francis's after only one year. He says: 'Tom was a rather weak student. He certainly did not make a *big* impression on us.'

Meanwhile, the teenager's mind was starting to focus on something altogether less serious than the priesthood. Tom was very shy and was afraid girls wouldn't like him because he was so short. He even asked one of the priests: 'When will girls be interested in me?' recalled another priest. The idea of celibacy was not so appealing after all.

By his second term at the seminary, however, Tom was sneaking out to the homes of local girls. 'We'd go to a girl's house in town, sit around, talk, play spin the bottle and I started to realise that I love women too much to give all that up,' he remembered years later.

Every weekend Tom and his pals would be allowed out to the Springfield Road shopping mall, just a short walking distance away from the seminary.

On one memorable occasion, Jeff Bayers, Tom's best friend from his brief stay at St Raphael's in Louisville, turned up at the seminary and the two boys had a great afternoon out in the local town, talking about their old friends back in Louisville.

Jeff never forgot how upset Tom still was about his parents' divorce. 'He wasn't real open about his family problems,' said Jeff. However, Tom was more revealing about his intentions to become a priest and told Jeff that he 'really wanted to join the priesthood' despite his frustration over how to handle the local girls. Jeff just hoped it would all be a passing phase.

Mass was held every day at the seminary and Father Kistner was spiritual director at the seminary at the time. This meant that he had to counsel pupils about their religious thoughts and knowledge. Interestingly, most of the boys saw Father Kistner at least once during that year but Tom did not seek his guidance at all.

Not even St Francis's was completely free of the sort of problems that have plagued most schools in the past 20 years. During the year Tom attended, one of the boys was expelled from the seminary for buying drugs from a narcotics peddler,

St Francis's Seminary closed as a school in 1980 because the number of students dipped below the 50 mark and it simply was not economical to run it as a school. However, most of Tom's teachers still live and work in the imposing building to this day. The heirarchy at St Francis's believes that, in the past 20 years, children have wanted to seek such a wealthy, luxurious existence that they feel no compunction to live the simple, relatively uncomplicated life of a priest.

Father Kistner is still disappointed by Tom Cruise's lack of interest in the seminary. In 1988, while filming *Rain Man* with Dustin Hoffman, the film's makers almost used the seminary for a number of scenes. In the end, they decided to film at a convent in nearby Crescent Springs and the nuns there told Kistner that Tom was very quiet and standoffish with them, unlike Hoffman who was happy to relate tales of his Hollywood life to the sisters.

For Thomas Cruise Mapother IV, one year at St Francis's seminary was more than enough, although he later described it as 'the best year I ever did in school'. He appreciated the good education that St Francis's provided for him at a very difficult time in his life.

Once, when Tom was back home for the holidays in the middle of that year, he and Jeff Bayers 'borrowed' Tom's mother's car. (They were both too young to drive at the time.) Tom was driving the wrong way up a one-way street when a Louisville police cruiser spotted the very short teenager who was barely able to see over the dashboard. Seconds later, Tom was pulled over and told he was going the wrong way up a one-way street.

Tom, ever the well-brought-up southern boy, thanked the officer for his advice and called him 'Sir' at least six times during the two-minute exchange. Then he turned the car around after Jeff volunteered to guide him into an opening. Seconds later, Jeff had to jump out of the way when Tom almost ran him over. Luckily, the police officer did not bat an eyelid as he watched from his patrol car parked close by.

For much of the summer after leaving St Francis's, Tom would 'borrow' his mom's car most evenings and go out cruising and looking for girls in the early hours. He tended to hang around playing pinball at the Bashford Manor Mall but, not surprisingly, there were few girls to be found at such a late hour.

During this period, Mary Lee had been trying to rebuild her life and she had met a man whom she believed could help strengthen her existence and that of her four children. He was, she thought, someone strong and dependable – a rock of stability who would bring her loving contentment for the first time in her life.

Mary Lee met Jack South at an electronics convention; he worked in plastics. They got married when Tom was 16. In the beginning Tom felt threatened by his stepfather. There was a part of him that was consumed with love for his mother and he found it difficult to accept another man in the household.

The underlying bad feeling between Tom and Jack was apparent to Mary Lee and her daughters. Tom was grouchy and sullen, like most teenage boys. Jack, desperate to make a good impression and painfully aware of the anguish suffered by Tom and his three sisters, knew he could never replace their father, but at least he deserved some respect.

To make matters worse, following his return from the seminary, Tom was sent to live for a brief time with his aunt and uncle – the Barratts – on the other side of Louisville. Mary Lee could no longer afford to rent a house and had to move into her mother's home, which was much smaller, so sending Tom over to her brother's home seemed to make sense.

Tom felt desperately lonely at the Barratts. He missed his mother and sisters terribly and knowing that Jack South was on the scene did not help to make him feel any more secure. For her part, Mary Lee fully realised that if Tom and Jack were to form a solid relationship she would have to get Tom back as quickly as possible. So she took on another extra job, allowed Jack to start providing a little for them and, within a few months, Tom was back in the fold. They were all together once again and that was all that really mattered.

'He has a charisma that needs exercising.'
Oliver Stone

When losing one's virginity, said Queen Victoria, one must close one's eyes and think of England. Attaching a little more lyricism to the act, the great romantics, from Cervantes to Byron, saw virgins as roses and their deflowering a poem to passions that would saddle lions.

Tom Cruise's first taste of real romance – not neccessarily the actual act of making love, but certainly a beginning – came when he met his first real girlfriend, a pretty 16 year old called Laurie Hobbs, who attended the nearby Sacred Heart School in Louisville. It was October 1978, and Tom, aged 16, had never had a proper girlfriend before.

'Tom struck me as being shy, sort of uneasy around girls,' recalled Laurie, now a 33-year-old housewife living in Louisville.

After weeks of brief exchanges in the street near Tom's home, Laurie found herself with no choice but to make the first move. She marched boldly up to his house, knocked on the door and asked the pint-sized teenager: 'Are you going to take me to the school dance or what?'

Laurie recalls: 'He was cute but not what you'd call cool. And he had a chipped tooth that embarrassed him so much that he decided to have it fixed.'

The night of the dance, Tom and Laurie went to a friend's apartment and opened a couple of bottles of wine to loosen up. However, as Laurie later explained, Tom was so shy that they hardly touched each other that first night and even conversation between the two teenagers was strained. The dance was a similarly frosty experience but Laurie was not easily deterred.

A few nights later she and Tom got high on champagne and once again she had to make the first move.

'I got things going by casually dropping a hand on the couch beside him. I can hardly describe how excited I was when he got hold of it at last and started playing with my fingers. Then we lunged towards each other, sort of kissing, only we didn't seem able to get our mouths in the right place at first.

'My head was spinning and I could hardly breathe. I could hear my heart banging away in my eardrums. First kisses are like that – you think you're going to faint. Once or twice, I opened my eyes to make sure his eyes were closed, and they were, so I knew he meant it.

'After that it was like we had just made love and could talk about anything. All we'd done was kiss, but a great obstacle had been removed. Things then got pretty hot and heavy. Hands shaking, knees knocking, you name it. My head was spinning and I could hardly breathe. I remember thinking how surprised I was that he could kiss like that.

'We just floated along clinging to each other. I even had to tell him to keep his hands to himself.'

As they kissed and cuddled, Laurie thought to herself: 'There is no way this guy is ever going to be a priest.'

Later she confessed candidly: 'I feel pleased with myself when people find out I dated Tom. But we were both only young and I was a Catholic girl. Although I might have let him slip a hand inside my dress and hold it there.'

Laurie, who lost touch with Tom years ago, also added: 'I often wonder what life would be like if Tom and I had got married. I guess maybe we'd probably be divorced by now. But now and then I flatter myself that I actually taught the world's sexiest male to kiss.'

Tom was still hiding the full pain and anguish of his parents' divorce, so being romantic was a kind of diversion, although he remembers that time with a definite note of sarcasm. 'I was going through puberty, that thrilling time we all remember as such an easy experience, particularly with the opposite sex. Who doesn't feel that way? You think, "If that girl just looks at me, my day is made." I was scared to death of being rejected and I was shy unless I got that look or that smile.'

Throughout all this period, Tom tried hard to keep in contact with his father's side of the family, despite the obvious complications created by Thomas Cruise Mapother III's decision to abandon his young family. On one occasion, Tom, then aged 15, and his cousin William, aged 12, accompanied Grandpa Thomas Cruise Mapother II on a sightseeing trip to Washington DC. It was an important event for young Tom as he and his sisters had long felt a little like the odd ones out as far as the rest of the Mapothers were concerned.

Grandpa Mapother later chuckled as he recalled to other family members how he had booked into an expensive hotel with the two boys and sent them out to get some lemon drops, only for them to return three hours later after 'getting lost' in the nightclub in the basement of the hotel, where they stood entranced by the sight of some pretty teenage girls.

Tom and his sisters were understandably disturbed by the initial intrusion of plastics salesman Jack South in their lives through his romance with their mother. It was difficult to cope with this stranger who had suddenly swept Mary Lee off her feet and they were suspicious of his motives. However, the girls – ever sensitive – soon started to appreciate how important Jack was to their mother. Gradually, it began to dawn on Tom too that here was a guy who loved his mother in a way not even his own father had.

There was also another aspect to Jack's relationship with Mary Lee. He was prepared to take on a readymade family and that took some courage. Gradually, the children came to appreciate it.

Jack started to take Tom out to bet on football games, although he was a terrible better. Tom, on the other hand, ended up making lots of money and in this way a bridge of friendship was built.

When Tom had completed his sophomore year of high school at St Xavier's in Louisville, Jack moved the family to Glen Ridge, New Jersey. This time, Tom and his sisters thought they might actually have time to make some real friends.

Glen Ridge is a small pocket of all Americana where a community of neat, tree-lined streets is tucked carefully into the centre of some of the rougher neighbourhoods of New Jersey. This mainly residential town is best known for the quiet glow of the Victorian gaslights which have become its trademark.

More than 90 per cent of the imposing houses in Glen Ridge were built between the years of 1870 and 1930, making it an area steeped in history when compared with many of the surrounding districts.

In the past 30 years there have been just two murders in the area and the local *Glen Ridge Paper* tends to favour front page stories about graduation days and noisy parties. It is the sort of place where drinking alcohol – except on very special occasions – is frowned upon.

Jack South rented an imposing clapboard house on Washington Avenue. It was by far the biggest house they had ever lived in and for the first time in years Mary Lee and her brood felt that they were leading a normal, happy life.

At Glen Ridge High School, Tom decided to take up wrestling because he reckoned it might help him to find some new pals as quickly as possible.

'He joined to meet other kids. He was a very nice, polite sort of kid. Very southern type of boy. Always saying "yes sir, no sir",' recalled the Glen Ridge wrestling coach Angelo Corbo.

Tom also proved useful at soccer, although his coach, Doc Voskian, later claimed he was a very one-dimensional type of player.

Essentially, however, Tom remained very quiet and reserved at Glen Ridge High, despite his efforts to mix with the other pupils. Wrestling coach Corbo was struck by his pupil's close knit family. He also noticed that they were having a problem fitting into the upmarket community. 'This is a very affluent community here. If you're from money you fit in. If you're not...' explained Corbo.

The wrestling team consisted of 12 boys and Tom tended to rate about number eight in actual wrestling ability. He wasn't one of the best, but he wasn't the worst either. However, Corbo conceded that the main reason he was in the team was because there was no one else in his weight classes of 115 and 122 pounds.

The rules and regulations for the wrestling team were just as tough as for any of the other school sports. Drinking alcohol meant an automatic dismissal from the team; everyone at the school had become especially aware of that regulation when six boys were barred from the soccer team after illicit boozing a few months earlier.

Mary Lee and Jack often turned up to cheer the youngster on. Mary Lee was particularly ready to get involved in the school activities of her children because she was convinced it would help to make them feel more readily accepted.

On 18 January 1979, Tom Mapother, as he was known then, made his newspaper début when his photo was published in the local *Glen Ridge Paper*. The caption under the photo of a very skinny Tom reads: 'Tom Mapother has full control over Jefferson Township wrestler in his JV match.'

A week later, on 25 January 1979, Tom's photograph was featured yet again, this time as he wrestled his first ever varsity match against Hillside School. He might have been a mediocre wrestler but he certainly had the ability to catch the eye of any cameraman present.

Years later, some of Tom's old team-mates in the wrestling side were surprised when the multi-millionaire actor did not reply to a request asking if he would be willing to donate $5,000 for a new wrestling mat. 'Maybe he never got the letter. But it would have been nothing to him and we would have put his name on it as an everlasting tribute to his generosity but we never got a response,' recalled Angelo Corbo. 'It would have shown that he cared about the area. He probably could have had the key to the town if he'd made the effort to come back here.'

However, Corbo also says that Tom's reluctance to return to Glen Ridge is understandable as the town has made little effort to commemorate the fact that he spent the happiest days of his youth there. 'It's typical of Glen Ridge. He's just about the most famous person to come out of the area but there's no plaque up outside his house and no one seems to care.'

Glen Ridge High School was not without its scandal either. In October 1979, one student, a Joseph Brennan, was issued with a summons by the local police after driving a four-wheel-drive vehicle over a newly laid sports field at the school. The school hierarchy was also perturbed by graffiti daubed on the high-school walls, which proclaimed: 'Zappa, Grateful Dead, ABB, Led Zeppelin, Santana', amid many additions of chewing gum and spit.

Around the same time it was reported in the *Glen Ridge Paper* that a number of Glen Ridge students were suspected of being heavily involved in drugs. Principal James Buckley revealed that all teachers had been assigned to an elaborate and regular patrolling system to keep an eye on all the bathrooms in the school. Even in a quiet middle class suburb like Glen Ridge, life had its problems.

Tom and his friends in the neighbourhood would frequently attend the Cloud 9 disco held at the Parish Hall of Christ Episcopal Church on the corner of Park and Bloomfield Avenues. The disco had been set up by the concerned parents of a Glen Ridge High School pupil, who felt it was better to organise a weekly event which would prevent pupils straying to the more dangerous areas of New Jersey just a few miles away.

In April 1980, Tom and his classmates took part in a bold protest against the sacking of the Glen Ridge High assistant principal, which earned them front page coverage in the local newspaper. Teacher John Curtis was known as a strict disciplinarian but he was admired and respected by his students because he was scrupulously fair to each and every one. 'The school is ruled with an iron fist but we'll still walk out for Mr Curtis because he's fair,' one angry student organiser yelled at a local journalist.

The group of young protestors sat down on the lawn in front of the school and refused to move. Banners were waved, proclaiming: 'CURTIS STAYS'. Some of the more daring students even began playing Jimi Hendrix music as they lay on a blanket on the grass. The teacher was reinstated.

Towards the end of that final term, Tom found himself exactly one pound overweight for his wrestling class. In order to lose that decisive pound, he dashed home to do a Rocky routine on the stairway, running up and down repeatedly, determined to sweat it off. Nearing his final lap, he slipped on a pile of homework papers his sister had inadvertently left on the stairs, and tumbled head over heels down the steps. To his horror, the fall left him with pulled knee tendons. Not only would he miss the match, he would be sidelined for the remainder of the semester. He was sorely depressed. His injury meant that he could not handle any other sport either. What was he to do with himself for the rest of the term?

Tom was desperate to focus in and do *something*. He knew he had energy and creativity. Mary Lee told him in no uncertain terms not to mope around the house but to find a new channel for his boundless energy. As it happened, he found an old one, one he had forgotten all about. He floundered briefly but then an inconspicuous miracle took place. He decided to turn his misfortune around and asked coach Corbo what he thought about him trying out for the school production of *Guys and Dolls*. Corbo – privately well aware that his student would not have done that well in the wrestling anyway – told him: 'Why not?'

Corbo listened patiently as young Cruise talked about his acting aspirations. To the wrestling teacher they seemed a mere pipedream. To Tom Cruise, however, those ambitions were about to become the driving force behind his life. He had carefully and quietly nurtured a fondness for acting instilled by his mother but, always the odd one out at school, had never told his classmates about his interest because that would have singled him out as being different from everyone else and he did not want to make himself any more unacceptable than he already was.

Corbo obviously enjoyed a close affinity with the young Tom Cruise and he has frequently considered showing up on location where the star was appearing to say hello. Privately, however, he admits he does not know if he would actually have anything to say to the new Tom Cruise. 'It probably would have been easier to talk to him when he was younger and did not have any money. Now, I don't know…'

Taking his teacher's advice, Tom attended the auditions and somehow landed the part of Nathan Detroit (the scheming gangster played by Frank Sinatra in the 1955 movie of *Guys and Dolls*, which also starred Marlon Brando) and took to the stage like a monkey takes to a banana plantation.

Mary Lee has never forgotten the glow of pride she felt as the family attended the opening night of the production: 'It was just an incredible experience to see what we felt was a lot of talent coming forth all of a sudden.' Even back in those days, Tom's mother never had any doubts about her only son's abilities.

A showbusiness agent who happened to be in the audience came up to Tom after the performance and declared him 'a natural'. The agent strongly recommended that Tom consider acting as a serious career and Tom needed little encouragement. With his characteristic energy and commitment, he jumped headfirst into his new-found passion. Daydreams of embarking on a hitch-hiking tour of Europe or enlisting in the air force (shades of *Top Gun* to come) were unceremoniously dumped. With professional encouragement on his side, he approached his parents with a new plan.

After the show, Tom arrived home and said he wanted to have a talk with Jack and his mother. He asked them for ten years to give showbusiness a try. They were stunned. Jack had genuine – and understandable – misgivings. Shouldn't he try and get a profession first just in case the acting did not work out? Mary Lee explained: 'My husband's thinking, "What's this gonna cost me? Ten years of what?" She howled with laughter. 'It's kind of a joke in the family. Sort of a joke and not a joke.' Tom was persuasively reassuring, however, and his enthusiasm was virtually infectious.

Mary Lee remembered years later: 'Tom said, "Let me see. I really feel that this is what I want to do." We both wholeheartedly agreed, because we felt it was a God-given talent; we gave him our blessing – and the rest is history.'

Tom himself was really happy at the reaction of his classmates to his performance in *Guys and Dolls*. They were really impressed – and that made Tom feel good. 'All the guys came and saw it and said, "Whoa, we didn't know that you could do that." I felt good about it. Not just the fact that they saw it, but I felt good about it in my heart,' he later enthused.

Tom was hooked. For the first time in his life he found he could express himself in a way he had never experienced before. 'I felt I needed to act the way I needed air to breathe.'

Graduation day at Glen Ridge High School was a difficult occasion for Tom and his family. He had already announced his intention to skip college and make a go of it as an actor, so the programme, which started with the national anthem followed by 'Pomp and Circumstance' and an invocation by the Rev. Lester Smith of the local Christ of Episcopal Chruch, probably went straight over his head.

As if to illustrate his role as an outsider at the school, when the senior poll came out, Tom did not even get a mention. The list – which featured the best looking, most intelligent, best dressed, funniest, biggest flirt, best athlete, most talented, most versatile, most likely to succeed, friend-liest, worst driver, cutest, quietest, best personality, to name but a few sections – did not rate Tom Cruise worthy of even a mention. It just goes to show how wrong people can be!

However, he did join in at the strictly non-alcoholic house parties with a Disneyland theme, which were held at various pupils' homes in the expensive neighbourhood near the school that summer. Local police officers even glided past some of the houses, taking snapshots with a camera as a subtle warning to students not to misbehave – that was the sort of place Glen Ridge was proud to be. By this time, Tom's appetite for girls had taken on healthy proportions. As his classmate Bobo Ahmed delicately put it: 'Tom was a ladykiller. He had a different girl every week.'

Tom conceded a few years later: 'It's a small place. You weren't allowed to date two girls at the same time but had to go steady with one.'

He admits he was a jock in those days – a serious-minded, slightly humourless character, interested only in the most basic things in life. 'I was a jock and I sang in the chorus. Jocks don't do that, so I always felt challenged. I always tried not to fall into that mould, not to judge people on where they came from or what they wore,' he recalled.

Later that summer, Tom held his own open party for his classmates at the house where the family lived. Without any of the inverted snobbery that seemed prevalent in the Glen Ridge area, Tom insisted that everyone from his year was welcome at the party. 'I couldn't stand parties to which some people weren't invited. Everyone in school knew about my party. Everyone who wanted to come, came. We had a big yard and around 200 people turned up,' he explained years later. It all went off without any problems.

Tom was incredibly protective towards his sisters. Once he was working as a busboy at a country club near Glen Ridge and he noticed a man looking at his sister 'the wrong way'. Tom immediately stared hard at the man as if to say, 'You son of a bitch'.

Another time, he was talking to a kid at school, who told him that he really wanted to kiss Tom's sister Cass. The youngster was really shocked by this admission and immediately told the other boy: 'If you touch my sister I will kill you.'

At the time the local cinema was showing *The Blues Brothers*, starring John Belushi and Dan Aykroyd, Tom and his friends made at least three weekly pilgrimages to see the film, considered a classic by high school kids across the nation.

Tom and his mother and step-father attended a special dinner for all the senior varsity athletes from the Glen Ridge High Class of 1980 a few days after graduation day. Tom who, along with more than 50 of his classmates, received a senior letter award for sporting achievement, listened to Bruce Harper, running back for the New York Jets football team, tell the audience that his own short height (just five feet eight inches, which is considered very short in professional footballing terms) had not held him back because he always had the determination to succeed.

Young Tom Mapother, still only about five feet seven inches at the time, took due note of his sporting hero's advice. He had already set himself a goal in life that would not be affected by his short height. Even with unemployment running at more than seven million people in the United States that summer of 1980, Tom did not seem worried about finding a job.

Later, Tom explained that all the schools he had attended and the difficult years of his young life had made him feel vulnerable a lot of the time and somehow that manifested itself in his desire to become an actor. 'I was constantly having to put up these guards to take care of myself. You didn't sit around with the guys and say, "God, that really hurt my feelings". What you said was more like, "Yeah, let's go out, have some beers and kick some ass." That was really frustrating for me.'

After Tom left Glen Ridge High in June 1980, his younger sister Cass continued the family involvement in wrestling by becoming team manager. Brother and sister were very close and her interest had been sparked by watching Tom the previous year.

Eventually, the Mapothers moved out of Glen Ridge and none of them ever returned. Even when Glen Ridge High became the focus of attention across the United States in 1989, after the arrest of a number of students charged with a sexual assault on a retarded girl, Cruise refused to be drawn into commenting on the controversy.

*   *   *

For most of his teens, Tom Cruise hardly ever saw his father, Thomas Cruise Mapother III. Occasionally, he would hear about his movements from Catherine, his grandmother on the Mapother side, during visits to their large house in Smithfield Road, Louisville.

Tom has never talked openly about what his father was

doing during these so-called missing years before his return, like the prodigal son, to Louisville in the mid-1980s.

Cousins Caroline Mapother and Professor Dillon Mapother say that Tom III 'went a little strange' during that period. He married a lady called Joan soon after his divorce from Mary Lee and continued to harbour a misguided conviction that one day he would make millions from some crazy invention or other.

'Thomas Cruise Mapother III's behaviour towards his children was appalling. I don't think anyone normal would go off and abandon a wife and four children like he did,' says Caroline Mapother.

Childhood friend Sue Downey, who knew Tom during those difficult years in Louisville, said she had heard that the boy's father had a terrible temper and that Tom was often so unhappy about his parents' split-up that he would cry himself to sleep at night.

Family members have now revealed that Tom's father was leading the life of a virtual hobo between the mid-seventies and mid-eighties. He seems to have spent much of his time travelling the highways and byways of Southern California.

He virtually vanished for a few years and his parents were beside themselves with worry. Catherine and Thomas Cruise Mapother II regularly sent their wayward son letters and cheques but they would all be returned to the family home in Louisville with 'Not Known' stamped on them. It seemed that Thomas Cruise Mapother III rarely stayed more than a few days in one place.

On one occasion, according to Cousin Caroline Mapother, on their way back from a trip to San Francisco, his parents made an ill-fated trip to try to meet their wandering son in Las Vegas.

'They had got word he was in Vegas and wanted to

make sure he was all right. They found out he attended a particular church that gave out food and bedding to transients and so they headed over to it. But by the time they got there, Tom had gone. He just didn't want to see them,' explained Caroline.

The few relatives who did get a glimpse into Thomas's life at this time report that he grew a long beard and had his hair in a ponytail for much of the time that he was wandering California and the far west of the United States with his new wife. Thomas Cruise Mapother III had basically become a man of the road – a virtual tramp who just could not cope with normal family life.

Cousin Caroline Mapother has noted with interest comments about Tom Cruise suggesting he had a deprived childhood, living on the wrong side of the tracks. 'These claims make me angry because his grandmother did everything in the world to try and help support those children, especially after Tom III went off,' explained Caroline. 'It has been implied that he was born into a blue collar family but everyone around him was from very respected backgrounds.'

She claims that after an article on Tom Cruise appeared in *Newsweek* some years after he made it as a Hollywood star, Tom's grandmother Catherine was deeply offended because he gave the clear impression he was born into poverty. 'Catherine was incensed. She wanted to put the record straight but never did get around to talking to Tom about it,' added Caroline.

She remembered hearing about Tom's story of the Christmas when the family was so poor that they recited poems to each other instead of giving gifts. Caroline says money was always available for Tom and his sisters but Mary Lee's pride may well have prevented them from going to the Mapothers for assistance. 'There has been a clear implication over the years that Tom's father's family abandoned them in some way, but that is not true,' added Caroline, a crusty, straight-talking lady in her mid-seventies with a strong southern drawl. 'Sad that it is, Tom Cruise comes from a broken family and that does not exactly make a pretty picture.

Whatever the truth behind the real feelings between Mary Lee and her in-laws, it is perfectly understandable that she might feel a little uncomfortable going begging to her husband's family. After all, she came from a poorer background, growing up on the other side of Louisville where families like the Mapothers were considered the landed gentry of the area.

Meanwhile, for Tom Cruise the struggle continued.

'There's no sense of a crest with Tom. His talent is young, his body is young, his spirit is young. He's a Christmas tree – he's lit from head to toe.'

Dustin Hoffman

To the outside world Tom Cruise is bright, witty, successful, talented and handsome but beneath that veneer lies a man in conflict with himself because of an invisible handicap, something that can be, at the very least, debilitating and, at worst, crippling. It is a common handicap which has become much more clearly recognised over the past 20 years. For Tom Cruise has suffered all his life from the learning disability called dyslexia.

As one of the United States' most famous dyslexics, Thomas Alva Edison, explained: 'I remember I used to never be able to get along at school. I was always at the foot of the class. My father thought I was stupid, and I almost decided that I was a dunce.'

The fact that one of the nation's greatest inventors should have been labelled an idiot at school provides the perfect insight into how Tom Cruise suffered as a child travelling from school to school across the country. Those never-ending changes must have made his 'problem' even harder to recognise because none of his teachers ever got to know him for long enough to help him with his disability.

Dyslexia is a very complex and confusing learning problem – one that educationalists are only now beginning to come to grips with. Along with other so-called learning disorders, such as attention-deficient hyperkinesia and hyperactivity, dyslexia is responsible for making life miserable for tens of millions of children and adults across the globe.

This invisible handicap comes in many guises: the case histories are endless. There are children who cannot understand their parent's commands; fathers who cannot read bedtime stories to their kids; people who have trouble working out the difference between a five pound note and a ten pound note. Then there are the thousands of people of all ages who have to think before tying their shoelaces, who get lost or disorientated easily, who cannot read a menu or a road sign, or have consistent problems articulating their thoughts.

All these problems come from one common cause – the brain of a learning-disabled person doesn't assimilate information in the same manner as the brain of an ordinary person. Every second of the day, the brain is bombarded with information. When this information becomes scrambled up, the person is thrown out of step with the rest of the world. Some dyslexics even have trouble analysing facial expressions. It's almost as if a link is missing from their chain of thought.

Tom's dyslexia made it difficult for him to deal with his schoolwork. He couldn't remember which way a 'c' or a 'z' went. Letters would magically switch themselves around and entire words and sentences appeared fractured and backwards. It was frightening, disorientating and, above all, frustrating.

'I was put in remedial reading classes,' recalled Tom. 'It was a drag. It separated you and singled you out,' he explained later. 'I didn't know whether a 'c' or 'd' curved to the right or left. That affects everything you do – how you deal with letters and which way they go, the way you pronounce things, your reading comprehension ... everything! My spelling was terrible. Fortunately, I was able to train myself to see letters the way they really were, but that took a lot of work ... and a lot of support from my mother.'

Tom's 'problem' was usually interpreted by teachers during his early school days as evidence that he was stupid or uncooperative, sometimes both. Some recognised that there was some sort of problem but they failed to establish precisely what it was.

'People would excuse me: "He's the new kid. We'll just help him through this year." I had to train myself to focus on attention,' he later explained.

Typically, at home Tom's confusion over which way to draw his letters did not alienate him from the rest of the family. It actually brought him even closer to them because it is considered almost certain that dyslexia is inherited. Mary Lee eventually spotted the condition in her son because not only did she suffer from it, but so did his three sisters. Gradually, she began to take decisive steps to help Tom.

Not only did Mary Lee appreciate the anguish Tom was going through, she also had professional expertise. She had worked with hyperkinetic and dyslexic children and she knew that, with patience and understanding, she could coach Tom and his sisters. Every evening she would carefully check their homework for major blunders and she gently coaxed the children through numerous crises of confidence sparked by their learning disabilities. Apparently, Cass had the worst problems and required almost constant attention just to get her through the most basic written work.

Gradually, Tom learned how to work around his dyslexia. It will never be completely cured but it is not now a problem that gets in the way of reading either for business or pleasure. However, there are still occasions when Tom finds reading the small print of a screenplay difficult.

They say that people with learning disabilities learn to compensate. A man who has trouble communicating verbally or otherwise may pick up a pencil or a paintbrush and become a great artist. It is suspected that Leonardo Da Vinci suffered from some sort of learning disability. At school, Tom compensated in his own way, by turning to athletics.

Sport helped Tom to fit in, especially in his teens. It at least gave him a focus, something that people with his handicap surely need. Simple tasks that were taken for granted by other children, like planning a career or daydreaming about what they would like to do when they grew up, had to be considered in a different light. At one point, Tom thought about being an astronaut but, with his problems, how could he throw himself wholeheartedly into his ambitions? 'I had to set goals and force myself to be disciplined because I always felt I had barriers to overcome. I was forced to write with my right hand when I wanted to use my left. I began to reverse letters and reading became difficult. I was always put in remedial classes. I felt ashamed.'

Sports provided short-term relief based on physical prowess and the kind of mental alertness that has nothing to do with telling the difference between the letter 'b' and the letter 'd'.

During the past 15 years, the general public has become much more aware of people with learning disabilities like Tom's. It is now estimated that at least 10 per cent of all schoolchildren may have the same kind of handicap and the problem is now more easily recognised. Tom was lucky because he was diagnosed as a small child and that gave him ample opportunity to work on his weak spots. Other dyslexics are not always so fortunate.

In recent years, Tom has definitely played a role in trying to bring worldwide attention to this learning disability. By talking openly about it, he has given many dyslexic children hope for a successful future and, even more importantly, he has constantly stressed the need to recognise and deal with the special requirements of dyslexics. In 1985, he received an award for Outstanding Learning Disabled Achievement. Along with other honorees – performer Cher and sportsman Bruce Jenner, businessmen Richard C. Strauss and G. Chris Anderson, and artist Richard Rauschenberg – Tom travelled to Washington to receive his award from the Lab School, which teaches both children and adults to deal with their learning handicaps. The six recipients met Nancy Reagan at the White House and the awards were presented by the then Speaker of the House, Senator Tip O'Neill.

At the Lab School, Tom was a huge hit, willingly posing for photographs with a long line of predominantly female students and answering their questions. 'Reading before the class was the most frustrating thing for me... I felt like I was dumb. I was real embarrassed... my teachers were upset because I made my "z"s and backward and I didn't know the difference between "b"s and "d"s,' he told the assembled group.

Tom then watched with a definite glint in his eye as superstar Cher told everyone that she didn't recognise her dyslexia until her daughter, Chastity, was diagnosed. Wearing her trademark-of-the-moment, an enormous black wig, Cher explained the nature of her impairment and its effect on her life. 'I'm a terrible reader. It took me a long time to be able to write cheques. I have a hard time dialing phones.

For me, it's very annoying but in another kind of work it would be devastating. If I read a script, I read it very slowly and memorise it the first time I read it,' she told the White House audience.

Former Olympic champion Bruce Jenner said he had to memorise his TV sports commentary because the tele-prompter poses a real problem for him.

Artist Robert Rauschenberg added: 'For years I thought I was just restless, just slow. The biggest help for dyslexic kids is to convince them it's not their fault.' Tom Cruise could relate very strongly with that comment.

Rauschenberg was upset that the press were excluded from the White House meeting and that First Lady Nancy Reagan neglected to make a statement. 'The only reason we're down here is to create some attention. Everybody in the group seriously believes our being here makes some difference in attracting national attention to a problem that can go undetected but can wreck your life.'

Tom's dyslexic problems had a happy ending but he'll never forget the battle he fought or the millions of people out there still trying to win the war, as he was later to prove.

'Nothing great was ever achieved without enthusiasm.'

Ralph Waldo Emerson

Tom set off for New York, to make both history and earn his bread and butter, with $2,000 saved from his various part-time jobs and little else but an ambition and a prayer. He could well have just blown the cash on a train pass and hiked around Europe like many of his classmates back in Glen Ridge. Instead, he bit the struggling-actor bullet and took odd jobs unloading trucks and bussing tables at places like Mortimer's restaurant. When he could afford to spare a moment, he'd audition or attend a workshop at the Neighborhood Playhouse.

Even before graduating from high school, he had managed to approach a manager who had been recommended by a classmate at Glen Ridge High who had appeared in some commercials. A few weeks before his full-time departure for the big city, Tom persuaded his mother to drive to New York with him in a dirty green Ford Pinto he had bought for $50 a few months earlier. Their mission was to get Tom signed up with that lady manager. Driving through thick traffic, Tom had a huge argument with Mary Lee, no doubt brought on by the tension he felt over this impending meeting with his first manager-to-be. It got so bad that they stopped talking to each other and sat in the car in crawling traffic in complete silence. Tom was angry because he knew that, at 17, he could not get a manager unless his mother co-signed a contract with him.

He was hardly well prepared for the most important meeting of his young life and did not even have any photographs of himself. By the time they got to the manager's office, they were running late so Tom jumped out of the Pinto and barked at his mother, 'Just park the car somewhere' while he went up to meet the woman, a part-time New York actress.

Within seconds of getting into the manager's office, she had young Tom do a brief reading of a Hershey's commercial script. As Tom later explained: 'It was one of those "Yeah, yeah, yeah, babe, you're beautiful, I'm going to make you a star," sort of situations.'

By the time a flustered Mary Lee arrived at the office, Tom had signed on the dotted line. His new manager was convinced she had discovered a potential star.

Just a few weeks later he landed his first role: the character of Herb in a dinner-theatre presentation of the musical, Godspell. Although both the role and the production were miniscule, none the less they validated his talent. It was his first professional experience in front of an audience.

Inside a month, Tom had fired his new manager because she had him doing errands for her. Nobody was going to get in his way. Tom now decided that an agent was quite sufficient for a young actor at this stage of his career. There was no need for a manager. Even then he did not mind flexing his muscles if necessary.

Tom presumed he'd be stuck juggling and struggling with day jobs and small productions for some time to come but he was also confident that his determination would earn him a breakthrough in the major league before long. He never saw himself doing odd jobs for the rest of his life: 'Otherwise, I wouldn't be striving to be an actor, would I? I'd be a professional waiter,' he said later.

As a child, Tom never excelled in any particular one of his many athletic undertakings; flitting from town to town and sport to sport left no time to develop true expertise in any single area. Now, after enduring all the shifts of scenery as well as the whims of athletics, the air force and even priestly vows, he had finally found his true calling. 'I wanted to be an actor,' he insisted.' I *want* it, *wanted* it very badly. I was *hungry*. I'm *still* hungry.'

Life in New York was a whole new experience for Tom. He managed to find a room-mate to keep his outgoings down but regularly hitched or rode a bus back to Glen Ridge for some of his mother's tasty home cooking. One actor who encountered him at that time described him as 'very New Jersey, less polished than he is now ... he was like a greaser – he had big muscles, he had his hair greased back. He had an angry edge to him.'

The truth was that Tom was still painfully shy and slightly overawed by New York and he was hiding his thoughts behind a seemingly angry exterior. He also believed that, as an actor, he had to fulfil a role in life and he clearly saw himself as a tough little guy with a good set of muscles and a cool hairstyle to match.

However, there was another aspect to Tom which others noted. 'He was handsome, and those who saw him then recall an urgency in his performing that was hard to dismiss,' says movie expert Chris Connelly.

That urgency was born out of a desperate need to

succeed at all costs. Tom had given himself ten years when he announced his intentions to Mary Lee and Jack but, privately, he reckoned he would have to make it as an actor much faster than that.

Tom's wrestling coach, Angelo Corbo, had a rare insight into what Tom was like just after he left Glen Ridge High, when he offered the teenager a ride in his car after spotting him standing on the corner of Broad Street in the town of Blomfield, near Glen Ridge. Corbo drove Tom to the end of ten-mile-long Broad Street where he could get a bus into New York City. Tom was full of enthusiasm for his new found profession. He bombarded Corbo with exciting sounding stories about life in the Big Apple. 'He said he'd got hooked up with an agent and was trying out for loads of parts. Frankly, I couldn't believe him. It had only been a few months since he'd left school. It seemed incredible that his career could be taking off so fast,' explained Corbo.

Then the fresh-faced Tom astounded his slightly cynical old teacher by announcing with childish fervour and a sly grin: 'I'm doing a movie with Brooke Shields.'

Corbo recalled: 'I really thought he was spinning a yarn when he said that. I laughed out loud and told him, "I hope you make it, kid." Frankly I didn't give him much chance.' A straight-talking Italian American, Corbo chuckled as he told the young Tom: 'When you make it, Tommy, remember me, I'll drive your limo.'

Corbo explained later: 'I dropped him off at the end of Broad Street and remember driving away thinking it was all a pipe-dream. His parents didn't even know anyone in the acting business. He had absolutely no connections. I just couldn't see it happening.'

Although Tom Cruise's rise to stardom was eventually to be incredibly swift, first of all he had to learn to deal with the rejection of going out on readings for insignificant parts.

Somehow he even managed to turn that often demoralising experience to his own advantage. 'I felt that the people rejecting me were there to help me in the long run. Sometimes it hurts but I truly believe that there are parts I'm supposed to get and parts I'm not supposed to get and something else is going to come along,' he later recalled.

Initially, Tom got turned down for dozens of small TV parts as well as a number of television commercials, which often provide struggling actors with a cash lifeline when the 'real' work dries up. A number of directors complained to casting agents that the fresh-faced New Jersey kid was far too intense. What none of them recognised was Tom's driving ambition and utter obsession to succeed. In a teenager, this was interpreted as intensity.

Yet, within a few months of arriving in New York, an inexplicable buzz was circulating about this young man, who had now dropped the Mapother part of his name, mainly because it was too much of a mouthful but also as a tribute to the women who had steered those Mapother men through so much troubled water over the previous five generations.

This period in Tom's career is clouded in mystery. It is known that he started out in New York by sharing a tiny loft with a male room-mate and that he definitely waited tables at Mortimers. Within a couple of months, he had managed to cut his living costs down even further by becoming an assistant/handyman to the superintendent of an apartment building on the West Side – a part-time job that brought with it free accommodation. However, it has been impossible to find out who it was that helped to guide his career so rapidly.

Tom seemed still to have a child-like innocence when it came to dealing with the sharper side of the acting profession. One time he was flown out to Los Angeles to read for a television series. The young actor had no idea just how competitive the acting market place was.

> 'I went in to read and this director was sitting there in his office – he thought he was the coolest thing happening. I read, and I knew I was terrible. And he said, "So, how long are you going to be in California?" And I'm thinking, "He's probably going to want me to come back and read again with someone else." I said, "Well, just a couple of days." He said, "Good, get a tan while you're here." I couldn't help it. I walked out and thought it was the funniest thing. Tears were coming out of my eyes, I was laughing so hard, I thought, "This is Hollywood. Welcome, Cruise."'

To all who met Tom Cruise at this time, he was nothing if not thoroughly focused. He loved to tell anyone who would listen about his auditions, his agent, his manager, the free flight for a movie test. He had just passed his nineteenth birthday and he was already frighteningly singleminded about his profession. Nothing and nobody would ever get in his way.

It was the beginning of the 1980s – a decade that was to be marked by big wages and self-motivated people driving onwards and upwards, taking few prisoners along the way. That was how Tom Cruise was starting to sound to his old friends but there was nothing offensive about his attitude – he was simply a kid with a mission to succeed. 'I focus on my craft, my work. That is the most important thing to me. And what people say, if I let it bother me, I'm going to be in a lot of trouble. I just focus in on what I want and what I want to do, and everything outside of that is just there, and it happens,' he told one of the first journalists ever to interview him, 18 months later.

The reference to Brooke Shields, which Angelo Corbo had dismissed as a joke when he gave him a lift in his car one rainy afternoon, had turned out to be accurate. Just five months after heading for New York, Tom bagged a small role in the film *Endless Love*.

Tom's movie début turned out to be a seven-minutes-in-heaven type of thing. Not that you'd miss him if you sneezed but you might miss him if you left the room during the first half of the film. Tom wasn't disappointed by the relative brevity of his appearance. In fact, he felt fortunate to get a break so quickly and equally fortunate that the movie was not necessary as a vehicle for his talent as it flopped in grand style at the box office.

He was still just 18, fresh-faced, determined and full of vitality. His superfit physique helped to gain him many admirers, both male and female, and he kept up his training by working exhausting hours as a busboy in restaurants.

Franco Zeffirelli – the director and driving force behind *Endless Love* – had made a name for himself in the United States thanks to his flamboyant spectacular, *Romeo and Juliet*, starring two unknown teenagers at the time. Despite this, Tom did not have a clue who Mr Zeffirelli was. In some strange way this complete and utter ignorance on the part of the young actor led to a blissful conclusion because Tom sailed through his brief audition, not a butterfly in sight. Director Zeffirelli reportedly exclaimed a breathy 'Bellissimo' after watching Tom in action. Already, he was starting to have that soon-be-renowned effect on both men and women.

Tom's character, Billy, was not exactly equipped with the sort of dialogue that would help Tom to make a worthy impression in his big-screen début. Basically, he was a young, gregarious jock who is a good friend of the leading male character. 'Billy' did not even merit a surname, although the few lines that Tom uttered so profoundly did determine the course of action for the entire second half of the movie. Tom had a role that might just about get him noticed if it was handled properly and carefully. Meanwhile, another member of the cast was grabbing most of the attention.

'I think she is the most beautiful person I've ever seen in my life. A miracle of nature,' gushed Zeffirelli in reference to *Endless Love's* leading lady, Brooke Shields. At that time, Brooke had become a national obsession: a teenage millionairess, the veteran of seven films and a string of Calvin Klein commercials. She had posed nude as a 14 year old and some of her movies – including the highly controversial *Pretty Baby* – had dealt with rather adult subjects like prostitution and underage sex.

Miss Shields had caused great outrage in Middle America, especially when it was revealed that she was managed by her mother. *New York* magazine once put both mother and daughter on its cover with the declaration: 'Meet Teri and Brooke Shields. Brooke is twelve. She poses nude. Teri is her mother. She thinks it's swell.' Enough said.

Brooke Shields was really 'hot', in Hollywood terms, at this time. She had just completed another titillating effort called *The Blue Lagoon* and, through her outspoken mother, was used to getting exactly what she wanted. Even the fact that the *Endless Love* script revolved more around the male lead than Brooke's role was duly noted and immense pressure put on Zeffirelli to alter it accordingly, otherwise Miss Shields might contemplate pulling out of the deal. It must be pointed out that Zeffirelli tried very hard to find an unknown actress to cast in the lead but, after a huge casting call, he decided on Brooke because none of the other girls had been as beautiful. The 16 year old got $500,000 plus 5 per cent of the first $5million in video rentals.

The male lead, Martin Hewitt, was almost as wet

behind the ears as Tom Cruise. He had graduated from Claremont High School in 1979 and went on to the American Academy in Pasadena. When he noticed an advertisement for auditions in the entertainment section of the *Los Angeles Times*, he was still a student earning some money by working as a parking valet.

Intriguingly, his starring role came about through sheer luck. Hewitt was not hired from the film's actual auditions; Zeffirelli noticed him while watching a TV programme made by entertainment reporter Rona Barratt about the business of auditions. Suddenly, he had his male lead.

The screenplay was based on the novel *Endless Love* by Scott Spencer. It was an extremely complex book, full of unusual characters and competing thematic eddies and swirls. The movie script was a very watered down version and a number of characters were added – like Tom Cruise's 'Billy', who was inserted into the film to eliminate some of the tangled web of people and plot.

However, a much bigger problem was caused by the original book's exceedingly graphic sexuality. 'When I read the book I put it down and thought, "There's a great film there but I don't know how,"' explained Zeffirelli. 'Then I decided it must be possible to handle daring material without offending anyone. And I think we succeeded.'

Unfortunately, those who try to sit on fences often fall off. The film did create a lot of interest but Brooke Shields used a body double after her mother put her foot down. This was further complicated when manager/mother Teri Shields insisted that the body double have a blemish on her bottom removed because 'Everyone's going to think that's Brooke's rear end, so there shouldn't be a mark on it.' This was the sort of headline story being sparked by the movie. Unfortunately the public's imagination was not caught by the film itself.

Zeffirelli has admitted that just before completing each of his movies, he was tempted to throw the entire film in the trash can and start again. Most people who saw *Endless Love* say he definitely should have done that with the end product this time.

Basically, *Endless Love* centres around a teenage couple who rush blindly into an obsessive and dangerous relationship. David Axelrod (Martin Hewitt) is the son of two left-wing lawyers. Their overwhelming concern for their fellow man leaves little time for their son. When David falls in love with Jade Butterfield (Brooke Shields) he becomes embroiled with her entire family, who seem so relaxed compared with his own parents, but there are some familiar problems lurking beneath the surface of this seemingly happy family.

Tom Cruise enters briefly as Billy the friendly jock who inadvertently suggests to David that he should set fire to his girlfriend's family's home after they turn nasty towards him.

Tom's portrayal of Billy offers an important contrast because he is animated, enthusiastic and boyishly gleeful. When put next to David's sullen depression, Billy highlights the leading man's distress. The final twist in this uninteresting tale came as Zeffirelli spouted on about what a great star Brooke Shields was about to come. Nobody present realised that the film's biggest star-to-be was that attractive teenager with less than a hundred words of dialogue.

Tom himself later admitted finding the entire process – which amounted to just one day on the set of *Endless Love* – as bewildering. 'It was a hell of an experience. The director kept grabbing at my chest. I wondered what was going on around here? He did it a couple of times, feeling me, and I walked away. It was all pretty strange. I was so naive. I didn't understand.'

Tom has never fully expanded on those comments and

it is difficult to interpret precisely what they mean. Is he talking about his own repressed fear of homosexuality or is he just referring to the physicality of the part and the method by which Franco Zeffirelli directs his actors?

Meanwhile, *Endless Love* suffered from bad word of mouth even before the movie was released in July 1981. A leak from someone who saw a sneak preview of the movie reported that many in the audience booed for the last 15 minutes because it was so corny. Most of the shouting was reserved for Brooke Shields. 'When she would deliver a line like "I'm hurt" or something like that in a heavy love scene, she came off like a little six-year-old with a boo-boo on her knee or something. The audience was just cracking up,' said one previewer.

In *TV Movies and Video Guide*, the film was labelled a 'bomb'. The magazine continued: 'Scott Spencer's deservedly praised novel ... is thoroughly trashed in a text-book example of how to do everything wrong in a literary adaptation. Rightfully regarded as one of the worst films of its time.'

Sheila Benson, of the *Los Angeles Times*, complained, 'Zeffirelli has turned the catharsis of the novel into a dread-ful sickly sweet sheen ... All of Zeffirelli's renowned lush-ness works against a story of dead-ahead urgency. But it may still have a happy ending – it may make thousands of new readers for Spencer's astonishing book.'

Even movie guide books are less than enthusiastic about *Endless Love*. Sentences like 'an overheated melodrama with unbelievable and unlikeable characters' stand out. In the *New York Times* the infamous Janet Maslin insisted that 'Zeffirelli and his screenwriter have bitten off so much more than they can chew that their film is virtually unintelligible.'

Feeble attempts to stir up interest in the movie among the dirty raincoat brigade interested in viewing teenager

Brooke in a number of steamy sex scenes, were fed by various cheapskate stories in the US tabloids, which blasted headlines like 'Censorship storm over Brooke's sizzling movie'. The truth was that the film's backers, Polygram, had financed a huge pup of a movie and they were desperately scrambling for any ticket sales.

Mind you, Zeffirelli was obviously in complete denial about the movie's dismal portrayal of young love. He told one journalist: 'I never think of anything I do in terms of financial success. The emphasis is not on sex, it is on the awesome power of love – and there's a difference.'

Poor innocent Martin Hewitt got taken to the cleaners in the tabloids as well. One quote he gave the notorious *National Enquirer* must have been the final straw for precious 'superstar' Brooke Shields. 'I decided it didn't matter that she was famous. She's still human and it doesn't make her any better than anyone else. I felt that I had to treat her like a normal kid.'

Hewitt had apparently spent much of the making of the movie trying unsuccessfully to get his pretty young co-star to go on a real-life date following their steamy sex scenes together.

When invitations to the film's glitzy opening party were sent out, an impressive array of stars, including Elizabeth Taylor, Diana Ross and Liza Minelli showed up, but no one bothered to ask the kid from New Jersey.

You could definitely say that Tom had lucked out. He had spent enough time on the screen to be noticed but he didn't have a big enough part to be associated with a flop on his first time out.

So far, stage one of his plan to become a star had worked out very satisfactorily.

'Life itself is a very humbling experience.
So that keeps you honest.'

Tom Cruise

Tom's life on the West Side of New York City was not much more than an extension of the difficult years following his parents' split up. He was juggling jobs and failing auditions with alarming regularity. Instead of a 4 a.m. newspaper round, he was getting out of bed at all hours of the day and night to repair leaking pipes and broken locks in his starring role as the handsome teenage handyman in the apartment block where he lived.

For Tom, however, not yet 19, there was one big difference from those painful times a few years earlier, and he kept reminding himself of it; he was doing what he wanted more than anything else in the world. The more he tried to succeed, the more confident he got. As one old New York acting friend recalled: 'There was no stopping that kid!'

So, when director Harold Becker held a huge audition in May 1981 for 2,000 young men, ranging in age from prepubescent to late teens, for his latest movie project *Taps*, Tom went charging in with all guns blazing.

'I guess *Taps* was where it all started for me. When I read for Harold Becker, I remember, I literally didn't have a dollar to my name. And even though I didn't have the role yet, I felt really good about the interview,' Tom recalled later.

Next, Tom had a meeting with the legendary producer Stanley R. Jaffe (*Bad News Bears*, *Kramer vs Kramer*, to name but two) and the director together. He explained: 'It was like a two-minute meeting – you know, "Pull your hair up; read this line". And that was it. I walked out of the meeting. I was going to see my family in Jersey but because I didn't have a dollar to take the bus home, I hitch-hiked.'

Later, walking up the driveway to the family house in Glen Ridge, Tom saw his mother, through the window, talking on the phone. She seemed very excited. When Tom let himself in with his front door key, Mary Lee rushed into the hallway and put her arms round her son. 'It's your agent. You got the role.'

Tom hadn't landed one of the two leads but he had managed to grab a reasonable part as a friend to one of the leading characters, David Shawn, an aggressive young Marine. Not bad for only his second movie appearance.

Tom considered the part a fantastic opportunity but when he met the actor cast to play David Shawn, his enthusiasm reached new boundaries. Director Becker – a master craftsman who cut his teeth as a director of highly rated television commercials – watched the sparks fly virtually from the first moment that Tom was introduced to the other actor. Tom had gone to the trouble of transforming himself into a chunky, physically intimidating rookie soldier. His role might have been small but Tom was going to give it everything he had. The nightmare for that other young actor had only just begun.

According to Sean Penn, who starred in *Taps* with Timothy Hutton, the other unfortunate thespian was completely overawed by Tom's infectious enthusiasm. Penn – who has regularly been accused of excessive behaviour both on and off the set in pursuit of his character's essense – watched the almost fanatical Tom Cruise focus in on his aims with cold, professional intensity, the likes of which he had never witnessed before in his life.

There was no question of Tom deliberately setting out to destroy his rival who was playing the so-called meatier role of David Shawn. That was not the way a well-brought-up kid like Tom behaved. There was no backbiting on his part – he just looked, felt and smelled right for the part. Simply put, he completely overshadowed the other actor from the moment he stepped out for rehearsals.

Harold Becker noticed what was happening instantly and found himself swept up by Tom's electrifying interpretation. He immediately halted proceedings and conferred with the movie's producers. They poured over the script for hours, trying to work out if something could be done to enlarge Tom's character – everyone present knew that this was too big an opporunity to miss out on.

Becker then came up with a solution; he proposed that Tom should take over the role of David Shawn. The teenager appeared horrified and embarrassed. He immediately went to the producer and insisted that he could not take over the part without the original actor's blessing. Sean Penn witnessed all this with a wry smile on his face. Here was an inexperienced actor being offered the chance of a lifetime and he was worried about hurting another actor's feelings.

Penn explained: 'Tommy had to get the part. Very

intense, 200 per cent there. It was overpowering – and we'd all kind of laugh because it was so sincere. Good acting, but so far in the intense direction that it was funny. The producers told him, "Look, buddy, if you don't want to do it, leave. We want you for this part, but we're not going to beg you." It was incredible how innocent and naive he was when he came to do *Taps*.'

However, what Penn, who had been brought up in a Hollywood family, did not appreciate at the time was that Tom's motivation had always been governed by what was right and what was wrong. In Tinseltown there might have been no guidelines but where Tom came from there most certainly were.

Tom explained: 'I said, "Thank you very much but I don't want to play David Shawn." I was in a small role and that's the way I wanted it to be. I was learning so much just being around, watching everything that was happening.'

There is no doubting the fact that Tom's behaviour was extraordinarily naive. After all, no actor worth his salt would admit to his "second" that he was a better man and graciously turn over his role. The most intriguing aspect of this entire incident was that not one person present believes that Tom deliberately set out to steal that starring part.

Anyway, Tom's apparent innocence did not prove a lasting hindrance as he finally accepted the larger part and became David Shawn, leader of Bravo Company. Tom had deliberately put on 15 pounds, thanks to a few gallons of high-density milkshakes. He more than made up for his lack of inches by making himself resemble an aggressive bulldog, much to the delight of director Becker who wanted David Shawn to fill the screen with unmitigated bodily chutzpah.

Just like a bulldog, Tom now had the bit between his teeth and he had no intention of letting go. The moviemakers were so inspired by his portrayal that they continued to expand his role in the screenplay as filming progressed. The character eventually grew into the classic, raving-lunatic cadet and Tom ended up appearing in more than 80 per cent of the finished movie. His career was taking off after only his second celluloid outing.

Tom was ecstatic. 'I felt like it was a chance for me, and a beginning. Me and Penn, I really don't know if we ever slept during that movie.'

Tom and his new friend Sean Penn would stay up all night just talking about the movie and their roles. There was little time to exchange the sort of information that one would expect two virile, good-looking young men to talk about. It was work, work, work.

'We were really scared and nervous and excited – we didn't know what was going to happen. It was a special time in my life because it was my first proper movie and it was Sean's too. You just felt that something special was happening,' explained Tom.

Besides the impressive Harold Becker, there was producer Stanley Jaffe. He had nurtured and carefully developed the script with a painstaking eye for detail. While other similar Hollywood producers of his stature tended to turn out two or three movies every year, Jaffe had averaged one every other year. He was a character who liked to be involved from conception to fruition. 'I buy the material. I work very, very slowly on it. I don't even bring in a director until one or two drafts of the screenplay have been completed,' he explained with meticulous understatement.

Taps also boasted some very high-brow talent in front of the camera, including veteran performer George C. Scott (who played the general himself in *Patton*, winner of seven Oscars, including one for Best Picture) and Timothy Hutton, who had walked away with an Oscar for Best Supporting

Actor for his impressive work on his first ever movie, *Ordinary People*.

Hutton, at 20 only a year older than Tom, was streets ahead of him in career terms. He was finding life as a celebrity tough to handle. Even the small matter of finding a suitable date seemed a nightmare scenario. During *Taps*, he explained in graphic terms a situation that would ring a few bells of recognition with Tom Cruise only a year later.

Hutton said: 'It would be wonderful to meet someone who doesn't know who I am. One girl said I made her feel good because I never take advantage of anyone. I said, "You got me all wrong. That guy on screen isn't me! What if I did take advantage of you?" '

Hutton even took a chance on a blind date, only to find that the girl knew in advance who he was. 'Everybody at the party knew,' he added with exasperation. Tom Cruise noted Tim Hutton's frustration and decided that whatever happened to his career he would make sure he avoided any such problems.

Taps was based on a series of tragic events at a military school, so the actors were sent by director Harold Becker to the Valley Forge Military Academy for four weeks and told to familiarise themselves with the tough, gung-ho lifestyle of real cadets. 'This film had to be founded in reality, every movement in it, every word in it,' explained Becker. 'We needed the environment to draw on and that became, as far as I'm concerned, our greatest single resource.'

Tom and his fellow thespians soon found themselves submitting to the school barber, a little initiation routine experienced by every new recruit. Then followed a fitting for a smart, tailored uniform with shiny brass buttons. Becker expected Tom and the rest of the cast to live their parts to the full so that they could reflect this reality when they started shooting the movie. This also included appreciating – and experiencing – the stringent rules and regulations facing every new recruit on entry to the military school, such as back-breaking physical discipline without any immediate rewards. *Taps* was turning out to be the nearest to the real thing any of the actors had ever experienced.

'I'm a great believer in rehearsals. In my other films we've had long rehearsal periods and in this movie I wanted it to be dedicated to turning our young actors into cadets,' explained the director.

Becker, a soft-spoken, highly articulate man, saw *Taps* as having a strong message in the society of the early 1980s. 'Any kind of closed situation is a dangerous one. The fictional school in *Taps* is also a kind of closed society, one that treats itself as a military post. Is that a suitable lifestyle for young boys who are enrolled at such a school?' It was a heavy, intense interpretation from Becker but that was the way he was and it had a profound effect on young Tom. He took every word of Becker's literally.

However, dress and discipline were not the only reality-based activities; there were daily weapon drills, parade procedures and every detail of military protocol. The regime included rising at dawn and stomping around in never-ending formation. Many of the actors moaned and groaned as they became immersed in the disciplined environment but not Tom – he loved every minute of it. This was his means to an end. If he had to eat dirt he would do it if it made him a better actor.

All these hardships were merely part of a day's work for the 19 year old. In any case, it provided a perfect outlet for his energy and enthusiasm, as well as legitimising his conviction that complete immersion in a role was essential for a good performance.

'To make the character as real as possible I have to find

out how I can relate to the character personally,' explained Tom to one journalist after completing *Taps*. 'I have to find out what is "real" in the character that I do ... there are going to be some points where you're going to have to be like a part of the character in terms of yourself, or else your character won't be real.' Tom could talk for hours about his art to anyone who would listen.

In *Taps*, Tom Cruise took a huge step forward in terms of his status and ability as an actor. The character of David Shawn was not an easy one to pull off because a delicate balance between Shawn and the other principals had to be maintained for most of the film. Considering the instability of Shawn, this was akin to crossing a tightrope with an all-terrain vehicle.

The role would have been a stretch for actors with ten times more experience than Tom but somehow he reached inside himself and pulled out a manic, dangerous characterisation – obviously something that had been lurking deep within him for much of his life. 'David Shawn ... is also a part of me, even though he was psychotic ... I pulled different things to different extremities, of course,' Tom explained, a few months later. He had somehow got a handle on the fact that Shawn was driven by two main emotions: fear and anger. Using those ingredients, Tom brought startling, almost frightening, reality to the role.

Yet Tom never once resorted to the sort of eye-rolling and drooling that so often stereotypes many movie madmen. His eyes became like angry slits, perpetually filled with hostility. He was like a ticking time bomb, humourless and cruel, waiting to explode.

With a certain degree of amusement, veteran George C. Scott sat back and watched the young turks beating themselves to death in order to give their finest performances. Twenty-five years earlier he had been a killer of a young actor just like them but now he preferred to amuse himself between takes by playing chess.

Later, as the youngsters began gaining confidence, they started to relax a little and Tom even got involved in some of those chess games with Scott, much to his regret. The old timer horrified Tom by telling him some highly unlikely stories about life when he was growing up. 'He told us he used to play chess for money after selling a pint of his blood for cash and using half of it to bet on chess and the other half of it to drink. Arghh! The good old days.' Tom lapped up every word the old master said, even though it did not sound exactly accurate.

Filming took place entirely in the Wayne, Delaware County area of Pennsylvania. Local businessmen were delighted by an estimated $5 million in revenue bought in thanks to the presence of the movie technicians and actors. At least 500 local people were also hired as actors, extras, carpenters and drivers.

Interestingly, a Twentieth Century-Fox Film Corporation handout about the film incorrectly gave Tom Cruise's age as 17 at the time of shooting. He was, in fact, 19 but it is believed that the movie's backers thought it might be advisable to give the impression he was somewhat younger in order to attract a young audience.

Tom was as enthusiastic as ever when he was quoted in the Fox press release as saying of his experiences at the military academy. 'I got into it the minute I got there. Being at the academy and making *Taps* has made me stronger. It's helped teach me endurance,' explained Tom, and he meant every word.

Intriguingly, paperwork, uncovered almost 13 years later, shows that Tom Cruise did not get a look-in when it came to the traditional Hollywood game of 'star projection'. A Fox legal document gives George C. Scott a 100 per cent guarantee of having his name above the title or in the last position reading – and GEORGE C. SCOTT as General Bache'. Tim Hutton is given a 100 per cent guarantee that his name would never be used in a size smaller than any other cast member. Tom Cruise's name is not even mentioned on this document – something that did not go unnoticed by the young actor as his performance in the finished product was considered head and shoulders above everyone else's. The situation was to be reversed more than ten years later.

The movie won praise in some quarters, although Z magazine declared: 'Taps' plot has more than its share of holes and contrivances ... but its remarkable cast is nearly flawless.' Other critics were also not too quick to hail the movie.

Time Magazine pointed out: 'Taps takes far too long to reach its bloody, predictable conclusion. Its big guns are loaded with nothing more lethal than Hollywood nerve gas.'

The Motion Picture Product Digest seemed to get a better handle on what the movie was intended to be.

'Taps starts out as if it's going to be a larkish movie – just the thing for the holiday season – about some students at a military academy who barricade themselves inside the campus grounds to prevent the 125-year-old institution from being shut down entirely by its trustees and the property converted to a lucrative condominium project.

'All too soon, however, this amicable notion is dispelled, and it is made clear that the film makers have more grave and didactic intentions in mind. They are out to deliver a pacifist, anti-military message, and the deeper they get into this element the more ponderous and shrill they become.

'*Taps* turns out to be such a downer, in fact,
it's hard to imagine it winning over a large audience
at any time of the year – much less than during a
period when the paying customers are in a festive
mood.'

In an outrageous article in *Village Voice*, columnist Stuart
Byron claimed that the film's success was due in part to the
fact that Oscar winner Tim Hutton represented, 'the quiet,
handsome, sensitive, student-body-president type that 11 to
15-year-old girls want as their fuck.'

Byron's opinions might seem a tad blunt but film
industry insiders who had predicted that *Taps* would bomb
badly and never make back its original $18 million budget
had to eat their words and were looking for all sorts of
excuses.

Veteran producer Jaffe explained:

'There were three things that nobody understood
about *Taps*. First, they didn't understand the
magnitude of the star quality of Timmy Hutton.
Second, they did not understand that this was an
unusual Christmas season in that an inordinate
number of the movies were adult-orientated,
which meant that a picture which could be sold to
youth could break through. And third, they did not
understand the considerable anxiety about military
matters which has gripped draft-age youth in the
wake of the return of draft registration.'

Note that not once was the name Tom Cruise mentioned –
not that that bothered the young actor.

Tom was delighted by the reaction to the film; it had
put him on a stage with two famous Oscar winners and

introduced him to an up-and-coming talent called Sean Penn who was to become a great friend. Tim Hutton and Sean were both in his peer group in terms of age, potential and, most important of all, personal commitment to professional excellence.

Meanwhile, critical acclaim for *Taps* continued to be mixed. Joan Tarshis wrote in *The Film Journal*: 'Is it fair to ask an audience to applaud assaultive sociopaths? Such is the demand placed on those who will see *Taps*, a film whose moral point of view is confused by its desire to shock and engross its audience while encouraging the fanatical actions of its paladin. *Taps* holds your attention by pointing a gun in your face.'

Unlike *Endless Love*, where Tom did not even receive an invitation to the gala premiere, the young actor was one of the guests of honour when Marvin Davies, owner of the movie's backers – Twentieth Century-Fox – hosted a glitzy bash at the AVCO cinema in Westwood, Los Angeles – although it has to be pointed out that Tim Hutton was still being hailed as the hero of the proceedings.

Tom was in a daze for much of that premiere. He could not quite believe that he, a gawky, 19-year-old kid from a broken home, was there among the rich and famous, including names such as Ali MacGraw, Michael Douglas and Dabney Coleman, to name but a few. At the gala dinner afterwards, he sat quietly with his good friend, fellow *Taps* actor Sean O'Brien, at a back table beautifully decorated with mirrors, black cloth, white orchids and tulips, feeling awkward in his tuxedo. The next day, Tom's name got no more than the merest mention in the showbusiness trade papers. In fact, another pint-sized star, Gary Coleman (all four feet two inches) of *Diff'rent Strokes*, caused the biggest stir by dancing with an assortment of stunning – and much taller – lady guests.

p: Tom with first wife Mimie Rogers, who introduced him to the Scientologists.

low: The near Olympic sized swimming pool used by Tom and other celebrities at the entologists' basecamp at Gilman Hot Springs, in the Californian Desert.

Top: Tom with second wife Nicole Kidman.
Middle: One of the heavily secured entrance gates to the Scientologists' basecamp featuring remote TV cameras and a special pass key.
Bottom: The bizarre looking clipper ship built into the desert hillside overlooking the Scientologists' basecamp at Gilman Hot Springs.

left: David Geffen, Tom's Hollywood mentor.

right: The well secured – and carefully hidden – entrance to Tom's vast Pacific Palisades mansion, near Los Angeles.

tom left: The nondescript entrance to Tom's vast apartment in one of New York's adiest districts.

tom right: The dingy hole-in-the-wall club on Hollywood's sleazy Sunset Strip, where m met an Asian girl during the making of *Losin' It*.

Top: Tom in his classic *Top Gun* pose.
Bottom: Mixing drinks in *Cocktail.*

Top: Tom in an off-guard moment with his wife Nicole.
Bottom left: Tom the business tycoon.
Bottom right: Director Oliver Stone celebrates his Golden Globe Award with Tom.

Days of Thunder may have flopped at the box office, but Tom really looked the part in his overalls.

p: Naval officer Tom in *A Few Good Men*.

ottom: Tom at the Los Angeles premiere of *Far and Away* with wife Nicole.

Tom accepting his People's Choice Awards in 1994, complete with floppy hair and designer stubble for his *Interview With The Vampire* role.

Later, articles in magazines like *New York* claimed that Tom, Sean and Tim were founder members of what became known as the Brat Pack – a play on words based on the Rat Pack, a group composed of Frank Sinatra, Sammy Davis Jr, Peter Lawford and Dean Martin, who worked together and rampaged through Hollywood and Las Vegas in the 1960s.

Taps was earmarked as the first Brat Pack movie. It was certainly a landmark movie in some ways because it blazed the way for a more substantial type of youth-orientated film and it featured a new type of young star. It is also widely acknowledged that those fresh young faces helped *Taps* to bring in a very healthy $20.5 million at the box office.

Following the gruelling shooting schedule on *Taps*, Tom headed off to his grandfather's log cabin on Lake Cumberland in southern Kentucky, to unwind and 'do some fishing'. Tom was desperate to recharge his batteries and spend some time alone thinking through the next step in his career. He had always felt the need for peace and solitude and the cabin, with its stunning lakeside views, was the perfect place. There was no phone, no people, just lots of water and forest.

However, there was another reason behind his self-imposed exile after *Taps*. The young actor was emotionally drained after playing that role. He had beaten himself up mentally to such a degree in order to play the highly strung, aggressive character that it was in danger of spilling over into real life. Years later, Tom admitted to friends that, after *Taps* wrapped, he was 'the most unpleasant person to be around'. His family told him to cool down and learn to relax. They genuinely feared that he would be burnt out before he reached his mid-twenties if he wasn't careful.

So Tom 'chilled out' by the lakeside and tried to get back to reality. His jaws ached from the tension of his performance on the set of *Taps* and he could not stop tapping his leg nerviously. A month or so in the middle of nowhere was essential if he was to retain his sanity.

A few months later, Tom's new found success brought an interesting response following the release of *Taps*. 'I have worked very, very hard for everything that has happened to me,' he said carefully, then laughed, 'But geez, I do get lucky!'

After *Taps*, Tom went to his agency and told them he was not interested in doing commercials or television – that, after his experience in *Taps*, he only wanted to make movies. The word was already out: Tom Cruise was a hot young property and he was about to learn that there were a lot of people out there who wanted a chunk of him.

'I would be shocked if this guy ever sells out what I perceive as a strong sense of purpose about the craft of acting, about being true to certain personal values.'

Robert Scheer

After his performance in *Taps*, the Hollywood buzz about Tom Cruise was phenomenal. Even before the movie was released in the Christmas holiday period of 1981, the teenager was signed to a two-picture deal with a Canadian production company. Tom had amply demonstrated that he could take a minor role and expand it until its celluloid power was tangible and undeniable. The next challenge was an out-and-out starring role … and such a part lay just around the corner, or so it seemed.

For no sooner had word got out on his *Taps* performance than he was facing that age-old movieland problem – type casting. 'After *Taps*, everyone said, "Okay, now we've got a good pyschotic killer,"' Tom observed a few years later. He was offered countless vicious bruisers but he felt certain his potential was being ignored. He might have only one major role under his belt but he knew where he was heading and he wanted to break the mould before it took over his career.

'I needed something that would be in sharp contrast to the brutal cadet on *Taps*,' Tom asserted and, as fate would have it, he got what he wanted, even that all-important top-billing status but, after it was over, he realised that he had made a terrible error. In his own words, his next film turned out to be 'the most depressing experience of my life'.

Losin' It was originally entitled *'Tijuana'* and Tom came on board the project shortly after *Taps* had wrapped. Tom read the script closely and even asked his pal Sean Penn for advice – they both concluded that it was in severe need of a rewrite. However, the two producers behind the project were a charming, enthusiastic pair and they convinced Tom that *Losin' It* would end up being the next *Breaking Away*. As is the case in probably 95 per cent of all movies, the good intentions could never be matched by the actual product.

'They were, like, pumping me: "Don't worry about the script right now; we're going to work on it". But the experience itself was not a great one, in terms of where I'd just been – working with Harold Becker, Stanley Jaffe, Sean and Tim. It was a totally different experience; creatively it was stifling,' said Tom later.

Tom tried in vain to explain why he did the film but his excuses sound a little weak today.

'Coming off *Taps*, I felt like, hey, everyone wants to make a great movie. Everyone who's doing this loves their work. It's too hard a line of work to not love it. You work as hard as you can and get everything and something has to work out. Then I did *Losin' It*. When I first read it, it was worse than the released film. I had this small agent at the time who said, "Do it. Do it." I worked hard, but it was a terrible time in my life.'

Losin' It centred around a quartet of Californian high schoolers who head way down south for a weekend on the loose in Tijuana, just inside Mexico near the border crossing. Dave (Jackie Earle Hailey from *Breaking Away* and *The Bad News Bears*) Spider (John Stockwell) and Woody (Tom Cruise) intend to visit a local brothel. Wendell 'The Wimp' has coerced big brother Dave into bringing him along so that he can buy illegal firecrackers for profitable resale in the United States. Wendell was played by John P. Navin Jr, an actor Tom met on the set of *Taps* and whom he recommended for the role. Along the way, they are joined by a renegade wife named Kathy (Shelley Long in a pre-*Cheers* performance), who is Tijuana-bound to secure a quickie divorce.

Losin' It's plot was based on a formula that typified the mentality of the early 1980s state-of-the-artless teen flicks. *Spring Break* director Sean Cunningham defined the narrative outline of such films as: 'Kids get drunk. Kids get laid. Kids go home.' Dubbed 'the dumb formula' by *Los Angeles Times* critic Peter H. Brown, it was, with minor variations, the essence of the teen movie. Unfortunately, *Losin' It* fitted in with this class all too well.

The gist of *Losin' It* is Woody's virginity and how he loses it. He accompanies his pals to the bordertown bordello to rectify his condition but finds the brothel atmosphere, with its ageing whores and dirty linen, an intimidating turn-off.

Kathy and Woody, both traumatised by the day's events, find solace in each other's company and cling to each other in the carnival of carnality the director depicts as Tijuana. Over a bottle of tequila they grow woozy and cozy until, driven by different needs, they end up renting a little motel room. There they fulfil each other's romantic longings. When they emerge, Woody has lost his virginity and Kathy has regained her feminine pride and self-confidence.

The movie certainly didn't do the same for Tom. 'You know when you're in trouble when it's a comedy and everybody making the movie is miserable,' he recalled.

While *Losin' It* is probably the least exceptional of Tom's movies, it was not a completely lost cause. There is definite evidence of some sort of socially redeeming value beneath its cheesy exterior – an underlying theme of prejudice versus tolerance is hinted at in the contrasting ways the four teens respond to their adventures in Tijuana.

From the minute the opening credits begin to roll, the differences between Woody and his companions are drawn out. Unlike Woody, Dave and Spider are painted as sexually and racially obnoxious; both betray a biased arrogance towards their south-of-the-border neighbours. The usually sullen and loutish Spider comes from a squalid and apathetic household – he stole his funds for the big trip from his mother's wallet. Dave is a vain slob who stuffs his crotch with a rolled-up sock and keeps his money hidden in the centrefold of a girlie magazine.

Woody, on the other hand, is sensitive to the feelings of others but is still true blue to his more vulgar friends. A touch of discriminating taste is suggested when he pulls *his* hidden money from a copy of the erotic masterpiece *Lolita*.

Dave and Spider stink up the movie with their condescension and bigotry, doing things across the border they would never try back home. Dave attempts to seduce a local girl by slipping some bogus Spanish fly (a reputed aphrodisiac) into her lemonade. He learns first hand that he's dealing with real people who are sick of being taken advantage of when the Mexican girl's brother defends her honour by abducting Dave and threatening his manhood with a blow torch. Hoisted up on a crane, helpless Dave is a captive audience to the Mexican boy's enraged protests. He shouts out that Tijuana is corrupt and dirty because outsiders like Dave have dirtied it with their sordid intentions and prejudices.

Losin' It's gestures against intolerance aren't enough, however, to disguise the fact that it's yet another lurid and trivial teens-amok movie. The producers tried to have their cheesecake and eat it too – by making an exploitative film about exploitation.

In the middle of all this misery, Tom became close friends with another young tearaway of an actor called John Stockwell, who later appeared with the star in *Top Gun*. Both were just 20 years of age and Stockwell has provided the first ever insight into the other side of Tom Cruise at this important stage in his career.

> 'Certainly lots of things happened on *Losin' It* but I just know he would not want these things disseminated. I have nothing against the guy – it is not to my advantage to say anything bad about him,' explained a nervous Stockwell during an interview at his West Hollywood home in the spring of 1994.
>
> 'Sure, it would be more fun to say something bad about him. Who needs to hear all that stuff about what a great guy Tom Cruise is yet again?'

Stockwell – now a movie director as well as actor – stated that he was very worried that anything he said about Tom Cruise could create big problems for him with the hierarchy that rules Hollywood today and includes a certain Thomas Cruise Mapother IV. However, he still managed to drop some pretty strong hints about the star's behaviour while on *Losin' It*. 'The stuff I know is wild, behind-the-scenes stuff but, unfortunately, I know he would not be too happy to hear it.'

Stockwell said that he and Cruise became good drinking buddies the moment the *Losin' It* production hit the border town of Calexico where more than 50 per cent of the movie was shot. 'Tom definitely knew how to relax. The problem is that if this ever got out, you know, the kind of things I could talk about could only have come from me. It was crazy out there. We were just kids.'

Another actor who got to know Tom during the making of *Losin' It* explained to me: 'Off the record? Tom was into girls and booze just like the rest of us. He had a healthy appetite and sure enjoyed himself during *Losin' It*.'

That same informant spoke in graphic detail about an incident Cruise got involved in at the notorious Lingerie Club on Sunset Boulevard in West Hollywood when the *Losin' It* production team were shooting in Los Angeles after the Calexico location had been wrapped.

'Tom and a couple of buddies were in the Lingerie one night and things got a little outta hand. Remember, these were the days when AIDS hardly existed. The club was filled with girls who were only about one step removed from street walkers. The atmosphere was electric.

'Anyway, Tom was knocking back the beers like the rest of us and he got dancing with this fantastic-looking Asian girl. She was gyrating all over him.

'As Tom danced closer and closer to her, he lent down and whispered something to the girl and the next moment she pulled a gun on him!

'We couldn't believe our eyes and Tom was terrified. She started shouting and swearing at poor

Tommy. He was completely out of his depth. She kept waving the gun in his direction. We grabbed Tommy and got the hell outta that club as fast as possible.'

This story is interesting because it shows that even career-obsessed Tom was capable of unwinding when he felt like it, although this incident does seem a rather ominous mirror of the role he was playing in *Losin' It* at the time!

According to John Stockwell, back in Calexico the young girls from the Mexican border town were forever throwing themselves at the handsome young actors starring in *Losin' It*. 'There were young girls everywhere. It was typically silly young men's behaviour. We got into everything.'

Some years afterwards, rumours of Tom's lack of interest in sex circulated. Back in those swinging days of the early-1980s, however, Tom was far from celibate. Says Stockwell: 'He was hardly a virgin!'

On another occasion, when the *Losin It* stars were holed up in the glamorous Westwood Marque in West Los Angeles, Stockwell and Tom linked up with *Taps* star Tim Hutton and headed out to the millionaire's playground of Two Bunch Palms in the Californian desert. On that particular trip, Stockwell said Tom once again 'proved he was no choir boy'.

Interestingly, Stockwell – one of the few people who knows Tom Cruise on a personal level ever to speak out – says that the actor has a side to him that 'always knew he would become a star. Even at the point where he had done nothing he was very aware of fans and treating people well.'

Tom, Stockwell and the other main stars of *Losin' It* had been living in a scruffy, two-star hotel throughout their earlier stay in Calexico. The young actor had the annoying habit of challenging Stockwell and the other young cast members to wrestling competitions when things got a bit tedious during the long, boring evenings. 'He was always challenging you to wrestle. He was very good at it and you'd always end up on the grass somewhere trying to put each into other headlocks or squeezing the life out of each other,' explained Stockwell.

John Stockwell's opinion of both himself and his soon-to-be-very-famous co-star is refreshingly unaffected. 'We were all so deeply superficial. We were typical actors who thought everything we were doing was incredibly important. It is all a mystery how anyone gets to become a huge star. There is no rhyme or reason.'

While he was very careful about revealing too much of the actor's personal life, Stockwell did describe his old pal's performance in *Losin' It* as 'awful'. 'I would have disowned that film if I had been him. It was a misguided project although, at the time, he was very serious about it and actually thought it was going to be a really important movie. He was very earnest about the way he approached it.'

One of the biggest surprises about *Losin' It* was that it was directed by Curtis Hanson, a highly regarded up-and-coming director who went on to direct the $100 million-plus-grossing *The Hand That Rocks The Cradle* in 1991. 'It doesn't matter how good the director is. If you've got a lousy script you may as well get a ten-year-old kid to direct – it's cheaper,' said one cast member on the movie.

Another, slightly older, actor in *Losin It* was Central American Mario Marcelino, who had just signed a lucrative contract to appear on the popular soap opera *Falcon Crest*. He got a completely different impression of Tom during the location shoot in Calexico. 'I talked to him one time and all he could speak about was his career, his agent. How he'd got his agent to put him up for some movie and how he was about to fly back to New York to do publicity on *Taps*. I felt as if I was in the presence of a whirlwind. I had never met a kid so intent on making it,' explained Mario, who was 31 at the time of the *Losin' It* shoot.

He said that Tom kept to himself and only hung out with the much younger actors. He also noted that Tom never once mentioned his own personal life. 'It was as if it did not exist. His energy and drive was apparent from the start but what depressed me was that his focus seemed more important than his acting skills. Here was a kid who was a lucky guy because he was not that good. Everyone will tell you the same thing.'

Fellow actor Kale Brown was just as stunned by work-aholic Tom's outlook during the *Losin' It* shoot. 'The kid was so focused. He was doing press-ups on the floor with that killer look in his eyes whenever there was a break in filming. I hope Tom has remained sane because it is so easy to get screwed up and insulate yourself. That's what stardom is all about. You form a wall around you and feel messed up.'

Mario Marcelino also recalled that Tom did not get on so well with his co-star Jacky Earle Hailey, who was given equal billing with Tom after his million-dollar-earning role in *Bad News Bears*. No one ever got to the bottom of the problems between Tom and Jacky and more than ten years later Hailey still refused to be drawn on the subject.

Mario explained: 'It was supposed to be Jack Earle Hailey's vehicle and it buried him. The premise was ludicrous, degrading and that's why it failed. It was all so clichéd. They even had a scene where donkeys were fucked on screen.'

The film's makers had decided to dress up the normally dreary town of Calexico and transform it into Tijuana because the logistics of filming inside the US were consider-ably easier. Mario was outraged by the way many of the cast and crew treated the local labour who streamed across the nearby border in the hope of picking up a day's work on the big Hollywood movie that was the talk of the town. 'They treated the locals pretty badly and paid them just $15 a day to work as extras. I was appalled. These people were very poor. They were not used to it. I thought the film ended up giving a lousy impression of Mexicans and that deeply offended me.'

Tom had learned the hard way that you never really know how low you can sink until you've hit rock bottom. Now he'd plumbed the depths of teenage schlock and could employ his newfound wisdom and experience to future advantage.

Tom admitted the importance of his one bad career move when he said: 'I can look at it and say, "Thank God I've grown." I thought anyone could make a great movie; all you had to do was knock yourself out. I didn't know anything about anything.'

Tom promised himself never to make another film like *Losin' It*.

'It was a real eye-opener. It made me understand how you really have to be careful ... you've got to examine all the elements of a project. I learned a great lesson in doing that movie. I realised that I'd have to learn how to survive in this business and not let it eat me up. I knew that the kinds of films I wanted to work on from then on had to be made by the best people. There I was, with the opportunity to be a working actor and I remember thinking that this wasn't going to last forever.

'Money was never a factor with me – I wanted to learn on a film. Money goes, but what you learn can't be taken away from you. Even though the film wasn't as bad as it could have been, it still wasn't the kind I wanted to be involved with.'

Tom was so determined not to get lost in the non-stop Hollywood shuffle of talent and end up being a disposable, average teen idol, that he turned down $70,000 and a first-class plane ticket to do a horror film simply because it wasn't something he wanted to be associated with. He wanted only the best and he was prepared to wait, however long it took.

Picking himself up by the bootstraps, Tom decided to try again. Having witnessed mediocrity, his next serious project was not his next movie role, it was to find the right agent. Within weeks he met Paula Wagner, not much older than himself and on exactly the same serious work commitment wavelength. He outlined his career aspirations to Paula: to grow as an artist, to work with the best people and not to care about money. She took him on and he soon found himself returning to the fold with a new seriousness and commitment to acting without any more sacrifices of his pride.

'I know where I am. I do my work, and that's the important thing. I'll let it speak for itself.'

Tom Cruise

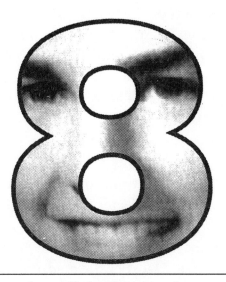

While *Taps* might well have gone down in Hollywood history as the first Brat Pack movie, Tom Cruise's next appearance on the big screen was considered the classic of its genre. The *Outsiders* went far beyond the usual parameters of the traditional teen flick. It was a sensitive, panoramic drama, devoid of cheap shots and naked cheerleaders. Its box office success was negligible but it is still considered a youth-market classic and the movie's overwhelming popularity as a video-cassette proves its durability. It is even reckoned that thousands of converts join the ranks of old fans each year, to watch the movie time after time.

It was around this time that Tom became aware of the fact that he was being described as a senior member of the Brat Pack and he was singularly unimpressed. 'I think I was in New York. Someone told me about the Brat Pack and that's when I realised I was a brat. "I'm a brat, Mom." "Girls,

I'm a brat." What are you going to say about something like that? I mean, how do I get lumped with that?'

What angered Tom was that he believed that being 'lumped' together with a group of other actors could seriously damage him professionally by encouraging the sort of type-casting he was desperately trying to avoid. 'The thing is there really isn't a community of actors, I mean that is false, absolutely false. There is not a community where we get together and sit down. The term Brat Pack is a bunch of crap, a lot of bullshit.'

Although *The Outsiders* hardly rated one decent review from film critics, it was an undisputed hit with its intended audience. For once, the quality of a film's ingredients – a classic story, a legendary director and a collection of talented young actors – won the day.

The movie also expressed an attitude towards teenagers rarely displayed in any facet of the media. Perhaps 12-year-old Todd Camhe, who reviewed the movie on its release, put it best: '*The Outsiders* is the first movie that's just about kids and their problems. I think that's important ... most movies and shows with kids in them are about senior proms and high school and buying convertibles. *The Outsiders* is a lot more realistic. The kids all have flaws. They're not the usual stereotypes.'

But then, this was a rare movie project for other reasons as well. The novel upon which the movie was based was located in classic Middle Americana – Tulsa, Oklahoma. Tulsa is a typical Midwestern city, with a heavy concentration of oil and agricultural industries. It's a sometimes uneasy blend of rural and urban and when author Susie Hinton was growing up in the sixties, the populace mainly defined its social order in monetary terms. In areas where religious and racial groups are fairly consistent, social conventions are usually reduced to one main priority – the 'haves' and 'have nots'.

The Outsiders was inspired when one of Susie Hinton's 'have-not' school friends received a severe beating at the hands of several 'haves'. The poor kids formed a gang called 'The Greasers' and the rich kids were labelled 'The Socs' (as in socials and pronounced 'So-shez'). Soon Hinton's initial essay had grown into a best-selling novel which was published in 1967. She even used a sexually ambiguous *nom de plume* so as not to alienate young male readers who didn't normally gravitate towards female writers.

It became, quite simply, a book that millions of American kids read. *The Outsiders* had a broad-based appeal that was obvious to publishers but for years it went unnoticed in Hollywood. Many later theorised that there simply was not anyone 'in touch' enough to appreciate the book's youthful message. In the end, it arrived on the big screen via extremely unusual circumstances.

Jo Ellen Misakian, a librarian at the Lone Star Elementary School in Fresno, California, noticed that many of her students seemed literally to idolise *The Outsiders*. She began to wonder why the book had not been scooped up by Hollywood years previously and, after much thought and consideration, decided to propose her idea to Francis Ford Coppola, the executive producer of another student favourite, *The Black Stallion*. Soon Misakian had managed to get up a petition which was signed by her students and she sent it off to the master director with a copy of *The Outsiders*.

Coppola immediately responded, recognising the novel's movie potential and assigning one of his producers, Fred Roos – who made *The Black Stallion* with him – to buy up the book rights and begin the process of getting a screenplay written. Writer Hinton asked for the not unreasonable sum of $5,000 for an option to film her book but Coppola's company, Zoetrobe, were in so much trouble at the time that

Hinton was persuaded to take a down payment of $500. Coppola – director of such movie masterpieces as *The Godfather* series – had originally intended to hand the movie over to another helmsman to direct but, as the months of negotiating and writing progressed, he found it impossible to let go of the project.

After much soul-searching and a little criticism within the media that Coppola – then in his mid-forties – was too old to handle such a youth-orientated subject, he officially got the green light on the movie. Even author Susie Hinton was welcomed on board the pre-production team. As a consultant, she would verify the authenticity of the settings, surroundings and general feel of the movie's backgrounds. She also insisted on having tremendous input in the casting, especially the hiring of handsome Matt Dillon to play one of the leading roles as Dallas Winston.

Word of *The Outsiders* reached the ears of young Tom Cruise during the Christmas holiday period of 1981. Bitterly re-educated about Hollywood, thanks to his awful experiences on *Losin' It*, he had already taken decisive action to rectify his career by hiring new agent Paula Wagner. The pair had agreed to look for quality rather than quantity. 'I learned the things I wanted and I didn't want,' he explained.

The Outsiders struck an instant chord with Tom because it was one of the few novels he had read in his youth, thanks to the reading difficulties caused by his dyslexia. He had started to cope with scripts by reading slowly through and conjuring up visions of what he read. However, reading *The Outsiders* had opened up his spectrum on life, as it had done for an estimated three million other young readers. He had been profoundly affected by the book.

Ironically, another agent who was touting for Tom at the time had laughed when Tom told him of his aspirations to appear in a Coppola movie. 'Francis! He's not going to pay you anything!'

However, Paula Wagner had a savvy eye for good projects and she had jelled so instantly with Tom that he felt complete and utter trust in her judgement. She seemed to be able to second guess his opinions and that magical mental shorthand made young Tom feel much more secure. Once again, a female was leading the way for him and he felt perfectly comfortable in that knowledge. Paula was already becoming like a fourth sister to him.

The go-ahead pair planned the actor's assault on Coppola with military-like precision. Tom was absolutely and utterly determined to get a part in *The Outsiders*. He had felt like one for most of his life and he was not about to let such a wonderful opportunity slip from his grasp. Paula suggested he pay his own airfare from New York to Los Angeles and fly to an audition that was being held the following week. He wasn't even necessarily after a big role – Tom just wanted any part in that movie. He called up his new friend Emilio Estevez on the West Coast and begged a free bed for his entire stay in Hollywood. Emilio had already been virtually assured of a major role in *The Outsiders* and he was naturally keen to encourage his pal to join him.

'I didn't feel I could carry a film. I hadn't learned enough and I felt that I would be eaten alive,' Tom later explained.

After the initial audition, Tom drew Coppola aside and pleaded: 'Look, I don't care what role you give me. I really want to work with you. I want to be there on the set and watch. I'll do anything it takes; I'll play any role in this.' It was a brave move – and it worked. He ended up with the relatively small role of Steve Randle. This part, as one of the 'have-not' Greasers, suited Tom right down to the ground. 'I took *The Outsiders* over a lot of other things. It was a small role ... but I was ecstatic to get that role because, at 19, I was going to work with Francis Ford Coppola.'

Tom could easily relate to the role of a poor kid rejected by most of his peers. 'Being the new kid in town was very intense. The cliques, you know. You've got your Democrats over here, your Republicans over there, your country-club kids, the athletes, the writers all over the place. And then there was me. I didn't fit into any group.'

Those experiences had also given him a self-destructive edge – an ideal ingredient for any angry young actor. Tom saw himself as 'reckless. I'm still that way, but in a more specific way. My recklessness goes through to my work. I was always looking for attention. I'd get into fights. I think it was out of a need to be creative because if you can't create, you eventually start to destroy yourself.'

Tom had the perfect background. Not for the first or the last time, he was fully intending to use his real-life experiences to help him gain invaluable momentum on a particular acting role.

When casting was finalised and contracts settled, the names lined up to appear in *The Outsiders* read like a millionaire boys club/future film makers of America roster: Tom Cruise, Emilio Estevez, Rob Lowe, C. Thomas Howell, Matt Dillon, Ralph Macchio and Patrick Swayze. Amazingly, all of these hot young names were apparently more than happy to share the limelight. It all seemed too good to be true. 'It was very chaotic,' explained Rob Lowe. 'But that's what was so great about it. Francis is like a giant chef. He'll say, "I need a little more of this and little less of that". He doesn't know exactly until he tastes.'

Lowe also had a very strange opinion of Tom. Shortly after filming completed, he lambasted his co-star in a flurry of fierce words. 'Cruise is this middle-class, kind of square, "Yes sir", "Yes, Ma'am" God-fearing American kid,' opined

Lowe, before thoughtfully adding: 'Something in the eyes says he'll snap your goddamned neck if you look at him the wrong way.' (Incidentally, Lowe went on to describe himself as 'a mixture of Matthew Broderick and Tom Cruise with a little European style'. Well, well!)

Coppola launched his mega-name production in Oklahoma in March 1982, for location filming. He insisted there was no substitute for the Midwest's wide-open spaces and gigantic skyscapes. Like an artist painting a canvas, he utilised the colourful sunsets and clear skies as an allegory. As is traditional for Coppola, his explanation for such filmaking was masterful.

> 'Even as we look at a sunset, we are aware that it is already starting to die. Youth, too, is like that: at the very moment of perfection you can already see the forces that are undoing it. *The Outsiders* takes place in an enchanted moment of time in the lives of all these boys. I wanted to catch that moment; I wanted to take these young street rats and give them heroic proportions.'

Like *Taps*, preparations for actual performances were very intense. Author Susie Hinton laid out meticulously detailed explanations of her characters' backgrounds and motivation to avoid any actor's interpretation ending up being flat and stereotyped. Pounds of pomade were coated on to Tom's dark locks as that was the Greasers' standard battle flag, waved by kids too poor to express themselves in any other material way. It was their identity ... their version of the varsity letter.

'I remember feeling very good, building up confidence in my own instincts on acting. And understanding more on each level; learning more about film acting and what I wanted to do,' said Tom.

Tom took on the task at hand with his customary intensity, even though his role ended up amounting to less actual screen time than anything he had done since *Endless Love*. His relentless determination to give 120 per cent, combined with his off-screen antics, managed to attract a healthy handful of publicity. His hair already doused with grease, Tom also removed the cap from his chipped tooth (a little souvenir he had received during a hockey match) and avoided showering for the majority of the next nine weeks. He was probably not a very desirable dinner companion but he certainly made his presence felt.

Increasingly, method acting motivated Tom's madness and he was delighted to find in 'Mr Coppola' (as he deferentially called him) a firm supporter. The director was an avid believer in thorough character analysis. He insisted that his actors digest their roles with incredible thoroughness. Coppola even created a specific environment, including stringent Nautilus, gymnastics and t'ai chi ch'uan workouts three times a day to shape the Greasers' bodies to perfection.

Typically, Coppola took this attention to method one stage further by insisting that the 'haves', the actors playing the Socs, stayed in fancy hotels and received their scripts bound in leather, were paid generous daily allowances and generally pampered and spoilt. Meanwhile, the Greasers – who were the real stars of the movie – got absolutely nothing. They had miniscule rooms with no maid service, a pathetic amount of pocket money and scrumpled, stained scripts.

Coppola was determined to create real antagonism and he succeeded with ease. His face lit up with delight when he attended a weekend football match between the Socs and Greasers, which nearly ended in a real-life blood bath as tempers frayed and fists flew. It was time to start shooting.

Tom wasn't the only actor doing his homework.

Virtually everyone seemed to be playing 'Let's pretend' off and on screen and it got so bad at one stage that people seemed to have completely forgotten the golden line where fact ended and fantasy began.

The most notorious episode occurred when Coppola suggested to Matt Dillon that he needed a little practical experience as a shop-lifter. A camera actually followed from a discreet distance as Matt and two other Greasers wandered ever so casually into a local shop, snatched some cigarettes and exited without being noticed by the store keeper.

Co-star C. Thomas Howell recalled later:

'Francis sent Matt Dillon, Ralph Macchio and myself to steal the cigarettes. He followed us with a camera. We stole the cigarettes and left but didn't know what to do with them. So we went back in and said, "We stole them." They threw a big fit but when they saw that we were actors it was OK. We got away with it ... actors have so many excuses.'

It is interesting to note that Tom Cruise was not involved in this escapade. One insider on the set said that he preferred to internalise his character by sitting alone for hours rehearsing a tough Greaser voice over and over again. In any case, Tom's honest upbringing by Mary Lee would never allow him to steal even if it *was* in the name of his art.

Heart-throb Rob Lowe was sent off to work in a real gas station to get into his character as a high school drop out who works with Tom Cruise's character, Steve Randle. That was only the beginning. Tom and the other Greasers were requested by Coppola to vacate their dingy motel rooms and spend a week with the real greasers featured in Hinton's book. 'Of course, now they're adults,' explained a bemused Rob Lowe. 'We'd talk with them ... I mean it was kind of a strange situation. I'd never met these people before. "Hi, I'm here to spend a few nights with you. Coppola arranged it." "Oh yeah, sure, come on in." A little bizarre.'

One day Coppola even herded his young goats into a crowded restaurant and encouraged them to act like the ultimate vandals and troublemakers. The guys harassed the waitresses, flung food everywhere and caused non-stop trouble while Coppola sat at another table (a safe distance away) and observed like some master-controller witnessing the antics of his slaves, a sly grin on his face and the odd raised eyebrow being the only evidence of his approval or disapproval. This was serious stuff on the method-acting front, and some of the youngsters, including Tom, felt uncomfortable about acting as hooligans in real life. He believed that the true sign of a real professional is his ability to get into a specific role, not perform for others before the camera even started rolling.

Coppola (many of the cast referred to him as 'Father Film') clearly enjoyed the danger. It was as if he was reliving his own youthful fantasies through the outrageous actions of his cast. He also admitted, rather strangely, that he had a special attachment to teenagers. 'I had been a camp counsellor when I was younger,' he told one rather puzzled journalist after shooting wrapped on the movie. 'I always got along very well with kids. I like being with kids rather than adults.' Papa Coppola was always available to any of the actors if they sought advice or wanted to go over the details of a specific scene.

Tom Cruise felt more at home with the cast of *The Outsiders* than on any other movie he had worked on. There was a comradely spirit, a feeling that they were all in it together. Egos had been dropped in favour of old-fashioned friendship.

C. Thomas Howell – who starred as the film's narrator

Ponyboy Curtis – remembers his times with Tom very warmly. 'Tom helped me a lot. He told me, "The minute you think something's going to be easy, that's when you have to put in even more work." ' Tom was no hypocrite. He was following his own advice to Howell with great vigour. However, like any healthy teenagers, the two actors did find time to play a few pranks in real life, too.

Howell recalled:

'Tom and I came out of the elevator [of the Excelsior Hotel] feeling crazy, so I pulled my pants down around my ankles and he came after me with a belt screaming, "I'm going to spank you! I'm going to spank you!" I was running around the lobby screaming, "No, no, no!" People freaked out. They couldn't believe it! They were going, "Oh God, what's going on?" But we didn't get arrested or anything ... we just got a warning from the hotel manager.'

Having kept a low profile at the start of the shoot, Tom started to gain confidence and come out of his shell. After all, he was there among true soulmates – actors with whom he could talk all day and all night if necessary. His dream had come true. Now he could relax among friends and a new Tom started to emerge, someone who could match any of the wildness on display.

In one extraordinary scenario, he put honey on co-star Diane Lane's toilet seat and inscribed 'Helter Skelter' on the mirror of her hotel room. The actress's response is unknown but some inside *The Outsiders* production felt it was a particularly tasteless episode and confirmed that Tom still had a lot of growing up to do. However, some of his young friends were full of admiration and pleasantly surprised – they had thought Tom was pretty square and not capable of any skulduggery.

Within a few days of the honey-on-the-toilet-seat episode, Tom's other great new friend Emilio Estevez retaliated by rubbing human faeces on his doorknob. Boys will be boys ...

A few days after this, an inexplicable and highly suspect incident occurred between Tom and Estevez, in which Tom ended up with a broken thumb after a brawl, being shot for the movie, apparently got out of hand. By all accounts, Coppola egged his young stars on and no one in the rest of the cast or crew could work out where the acting finished and real life began. The director was delighted and Tom and Emilio remained firm friends, despite this little hiccup.

Tom was also suspected of rearranging Rob Lowe's hotel room as well as taking a bath, fully clothed, with some other Greasers in the fountain in the hotel lobby. Papa Coppola had wanted real louts – now he had them.

All the Greasers, including Tom, faced a barrage of about 500 lusting teenage girls each time they stepped outside the Excelsior Hotel in Oklahoma. According to one witness who spent some time at the location, besides the horseplay and beer guzzling there was a lot of sex between the visiting celebs and local girls. Even the computer games Coppola had installed in his production offices weren't enough to cool off the hot libidos.

Life off-camera revolved around a couple of discos and one raunchy evening Tom and his co-stars attended a women's mud-wrestling match in Tulsa.

'These teenage girls were desperate to go to bed with Matt, Tom and all the rest of the stars. They hung around all day hoping for a date and many of them ended up back at the actors' hotel,' said one member of the crew.

Unit publicist Beverly Walker played mother hen for

much of the production and she was even responsible for killing the first set of still photos taken for publicity purposes because of too much crotch posing by Tom and the boys – great for gays and wishful females but not the class act one expects from a Coppola production. Meanwhile, Susie Hinton, who was present throughout the shoot, got a distinct crush on Matt Dillon to whom she gave constant, motherly attention. Meanwhile, the area's notoriously unpredictable weather conditions, led her to observe: 'Francis thinks he can stop the rain.' To which Coppola snorted in response: 'Fuck the budget. You can't be penalised for an act of God.'

Ultimately, the incident of the crotch posing high-lighted a problem for the movie's makers. Whether they liked it or not, they had a cast filled with heart-throbs out of the pages of *Sixteen* magazine. In the end, a happy medium was found in which actors gave both serious and trivial interviews for the sake of the film. In one teenage girls' mag, Tom was written about in gushing terms.

'When it comes to physically getting into character – there's really no one who went to greater lengths than Tom Cruise. Already building a reputation via his work in *Endless Love*, *Taps* and *Losin' It*, Tom has always found a way of making his character stand apart, no matter what the original script said. A believer in the showbusiness dictum: "There are no small parts, only small actors", Tom once again found a way to make you really sit up and take notice of his character ...

'Tom describes Steve (his character) as a really poor "grease monkey" – referring to his job at a gas station – but little else was written in about Steve from the start. "It was really left to my imagination as to how to play him," confided Tom. For Steve's looks, Tom wanted to go beyond greasing his hair back – and he did. Not only did the young actor have a tattoo painted on his arm, he also went to the trouble of going to the dentist and having his front tooth chipped! That's going a long way to make a part realistic – but Tom Cruise could never do it any other way. He's that serious about acting – no matter what the part is. His character's loyalty to his group of greasers is clear in Tom's hand-written note to you:'

Then the article printed a carefully scrawled, cringe-making note from Tom signed in the name of his *Outsiders* character Steve. It reads: 'Are you are all glad you're part of it – grease is the only way!!!'

Overall, it was a happy set. Coppola enjoyed the kids and they got an equal kick out of him. He paid them the ultimate compliment of treating them just like grown-up actors, encouraging their input, allowing them to improvise dialogue, letting them devise details to bring their characters to life. Emilio Estevez even dreamed up his own hairdo, a grotesque Vaselined ducktail with a front flip that no pro-fessional hairdresser could ever (or would ever wish to) get just right. Furthermore, given the unlimited amount of beer Tom and the others were allowed to guzzle after each day's shoot, the kids didn't even mind the long workdays which sometimes hit the 18-hour mark. Then there was Coppola's home-made pasta. He often would cook up some tasty dishes for the assembled youngsters and watch them hungrily devour every morsel. *The Outsiders* was certainly not the traditional Hollywood movie by any means.

About half-way through the shoot, Tom invited his cousin William R. Mapother Jr to join him on the set for a few days. By all accounts, the young Louisville resident had a great time hobnobbing with some of the world's most exciting young actors. He played racquetball with Rob Lowe and found Matt Dillon 'a really nice guy. He usually plays a redneck but he's not like that at all.' William – one of Tom's closest confidants – later joined Tom's production company in Los Angeles as head of film development.

Tom's own part in *The Outsiders* was always small but, plainly, something was missing in the final version of the movie where there are several scenes where Tom is in the background but doesn't participate in the action. Unfortunately, much of the action ended up on the cutting-room floor, along with a large chunk of other footage, including much of Rob Lowe's performance. Francis Ford Coppola was overruled by studio executives who, having spent $10 million on the production, did not approve of the version presented to them by the director. Even so-called powerful directors like Coppola often lose control of the final cut of a film if the producers have retained the power to make artistic decisions.

Meanwhile, within weeks of wrapping *The Outsiders*, Coppola was planning another tough production, this time of a project called *Rumble Fish*, based on another S.E. Hinton novel. Tom, along with many of the cast and crew from *The Outsiders*, was approached to appear in the new movie production but he had already lined up something very special which he had kept secret from everyone on *The Outsiders*. Reluctantly, he rejected Coppola's offer of another film and Coppola has rarely even given Tom a mention when talking about his experiences on *The Outsiders*, although he regularly refers to Matt Dillon as 'one of the best young actors to emerge since the Brando-Dean era'.

Not surprisingly, the film opened to mixed reviews after

being deliberately moulded with an adult audience in mind. *Time* magazine said it all in one headline: 'Playing tough, going nowhere'. In the *Los Angeles Herald Examiner* Peter Rainer called it a 'gutsy, overblown vacuum'. In *The New York Times*, Vincent Canby labelled *The Outsiders* as 'spectacularly out of touch ... as if someone had handed Verdi a copy of 'The Hardy Boys Attend a Rumble' and, holding a gun to the poor man's head, forced him to use it as a libretto.' There were even stranger reviews, like that by David Denby of *New York* magazine who dubbed it 'the cinematic equivalent of purple prose'. However, John Engstrom of the *Boston Globe* hailed it as 'a small, sincere and nearly perfectly realised film about adolescence in Oklahoma' and praised Coppola's 'cool restraint', while *Variety*, often a down-to-earth judge, regarded the production as being like a 1950s drama about problem kids.

Probably the most comprehensive summing up of the movie came from John Osborne in the *Hollywood Reporter*. He wrote: 'Box-office waves, if any, will be as interesting to contemplate as the idea of how *The Outsiders* might have played if put on the screen by talents closer in age to the subjects they're X-raying.'

The most damning review came from Andrew Sarris in the *Village Voice*. He complained: 'Coppola has treated very slight material with an excess of emotional display that is embarrassing to watch with a straight face. Much of the dialogue is so yearningly "sensitive" that many of the lines sounded like song cues, and many of the images are so blatantly homoerotic that I was tempted to look in the final credits for Kenneth Anger's name as a consultant.' Hell hath no fury like a critic scorned.

However, at least the young actor's tens of thousands of lusty young female fans were satisfied. As Tom's cousin William explained after attending the movie: 'The majority of the audience were seventh and eighth-grade girls who were screaming and yelling over Matt Dillon and the other guys. When one of them took off his shirt, they really freaked out!'

When asked his own opinion of the movie, William tactfully replied: 'Well, I'm not a movie critic, but I thought some parts were good and emotional and other parts could have been acted better. The movie ended on a depressing note, not upbeat.'

After the movie's release, some of the stars found themselves under siege from disappointed fans. Rob Lowe explained: 'A lot of irate kids have come up to me and asked what happened to the movie. I hope the people responsible for the way it turned out get the same complaints I do.'

Tom was much more optimistic and upbeat. 'It was never a main role but I created something. That was where I learned I had a sense of comedy. I still want to work with Francis again.'

Todd Camhe, the youngster whose interpretation of the film is still considered the most worthwhile, put what many consider to be the correct interpretation on the movie.

'Most of the critics are looking at the kids in the movie as characters with problems, but they don't really identify with them because they don't care. I don't think it's true that kids never talk about poetry or sunsets. The kids in the movie are talking to their best friends, so they don't have to worry about acting cool or tough ... the reviewers have been saying that *The Outsiders* is only for kids, but I think it's for grown-ups as well. People over fifty probably won't like it, but they don't like many movies anyway.'

Tom Cruise was perfectly happy with his performance in *The Outsiders*. He felt it had put him back on track and he and agent Paula Wagner had already secretly cast around for the perfect starring vehicle which would help to lift his career towards superstardom.

'The dream is always the same.'
Joel Goodsen in *Risky Business*

Tom's eye for the main chance had proved itself when he managed to slip quietly out of Oklahoma during the later stages of filming *The Outsiders* to fly to Los Angeles to read for a leading role that was to catapult him to superstardom.

Young writer/director Paul Brickman had originally fought strongly against having the young actor even come in for an audition for his teen-orientated movie project entitled *Risky Business*. After seeing him play the crazy rookie in *Taps*, Brickman believed that Tom was 'too much of a psycho'.

The director had in mind someone altogether more gentle and charming for the lead role in his carefully nurtured project. The character Brickman was thinking about was called Joel Goodsen, a basically nice teenager who ends up in a heap of trouble after his parents decide to leave him alone at home for the weekend.

Brickman seemed flat, almost uninterested when Tom

turned up at the audition. However, the young actor and his agent Paula Wagner had seen the script of the movie and they both knew it was the perfect starring vehicle for Tom. Up until then, his potential as an actor had been barely tapped – the roles he played had either been too small or had lacked the depth needed to demonstrate his capabilities.

Over lunch with producer Steve Tisch, Paula Wagner had come up with an outrageous ruse to get Tom into the casting meeting. 'The idea was', explained Tisch, 'that he'd drop in on me as if we were old friends and I'd take him to meet Paul Brickman.'

That is precisely what happened. Cruise and Tisch even persuaded Brickman to agree to meet them at 5 a.m. on a Sunday morning, much against his better judgement. To make matters even more dubious, Tom looked about as far removed from a pampered teenager as one can get because he was still tattooed and greasy, as well as bearing the sinuous muscles of the street brawler he had been playing in *The Outsiders*. A flash of that famous smile even revealed a chipped tooth. This was going to be an uphill struggle for the young actor.

Director Brickman's apathy was initially fuelled by Tom's extraordinary appearance. He was physically completely pumped up and still talking in an Oklahoma accent when the reading began. However, once Tom settled down and began adjusting his reading of the *Risky Business* script, Brickman sat up and began to take notice. 'When he read for the part, he stopped himself halfway through and said: "Wait, I think I can go in this direction," and started over again,' recalled the director. 'That was a courageous thing for a 19-year-old to do, but Tom is a courageous guy. He's got a will for excellence.'

It's a telling testimony to the expressiveness of Tom's acting ability that he managed to convey Joel Goodsen's warmth and candour despite his hard-edged appearance. When Tom returned for a final tryout, his schedule was just as tight – flying in at 1 a.m. for another early morning appointment and having to get back to *The Outsiders* set in Oklahoma by ten the following evening.

This time he looked even worse than before; his hair greasy and wearing a preppy Adidas shirt – and he was stunned to find his co-star Rebecca De Mornay sitting there! She had already been cast and the director wanted to be absolutely certain that the two would have a certain chemistry. Somehow Tom got over that hurdle as well.

'We were after that combination of youth, beauty and talent,' recalled casting director Nancy Klopper. She was particularly on the lookout for a young Dustin Hoffman who would have both the innocence and naivety for that side of the character and also the sex appeal and pzazz that young girls would find attractive.

For his part, Tom felt completely at ease with Brickman the moment he saw the look in his eyes following his decision to start reading all over again. The director could have been impatient, fed up with the indecision. Instead, he was impressed that this kid from New Jersey had nerve. Later, Tom conceded: 'My best work comes when I'm really communicating with the director and I work great with Brickman.'

The interesting thing about *Risky Business* is that, like *Losin' It*, it was essentially about a teenager who loses his virginity. However, there was an edge to it, a sophisticated approach that would put the movie on a much higher rung than the sort of ghastly teen flicks produced since the phenomenal 1982 success of *Porky's* which took in a staggering $160 million at the US box office alone. Since then a torrent of similarly mindless sexploitation flicks had flowed unabated, threatening to submerge popcorn-munchers from coast to coast in North America.

Before finally fulfilling Brickman's vision of the perfect actor to play Joel, producer Steve Tisch and Jon Avnet had found the perfect actress to play the role of Lana, the prostitute who transforms Joel's life. They were healthily besotted by blonde Rebecca De Mornay, who just happened to have made her memorable screen début in Francis Ford Coppola's *One From the Heart*, a sentimental, highly stylised and extremely expensive fantasy of Las Vegas nightlife, which bombed appallingly at the box office. Rebecca's one and only line in that entire movie was the immortal utterance: 'Excuse me, those are my waffles.'

Rebecca had an interesting background. She was in a rock and roll group at 15 and starred in a Bruce Lee kung-fu movie only a few years later. She had just the right balance of inaccessibility and cunning. As she herself put it so aptly: 'Lana isn't exactly Miss Warmth. So that's what I gave him.' Combined with Lana's growing sense of attachment and love for Joel, these emotions added to her depth, shading her enigmatic and erotic allure.

Meanwhile, Tom plunged himself head first into his own part as Joel by travelling down to Florida to jog off the 14 pounds of weight that he considered his character simply would not be carrying. 'Florida's hot, really hot,' he explained breathlessly. 'I wanted to sweat as much as possible and I also wanted to get away, to focus myself.' That old familiar word 'focus' was coming into the frame yet again.

After reaching his weight goal, Tom stopped exercising 'so I could put on a little layer of baby fat'. He explained very matter-of-factly: 'He's a vulnerable person. I didn't want any physical defences up for him. No muscle armour at all.'

Once again, Tom immersed himself in the part of Joel by travelling to the Highland Park area where the script was located. There he hung out with the local rich kids for a few weeks, getting a feel for their dress code, speech and mannerisms.

The preparation was half the fun for him. He explained: 'I enjoy the pressure of making a movie. It's like getting psyched up for a wrestling match – but with higher stakes. I thrive on it.'

Tom's character, Joel, was basically an average all-American kid who just happens to have wealthy parents who want him to attend the prestigious Princeton University. To a lesser degree, he also shares that desire but the movie chronicles what happens after his parents head off for the weekend, leaving him in charge of the house.

Everything goes fine until Joel's sexual urges convince him to contact a call girl – played by Rebecca De Mornay – whom he asks around to the house. This eventually leads to a clash between Rebecca and her pimp and later Joel's father's Porsche is accidentally wrecked.

Meanwhile, Rebecca makes Joel an offer he can't refuse; if he'll let her and her call-girl colleagues use the house as a brothel for one weekend, he could work as their pimp and use the money to pay for the damage to his father's car. It sounds like the perfect plan but in Hollywood movies such schemes always end in disaster – unless you happen to have Tom Cruise in the lead role.

In the young actor, Brickman found the perfect embodiment of his screen protagonist Joel. In developing this complex character, Brickman employed the full capacity of his scriptwriting expertise, enlivening him with a wealth of autobiographical touches. Even Highland Park, where filming commenced in the autumn of 1982, was an area where Brickman had spent much of his youth. This gave Tom an excellent opportunity to dog into Brickman's persona for his inspiration.

Risky Business has two sequences which stand out more than any others. The first is when Cruise plays air-guitar to Bob Segar's 'Old Time Rock & Roll'. Tom later explained that this was nothing more than a brief description, saying 'Joel dances in underwear through house' until the confident young actor decided to put his own personal stamp on it.

'I tried it a couple of ways where it didn't work so I put on my socks, waxed the floor and then put dirt around the area so I could slide right out to the centre of the frame. Then we did the thing with the candlestick – using it as a microphone – and made it into this rock and roll number.'

Moms and daughters alike would swoon at the wondrous sight of Tom coming on like a junior member of the Chippendales as he made his entrance clad only in sweat socks, BVDs and a pink, button-down shirt. Tom improvised all his dance moves on the spot, delivering his impression of a strutting, rocking cock o' the roost. He was dancing and bouncing off the living room furniture, even shimmying on the couch and doing 'the worm'.

The only person on the set not surprised by Tom's off-the-cuff routine was director Brickman. 'Tom is able to bridge innocence and heat. It's a difficult range, but he'd got it naturally.'

Singlehandedly Tom transformed a somewhat banal scene into one of the most memorable movie sequences in modern movie history. He later revealed that he got his inspiration from watching disco movies like *Saturday Night Fever* back in Louisville. 'If you couldn't dance you couldn't pick up the girls. All the girls loved to go dancing on Saturday night. I used to watch *American Bandstand* and *Soul Train* all the time and I'd rehearse dancing so that, when I showed up at a disco, I could ask girls to dance. I taught myself how to do the robot, spinning and stuff like that.

That's what acting is. Finding yourself in roles and bringing aspects of yourself to life. Not being afraid to do that.'

Tom gyrating in his underwear garnered much attention on its own. TV viewers were treated to it daily in a television ad for the movie and a rock video for Bob Seger's big hit also featured the clip. It was no mean accomplishment and would no doubt have delighted Joel himself.

Enthused Tom: 'With kids, to be a rock star is the ultimate. When their parents leave, they turn the music up. Dancing with your pants off – it's total freedom.'

The second sequence that raised temperatures and consolidated Tom's image as a teenage heart-throb came when he made love to Rebecca aboard a train – a scene that is almost surreal in its erotic imagery.

Tom and Rebecca had enjoyed a love-hate relationship during shooting of *Risky Business*. It was a situation that eventually led to a long-time, real-life, live-in love affair. However, at the time of filming this controversial scene, it seems that love was the furthest thing from both of their minds.

'I remember it was uncomfortable,' recalled Tom with classic understatement. 'A love scene can really step over the line sometimes. I don't mean that I step over the line or that the other person steps over the line – it's just, how far do you go? And although it may be exciting and romantic for the audience – you hope it is, otherwise you're doing it for nothing – it's just kind of uncomfortable.'

When *Playboy* magazine asked Tom who would be his ideal couple for the erotic train scene, he paused and then replied: 'Hmmm, who would I like to see make love on a train? Sean Penn and Madonna? Bruce Willis and Cybil Shepherd? Actually, I see more of Kim Basinger and ... Paul Newman. I'll throw him in there so he can have a good time ...'

WENSLEY CLARKSON

The movie proved very popular with the so-called MTV generation as it turned out to be a hell of a ride, a real standout within the teenage comedy genre. In fact, it ranks among the top three, which include Rob Reiner's *The Real Thing* and John Hughes's *Ferris Bueller's Day Off*.

As *Risky Business*'s producer Steve Tisch explained: 'The teen audience has a finely tuned antenna for being hyped. The interest from the studios waned because they could not design movies that worked for that audience. These movies can't be ordered like you order a pizza. It's just as difficult to make a good teen movie as a good thriller or action movie.'

In *Risky Business* Tom managed to make sure that Joel never became a caricature, always managing to make the character a real one. Rebecca De Mornay proved the perfect sexpot but a great deal of the credit for the movie's success went to writer/director Paul Brickman, who refused to compromise and take the easy path of gratuitous sex or sophomoric humour of any fashion.

Tom knew that he and Rebecca had pulled off a performance that he could display with pride. 'Hurrah!' he proclaimed. 'Finally there's a love scene with some taste that teenagers will see.' Tom keenly defended the open sexuality of the movie: 'It's not a woman-being-exploited movie, a T-and-A film with girls' bras popping open and stuff like that. I feel the scenes were shot in a very stylish way and young people appreciate that.'

Somehow, Tom even managed to find that he shared something in his background with Lana the prostitute: 'As an actor what do I do except sell myself? I am hired to put my soul on the line. My self. Bring myself into character.'

Within days of the film being edited, rave word-of-mouth praise started to circulate about *Risky Business*. It was what is known in Hollywood terms as a 'sleeper' – a movie that no one expected to be a big hit while it was being made.

Tom was certain *Risky Business* would provide the perfect step up the stardom ladder in Tinseltown. 'It is the first film I carry. It has given me freedom, opened up doors. I'm getting better scripts, a wider variety of characters to play. Producers and directors don't feel like it's a risk letting me star in a film. They trust me.'

Tom Cruise's risk-taking had paid off handsomely. Before *Risky Business*, he explained, 'I'd go into a meeting and have to work hard to make them see me, do my juggling act, prove myself to them. Now they say, "I know he can do it." They tell my agent, "I'd like to meet him." ' Strutting his stuff in a lead role, Tom had proved to the world that he was every inch a star.

Like all good Hollywood movies, there was a major battle over the ending of *Risky Business*. Originally, there was a big emotional scene in the restaurant, where Rebecca sits on Joel's lap and it just ended at sunset with Joel stroking her hair and her head on his shoulder. The scene then cut back and forth and Joel exclaims 'Isn't life grand?'.

The producers, Geffen Films, wanted the movie to end on a more upbeat, commercial note. At one point, Paul Brickman threw a tantrum and refused to film the new ending. The Geffen producers started casting around for a new director to finish off their very expensive investment.

However, Brickman had a keen supporter in Tom Cruise. The young actor was determined not to see his character, Joel, sell out at the end. A compromise was finally reached, which left director and star content if not exactly enthusiastic.

'Joel has to know in his heart that this woman is more important than money. That's what I wanted to get across. A lot of people, when I discuss the ending of the film with them, say Joel didn't sell out – some say he did. It's a subtle film and you walk out with what you want to walk out with. It has so many different levels.'

Risky Business paid off for everyone concerned. The Geffen Film Company had backed the movie on a budget barely exceeding $5.5 million and it went on to gross more than $60 million at the US box office. The movie also made millions more on cable TV networks and in video sales.

David Geffen – head of Geffen Films and his own highly lucrative music record division – had made tens of millions of dollars from musical megastars like Don Henley and John Lennon, but his previous attempts at film making had ended in heavy financial losses. *Risky Business* made Geffen personally at least $5 million because of the complex nature of the financial backing of the movie. Geffin – probably the most powerful individual in Hollywood over the past five years – never forgot the actor who made all those millions of dollars' worth of profit possible.

Ironically, Tom had not been given any percentage share of the profits from *Risky Business* as he had signed for the lead role at a time when his box office viability was unknown. His fee was understood to have been in the region of $200,000. But then, no amount of cash could have bought in the kudos that came with the success of *Risky Business*. Besides, Geffin became an overnight fan of Cruise and would have a very substantial influence on the young actor's career from that moment onwards.

After the film's release, Tom still insisted that starring vehicles were not his only aim in life. 'I am not interested in just starring roles. I'm still interested in character roles. Good films. If I was going to carry a film, I want it to mean something.' He was even insisting that he had been turning down other lead roles because of his wish to do only quality projects.

Despite its heavily pro-youth slant, *Risky Business* got relatively good coverage from the movie reviewers.

Just after the opening of the film, Tom took his mom, stepdad, Granny Kremer and three sisters out for a slap up meal as a belated celebration of his twenty-first birthday, which had fallen a few days earlier. They all wondered if Tom would bring his mystery new girlfriend but he turned up alone and burst into fits of laughter when Granny Kremer gave him three pairs of sexy underpants as a gift.

Perhaps the least-expected success story resulting from *Risky Business* was the phenomenal boost in sales of Ray-Ban's classic 'Wayfarer' sunglasses. This particular model, first introduced in 1952, tripled in sales after audiences got a peek at Tom sporting them in the movie. He dons the shades halfway through the film, transforming Joel into a not-so-naive, slick-talking guy.

The whole art of wearing sunglasses took on new social significance. According to New York fashion consultant David Wolfe, if you're wearing Ray-Bans 'you look like you know what you're talking about'. Tom Cruise helped to make 'Wayfarers' Ray-Ban's number two best-selling sunglasses. The 'Aviator' shades he wore in *Top Gun* are rated number one by the company.

Tom even dropped in on his old Louisville friend Jeff Bayers and gave him some tickets to go and see *Risky Business*. Afterwards, Jeff was convinced that his one-time shy loner of a friend was on the verge of superstardom. Tom also stayed for a few days at Jeff's Louisville home while he was passing through shortly after the movie's release.

After the success of *Risky Business*, a sequel would have seemed an almost certain proposition but producer Steve Tisch killed the idea stone dead when he told the *Los Angeles*

Times that he 'never felt we needed to selfishly capitalise on the success of the movie by rushing out and doing a sequel'.

It seemed very commendable but there may well be an even simpler answer: Tom Cruise never does sequels, well not yet he doesn't. As far as the brand new star was concerned, money-spinning follow-ups were to be frowned upon because they would divert him from his predestined goal of becoming the world's most successful actor.

'My agent handles the money. I'm interested in the characters. What's important for me now is to keep in focus, keep my mind straight. Right now, we're building a firm foundation for a career. We're looking for growth,' he said with great maturity for one so young.

It all sounded more like the business plan for a major corporation rather than a highly talented artist on the edge of incredible success, but that was the way Tom wanted it to be.

'I want someone extremely bright and creative. That kind of woman is likely to be pursuing her own vision in life.'

Tom Cruise

10

The nightclub was virtually steaming with atmosphere. Beautiful women of all types seemed to be lining the walls. Throbbing salsa music was coming from the dance area. The constant hum of conversation, combined with the clink of bottles and glasses, dominated the dining section.

As the two handsome young men tried to make their way through the crowds, every pair of female eyes within range locked on their hunky targets. Tom Cruise and Sean Penn had just arrived and word was spreading through the New York nightspot like wildfire. Pairs of women whispered in each other's ears. There were admiring glances from others, unashamed looks of sheer passion from the bold ones. Then a gasp: Robert De Niro and Mickey Rourke were following just behind the younger stars. This was turning into most women's fantasies all rolled up into one.

Tom was probably the only one that night who felt just a little uneasy at the sight of all those pouting lips and wiggling hips. He was more used to cooking himself some pasta at home and sitting back to watch videos of his favourite films, *Casablanca*, *Women In Love* and *Annie Hall*. He looked away each time any of the sensual sirens caught his eye, while Bobby and Mickey just soaked up the atmosphere and the beautiful bevvy of women who went with it. The evil grins on their faces said it all. There was a confidence in their swagger that said they had been down this path many times before.

By the time the Hollywood foursome reached their table, everyone in the nightclub knew precisely where they were seated, such is the power of being a celluloid hero. Sean Penn tried to relax his young friend. He had known ever since the pair became close pals during the making of *Taps* that, beneath the arrogant, confident, ever-focused exterior, lay a shy, complicated character who was still a 'short-assed kid from New Jersey' in reality. *Risky Business* had just been completed and the word in Hollywood was that it would be a smash hit and its star was going to get a million dollars for his next movie without any difficulty.

Each of the stars ordered a beer and swapped titbits of conversation as the older, more experienced stars, Rourke and De Niro, let their eyes drift casually around the room before locking on some delightful looking woman or other. Tom, meanwhile, kept his eyes fixed on the table in front of him and on his three male companions.

Suddenly, out of nowhere, a well-manicured finger tapped him on the shoulder. Tom nearly jumped out of his skin. He turned to find a truly magnificent-looking girl, with gorgeous olive skin, leaning in towards him. Her tight black mini-dress seemed to grip every curve on her body.

'Hi,' she said, ever so calmly. This was the sort of club where old-fashioned etiquette about men only trying to pick up women had long since disappeared.

'Hi,' came the superstar's slightly hesitant reply.

'Mind if I sit down?' This girl had guts and she did not mind showing them.

'Sure,' Tom mumbled back, not quite sure why he even responded but still taken aback by her forwardness.

The following five minutes were taken up by what can only be described as harmless tittle-tattle; polite conversation peppered with long luscious smiles on the part of the olive-skinned beauty, but absolutely no reference to anything personal. Tom was starting to relax – a little anyway but there was an edge in his eyes throughout.

Sean Penn was the only one of the remaining threesome who witnessed what happened next. Mickey and Bobby had long since become distracted by some shapely piece of femininity.

Tom's new best friend leaned in especially close and whispered something in his ear about him coming back to her apartment to continue their in-depth conversation. The young actor's eyes turned instantly to steel. 'I have a girlfriend I'm in love with,' he exclaimed.

Sean Penn heard every word and was astounded. It was the first time Tom had ever publicly referred to the fact that he was living with Rebecca De Mornay, his beautiful blonde co-star in *Risky Business*.

'That girl just wanted Tom for his body and she told him, "You should have told me that five minutes ago!"' explained Penn.

This was a significant moment in Tom's career. By rejecting the girl's advances, he was putting on record his determined intention never to become embroiled in the seedier side of superstardom, something that his three companions that night had enjoyed more than a brief taste of over the years.

Tom's attitude towards women had been shaped by his

admiration and love for his mother and his three sisters. They had guided him through poverty and heartache, not to mention countless awkward teenage moments. Tom could never treat women as mere cattle to be traded up – or traded down – on a whim. He had total and utter respect for the female sex and watching them all lined up, waiting to be wined and dined in that New York nightclub, was almost offensive to him.

Tom never doubted his own tastes and preferences where women were concerned. He deeply values mutual challenge, respect, commitment and independence. 'I like bright, sexy, very sexy women,' he has explained in the past, 'and strong, someone whom I'm not going to run over, someone strong enough to stand up to me.' Tom has great admiration for self-sufficient women with their own careers and personal goals. He sees this quality as an essential ingredient in all relationships. His idea of the perfect woman – even in those far-off days when megastardom was still around the corner – was someone stable, but not boring.

'I don't get into habits with someone; the same thing every night,' he confessed. 'I don't want someone ... depending on me for everything, because I do need a lot of time alone.'

The key phrase for Tom is independence. His lonely childhood, drifting from school to school, made him very self-sufficient and he cannot abide people who are in desperate need the whole time. There were also the classic problems of being in a relationship with someone who might spend three quarters of the year away from home.

In his terms, a successful relationship required some very special preliminary 'clauses'. He explained: 'You can't say, 'OK, let's keep that thought – I'll be back to you in a couple of months when I finish this.'

Those ideal ingredients seemed be possessed by

Rebecca De Mornay, Tom's first serious girlfriend, although no one present during auditions and the first few weeks' shooting of *Risky Business* would have guessed there was an iota of passion between them.

Their first encounter came when Tom – still in Greaser mode for his role in *The Outsiders* – turned up for his second audition for *Risky Business* director Paul Brickman. Tom later admitted he took one look at his soon-to-be co-star Miss De Mornay and his libido sounded a red alert. 'I walk in and see this stunning gorgeous woman sitting there looking at me and I'm thinking, "Oh my God," he later recalled.

However, things got worse, rather than better, between the two actors. Steve Tisch, one of the *Risky Business* producers, has privately retold the following classic Hollywood insiders' tale. After a hard day's shooting, Tom apparently approached Tisch, his partner Jon Avnet and the film's director Brickman because he was concerned that his co-star Rebecca De Mornay was miscast. Things just weren't 'working' between them.

'We explained to Tom that, from our point of view, she was not going to be replaced and that she was doing a terrific job,' explained Tisch. 'We told him that, as production went on, they were going to have to play a number of scenes together and there had to be this illusion these two characters were falling in love.'

In other words, Tisch told Tom to find a way to make it work. The young actor, whom Tisch insists on describing as the 'most sincere and authentic guy I know', nodded seriously and marched out to give it his best shot. Two days later he informed Tisch he would no longer be needing his location hotel room because he and Rebecca were now sharing a suite!

The story perfectly illustrates Tom's penchant for 'tinkering' in the making of a movie and it also shows how strangely love can grow from intense dislike because there seems little doubt that, initially, Tom and Rebecca could not stand the sight of each other.

This story was subsequently denied in very strong terms by Tom's personal publicist more than eleven years later. His PR woman insisted: 'I was on the set and that never happened. Tom was very, very grateful to be in this movie, which was his first lead role. He never would have asked for the lead actress to be replaced.'

Director Paul Brickman was just as reluctant to discuss the 'truth' of the story. He said: 'I don't really remember. It was eleven years ago, but I remember there were some problems in the beginning, and everybody was getting testy. We just had to cool it for that day.'

When Los Angeles-based writer Rod Lurie was working on the story, he got calls from Tisch and others involved, all insisting that their stories should be altered or removed from the article he was writing. It was made clear to him that Tom Cruise did not appreciate seeing their names in that article. Why Tom should be in the slightest bit bothered by such a story remains to be discovered. It simply offers an interesting insight into how his relationship with Rebecca De Mornay got started.

As Lurie put it: 'It was the kind of damage control you would not come up against if you were trying to talk to the President.'

However, Paul Brickman did make some revealing comments about the sex scenes in *Risky Business* which provide ample evidence that true love was always lurking somewhere in Tom and Rebecca's hearts. 'We were able to make the sexual scenes work because of the trust we had in each other. To begin with, I cleared the set except for the cameraman – even the sound people weren't there. I wanted to make it as private for Tom and Rebecca as possible,' explained the director. 'If you want to know the truth, those sex scenes were hard work. It was hard to get them [Tom and Rebecca] started, but it was harder to get them to stop!'

Around the time of his alleged attempt to get her fired from *Risky Business*, Tom bumped into Rebecca in a 7-11 convenience store in West Hollywood. They got talking and, as they say, one thing led to another. They didn't, as was claimed, move into a hotel suite together instantly, but the relationship began to grow into something special.

Rebecca was stunned by the change in Tom's attitude. All their on-set tensions seemed to have disappeared. He saw it a totally different way; that was business, this is pleasure. In other words, his on-screen tensions were solely connected to his work-orientated, highly competitive nature. He saw nothing strange in becoming good friends with someone whom he had tried to get bumped from a movie they were starring in together. Such is the mind of a highly focused, incredibly ambitious film star like Tom Cruise.

As the couple became reaquainted, Rebecca found herself inexplicably drawn to the vulnerability that Tom had hidden so carefully during work hours. They discovered that they had much in common. Both had survived the spectre of painful parental divorces and the hardships of growing up without a father. Rebecca's father – well-known Californian right-wing talk-show host Wally George – had separated from her mother Julie when she was just an infant. Julie had remarried but Rebecca's stepfather Richard De Mornay had died only two years later.

Rebecca later described her mother as a bohemian but that lifestyle only took over for Rebecca and her little step-brother Peter when her then recently bereaved mother decided to embark on an extensive journey through Mexico, Jamaica, Bermuda, England, Germany, France, Spain, Italy and Austria. The young Rebecca learned to adapt to the ever-shifting customs and languages of her many homes.

'I was desperate to fit in ... so I'd adopt a local accent as soon as possible,' she explained. 'I learned to speak German with a perfect Austrian accent.' It sounds like shades of Tom Cruise's own upbringing.

Rebecca also become fluent in French and British English as opposed to the American version. 'When we lived in England the children used to mimic my American accent so I wound up speaking like a Cockney.'

By the time Rebecca returned to the United States, she felt as disorientated as Tom had by the time he reached Glen Ridge, New Jersey. 'I've always been an outsider trying to fit in,' she explained. 'I worked hard to be accepted.'

However, Rebecca harboured no regrets or bitterness about her unorthodox upbringing. 'It was a great learning experience. I'm very American in the way I look at things but I do know there's another world out there.'

That was where Rebecca differed enormously from Tom. He had not been any further than Mexico or Canada by the time they first fell in love. However, Tom found her strong personality and individual resourcefulness very attractive. Soon the couple were dating very regularly. Within months they were living together.

'Rebecca was my first serious girlfriend,' Tom said. 'Living with her was fantastic. She's bright and talented.'

For her part, Rebecca described Tom as 'a pure person ... there's something earnest and virtuous about him that's quite rare.' The contrast in descriptions is significant. In Tom's eyes, Rebecca was a wildly extrovert, exciting girl. To Rebecca, Tom was solid, dependable, almost safe.

She had this interpretation of why their relationship evolved. 'There's definitely something different about kids who come from broken homes. They have this sort of searching quality, because you're searching for love and affection if you've been robbed of a substantial amount of time with your parents. I think that's true of Tom.'

Rebecca also had a very sympathetic understanding of Tom's learning disability because she had a nephew with dyslexia. She constantly helped Tom with script reading and when he got overworked and stressed out – a condition accentuated by dyslexia – she would take extra special care of him.

Tom, in turn, spent hours poring over various nuances of acting technique to help to get even better performances from Rebecca. He taught her to polish and repolish every sentence until it was absolutely perfect. There were no half-measures with Tom Cruise.

> 'She is so strong and honest. I'm already a better person and a better actor because of our relationship. She has a true understanding of what I'm going through, and I also know about the room she needs. Being in the same business can be difficult, though. I go to a movie and see Rebecca doing a love scene with another guy, telling him that she loves him. I'm always facing my fears.'

Tom's stardom – and the intrigue of his relationship with De Mornay – turned up the flame of public interest. *People* magazine asked him and Rebecca to pose for a cover; paparazzi stalked them outside their New York hotel. The public started discovering how wholesome, gracious and kind he could be. But there were still areas of his life he hadn't yet come to terms with.

One day, he stayed on the set of a movie entitled *The Slugger's Wife*, in which Rebecca was starring, and helped her to perfect a southern accent. Cast and crew were astonished to discover Rebecca and her lover going over her lines again and again late one night.

During the latter half of filming on *Risky Business* what had started as a tense battle of egos had transformed into a lovey-dovey hand-holding scenario which had very good side effects for the movie's director Paul Brickman. Tom and Rebecca's sizzling train sex scene near the end of the film was made all the more authentic by the couple's real-life love affair.

The biggest test of their relationship came when Tom shipped himself off to London for *Legend*. The film hit major technical difficulties and he spent the best part of a year stranded in Britain, although Rebecca, who had many old friends in London, did travel over a couple of times.

Ironically, it was after Tom's return to New York that their relationship suddenly began to founder. They discovered that they had little left in common and parted. It was all done quietly and discreetly – not one word appeared in the press for months.

There was no denying that Tom and Rebecca's break-up was very painful. For Tom it was probably the most emotionally difficult period of his life since his father had walked out ten years earlier. For years afterwards, Tom refused even to talk about Rebecca. Later he did refer to the split, saying: 'It wasn't like, "Hey, shake hands. It's been great, baby, let's have lunch." When you care about someone that deeply it's always difficult, but it wasn't ugly.'

Rebecca was more open about the problems. She hinted at creative difficulties between the couple. Certainly, a clash of egos would not be surprising in the circumstances. 'There's the potential threat of competition, there's a continual threat of long separations, of major love scenes, of adverse publicity, and of the transitory nature of the business itself,' she explained with remarkable coolness. Then she cited one vital factor that might well have been missing, ultimately, from her relationship with Tom. 'Total understanding of what each other does.'

As far as Tom was concerned, the competitive edge between himself and Rebecca was perfectly healthy. Both were successful, ambitious actors. Surely they could continue to separate work from their home life? But it's never as easy as it sounds.

Tom hinted at the situation when he explained: 'You have to have the strength to separate. People are more prone to stay together for the security, which is something in my life that I have really not done ... if something's not working you've got to face it and move on.' And that was precisely what Tom did.

The break-up was done in a highly civilised fashion. No plate throwing; no bitter fights over possessions; no hurtful jibes in the tabloids. The parting of the ways for Tom and Rebecca took place in a very cool, controlled atmosphere – just the way Tom liked running his life.

Years later, he was positively gushing in his praise of Rebecca. 'Living with her was fantastic. She's bright, talented.'

However, Rebecca did say later, rather coldly, when asked if they had stayed on friendly terms, 'No, we're not friends. But we're not enemies either. Tom is a lovely guy, but success caused too much friction. We were both ambitious and hard-working. I'm afraid the ending was not very amicable.'

Tom was relieved – even pleased – that he had avoided being accused of behaving like his lady-killing, fellow Brat Packers such as Emilio Estevez, Rob Lowe and, of course, Sean Penn.

All that changed in 1985, when Tom, then 23, went to the White House for the special dyslexia fund raiser and ended up meeting singer Cher, aged 39. The event – intended to help to raise cash for the Lab School which helps students suffering from learning disabilities – was overshadowed for Tom by the spark that ignited instantly between the two stars. Wearing a 1920s gangster-style suit, Tom looked positively conservative in comparison with Cher's black and grey gabardine outfit, complete with a vast, jet-black, punk-style wig.

At the time, Tom was already being hailed as a major star following the phenomenal success of *Risky Business*. Even his demeanour – which had earlier been that of a slightly baby-faced, chubby-cheeked boy rather than a man – had changed. By 1985, a butterfly had emerged from the gawky, unformed cocoon and the new Tom Cruise was strikingly handsome and full of confidence and inner assurance.

Cher was riveted from the first moment she saw him. To her, he was handsome in a manly kind of way, yet with oddly boyish expressions and mannerisms. She had also suffered the same sort of chaotic early life and within minutes of meeting at the White House they were comparing notes on their dyslexia-ridden early years. Later conversations between the pair were to have little to do with learning disabilities.

'Cher was truly mesmerised by Tom at the beginning,' explained one of Tom's former business partners, Stephen Clark. 'She said, "I can't take my eyes off the guy. He's so damn handsome all I want to do is stare at him. Have you ever seen a man with a face like that? And a body like that?"'

At the beginning, Cher devoted herself to Tom because she did not believe in going out with more than one man at a time. Her previous lover, movie executive Josh Donen, was pushed aside and Tom and Cher spent long evenings together, talking and watching old movies at his New York apartment. The singer told one friend: 'He drives me wild!'

On other occasions during the relationship, Cher would cook meals for Tom at her Malibu home so that they did not have to go out in public and risk being photographed together. At the time, the romance was one of Hollywood's best kept secrets. Tom got along well with Cher's children, Chastity – then just eight years younger than Tom – and Blue, then nine.

Cher and Tom dated off and on for several months. Cher spent a lot of time at Tom's New York apartment, hanging out there for days at a time when Tom was on the West Coast. Reports that Cher had moved into his place were sparked by sightings of her at the entrance to the apartment block. However, she was actually taking advantage of Tom's offer of free use of the apartment while he was away. They never lived together.

In fact, at this time, Tom also started seeing another older woman – an actress called Mimi Rogers – but he never considered that he was being disloyal to Cher because he did not look on the relationship with the singer as serious. Tom's romance with Mimi was so slow to develop that he managed to keep it a secret for months.

Inside Hollywood, stories about Cher and Tom began to circulate because they were getting into juicy – and slightly tacky – kissing scenes at Tinseltown parties, such as a party hosted by Paul Newman. It should be pointed out, of course, that neither was married at the time, so there was nothing morally wrong with what they were doing – it was just considered a little immature, especially on Cher's part.

Tom actually went to the trouble of denying the romance in public because he worried about what it might mean for his carefully nurtured image. He insisted to *People* magazine: 'Cher is funny and bright and we're good buddies and that's it.'

Cher looked on Tom as a good, handsome young catch at the time. 'But it is debatable whether she ever took him all that seriously as a lover,' explained one Hollywood insider. Later, Cher even admitted that one of the risks about dating younger men is that they often fall for someone else. 'When you date younger men you gotta be prepared that they might want to try other experiences. It's the risk that you take.'

When it did end, Tom was a little guilt-ridden about his romance with Cher. During their relationship, he felt a little embarrassed by the fact that he was dating such an obviously older woman but he was attracted to the fact that she was so independent. She did not need him and that made him feel more secure in a strange way. When the affair ended, he was also genuinely worried that he might have upset Cher when she later found out about his relationship with Mimi Rogers.

After the break-up, it was suggested by friends of the singer that Cher was so crushed by Tom's rejection that she has never got over it and that she now compares every man she dates with her 'lost, beloved Tom'. The truth is probably far simpler – they had a passionate fling which taught Tom how to handle older women and Cher got to date the man who went on to become the world's most successful movie star.

There was never any question of Cher planning any-thing serious with Tom, although her ego might have been temporarily damaged when Tom chose to get into a proper relationship with Mimi Rogers, the actress who went on to become his first wife. In retrospect, what really drew Tom and Cher together was their shared dyslexic incapacity and the memories of a difficult childhood. Years later, Cher proved she had no hard feelings towards Tom by saying she felt genuinely sorry for him when he failed to get the Best Actor Oscar for *Born on the Fourth of July*. 'He deserved it so much!' She went on in reference to her own Oscar win, 'But I got one eventually – and so, I'm positive, will Tom!'

Other relationships that did reach the popular press included rumours of a hot romance with actress Darryl Hannah. Tom laughed that one off when a friend asked him what she was like when they went on a date. 'I did?' Tom asked incredulously. 'How was I?' He'd never even met Darryl Hannah. 'I don't know why people think I'm running around with everybody.'

Top Gun director Tony Scott – himself something of a ladies man to say the least – described Tom as 'a magnet for women', but the truth was that, even then, the young actor was desperate to settle down. Casual relationships were not his favourite way of life.

One time when Tom, dressed 'inconspicuously' in 'Aviator' Ray-Bans and a bomber jacket, was dining on romantic chilli dogs with a date at the New York celebrity hangout Serendipity 3 when he became increasingly unnerved by a quartet of giggling girls standing nearby gawking at him. When the waiter intervened and told the girls to stop annoying Mr Cruise, Tom rewarded him by paying a $17.50 check with a $50 bill and instructions to keep the change.

However, another, much more serious, incident really freaked the young star out. It occurred when he was living in a classic New York loft on the west side of the city. Over a number of days and nights he started to notice that someone with a set of binoculars was spying on him from another apartment block across the street. At first Tom thought that maybe they were not actually aiming their spy gadgetry at him and he ignored it. By the third night, he was convinced that the binoculars were trained on him.

In a remarkable piece of one-man detective work, he calculated which apartment the spies were using and confronted the bewildered owner of the flat that same night. The man had no idea that his two young daughters had set up the ultimate peep show for their friends. The shocked, and deeply shamed, parent immediately offered to board up the girls' window and ground the young peeping toms for a month but Tom came up with his own solution, which seemed completely out of character for the shy, reserved young man most knew him to be. He told the father he would take the girls to lunch if they promised not to spy on him ever again. Naturally, they agreed.

Tom did not consider his friendship with Cher to have been a proper relationship. Following the split with Rebecca De Mornay, he was also in a rather confused state about whether it was better or worse to date women inside the entertainment industry. His earlier opinions had been altered somewhat by his most recent experiences and he even went to special lengths to go out with women outside the industry, like lawyers, writers and artists.

'I'm not really sure whether it is an advantage to be with someone in the business. I know I need someone who is adaptable, someone who can go from one extreme environment to the next and not go crazy. Sometimes I get up in the middle of the night and want to work. Other times, I can sleep for days,' explained Tom.

Tom did date blonde *Dynasty* actress Heather Locklear briefly but that relationship seemed to be put together for the paparazzi, rather than reality. In the middle of 1986, US tabloid *The Star* ran a whole page headlined 'Why Hollywood's hottest new hunk can't find a girl to love'. It kicked off by stating glibly: 'Tom Cruise is suddenly the hottest hunk in Hollywood – and also the loneliest.' While the article mainly consisted of excerpts from other publications' interviews with Tom, it did have a good point.

By the middle of 1987, Tom was topping just about every eligible bachelor list in America and Britain. *US* magazine featured him on the cover with Charlie Sheen,

Corbin Bernsen, John Kennedy Jr and Jon Bon Jovi as a few of the country's hottest single men. The viewers of the popular American television show, *Entertainment Tonight*, voted Tom 'Sexiest Man in Hollywood' with 27,000-plus votes (Don Johnson followed with just 19,000).

In reality, Tom was still the same loner he had always been. He told friends at the time that it did not bother him, but it had to have some effect. As he admitted to movie director Cameron Crowe in 1986: 'It's not easy. I spend a lot of time alone. I mean, a lot of time alone. But I've spent time alone my whole life and it doesn't bother me. I feel lonely at times. It takes time to get to know people.'

It was ironic really. On the streets of New York his success in a string of movies had made Tom a very famous face, even though he had a great deal of trouble getting used to being stared at all the time. 'I used to think "Jesus, is something hanging out of my nose?" It took time to get adjusted to it.'

A purely platonic meal at Lusardi's restaurant in New York with Demi Moore and Kelly McGillis nearly ended in a riot after word got around of Tom's visit.

Meanwhile Tom was still waiting for his perfect woman to appear on the horizon. 'In the final analysis, it's just the person, isn't it?' He remarked once while discussing the ups and downs of finding Ms Right. 'Who knows? One day, I'll just be walking down the street and there she'll be.'

*'I didn't become an actor for money;
the money isn't why I work.
It's great to have, though.'*

Tom Cruise

The onset of stardom which arrived with the runaway success of *Risky Business* caught Tom Cruise completely by surprise. Suddenly he was inundated by press and television coverage; an obligatory media blitzkrieg which included the public's natural curiosity about aspects of Tom's private life that he found it very uncomfortable talking about. The questions were neverending and concerned his love life, his childhood and even the pain of his parents' divorce. Tom was completely unnerved by the entire experience. No one had prepared him for it and he did not know how to respond. 'I'd say to myself, "My God, I've never told anyone about these things before in my life." '

Tom was baffled by the media's obsession with him. He felt mightily awkward being asked such intimate and prying questions. 'You know how it is when you're a kid and you aren't wearing the right kind of shoes and they hang you up in the locker room for being a nerd? Well, I was never wearing the right shoes,' was his cryptic explanation.

During his childhood, Tom had always been the new kid in town and he had devised a clever routine to make people accept him easily. He would create new personalities and backgrounds to fit each new bill. But this was different. This was the big, wide, grown up world and there were a lot of inquisitive people out there wanting to know the truth about Tom Cruise. 'When you travel like that, you can make up who you are. But I couldn't do that in interviews,' he explained.

After *Risky Business*, there was also the little matter of Rebecca De Mornay. Their love affair seemed a movie publicist's dream and some cynical members of the press even tried to suggest that the entire relationship had been created to help to promote the film. As we already know, however, Tom and Rebecca's relationship had got off to such a rocky start that it would have been impossible to manipulate the affair.

The whole media circus surrounding *Risky Business* terrified Tom and once he had performed his contractual obligations in terms of interviews and television appearances, he backed off the publicity merry-go-round. 'I had to say, "Listen guys, for myself, I'm just not personally ready to do this." '

Tom was already starting to shape his attitudes towards the press and their intrusion into his life. He was later to state that he learnt a lot of lessons during those early years, lessons which convinced him to try to take complete and utter control of the flow of interviews and photographs about him in a way no other star has ever attempted. He made no secret of his opinion that the proper perspective on the acting profession places integrity in the foreground and publicity way back on the horizon. 'My art, my craft is the most important thing to me. Keeping my integrity is important, keeping my base … When I look at myself in the mirror, at first I think, "Oh God, why can't I do better work?" But then I see I'm really proud of what I've done.'

Tom was becoming fairly obsessed about his work. He had even stopped cracking vaguely amusing one-liners during press interviews. As he told one journalist: 'I guess I do get very serious when I talk about my acting but it is very important to me. I hate that word "career". I try not to focus in on thinking of it as a career. Career sounds very money orientated … I just want to keep focued on my craft.' Whatever way Tom said it, it sounded like he had a one-track mind. And that word 'focus' would not go away. It was Tom's priority even back in those days. The other key word was 'quality' or at least what he deemed to be quality. However, the success of a movie is not made or lost by one person. It is a team effort, consisting of the skills and failings of hundreds of people and, because of that, every actor, director and technician will make his or her fair share of disappointing films during a career.

At that time, Tom sincerely believed that he had learnt all his lessons right at the start, thanks to the appalling *Endless Love* and the sloppy, silly *Losin' It*. He was insistent on maintaining his integrity and beside choosing his movie projects with incredible caution, he also completely clammed up, refusing to give any interviews for the next couple of years.

There was some clever thinking behind his decision. His silence helped to create an even greater buzz about himself. Hollywood's main-line players don't read the pages of the tabloids, they concentrate on trade papers like *Variety* and the *Hollywood Reporter* and both of those publications were attaching Tom's name to just about every major project in Tinseltown that required a leading man under the age of 30. The trades also ran daily columns filled with snippets of inside gossip that fuelled that day's discussion at lunches in restaurants like Spago's and The Ivy.

When one columnist reported that Tom's per picture fee had rocketed to $1 million, producers all over town took that as confirmation that Tom Cruise was the hottest male actor in Hollywood and they presumed his fee would keep climbing. Many of them started swamping Tom's agent Paula Wagner with screenplays.

Most of the projects on offer were the sort of teen flicks that Tom thought he had turned his back on since *Losin' It*. Both he and Paula Wagner soon realised that if his career was to develop on a healthy arc rather than adopt a short-sighted money-grabbing mentality like many others before him, he should throw every one of those lucrative movie scripts in the rubbish bin and wait until something with a little more depth came along.

So, despite his enviable negotiating position, as his next film Tom chose a rather low-key project which he was convinced would test his acting skills rather than inflate his bank account. Choosing the correct film is a finely balanced decision for a movie star because if the subject is too dense and heavy-going then the movie will probably get nothing more than a limited release before diappearing into movie oblivion. Choose a rip-roaring piece of commercial tripe and you are more than likely to be laughed out of town by the critics.

Unfortunately, Tom agreed to play the lead in a film that was almost certainly predestined to be overlooked by a mass audience due to its sombre, almost depressing over-tones, not to mention a complete lack of Hollywood sparkle. The movie, entitled *All the Right Moves*, featured Tom in the role of Stefan Djordjevic, a high school football star with more than a passing resemblance to *Risky Business*'s Goodsen.

Stef's main characteristics were just the sort of things Tom felt he could relate to: anxious, insecure, honest, forthright, incorruptable but also determined to win no matter what. There were also elements of Stef's family background which mirrored his own.

'There were times when my father was working,' reflected Tom. 'I remember that for about a year we lived in a nice house in a nice neighbourhood. Then, later on, times really got tough. But it was exciting, it was challenging. And there was a sense of teamwork. We all worked together and when the team broke down, there were problems. It wasn't easy.

'I think on certain levels I could identify with the guy. But I didn't need the ticket out. I didn't feel that trapped. I was lucky enough to live in places where I could always make the money.'

Tom's ever-improving ability to remould his body and mind to fit any character he was playing resulted in a complete physical transformation for the role of Stef. He underwent an intense weight-training course and exercise regime to regain the kind of hard-edged physique he had when he portrayed Steve Randle in *The Outsiders*.

It seemed as though no detail was too small for Tom's cosmetic scrutiny. He wanted to ensure that his character would fit in perfectly in the grimy, grey town of Johnstown, Pennsylvania, which was tranformed by film makers into the fictional Ampipe, Pennsylvannia. Tom died his hair jet black and took on the demeanour of a pale, scrawny youth to such good effect that if it hadn't been for his bulging biceps he would have looked extremely sick.

The essence of the story is Stef's dream of escaping the

steel mills of Ampipe to make it as a bigtime football player. His coach, Vern Nickerson, was played by well-known television actor Craig T. Nelson. He is just as keen to escape the drudgery and the movie builds up to the game that ultimately will decide if either of these characters can finally realise their dreams.

In *All the Right Moves*, Stef's girlfriend was played by Lea Thompson, who went on to find fame and fortune in movies such as *Back to the Future* and *Space Camp*. It was Lea's first starring role and her preparations were just as demanding as Tom's. She had to go undercover at a local high school in order to absorb the way of life in such a tough, gritty steel town. Lea needed to know the dreams and fears of girls raised in such an environment. Her character, Lisa, is in a predicament even more desperate that Stef's; she aspires to study music but she's painfully aware that only those with footballing talents ever escape Ampipe.

Tom and Lea hit it off as friends from the moment she was introduced to him during a reading, unlike his initially antagonistic attitude towards Rebecca De Mornay. They shared very similar views about movie making and acting and Lea had very strong, forthright opinions about the sort of roles women are expected to play in films. 'I read a lot of scripts and most of them are about men. Women are just there to be cute and look nice in a bikini. Well, that's absurd. Young women have the same problems growing up that guys do and I think audiences are starting to want more strong female parts in movies, young women who are fun and smart.'

Lea's opinions mirrored almost exactly those of Tom's mother and three sisters and he felt very much at ease in her company.

Tom was especially attracted to the part in *All the Right Moves* because the director, Michael Chapman, had been

Martin Scorsese's cinematographer on *Taxi Driver* and *Raging Bull*, a film that Tom had seen at least five times with Sean Penn when they became close friends during the shooting of *Taps*.

Tom and Chapman hit it off immediately and before actual production of the movie the pair would meet at Chapman's house to rewrite certain lines of dialogue to suit Tom's instincts about his character. The young actor had very strong opinions about dialogue and he always insisted on altering elements, even without the involvement of the screenwriters if neccessary. Tom believed, and still does to this day, that, ultimately, he was the one who would be damaged by sloppy dialogue and he was determined to ensure that every word he spoke would be completely believable. Like a master craftsman, he would sometimes toil for days on the shape of one sentence just because he felt it did not flow correctly.

Chapman and Tom also held little gatherings at the director's house each Sunday night and invited other actors over to their sessions to discuss the characters with them and rework other elements of the script as they went along.

Lea Thompson was very impressed by her young co-star's analytical approach to acting. 'He's astonishingly smart the way he knows how to break down scenes in a script before playing them.' Lea was also astonished to discover the full range of her co-star's acting talents. 'He can act younger and more innocent than he really is,' she enthused.

Tom actually related more to the character of Stef than any other part he had so far played. When the plot called for him to act out the despair and disappointment of being dropped from the football team, he remembered back to the time when he was sidelined from the wrestling team at Glen Ridge High. He also insisted that no doubles be used in the football sequences and – apart from several staged shots –

no one was spared the rigour of full-contact play, even if that risked actual bodily harm. Tom relished the physical contact. It was a bit like being back in school, only the big difference was that, this time, he got to make the football team.

One day, after a series of head-knocking, open-field collisions for the camera with fellow actor Paul Carafotes, Tom showed up looking so cock-eyed that director Chapman had him sent to hospital, where tests revealed a minor concussion. The film's consultant for these blood-and-guts sequences was local high school coach Don Yanessa. He said admiringly: 'I think Carafotes went for the hit so hard 'cause it was his job and I think Cruise really liked it!'

Some critics were very generous in their praise of *All the Right Moves*. Roger Ebert, noted reviewer and television personality, proclaimed in the *Chicago Sun-Times*: 'It is an astonishing breakthrough in movies about teenagers.'

ABC-TV's Katie Kelly declared: 'Tom Cruise proves once again he is an actor to watch. I really like this one.' Kathleen Carroll of the *New York Daily News* wrote: 'Tom Cruise is exceptionally appealing and his sensitive performance more than matched by that of Lea Thompson. It is a gritty, dignified movie.'

The film itself fared poorly at the box office and *Time* magazine noted: 'This was no chic adolescent fantasy, just a drab ring around the blue collar, and suddenly Cruise has lost what he earned in *Risky Business*.'

Movie pundit Edward Gross wrote: 'With the exception of its fairy-tale ending where everything works itself out, *All The Right Moves* is a downright depressing film.'

Premiere magazine probably summed up the movie perfectly when it stated: 'For Cruise's career, it was the time. It solidified his now pre-eminent position among Hollywood's young actors.'

Tom's gamble with *All the Right Moves* had paid off handsomely because he was establishing himself at the top of his class rather than sacrificing art for money, or so he thought. Reviewers admired the 'accessibility' of Tom – ironic when one considers the extraordinary efforts he has made to remain a very private star. Next to him, fellow Brat Packers were coming off a poor second: Matthew Broderick was compared to Walter Matthau in knee pants, Matt Dillon dubbed a male-model fantasy (despite Coppola's raving admiration) Sean Penn was simply earmarked as frighteningly intense – and a troublemaker to boot.

'Cruise's dark eyes, jutting cheekbones and nosebone-smooth jaw are natural tools for conveying moods ranging from astonishment to deep hurt to scant amusement,' gushed writer Fred Schruers. His assesment of Tom's image as conveyed in *All the Right Moves* perfectly sums up the state of his career at that stage.

> 'Though Cruise is supposed to be a tough guy, he's not allowed to look bad. He may bumble and screw up, but that girlishly attractive face was never meant to get kicked. When some thugs beat him up, he wears an adriotly placed light-blue bruise; smudged with blast furnace soot, he's all the more fetching, and we know that any minute now the story line is going to lift him up where he belongs.'

Just after completing shooting on *All the Right Moves*, Tom told friends he wanted to try his hand at some New York theatre work in an effort to stretch his acting skills even further. Home, at that time, tended to be a Samsonite suitcase but the young star insisted that his 'emotional base' was strong and that was all that mattered.

Amid all the adulation and stardom, Tom's emotional

base came crashing down in late 1983 when he learned that his father, Thomas Cruise Mapother III, was seriously ill with cancer. The prognosis was bleak. While Tom had been making *All The Right Moves*, his father had been operated on but doctors had found that the disease had spread to other parts of his stomach.

Since he had walked out of their lives ten years earlier, Tom and his three sisters had received only the barest snippets of information about their father and, understandably, Tom has remained very sensitive about the subject to this day. It is not even clear if Tom actually knew anything about Tom Sr's transient travels across the United States in the years after he and Mary Lee separated.

The very thought of being reunited with his father brought a rush of mixed emotions through Tom's mind. He couldn't help but remember some of the brutality he faced at the hands of his father before the family split up. It was violence that was only directed at him, not his mother or sisters. But it was something he could never forget...

Throughout this period Tom's cousin, Caroline Mapother, was a confidante to Tom's grandmother Catherine, so she gained a unique insight into the whole sad scenario. She says that after the split-up Tom Sr 'just vanished'. He remarried and drifted across the western side of the United States with his new wife, picking up odd jobs wherever he could, still harbouring a dream that one day one of his inventions would earn him a fortune. 'He was a drifter. I felt so sorry for him. He obviously regretted what happened between himself and Tom's mother,' explained Caroline Mapother.

Cousin Dillon Mapother – self-appointed family historian – said: 'He was living a hand-to-mouth existance. It was very sad.'

Some time during his travels, Tom Sr parted with wife number two and then became ill so he finally abandoned his tinpot ambitions and headed back home to Louisville. It was a sad homecoming. The city where his family had always held their heads high and had enjoyed political and legal influence for at least four generations did not exactly welcome him back with open arms.

Tom Sr's parents, Thomas Cruise Mapother II and Catherine, were naturally relieved to see their wayward son finally come home to the fold. However, Tom's father's wanderings had turned him into an eccentric character not really capable of blending back into a society like the one that greeted him in Louisville. With some financial backing from his parents, he rented a small, cheap apartment at the Crestview complex, on Brownsboro Road, Louisville – a tatty block on a busy main road. Then he persuaded his family to provide financial backing for a book he intended to write, on how to invest money wisely – an ironic subject considering his own chaotic working life.

Shortly after that he met and fell in love with Jill Ellison, the wife of a local newspaper executive, and caused another mini-scandal in the tight-knit community by moving her into his apartment. Jill was in her early thirties while Tom Sr was close to 50. The cancer was already spreading and Tom Sr realised that his decision to move back to familiar surroundings had been rather fortunate. He remained hale and robust right up to the end and he was just as reluctant to talk about his son as Tom was to talk about him. He did not deny that he had failed to keep in touch with his son and he never once tried to take any credit for Tom's success. As for criticising his son's films, Tom Sr would never have dreamt of doing that. He did not actually get to see one of those movies before his untimely death.

Caroline Mapother says she doesn't know how much Tom is aware of about his father's last few years. 'Maybe he doesn't know about it all. It's all so sad.'

Bill Ellison, the husband of the woman that Tom's father lived with, said he had no idea where his former wife was now living. Mr Ellison, who works as an editor on the *Louisville Courier-Journal*, said: 'I don't feel this is something I can talk about. I don't know where my former wife is now but I can tell you that she never actually married Mapother. It was a very difficult time for us all.'

One of his colleagues reiterated: 'It is a very delicate matter.'

Caroline Mapother last saw Tom Sr shortly before his death when he hosted a book-signing session at the Hawley-Cooke bookstore in Louisville. It was for his self-published effort entitled *Winning Through Intimidation*. Interestingly, he steadfastly refused even to attempt to cash in on his son's famous name and insisted on writing under the *nom de plume* of Thomas May. Tom Cruise did not show up at the signing.

'He was very ill even then,' explained the manager of Hawley-Cooke. 'His woman friend at the time did all the negotiating for him. She seemed very supportive.'

The book was geared towards the money-grabbing 1980s – a decade that later adopted Tom Cruise as its favourite son. 'The theme was somewhat aggressively saying that you should save yourself first, look after number one. It was a pretty aggressive tone, as I recall,' said store manager Bill Schwartz, who hosted the signing.

A year later, shortly after Tom Sr's death, his girlfriend called the store manager and asked if he wanted to buy some extra copies of the book that Tom Sr had kept. The store manager put them out on his bargain book counter, but virtually none of them sold. The book, sadly, was a complete flop.

The Thomas Cruise Mapother III that Cousin Caroline met that day at the book signing was a mere shadow of his former self. He had a long flowing beard and hair, was wearing scruffy jeans and, as Caroline explained: 'He looked like he had, as they say in Kentucky, come from the country and was in trouble. I suppose you could call him a hippy really.'

After news of Tom Sr's illness got out, Tom and his sisters rushed to their father's side. It had been many years since Tom had last seen his dad. Tom Sr never tried to take any credit for his son's success. He knew his own failings as a parent but he could not help feeling proud of Tom and, having seen his photo in so many newspapers and magazines, he longed to see him one last time.

But Tom's father only allowed his son and daughters to visit him on his deathbed if they agreed not to ask him any questions about those missing years. He even told his only son that he was looking forward to getting out of hospital and sharing a beer and a steak with his long lost child. But that never happened...

Father, son and daughters cried without shame. They showed a level of forgiveness that is admirable and they probably made their father's last memory of them a happy, loving one. Tom Sr had never really expected ever to be reunited with his children again.

Tom Cruise was understandably torn apart by the reunion but at least it cleared up a few of the many unanswered questions about who his father really was and why the family fell apart in such tragic circumstances ten years earlier. Tom knew that his father felt deep remorse for what had happened and he greatly regretted that his father had not been a bigger influence on his teenage years.

Caroline Mapother remembers being stunned by the news of Tom Sr's death and the fact that so little was mentioned at the time of his illness. 'It was as if the memory of Tom's father was just wiped from the face of the earth,' she said.

Tom Sr's funeral was a very quiet, very small affair. Today, the grey gravestone at the Calvary Catholic Cemetery on the outskirts of Louisville is virtually unreadable because of the overgrown plants surrounding it. It reads simply: 'Thomas Cruise Mapother III Oct 15, 1934 Jan 9, 1984'.

In 1986, the coffin containing Tom's grandfather, Thomas Cruise Mapother II, was lowered next to his son, following his death on 17 January that year. Officials at the cemetary say they have rarely seen Tom visiting his father's or grandfather's graveside.

In 1984, Tom's father's death was his first experience of the death of a loved one and he wondered how he would have coped if he had not had a serious multi-million-dollar career to throw himself into. Just before his father's death, he had agreed to star in the $30 million movie *Legend*, to be directed by British helmsman Ridley Scott, a man reputed to be capable of painting truly vivid images with film following fantasy world epics *Blade Runner* and *Alien*. Tom knew it was going to be a tough, slow process to make the film but gallantly refused an offer from agent Paula Wagner to get him out of his commitment to the project. Tom felt that he had made a promise and could not break that pledge to Scott and, because of his father's death, he explained later, 'I had this thing, like I had to go through with it.' Tom wanted to refocus his mind away from the heartache and anguish that he had left behind in Louisville.

Legend also seemed the perfect opportunity to prevent Tom from being pigeonholed in any particular category.

By the beginning of 1984, Tom found himself in London for the *Legend* shoot, cut off from his support system: his family, Rebecca De Mornay and the US movie-making community. To pass the time, he began hanging out on the set for hours on end, even when he was not needed by meticulous mastercraftsman Scott, a gritty Geordie who had already amassed a multi-million-dollar fortune by directing some of the most significant television commercials of the sixties and seventies.

Scott fully appreciated what a gamble the role was for Tom. 'For him to do this movie is very brave ... as a career step it's very challenging. Suddenly, he's stepping out of the usual kind of role that a 23-year-old guy is going to do and into a much more theatrical situation,' said Scott.

This was a very difficult time for Tom. He took long walks by himself around Hyde Park to try to relieve the boredom and isolation. Thoughts of his father still drifted back uncomfortably. Certainly, Tom liked to be alone but not all the time and he found London a cold, grey place where people were not always as instantly friendly as in Kentucky or New Jersey. As usual, he tried hard to immerse himself in the character he was about to play. 'He's very unassuming. He doesn't judge people. He has a great capacity to love. And he's magical, which is nice,' he explained.

Legend's elaborate sets at Pinewood Studios near London looked like a sensuous fairy tale, similar to Disney meets Cocteau's 'Beauty and the Beast'. The main stage was on the set originally built for the Bond film *Moonraker* and even the extras were having to submit to four–five hour make-up sessions to transform them into elves and fairies. Scott – a former art school student and artist – refused to shoot until everything was absolutely perfectly set up, so the actors, including attractive Mia Sara and British actor Tim Curry, and crew endured painfully long gaps between camera set-ups. Sometimes they would end up working on a scene that might last 30 seconds in the film but take a week to shoot.

Then, to make matters even worse, halfway through filming Tom injured his back and spent the following few days bent over like Quasimodo. There was also the cute little fox that Tom had to cradle in his arms for one scene and which ended up merrily scratching the skin off Tom's legs while he had to sit there looking tranquil. Then came the bird which flew towards Tom, supposedly to land on his hand, yet kept on going. The whole crew was mobilised to shimmy up the walls with nets in search of the errant fowl. It seems the trainer had decided to economise and it was the only bird they had.

By the time Tom's agent Paula Wagner and her husband dropped in on the *Legend* set during a honeymoon trip to London, the young actor was feeling at a fairly low ebb. It was the first time Paula had ever visited her precious young client on a film set and the threesome headed off for lunch together, hoping to lighten Tom's dampened spirits.

Unfortunately, while they were eating, a phone call came through to the restaurant to say that Ridley Scott's pride and joy – *Legend*'s multi-million-dollar fantasy world set – was engulfed in flames. Two stagehands and four firemen were injured tackling the blaze and an estimated $3 million worth of props went up in smoke. Things were definitely going from bad to worse.

Somehow Tom managed to find a light side to this disaster. He turned to Paula – by this time probably his closest, most trusted confidante in Hollywood – and said: 'I hope you'll understand when I ask you never to visit a set of mine again.'

Tom rushed back to the set to inspect the damage and was devastated by the charred remains of the elaborate forest that had been created. Suddenly, across the burnt set, he spotted director Ridley Scott wandering in a daze among the ruins and called to him: 'Rid …' but he did not know what to say.

The gritty Geordie looked up at young Tom, by now terrified that he might have encroached upon his director at an awkward moment, and said: 'Well, I'm going to go play some tennis. How about meeting me for dinner later? Does that sound fine to you?' Tom was stunned – and then mightily relieved. The two became firm friends from that moment onwards.

The fire put Tom in a very difficult position. The shoot was seriously delayed and he had dozens of other top quality scripts waiting for him to green light back in Los Angeles. 'I really had to make a choice. When the set burned down, it was like, "What are we going to do now? Where does this take us?" I said, "I can sit here and feel shitty and wallow in my frustration" and, banging your head against the wall, you say, "Okay, that happened, now what do we do? Let's go ahead." '

Tom saw his experiences as yet another test of character and determination. Every mountain was there to climb but no peak would get in his way, however high. 'I mean, I always had that ability to just deal with things. My whole life has been like that: "OK, what do I do now?" '

In *Legend*, Tom's character of Jack O' the Green – who wears a green outfit and resembles the son of Robin Hood – spends a lot of time talking to unicorns. You could safely say it was something completely different for the young actor. Tom insisted he was grabbed by the character of Jack after watching Ridley Scott develop the character through a poetic script. This time, Tom's traditionally thorough, muscle-obsessed research required a new type of intensity.

Tom carefully wrote up a background for his character, to create a sense of history, and then practised his backflips and grew his hair long.

Scott, a man of few words, said admiringly: 'It's always good if a large amount of input comes from the actor. He's the person doing the work. If Tom can get inside the role and brings to it what I hadn't thought of, then that's the best way to operate.'

Interestingly, Tom was rather non-committal when asked about the movie's box office potential. 'I can't predict what is going to be box office and what is not. I think anyone who says, "This is going to be a hit" before the thing is made really doesn't know. Nobody knows. So you'd better do something you believe in and you love, because if it's not financially successful, you'd better walk away with some-thing.' It almost sounded as if Tom already knew how *Legend* would fare.

Mind you, at one point, studio executives seriously considered not even releasing the movie and cutting their losses after they received reports that audiences who sneak-previewed the trailer laughed at Tom's hair. (Just two years later long hair for men came back with a vengeance!)

Legend opened in America as that week's top-grossing film and then promptly sank without trace. Hollywood interpreted this to mean that Tom had become such a box office pull that even a film as poor as *Legend* could open well because it had such a magnetic name in the starring role. All his pre-production handiwork had certainly helped him to salvage a decent performance even if the movie itself was very disappointing.

The critics were united in their dismissal of it. Richard Corliss described it in *Time* magazine as 'landscapes too remote. Quests too familiar and special effects too rudi-mentary'. Kevin Thomas of the *Los Angeles Times* wrote:

'According to Ridley Scott, legends are born of the eternal struggle between the forces of light and darkness. Perhaps so, but it's hard to imagine his *Legend* living up to its name.'

Tom himself even admitted later that he had been 'just another colour in a Ridley Scott painting'. Publicly, he insisted that all the delays had not affected the movie's final outcome.

The truth was that there were a lot of post-production problems. Ridley Scott had made a fairy tale, something he believed was a breakthrough visually but the project's main backer, Twentieth Century-Fox, thought the whole piece was a little too romantic so Scott had to go back and re-edit the film to give it a harder edge.

Tom later described *Legend* as a 'tortuous experience' which he never wanted to endure ever again. 'Making that movie was exhausting.'

All in all, the making of *Legend* was a severe test of his patience and ability to enjoy his work. When he got back to Los Angeles he had already decided that his next project would be the complete and utter opposite of that lengthy, heavy-handed experience, something filled with comic-book-style heroes and adventure.

'I feel the need, the need for speed.'

Maverick, in *Top Gun*

12

The first thing you pick up on is the sound – the ear-splitting, brain-busting, bone-shaking rumble; the rumble that shatters as though it were the end of the world. Tom heard the sound and turned away from his lunch directly towards its source, an F-14 Tomcat roaring down an adjacent runway. His concentration broke and a smile slipped across lips so tight they seemed on guard duty. As the jet screamed into the atmosphere, the smile took on an afterburner's glow. 'Ah,' sighed Tom, searching the sky through 'Aviator' lenses, 'the sound of freedom.'

Throughout the trials and tribulations of making *Legend* for the best part of a year in London, Tom somehow held his relationship with Rebecca De Mornay together. On his return to New York, however, the couple found that actually having to live together for any length of time was not the pleasurable experience it had been before Tom's departure to Britain. It was, as they say, by mutual consent that Tom and Rebecca decided it was time to call it a day and the actor, still only 24 at the time, immediately committed to a project that was to accelerate his career more than any other single movie before or since. He needed his freedom in a big way.

The film was called *Top Gun* and it had been carefully developed by two of Hollywood's sharpest young producers, Jerry Bruckheimer and Don Simpson. The project's conception occurred when Bruckheimer was skimming through a copy of *California* magazine in the duo's office and he spotted an article by writer Ehud Yonoy entitled 'Top Guns'. The piece was an in-depth look at a flight school for the US Navy's best fighter pilots. Bruckheimer was immediately hooked. 'I thought, "This looks like *Star Wars* on earth," ' he later recalled. 'I flipped it over to Don, who read the article and said, "We've gotta buy this." '

Within two months the dynamic duo were presenting their movie idea, based on the article, to Pentagon top brass in an effort to recruit the US Navy to their cause. Simpson adlibbed a story outlining the film he wanted to make and the admirals gave it their enthusiastic approval and promised to lend their considerable technological muscle to the project. The navy's thinking was pretty basic; they knew that an action-packed hero flick would help the navy's image enormously and breathe life into the recruitment slogan: 'Not just a job, but an adventure'.

Bruckheimer and Simpson then visited the Miramar Naval Air Station in San Diego, California, just 90 miles south of Los Angeles. They encountered pilots who looked as if they had just walked out of central casting – charismatic, young, sexy, confident characters with wild monikers like Snake, Jambo, Mad Dog and Jaws. They were guys who really lived life on the edge.

The 'rock n'rollers in the sky', as Bruckheimer dubbed

them, would provide perfect raw material for a supremely popular movie. The two producers were just as convinced as to who would make their perfect leading man. 'From the first time we went to Miramar, ' recalled Bruckheimer, 'even before the script was written, we said, "These guys are Tom Cruise!" '

Added partner Simpson: 'He represents the all-American, straightforward, proper young man.'

(What Bruckheimer did not say was that before Tom came into the frame for the role, his old friend Sean Penn had been the producers' favourite.)

In Hollywood terms, Tom had already established himself as the archetypal, high-profile, clean-cut, all-American performer. He was up there with the Harrison Fords, the Warren Beattys and the Arnold Schwarzeneggers even though he had yet to make a really huge, blockbuster hit movie.

Simpson and Bruckheimer were old hands in Tinsel-town terms and they had proved themselves a very astute pair, capable of delivering hugely successful films. They grossed a massive $270 million with their very first effort, 1983's *Flashdance*. The following year, the incredibly popular *Beverly Hills Cop* made $350 million thanks to a blend of Eddie Murphy's sassy comic routines and a fast-paced cops-and-robbers drama.

The producing pair were as flamboyant as they were rich by the time they started developing the *Top Gun* project. Hollywood mansions, Rolls-Royces and a particular penchant for the good life outlined their reputations in movieland. They were a very powerful team who insisted on overseeing every aspect of film production. They tended to work hand in hand with their instincts and few people were ever allowed into their carefully managed world.

In vastly over-the-top terms, Simpson told *Life*

magazine that he and Bruckheimer 'like pictures about triumph'. His partner then chipped in with uncharacteristic modesty: 'What we like, other people seem to like.' With a $15-million budget, including allowance for vast amounts of incredibly expensive jet-fighter fuel that ran at $8,000 an hour, *Top Gun* was going to be an expensive route to reality.

So, with screenwriters Jim Cash and Jack Epps working around the clock to come up with a script that would meet their approval, Simpson and Bruckheimer approached British director Tony Scott, who just happened to be the brother of Ridley Scott with whom Tom had worked in London on the *Legend* project. Tony had only made one movie before and that – entitled *The Hunger* – had been panned by the critics and failed miserably at the box office. After its failure, Tony who, like his brother had already amassed a fortune by making lucrative TV commercials, had a hard time bouncing back into the feature film market. He even confessed at one stage that he 'couldn't get arrested' let alone get hold of a new project.

In 1984, while accompanying his friends Bruckheimer and Simpson on a perilous raft trip down the Colorado River, Tony heard all about the *Top Gun* project, which the pair had already earmarked for another director. Tony was disappointed as he could see what a potentially great movie it might turn out to be. For months afterwards nothing was mentioned about *Top Gun* until the two producers called up Tony Scott out of the blue and offered him the movie. 'I jumped at the chance. Who wouldn't,' said Tony later. They never explained what caused them to change their minds about their original choice of director.

The pair also informed Tony that Tom Cruise was attached to the project. Tony had no objection; he had even met Tom during the actor's lonely stay in London during the making of *Legend*. 'I felt he had just the right arrogance in

the best sense of the word,' explained Tony, a more flamboyant, gregarious type of character than his older brother.

The initial draft of the *Top Gun* script was actually first
shown to Tom for his approval before *Legend* wrapped. It
seemed a welcome piece of light relief compared with the
British-based project. 'I was hungry for it,' said Tom later.
He found the coincidence of working with Ridley Scott's
brother 'weird – I feel like a member of the family'.

Tony Scott had an interesting view of Tom. 'Tom is
frighteningly polite. He's so nice he's sick,' he said with
more than just a hint of healthy British cynicism.

The project should then have gone rapidly forward to
actual production except that Tom Cruise was about to
prove he was no ordinary movie star. He had studied the
script very closely and was very unhappy about how it was
shaping up. It is worth remembering that Tom had long
since decided that he would make all the demands he felt
necessary if a screenplay seemed substandard.

Tom wanted the writers to go back and rethink certain
important aspects as well as to improve the way the main
characters were being projected. 'It was important to me
that we made a movie about characters and the human
element – not just a war picture.' Tom wanted the emphasis
to be on 'competition, not killing'.

Tony Scott, Bruckheimer and Simpson might well have
told certain stars where to get off at this stage, but not Tom
Cruise. They knew how much they needed his name in their
project and they were also well aware of his reputation for
meddling with scripts. They conceded that he had a very
good point about the script not being right. Tom, for his
part, had been intensely involved in rewriting *All the Right
Moves* and he felt he had the experience to influence the
direction of the screenplay.

The two producers then made an unusual arrangement

with Tom, which few actors in the world would have had the clout to achieve. Simpson and Bruckheimer agreed to let Tom have two months to work on the script, to develop the character he was being asked to play – then he would sign a contract to perform the lead role.

It was a remarkable agreement because Tom was basically saying that he preferred to risk investing his precious time in extra work that might not result in a deal, rather than be stuck with an unsatisfactory screenplay or an underdeveloped role. Tom was fully aware that the two producers had nothing to lose because they would end up with a better script and an opportunity to attach all sorts of big names if Tom pulled out. The development of the *Top Gun* script was probably the most savvy thing Tom had ever done up to that point in his career.

Simpson and Bruckheimer were not that keen on Tom's proposal at first because they presumed there would be a non-stop battle of egos over the size and structure of his role. Explained Simpson: 'I was against it because I like to run things. To me, an actor is generally a hired hand. But we talked at great length and he proved himself to us.'

When that particular meeting was over, Tom stood up, shook both producers firmly by the hand and told them: 'Gentlemen, I'm on board.' He was already sounding more like a 'top gun' than an actor. Later, Tom even managed to get Simpson and Bruckheimer to allow him to have approval of his co-stars. Tom was wielding awesome power for one so young. 'I've got a strong point of view and I like to get it across in the films I do,' defended Tom. 'Everything that I've done to get involved in this was to benefit the piece itself.' That naturally included benefiting the character he was playing in the movie.

As Simpson later admitted, the script development sessions with Tom were 'terrific. He would show up at my house, grab a beer and we'd work five or six hours on the script. Sometimes we'd act scenes out. The guy doesn't see things from just a couple of perspectives – he can really wrap his arms around something and see it from all angles. We had a lot of fun.'

As was becoming traditional for Tom, his research into the lead role in *Top Gun* was meticulous. He went to the Miramar naval pilots' school three months in advance of the shoot to soak up the heroic real-life characters. He went to 'top gun' classes and 'What I discovered was a group of men who enjoy flying above almost anything else you can name.'

However, Tom's stint at Miramar was hardly a bed of roses. As he later explained: 'These guys took one look at me and said, "We are going to kick your ass." Somehow, Tom turned them around and, within days, he was eating, drinking and sharing the lives of these brave pilots. To get a chance to tag along on one of the F-14 fighter plane flights, he had to prove he was physically and mentally capable of withstanding lightning-fast changes in the environment. Tom deliberately put on weight and trained himself to a comparable state of physical fitness.

To prepare for the film's spectacular dog-fight sequences, Tom and the other principal actors had to go through several days of psychological testing for F-14 certification, learning how to withstand high G-forces, eject and escape an ejection seat in water. It was, as Simpson later described, 'literally a crash course'.

Tom ended up being taken up in an F-14 fighter jet three times. They turned out to be unforgettable highlights of his life. 'Those jets rip through the clouds,' he later recalled. 'It's very sexual. Your body contorts, your muscles get sore, and the straining forces blood from your brain. You grab your legs and your ass and grunt as sweat pours over you. It's just thrilling. I had this grin on my face that wouldn't leave.' To Tom it had been as marvellous as any sexual experience.

Tom also allegedly matched the fighter pilots drink for drink during boistrous Wednesday-night 'animal night' traditional boozing sessions at the navy school's officers' club. Rumours circulated that, one particularly alcohol-riddled evening, Tom managed to be violently sick all over co-star Anthony Edwards's new BMW! How much of this was true is left open to doubt as Tom was barely drinking alcohol by this stage in his career. He did not like to be out of control for a moment longer than was necessary.

However, there is no doubting that Tom was swept along by the patriotic fervour and adrenalin-inducing life-style of the navy pilots he encountered. As one naval commander said,

> 'They're the last of the cowboys. Back in 1836 they would have been gunfighters squaring off against the bad guys. A century earlier they would have been pirates. Even earlier, they would have been gladiators fighting in the arena amid the sawdust, playing for the big chips with no way to walk out unless you win.'

When Tom finally delivered his version of the *Top Gun* script, Simpson and Bruckheimer were delighted. He had introduced elements no one had ever thought about and had tightened up the action. The gamble had worked and now it was down to Tom and director Tony Scott to make sure it all held together on celluloid when shooting started in June 1985.

The first concern of Tony Scott was the photography. As a former art director and meticulous TV commercials maker, he had a definite eye for the light and colours that

go towards making a movie look beautiful. He was determined to make sure the cinematography was the closest
most people would ever come to actually being in the
cockpit with those pilots and that is precisely what was
achieved.

Tom's character, Pete 'Maverick' Mitchell opens *Top
Gun* in the middle of an emergency with his partner 'Goose',
played by dashing Anthony Edwards. The two actors worked
perfectly together. Edwards's other films included *Sure
Thing* and *Gotcha!* He is an independent, easy-going
character with a healthy, down-to-earth attitude towards
movie stardom. 'For a lot of actors, movies and publicity are
a way of life. Me – I'd rather go sailing,' he said proudly.

In the film, Maverick and Goose are supporting fellow
fliers 'Cougar' and 'Merlin'. Cougar was played by John
Stockwell, Tom's old drinking pal from *Losin' It*. More than
three years had passed since that low point in Tom's career
and John Stockwell noticed a big change in his personality.

'In *Top Gun*, Tom was clearly a star and much more
careful about what he did. He was much more reserved,
much more aware. Those good old days were over and he
was very careful about preserving his image,' explained
Stockwell, who revealed that Tom kept well away from the
crazier actors – himself included – who still liked to head off
for some fun once the day's shooting wrapped. Sometimes
Tom would join them for a beer in a bar but then disappear
the moment 'things got raunchy', explained Stockwell. 'He
never got involved.'

Tom's character of Maverick is so volatile that he turns
on the heat without hesitation or forethought and he is
constantly battling against his main rival and personal
nemesis, the aptly named 'Iceman' Kazanksy, played by Val
Kilmer who later married beautiful British actress Joanne
Whalley, as well as starring in movies such as Oliver Stone's

The Doors and a highly acclaimed performance in *Tombstone* in 1994.

The two actors – both intensely in favour of the method school of performance – did not exactly hit it off. As sworn enemies on the screen, they both decided to continue their bad relationship off duty as well. There was speculation that the fact that Val had enjoyed a fling with Cher two years before Tom met her at that dyslexic fund raiser at the White House might have caused a little friction between the two stars.

Kilmer graciously side stepped the issue when confronted about it years later and, in fact, has said little about what really happened on the set of *Top Gun*, although it is clear that he felt the movie was not exactly a healthy stepping stone for his own career.

After meeting director Tony Scott, Kilmer was bluntly critical of the *Top Gun* project and told Scott: 'Frankly, I don't like this.' He explained later: 'I loved what I had seen of Tony Scott's work but I just didn't want to do that movie. Tony said, "Don't worry, your hair will look great." He thought that would make a difference. He was infectious that way.'

It is worth remembering that while Val Kilmer might not really have wanted to be in *Top Gun* with Tom Cruise, the star himself felt the opposite way about Val as he approved Scott's casting of the young actor.

Later, reflecting on his experiences in *Top Gun*, Val explained: 'I have very definitely had a different kind of career than Tom. You never know if a job has commercial success written all over it. I just think life's too short to worry about that.'

Tom and Val's rivalry on screen brought two very exciting talents into direct competition. Besides pitting their strengths against each other in the air, they also take part in a no-holds-barred volleyball match which was criticised by many as being a flimsy excuse to titillate the audience with some torso muscles and bronzed physiques. Tom insisted this was not the case when he later said: 'It shows that, to fighter pilots, physical prowess is very important. Plus the scene shows the constant competition between these guys – how they compete on every level.'

Tom was privately infuriated by the accusations that he was purely a beefcake star in *Top Gun* – and this was before the shooting of the movie had even been completed. As a result, he insisted that shots of him topless could not be used to help to promote the film once it was released. 'If you notice, none of the *Top Gun* TV commercials or stills being released show me with my shirt off. And you don't see posters of me like that. Any poster that's ever been made has been black market – I've never authorised anything,' he admitted later.

Tom was attracted to the character of Maverick for all sorts of reasons. He loved the fact that he was completely unpredictable. 'He doesn't do anything by the book,' said Tom. 'He's kind of wild and he experiments with different ways of flying. The film is about a guy who has an absolute passion for something, a guy who wants to live at one hundred and fifty per cent afterburn all the way.'

However, the aspect of the character that really pulled Tom in was that Maverick's father had died after his plane was lost during a mission 20 year earlier. Losing a father was certainly something that Tom could closely identify with in real life. He openly acknowledged that bond with his character by saying: 'Obviously my father wasn't a fighter pilot and didn't die a hero, but I think a lot of the gut level, emotional stuff – the love of father and the conflict in that – is there.'

Tom's love interest in *Top Gun* was played by blonde

actress Kelly McGillis as the civilian instructor Charlotte 'Charlie' Blackwood. Maverick gets off to a bad start when he tries to seduce Charlie in a bar without realising who she is. The slightly sick-making sequence involved Tom crooning 'You've Lost That Lovin' Feeling' and some said the relationship smacked of cradle snatching.

Kelly was Tony Scott's first choice for the part, although Tom, Simpson and Bruckheimer definitely played a part in selecting the actress. Scott explained: 'I think she's just right. She had to be a mature-looking actress to fit the role.'

Initially, stories about the casting session circulated in Hollywood, suggesting that Tom had vetoed Demi Moore in favour of Kelly because he was infatuated with her. That could not have been further from the truth.

The actress radiated a certain mysterious femininity yet retained a lot of strength and independence. Kelly herself scoffed modestly at such praise by saying: 'It's all luck. I think I'm the least appealing cinematographically. I'm not Kim Basinger. I don't think about those things. I can't and I don't want to.'

Naturally a brunette, Kelly bleached her hair blonde and the scenes featuring her and Tom literally sizzled on screen, despite criticism from reviewers who complained that they found the relationship between Maverick and an older woman 'unbelievable'. The public certainly did not seem to mind.

Off screen, rumours of a romance between Tom – now single again after breaking up with Rebecca De Mornay – and Kelly persisted and spread like wildfire. The outspoken actress was flattered but incredulous. 'It's just not true!' she protested. 'But it's fascinating how people love to pin the leading man and the leading lady together.'

The true situation between the two actors was that Tom

was having great difficulty 'relating' to Kelly because she was a blunt, carefree character who approached her acting in a very different way from the young star. At one stage things got so frosty between them that there were serious worries that it might affect their respective performances. Ironically, it was later claimed that this was a deliberate policy on the part of the two stars because they wanted to instil some sexual chemistry in their respective performances. It certainly worked! Not since Tom's early clashes with Rebecca during the making of *Risky Business* had he had such a breakdown in communication with a leading lady. This time, however, they were not destined to turn the situation around.

Kelly was dating handsome actor Barry Tubb – known in Hollywood as the most famous non-star in Tinseltown. He played 'Wolfman' in *Top Gun* and Kelly would walk straight off the set at the end of a hard day's shooting right into the arms of Barry. Some months later, the *New York Post* spotted Tom and Kelly dining in the same Big Apple restaurant – on opposite sides of the room. Tom wore dark glasses and chatted with family friends and their children while Kelly was huddled with a guy on the other side of the restaurant. They never even acknowledged each other.

All this friction did not prevent Tom and Kelly from pulling off some very steamy scenes together on the set of *Top Gun*. Director Tony Scott even shot an extra love scene, featuring the two co-stars in an elevator, which most Hollywood insiders consider so steamy that the producers were lucky to get the movie an all-important PG rating in America, which would enable all those teenyboppers to queue up and see their idol.

One of the more ludicrous observations about *Top Gun* came when some critics claimed that there was an underlying sexual dynamic searing through the entire film and that it was deliberately planted there to make the movie attractive to both heterosexuals and homosexuals. For example, one pilot not only seems to get aroused whenever he enters the cockpit but even gets excited thinking about fighter planes. Some claimed the very landscape at Miramar was littered with phallic imagery, while others insisted that the buddy-buddy pilots seemed overly intimate and theorised that there were homoerotic undertones to the film.

Tom was made to feel very uncomfortable when confronted about these aspects of *Top Gun* during one interview. He tried to ignore the question and then mumbled: 'Of course they're friends – they spend months together' in reference to the abundant male affection expressed in the film. 'There is camaraderie and also that competition ... they want to beat each other; they all want to be the best.'

The pilots certainly seemed constantly to be projecting a macho and sexually aggressive image. After the film was released it was noted that a large number of homosexuals went to see *Top Gun* over and over again because they enjoyed certain scenes in the movie. There is no doubt that the alleged gay elements in the film created problems for Tom later in his career.

Many of the movie's action scenes were shot 'live' and that meant dicing with danger for Tom and the rest of the cast and crew. When the movie's most dramatic rescue scene was shot, Tom had to bob about in icy waters off Point Loma, California for hours while being saved from the sea by air-sea rescue helicopters. As he leaned out of a small lifeboat and yanked what was supposed to be his colleague Goose from the water, the lines of his parachute became entangled in his watchband. The chute, heavily saturated with seawater, caused Tom to lose his balance. He became trapped in a chaos of ropes and was then pulled beneath the choppy waves of the Pacific Ocean.

The production crew tried frantically to free him and, fortunately, two real-life navy divers were on hand to tackle the emergency. The divers leapt into action and Petty Officer 2nd Class Darryl Silva was the first to reach Tom. 'He was three feet under water. I grabbed the shoulder strap of his flight suit but couldn't lift him, so my partner also grabbed the strap,' he explained later.

Silva then went back under the water and started desperately trying to untangle the parachute lines from Tom's wrist. It was a battle against the clock. He managed to haul Tom into the raft, where the young actor began coughing and spitting up huge quantities of salt water. The officer administered mouth-to-mouth resuscitation, something that millions of women throughout the world would no doubt have liked to do! Tom came round and muttered thanks to Silva for saving his life. An hour later, he was before the cameras once more, proving himself the ultimate professional.

Tom also proved he was determined to stay with the project every inch of the way, even after the shooting of *Top Gun* was completed. He sat in on much of the post-production process and had some fairly harsh words to say about the rough cut of the film (the first roughly edited version). He told *Premiere* magazine: 'In the rough cut the aerial story just didn't work. Tony Scott had miles and miles of aerial footage. He had to go back and tighten it up, define the story more. I always try to look at a rough cut like, "The movie's not out yet – you can fix it." '

Behind the blunt words lay a complex scenario because Tom was undoubtedly interfering in the film making process more than virtually any other actor in Hollywood. However, he already had the clout to do so because director Tony Scott, plus Simpson and Bruckheimer, knew that Tom was the key to their success. Normally, they would have told an actor where to get off for daring to pass an opinion on such matters as the editing process.

Tom saw it a different way; he was not interfering but helping to guarantee that the end product was as near to perfection as one could get. 'Once a film comes out,' he elaborated later, 'they say, "Oh, of course, that's why he took it. It's a commercial movie; a hit! Why wouldn't he want to do that?" People don't understand the risk factor. It didn't start out as a commercial movie. Nothing is a sure thing! Nothing is a sure thing! And if you looked at the script beforehand and saw what might have happened ...'

Director Tony Scott saw Tom's active interest in all aspects of the film as the actor being 'like a terrier. He locks on and hangs on.'

Another aspect of the lead up to the movie's release was Tom's whole-hearted decision actually to go out on the road and help to promote *Top Gun* following his self-imposed silence of more than two years after the problematic work he did to help to promote *Risky Business*, which turned into a stressful situation for the then press-shy Tom. It wasn't as if he had now decided that he loved the media and did not mind revealing his innermost secrets to them. He had simply grown up considerably since *Risky Business* and appreciated that giving hundreds of banal interviews was an important part of the movie making process if he was to maintain his newly found spot at the top of the Hollywood pile.

Cruise's coverage for *Top Gun* was truly awesome. He did his first 'grown-up' cover for the arty New York magazine *Interview* (up until then he had only been featured on hundreds of teeny mags). There were also Cruise articles to be found in *Rolling Stone*, *People* and *US*. He schmoozed with newspapers at a New York junket. In Los Angeles, he did interviews with *Associated Press*, *New York Times Syndicate*, *Knight-Rider Syndicate*, *USA Today* and some radio. There were also TV appearances on *Good Morning America*, *CBS Morning News*, *Entertainment Tonight*, the *Movie Channel* and *CNN*.

The younger, inexperienced Tom had found it virtually impossible to deal with prying questions about his parents' divorce and other personal matters. For the *Top Gun* publicity roadshow, however, journalists seemed more interested in finding out how much money Tom was getting and that was something he found easy to cope with. 'I make it my policy not to talk about money,' he would respond coolly. 'In choosing a role, money is not an issue if I want to do something.' Really?

In all interviews he remained the essence of politeness and seemed overly concerned about making sure each journalist was being looked after properly. While there was no doubting Tom's good manners, in reality he was undoubtedly hiding his true feelings about the press as he would later prove. For the moment he had a major movie to promote and if that meant being pleasant towards a bunch of blood-sucking journalists then so be it ...

Even when reporters pressed Tom about the fact that many moviegoers perceived *Top Gun* to be a blatant exploitation of handsome young male bodies, he kept his cool. 'I don't take my shirt off to sell tickets. The way I look at it is, let a good movie bring the audience in,' came his ever-charming reply.

*   *   *

Top Gun opened with a winning $8.2 million take at the US box office in its first week of release. However, the public's relish for the movie did not exactly match critical acclaim. Most reviewers sneered at its over commercialism. '*Top Gun* is little more than a glitzy, superbly photographed recruiting movie for the US Navy flight school. It is also a visually stirring if somewhat aimless movie,' was about the best of a bad bunch from *Video Review* magazine, and reviewer Jeffrey Lyons summed up: 'It's trite, it's hokey, it's manipulative, but *Top Gun* is perfect for unchallenging, exhilarating entertainment.'

Movie historian Edward Gross got a slightly better grasp of the subject matter when he wrote: '*Top Gun* is a full-length cartoon, though a highly effective one.'

There were also some highly personalised attacks on Tom by the reviewers, including the *New York Times'* Walter Goodman who wrote that 'Cruise brings little but a good build to the role' and *USA Today's* Jack Curry went one step further by proclaiming: 'Supposed to be a super flyboy, he comes across more like just a fly or a boy.' *Newsweek's* David Ansen did at least concede: 'The likeable Cruise is simply miscast. He's not the dangerous guy everyone's talking about, but the boy next door.'

Tom was deeply hurt by some of the more personal attacks on him. He knew perfectly well that the movie was a highly commercial comic-book style adventure but he could not understand why the critics were taking it all so seriously. However, inside Hollywood the beefcake sneerers were more than silenced by the cold hard fact that the film's phenomenal success (it went on to make more than $170 million in the USA alone) had firmly established Tom as the world's biggest box office attraction at the age of 24.

The public did not seem to care either, because the movie became the biggest grossing film of 1986 and then went on to be the first blockbuster to surpass its box office take on video tape, resulting in over half a billion dollars total gross.

Obviously, the question on everyone's lips following *Top Gun's* success was, 'When is there going to be a sequel?

Tom had other ideas on the subject. It wasn't even a matter of when, or if. He told friends he had no intention of making a second version of the movie. Every few months, articles would appear in the tabloids or the industry press suggesting that Tom was about to sign up to replay the role for some vast sum of money ($25 million at the last count). Simpson and Bruckheimer held on to the sequel rights and they were as keen as Tom was opposed to making 'Top Gun II'.

In 1992, there were reports that Tom had secretly purchased the sequel rights from the producing duo for a sum in excess of a million dollars. These claims have never been officially confirmed but, according to Hollywood observers, Tom either planned to sculpt the perfect script for a sequel or he deliberately bought the rights to prevent Simpson and Bruckheimer from ever making another *Top Gun* movie.

As recently as August 1993, there were reports that location scouts were out looking for good sites to film the sequel and Jack Epps, who wrote the original *Top Gun*, was said to be hard at work putting together a script for the sequel. By the summer of 1994, however, the movie project had still not materialised.

While Tom was well and truly perched on top of the fame mountain, his love life was going from bad to worse. Rebecca had gone and the few dates he did have time to go on just did not work out. One time he went to a celebrity bowling session at New York's Madison Square Garden but ended up snapping at a photographer and staying only ten minutes. The fact that old flame Cher was among the other famous faces in attendance that night might well have had an influence on his decision to leave in a hurry.

Tom later admitted that this was a very lonely period in his life. He had all the trappings of power and success but no one to share them with. His problem was a classic symptom of the 1980s where wealth and success so often took priority over actual happiness. Tom knew he was getting more and more sucked in by the Hollywood system and all he really wanted was someone uncomplicated to share his life with.

The extraordinary success of *Top Gun* actually forced the young actor into even more of a social shell. A simple trip with his sister and her baby to the Smithsonian Institute turned into a horrific experience when hundreds of fans started pointing at him and staring. Then some began demanding autographs. Tom felt particularly responsible for his sister and niece so he ordered them out of the building and slipped out of the back entrance. That experience simply fuelled his desire for solitude even though he was still as desperate as ever to find someone to love.

Top Gun's success and Tom's very intense involvement in the entire film making process finally persuaded him to open a production company to develop projects specifically for himself. TC Productions was given a very loose development deal at Columbia Pictures and soon dozens of scripts were pouring in every week. In the preceding three years Tom had been very careful to try to get a feel for every aspect of film production, from development through to distribution, and now he brought in his cousin, William Mapother, as head of development in the first of many moves to install his own family members in positions of trust within the Cruise empire.

A few years earlier, efforts to write a screenplay with his friend Emilio Estevez, based on a novel by S.E. Hinton – the same novelist who wrote *The Outsiders* – had foundered mainly because neither actor really fully understood the screenwriting process. Now Tom would hire his own screenwriters to convert his ideas into movie scripts before adding the sort of finishing touches that had helped to turn *Top Gun* into such a huge success for everyone.

Tom even toyed with the idea of starring in the lead role of a screen adaptation of Jay McInerney's novel entitled *Bright Lights, Big City*. 'It's an interesting role, but I'm learning that I can't just jump into something. I like to take my time and make sure I feel good about it.' Eventually Tom shyed away from the project because it dealt explicitly with excessive drug taking among New York's rich and successful. Tom – the homespun boy who had never even been near a cannabis joint – was concerned that such a role might damage his image.

Since then, Tom had adhered to a game plan in which the role and the project were the main priority. He actually believed that his popularity was not his concern. 'I've got enough just to deal with what I have to deal with. Let someone else figure out who's hot and who's not and all that kind of thing. I'll be happy just to work.'

'I don't like my part too much, it's just an OK part, but I can learn so much from those two guys.'

Tom Cruise

13

Actors who make films in which their good looks are amply displayed are, more often than not, demeaned by hostile critics as 'just another pretty face'. Tom Cruise had already suffered his fair share of such accusations and, 25 years earlier, another matinee idol called Paul Newman had faced precisely the same sex-idol label. Just as Tom had steadfastly navigated around the pitfalls of beefcake and Brat Pack pigeonholing, so Newman had faced up to similar battles during his early career.

'My fame came with a beefcake stereotype,' admitted Newman. 'All people asked about was my blue eyes – ladies still ask me to remove my sunglasses so they can see them.'

In 1961, a tough young pool player named 'Fast Eddie' Felsen provided moviegoers with a precise demonstration of the game's finer points when *The Hustler* was made – and provided Newman with an escape route from those hunky roles. In 1986, he did the same thing for Tom when he handpicked him to star in the better-late-than-never sequel *The Color of Money*.

Newman brought Fast Eddie back from beyond but with him came a youthful warrior, a true contender for the title: Vincent Lauria, to be played by Tom Cruise.

The inside story of how Tom came to be paired up with one of Hollywood's most respected stars began late in 1984 when Newman approached director Martin Scorsese (*Mean Streets*, *Taxi Driver*, *Raging Bull* to name but a few) to discuss the possibility of directing *The Color of Money*. There was one problem; Scorsese never directed sequels. He preferred to avoid them like the plague they had become. However, there was something about this particular project that was special and irresistible. 'I love Paul Newman's work – especially *The Hustler*, and I like the ambiance of that film,' explained Scorsese.

This was to be a very special project indeed. The screenplay had been carefully developed by Newman through writer Walter Trevis, the author of the novel upon which the movie was based. Then Scorsese, ever the perfectionist, threw that draft out and insisted on starting again. As his collaborator, he chose Richard Price, an experienced New York author best known for his tales from the dark side of life in the city's Little Italy neighbourhood, where both Scorsese and his great friend Robert De Niro grew up. Price shared the director's predilection for heroes with a twist. 'Marty and I like mean things,' explained writer Price. 'The meaner the better because the greater the shaft of light at the end.'

Both men knew they had to get the script absolutely right otherwise a complex financial and distribution deal in place with Disney's Touchstone Pictures might collapse.

When Paul Newman inspected Price's early efforts he became very concerned because Scorsese's slant seemed to be making hero Fast Eddie extremely dark and twisted – characteristics that no self-respecting movie star likes to see dominating their character too much. 'One thing I was sure of, if I ever made a sequel, it was damn well going to be better than the original,' he insisted.

From that moment onwards, Newman decided to attend every single script session to make sure his baby was going to be reborn in exactly the way he deemed right and proper. It was during one of these meetings that Newman started to notice that Vincent Lauria – the young hustler who was Fast Eddie's protége – was beginning to bear an uncanny resemblance to the young star he most admired – Tom Cruise. 'He seemed innocent and sweet, the kind of character this boy would be,' noted Newman.

Scorsese was not impressed with the suggestion at first. He had been hoping to sign the lesser known, up-and-coming New York actor Vincent Spano, who had starred in *Creator* and *Alphabet City*. However, this was Newman's project and he put his foot down firmly. Scorsese, who had met Tom when they shared a pizza in a Los Angeles restaurant in 1983, gave in because he had been impressed by Tom's performance in *All the Right Moves*.

There was a problem at first when Tom turned down Newman and Scorsese's first indirect approach to him because he feared *The Color of Money* would turn out to be a Newman vehicle which would leave him looking like a redundant hero. Tom had a naturally cautious streak in him as well as being slightly overawed by the magnitude of working on a movie with two of the biggest names in film history. However, Paul Newman knew that Tom was his man and he pursued him relentlessly, finally persuading him to attend a meeting. 'When we met, we hit it off from the start,' explained Newman.

One associate described the relationship perfectly:

'They are genuinely fond of each other. They have a nice, jokey sort of rapport and I think it's one of those good, solid exchanges that's going to go on.'

Secretly, Tom's stomach was turning cartwheels at the prospect of starring opposite Newman. He later confessed to feeling sick with nerves during that first meeting but the professional side of him knew that *The Color of Money* was a superbly scripted project. 'I'd be a liar if I said I felt totally confident and relaxed,' he conceded later. 'But the screenplay was so well written and we had a two-week rehearsal period. Newman really took the time to make everyone feel comfortable – he's very supportive and generous with his time as an actor and a person. We became good friends.'

Rapidly, Tom recognised the potential in his role and the fact that it presented him with a unique opportunity to take his career in yet another direction. 'I want to go all the way,' he proclaimed. 'Look at Newman, look what this man has created as an actor and a human being.' Behind the scenes, while there is no doubting Tom's words, it has to be noted that Newman received a smaller fee for his starring role in *The Color of Money* and both Newman and Scorsese put up one third of their salaries each to help guarantee that the film got made.

There was no doubting that Paul Newman was impressed with Tom.

'He's prepared to hang himself on a meat hook. He'll hang himself out to dry to seek something. He's not afraid of looking like a ninny. He doesn't protect himself or his ego. And he's a wonderful experimenter. Of course, like any actor, when the material is poor, he falls back on his successful mannerisms: the happy kitchen. I don't know that he's a great mathematician or a theoretical physicist, but he has what he needs to be a good actor.'

The movie had not even begun shooting and the Newman/ Cruise team were already sounding like a mutual admiration society.

Tom threw himself into researching the role of Vincent Lauria with his customary enthusiasm and began cruising the pool halls of New York to get a feel for his character through watching some of the reallife Fast Eddies. He especially enjoyed watching the hustlers trying to hustle each other – by telling tales of sprained wrists and failing nerves to guys who had used the same stories themselves a hundred times, all for the joy of pulling off a good one. "It's not the money for these guys; it's the hustle," Tom explained. "One day they're up a hundred thousand dollars. The next day they'll go to the track and blow it all. They justify it, the morality."

Paul Newman did have one distinct advantage over Tom – he knew how to shoot pool. The younger actor went on a crash course to learn the finer points of the game and he was soon potting everything in sight. Michael Sigel, the professional hired to squire the two actors-turned-pool-sharks around the table, was very impressed by his youthful pupil and Newman was positively amazed by Tom's skills on the felt. 'It took me a long time to get OK. It took him very little time to get very good.' The two actors even kept their skills polished by constantly playing for bets between breaks in rehearsals and the actual movie shoot, which was to be a tight, 49-day schedule shot mainly in Chicago.

Newman even leapt to Tom's defence publicly when a Chicago newspaper slammed the younger actor's technique. The veteran star wrote personally to the editor, insisting that Tom was a fine pool player in his own right.

The Color of Money marked a notable development in Tom's career for another reason – he wore an earring for the one and only time on film. In fact, the diamond stud seen glittering on his left earlobe was a present from his granny on his mother's side. Tom had it gold-posted and wore it for a couple of months following the shoot, but then decided to stop wearing it after being warned that it might damage his chances of getting the sort of serious roles he hankered after.

The Color of Money was painstakingly shot as master-craftsman Scorsese began fitting all the pieces of the filmic puzzle together. Tom recalled later:

> 'I worked day and night for months. For one shot, Marty told me, "OK now, the camera's just going to follow you around the table, and you got to clear off the whole table. You think you can do that, kid?" I go, "Yeah," and I went home, and I was just sweating. So I really had to learn how to play. But for me, that's exciting. The more I learned about playing pool, the more confident I became. I love pool now.'

For the first few weeks after their first meeting, Tom insisted on calling both Newman and Scorsese 'Sir'. It was a classic example of Tom's good upbringing and it made tough New Yorker Scorsese feel very uncomfortable. Eventually a meeting was organised with the express purpose of persuading Tom to stop calling people 'Sir'. He eventually obeyed their command but continued to find it very difficult not to show great respect for two such movie making giants.

Scorsese also had another important priority – he wanted to ensure that *The Color of Money* could stand on its own and not be judged purely as a sequel to the *The Hustler*. That meant he was constantly trying to imprint his own unique film-making stamp on it. Scorsese explained:

> 'We wanted this movie to stand on its own. The only link to *The Hustler* is the character of Fast Eddie. He's no longer a pool player. He's now on the outside of the game looking in, and with a whole new perspective.
>
> 'Our movie is about a man who goes on a journey towards self-awareness. A man who changes his way of living, changes his values. The movie is about a deception and then a clarity – a perversion and then a purity.'

From these words, one can tell why Scorsese commented later that the finest compliment he could ever receive would be to be described as an artist. On *The Color of Money* he had another reason to be satisfied because he managed to come in $1.5 million under the film's original $14.5 million budget. That's the sort of stuff sainthood is made of in Hollywood.

Tom's character, Vincent, has a girlfriend called Carmen throughout much of the movie. She was played by Mary Elizabeth Mastrantonio and the two actors had to perform a number of steamy bedroom scenes. For once, Tom was not romantically linked with his attractive co-star, despite the sexy scenes in the film itself.

In August 1986, there was a sneak preview of *The Color of Money* at a cinema in Paramus, New Jersey, not far from Tom's old home in Glen Ridge. Paul Newman, his wife Joanne Woodward and Tom drove down together from Connecticut, where Tom had been staying as the Newmans' houseguest. Scorsese came from New York. Audience reaction to the movie was good, and Touchstone executives, plus the stars and director, decided that perhaps the movie's release date could be moved up, so it was scheduled to open in America in mid-October, rather than December.

Meanwhile Tom – dateless and feeling a little left out in the romantic stakes – went off to a Bruce Springsteen concert in New Jersey in order to unwind after his exhausting year. The concert proved a welcome opportunity to recharge his batteries in more ways than one, for Tom briefly went out with Patti Sciafla, who went on to become the mother of three children by 'The Boss', who was still married to his first wife at that time.

Cruise, Newman and Mastrantonio all received enthusiastic praise for their performances from many reviewers following *The Color of Money*'s release. In *Time* magazine Richard Schickel took note of Tom's duality: 'There is something funny about his knot-headed exuberance and something unsettling and dangerous about it, too.' He continued: 'There is a ferocity in Cruise's flakiness that he has not previously had a chance to tap. That, in turn, gives Newman something to grapple with. There is a sort of contained rage in his work that he has never found before, and it carries him beyond the bounds of image.'

Newsweek's David Ansen touched all bases when he wrote:

'At the improbable age of sixty-one, the old bull – arguably America's best loved male movie star and certainly the most durable – has come down from the ridge in Westport, Conn., to play an aging but still hustling Eddie. The casting of Newman and Cruise is more than just the casting coup of the year. Anyone who doubted Cruise's seriousness as an actor will have to think again after seeing this whirlwind display.'

In Britain, reviewers were just as supportive. Neil Norman wrote in *The Face*: 'The moral dilemma of competitive motivation – play to win or play for money? – means that Scorsese's film is littered with human digressions. This is the most satisfactory aspect of the film as it allows actors … to create flesh and blood characters without the constraints of a thema⁀ic straitjacket.'

All this high praise had one very important knock-on effect, besides naturally helping *The Color of Money* to succeed at the box office. The Academy Awards were only a few months away and word about the movie was gaining momentum and building into a deafening media roar. In plain Hollywood terms, there was a powerful Oscar buzz accompanying the movie. Newman's name on anything was enough to guarantee attention because he had already been nominated six times for Best Actor – and lost every time. Now the media was pushing hard on his behalf, believing that the Academy could not turn him down a seventh time.

'The Newman-Cruise combination is irresistible to editors,' explained *Newsweek* magazine's David Ansen. Soon Paul and Tom's smiling faces were appearing on covers of *Life*, *Newsweek*, *USA Today*, *The New York Times Magazine*, to name but a few. In the *Life* spread, the cover photo was shot two different ways, with Newman and Cruise lying in opposite directions on a pool table in Newman's Connecticut home. In deference to equal billing, *Life* distributed covers with Newman facing upside down and Tom right-side-up in the western half of the United States; on the other side, the other version was used, with the positions of the actors reversed. In an experiment to see which version would outsell the other, *Life* displayed the alternative covers side by side at 20 selected news-stands. Tom Cruise won by 55 per cent.

On the Oscar front, Paul Newman seemed to be out in

front as the leading contender for Best Actor. *The Color of Money* had become a highly acclaimed movie which grossed $6.4 million in its first weekend in the United States, earning an average of $10,000 per screen as it opened in 635 cinemas across the country. An array of celebrities attended the New York premiere at the Ziegfield Theatre and the bash after the screening was thrown downtown at the Palladium nightclub, where 1,200 guests danced the night away beneath hundreds of billiard-ball balloons. Tickets for the event had sold at $250 each and raised more than a quarter of a million dollars for the Actors Studio, then in serious financial trouble.

The celebrities included Helen Shaver, Mary Elizabeth Mastrantonio, Martin Scorsese, Ellen Burstyn, Emilio Estevez, Mariel Hemingway, Jennifer Beals, Aidan Quinn, Danny De Vito, Bianca Jagger, Shelley Winters, Michael Douglas and Calvin Klein. The chic nightclub was especially made to look like a New York pool hall. Guests even received chits to play roulette, blackjack and craps and, if they were lucky, won *Color of Money* sweatshirts, suspenders and pool cues. Decked out uncharacteristically in a blue suit and red tie, Paul Newman greeted Tom's grand entrance in plaid suit and grey cowboy boots with a whistle and a 'nice boots, cowboy'.

Tom was very proud of *The Color of Money*. 'As long as people keep hiring me', he said. 'I'm gonna take a lot of chances and make some really good movies. And some not very good movies – hopefully not too many.'

Many Academy insiders confidently predicted that Paul Newman would win the Oscar simply on the basis of his past acting achievements and because he had been so unfairly overlooked before. The experts were absolutely right and, *in absentia*, he was awarded the Oscar for Best Actor.

What the tens of million of film fans watching the ceremony across the globe did not realise was that Newman had been wracked with guilt about his nomination because he believed that Tom equally deserved the award for his performance. Before the ceremony, Newman secretly sent Tom a telegram of condolences when he learned that the younger actor had not even been nominated for Best Supporting Actor. Paul assured his young friend that he did deserve a nomination and even added: 'If I win, it's ours as much as mine because you did such a good job.'

Tom was moved to tears when he received the telegram and had it framed and hung on the wall of his New York apartment.

Newman would tell anyone who would listen about Tom's great talents. 'Tom has such instinct – he knows a lot more at his age than I ever did. He's got guts too – I called him "Killer" because of his tremendous courage. He's always saying. "I'll give it a whack!" '

Behind Newman's praise lay the foundations of a very special friendship between the two actors. The veteran had become a virtual father figure to Tom, giving him advice and encouragement whenever it was needed. For Tom the bond was especially close because he genuinely saw the older actor as someone he could turn to. In many ways, Newman became the father Tom had so desperately needed since the age of 12. Certainly, they built up a touching rapport that exists between very few actors in their league. Explained Tom:

'Paul is very easy. Very down-to-earth, really open. We would go over and eat at his place; he'd cook. We all got so fat – oh yeah, I would go over to his trailer, and we would have lunch every day, dinner every night. It was like this family working together. Gained about a hundred pounds. We had a blast. He is an extremely bright man, very eloquent, gracious, generous, knows how to tell a good joke.'

Tom took in everything Paul told him about Hollywood. He duly noted Paul's warning that movie audiences had a fickle attention span. 'They're like Romans, forever looking for a fresh Christian to feed to the lions.' Newman also disclosed his own low opinion of the movie industry as a whole. 'Success is measured by one thing: box office.'

Tom admired Newman more than any man he had ever met in his entire life. 'He lives a normal life. He's got several businesses, a wife, a family. That's good for me to see,' noted Tom, who one day intended to emulate his hero in every way.

Tom's only consolation about not even being nominated for the Best Supporting Oscar came when he received the 1835th star on the Hollywood Walk of Fame. The ceremony took place on Hollywood Boulevard, near the corner with Orange Avenue, amid a touch of controversy caused by some Tinseltown stalwarts who claimed that Tom was far too young to be given a star on the pavement. Unfortunately, in 1990 it was discovered that Tom's star had been virtually completely removed by fans who had been helping themselves to chunks of it as souvenirs. It was the first time in the Hollywood Walk of Fame's 30-year history that anyone had ever vandalised a star.

There were times when the father-son relationship between Paul and Tom was reduced to something that made the pair resemble a pair of childish adults playing silly pranks. During the making of *The Color of Money*, both indulged in endless silly jokes, like the time Tom gave Newman a suspender belt and bra for his sixty-first birthday.

However, the biggest influence Newman had on his younger co-star was to pass on his own fascination with the high-speed thrills of car racing. This passion for speed was, it seems, highly infectious. As Newman explained: 'I asked Tom if he wanted to try my car and he said, "You bet!" Now he's hooked and he's very good.'

Tom rapidly graduated from racing lessons to car clubs and then to his first professional race: the Road Atlanta series, held in Brazeltown, Georgia. Paul Newman raced in the same series and finished fourth with $4,000 in prize money. Tom's début was marked by several mishaps, including a near miss during a practice run in his Nissan 300ZX. Then, during the actual race, he fishtailed twice, forcing one contestant off the track and then went into a complete spin-out when negotiating one tricky turn.

Despite all this, Tom emerged unscathed from his trial by fire and commented nonchalantly: 'Smooth as silk.' When asked some pointed questions about his disaster-prone first effort, he replied: 'I drive faster going to work.' Tom ended up finishing a reasonable fourteenth out of 44 entries – not bad for a neophyte.

By taking a youngster like Tom under his wing, Newman could not have been unaware of the inevitable presumptions that he was working out his parental feelings by 'adopting' a surrogate son to share his acting and racing career. There was a genuine bond holding Tom and Paul Newman together, besides the young actor's desperate need for a father figure in his life and the fact that Newman had lost his only son through a drug overdose. In each other the two stars had found the same profound respect, trust and caring that many long for, whether famous or obscure, young or old.

'If you marry, you will regret it. If you do not marry, you will also regret it.'

Soren Kierkegaard

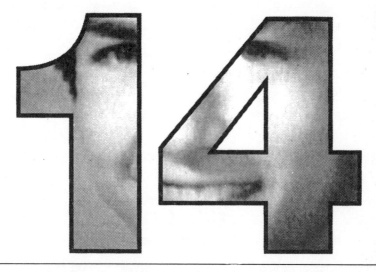

14

One week after the glamorous launch party for *The Color of Money*, Tom went down to Georgia for the 19 October Valvoline Road Racing Classic to join his recently acquired best friend Paul Newman and indulge in his newly found passion for automobile racing. What made this event so significant was that he decided to take along his new girl-friend, an actress called Mimi Rogers. It was her first public outing as partner to the world's number one star.

To the devoted clique of Tom's millions of fans – those mainly prepubescent girls whose bedroom walls were adorned with posters of his handsome face – the idea of dating the modern-day matinee idol is enough to render them breathless.

The couple had first met each other at a crowded dinner table at a friend's home in Los Angeles more than a year earlier. Unfortunately, Mimi had been dating an associate of Tom's, so the friendship never got beyond the stage of furtive glances and the occasional smile.

Mimi – a statuesque woman with a thick halo of soft, auburn hair and a polished, modulated voice – had recently finished a very serious, long-standing relationship with another actor called Tom Selleck. At one stage she had been set to marry the six foot four inch star of *Magnum*. The mustachioed heart-throb told one friend: 'She's the main woman in my life.' The couple openly smooched on the set of movies and generally seemed at ease in each other's company. Then something inexplicable occurred between them and they were no longer an item. Mimi never explained what it was that caused her split with Tom Selleck.

Back in Georgia that afternoon with Paul Newman, Tom Cruise and Mimi Rogers held hands as they greeted Newman with a good luck floral arrangement, complete with a card that read: 'These are for your garden. Go get them. Love Tom and Mimi.'

Encouraged by Newman, Tom took a one-day driving seminar at the Chesnut Mountain, Georgia racetrack, with Newman's Nissan team-mate and Road Atlanta's chief driving instructor, Jim Fitzgerald. Newman even rented a half-mile track for him and his Hollywood pal to do a little race practice on.

'He took me out and spent a lot of time talking about it,' Tom later recalled. 'I've always loved cars and motor-cycles and stuff. Racing is one thing I said I wanted him to get me into.'

While Newman was gushing about Tom's 'star status', the young star never strayed far from Mimi's side. Mean-while, race track officials were predicting big things for Tom. 'As far as Tom is concerned, he shows a lot of ability and potential as a racer,' said Road Atlanta operations manager Janet Upchurch. 'He's a smart young man and we're hoping he gets into road racing. He seems to enjoy it very much.'

Actress Mimi – an impressive lady with a million-dollar smile and a curvaceous body to match – looked on intently as her young lover and one of Hollywood's elder statesmen continued their mutual admiration society. She seemed completely unfazed by the press attention her visit was provoking and even insisted: 'I've never given it much thought. It was never an issue with us.'

Mimi had had her first break in television's hugely successful *Hill Street Blues* but her next two series did not do so well. There was a starring role in the eminently forgettable *Paper Doll*, an ABC-TV pilot that Mimi was very relieved never went into a full series.

Her following project was a series entitled *The Rousters*. That also failed miserably, although Mimi, ever the resolute professional, bounced back with a highly acclaimed play called *The Last Prostitute Who Took Pride in Her Work*, followed shortly afterwards by a major feature movie entitled *Gung Ho*. Director Ron Howard – once Ritchie Cunningham in *Happy Days*, who went on to become a director of such popular pieces as *Splash* and *Cocoon* – chose Mimi to play the role of Michael Keaton's girlfriend in the 1986 comedy about cultural differences between a Japanese company and its American workers. *Gung Ho* was later made into a short-lived TV series but without Mimi in the lead.

Mimi's best movie part to date had been playing Christopher Reeves's girlfriend in the movie *Street Smart*, a vastly underrated production which elicited some fine all-round performances from a number of actors, including Mimi and Christopher, but particularly Morgan Freeman, who later gained worldwide attention through *Driving Miss Daisy*.

'Mimi was a smart, sexy lady who had lived life to the full. You could say she was more than a match for Tom,' explained one member of the *Street Smart* crew. They vividly recall watching Mimi squeeze into a variety of very shapely outfits for her role. 'She is the kind of woman who sticks out in any crowd. There is something about her – she exudes a certain type of sensuality. It is quite remarkable.'

Tom had never forgotten how impressed he had been by Mimi's intelligence and stunning good looks at that dinner party a year earlier but he had done nothing about it at the time because well-brought-up boys like Tom do not steal girls off other guys. He also had very strong ideas on what he expected from a woman. 'It's all relative. I like bright, sexy women. And strong, someone whom I'm not going to run over, someone strong enough to stand up to me. She's also got to have her own thing going. I don't want someone living for me.'

Mimi Rogers's most vivid recollection from that first dinner party meeting was simple: 'I guess we both thought we were kinda cute. You just know.'

However, Tom's penchant for bright, attractive girls meant that when the couple bumped into each other again 24-year-old Tom and 31-year-old Mimi instantly clicked as a couple. The thing that really swung it for Tom was that Mimi had been a child when her own family split up. It was as if Tom could only really relate to people who had experienced some of the same sort of personal anguish as him.

Mimi, born in Coral Gables, Florida, told Tom how her parents got divorced when she was just seven years old. Her mother had moved across state, leaving her father to look after her and her younger brother Paul. Then followed many years of moving annually with their father – an engineer like Tom's father – to wherever his work took him. Mimi learned to be a chameleon, fitting in wherever they went – Tucson, Washington DC, Detroit, LA – the Bay Area. Mimi – a science whiz in school, skipped grades twice because she was so intelligent but her unconventional childhood made her more of an outsider than most kids, except for Tom Cruise.

Tom did not give a moment's thought to the age difference between them. After all, this was the mid-1980s and Hollywood was well used to women being wooed and won by younger men. Some memorable relationships spring to mind: actress Juliet Mills, 44 (*of Nanny and the Professor* fame) wed Maxwell Caulfield, 25 (of *Grease 2* and *The Colbys*). Like many of these pairings, they met through professional connections. Joan Collins, aged 53, had set the pace in 1985 when she married 39-year-old Swedish businessman Peter Holm; Olivia Newton-John, 38, married 24-year-old actor Matt Lattanzi; and 43-year-old Britt Ekland (ex-wife of Peter Sellers) wed drummer Slim Jim Plantom, formerly of the Stray Cats, when he was just 26.

Adding to her mystique, Mimi refused to discuss her age in all press interviews after she met Tom and estimates of her age varied enormously. She seemed to be between six and ten years older than Tom, depending on which newspaper you read.

Besides Tom Selleck, Mimi had also been romantically linked with the likes of Ed Marinaro and Bobby Shriver, a member of the Kennedy clan. Before those relationships blossomed she had been married briefly to a Scientologist counsellor named Jim Rodgers. The moment the press got wind of Tom's relationship with Mimi, a vast trawl of her background was ordered by the notorious US tabloids.

Mimi, 'the older woman', was painted as some sort of sexual siren who would teach Tom a thing or two about lovemaking. In fact, the two enjoyed an immensely equal relationship in the early days of their love affair. There is no doubt that Tom looked up to Mimi (she was an inch or two taller than his five feet nine inches!) but she enjoyed the warmness of their friendship and the fact that Tom was not one of those brutal macho characters who would throw his masculinity in her face all day long.

It has also been suggested that Paul Newman – the nearest thing to a father figure in Tom's life at the time – was instrumental in getting the couple hitched. One night Paul and Tom were out to dinner and Tom made a real point of mentioning how much Mimi meant to him and how the age difference did not really matter to him one bit. He told Newman he was confident that she was a good, strong woman but he was nervous about whether actual marriage might damage his career. That old Cruise obsession of 'remaining focused' was coming back into the frame. Love versus work – it was a dilemma that would haunt Tom for a lot more time to come.

He even admitted: 'When you don't feel like getting married, marriage is just a piece of paper saying two people own each other ... I have a very cynical attitude about it.' Tom's attitude was hardly surprising considering his parents' divorce. But then he remembered his sisters and added: 'They're married and happy.' In some ways it would have been easier for Tom to say 'no way' to marriage if the debris of matrimony was scattered all around him.

Newman listened carefully to Tom's comments and then recounted his own personal experiences. Mainly, there was his own thriving marriage to Joanne Woodward, which had neither damaged his sex appeal nor altered his status as a serious actor. Newman urged Tom to set a date for marriage to Mimi.

Tom took note of his friend's advice. No one had ever spoken to him on this sort of subject before in his life. He began to realise just how much he had missed in not having a father to bounce such things off. Paul Newman made Tom realise how important marriage was. Tom knew all along that Paul was right but he just had to hear it from Newman before he realised it himself.

There was another motive behind his decision to marry Mimi. Tom sincerely wanted to try to ease up on his enormous workload and actually start to enjoy life instead of dashing from one movie to the next without ever pausing for some fun. 'I know it's not the norm to be my age and this successful. I can't say I felt totally great about it in the beginning, but then I thought: "Tom this is where you want to be,"'' he explained.

'You see some people destroy themselves because they become successful and feel guilty about acknowledging it – and then it goes away. Now I'm trying to enjoy myself and what's happened to me. I think I've settled in a little more. Even after the financial success of *Top Gun* I have trouble enjoying it instead of taking the moment to say: "Hey, this is really amazing" '

On 9 May 1987, Tom took Paul Newman's advice and married Mimi at a secret ceremony that, ironically, Newman could not get to because he was premiering his next movie *The Glass Menagerie*. The couple hardly told a soul. Unlike his great friend Sean Penn – whose marriage to Madonna had been eclipsed by a media circus that included helicopters hovering overhead and boats bobbing about on the ocean – Tom succeeded in marrying without any member of the media knowing about it.

Even the so-called well-informed gossip columnists like Liz Smith of the *New York Daily News* were left red-faced and empty-handed. She complained in her column: 'Why didn't any of my thousands of spies out there bother to tell me Tom Cruise was marrying Mimi Rogers last weekend?'

Tom even kept his publicist Andrea Jaffe (publicity agent for both performers) in the dark about their marriage plans. Two days after the ceremony she admitted: 'Guess what? I got a phone call today telling me. I didn't get any details. I don't even know what day it was.'

The secrecy surrounding Tom's wedding to Mimi was just another example of the young actor's increasing obsession with privacy. He might have owed his multi-million-dollar salaries to the public who flocked to see his movies but that did not mean they owned a chunk of Tom's personal life. In the few days leading up to the wedding, Tom decided not even to tell some of the Hollywood associates who had grown close to him for fear that news might leak out and he'd face the sort of chaotic scenes that greeted Penn and Madonna. He told the people who were invited that he was having a 'spring bash' at the house and did not reveal the marriage plans until after everyone had arrived.

What few facts can be gathered about the ceremony go as follows: best man was Emilio Estevez and Tom's mother, Mary Lee, later conceded to *People* magazine that the wedding was 'very small, intimate and beautiful'. A short Unitarian service was held in a large Victorian house that Tom and Mimi were renting in Bedford, New York State. Besides Emilio, the only non-family members in attendance were a girlfriend of Mimi's, who acted as bride's attendant, and the Unitarian minister who presided over the union. Initial reports that actors Judd Nelson and Charlie Sheen were among the guests were later emphatically denied.

The couple and their guests dined on food prepared by Tom's mother and his sisters. Even the wedding cake – chocolate with white marshmallow icing – was baked by one of Tom's sisters.

'I couldn't be more blessed,' exclaimed Mary Lee.

Publicist Andrea Jaffe told *USA Today* that Tom and Mimi had deliberately kept the ceremony as quiet as possible. That was a shocking revelation! 'A lot of people didn't know about it until they got there,' she said in hushed tones as if revealing some sort of state secret. According to Jaffe, the privileged guests, numbered 'fifteen tops'.

Tom and Mimi were said to be too busy to consider a honeymoon of any sort; instead, they combined business with pleasure and headed for Los Angeles to visit friends ... including Mimi's best friend actress Kirstie Alley and her husband Parker Stevenson. So much for Tom's intention to ease up on his workload. It was disappointing for Mimi whose romantic image of marriage considerably differed from Tom's real, ambitious aims which could not be effectively watered down by his wedding.

Just before the marriage ceremony, Mimi said optimistically: 'If I were offered an unbelievable role that was shooting in Tunisia for three or four months and Tom couldn't go ... well, Tunisia would have to wait.' Mimi even talked in glowing terms about having children with Tom and insisted that Tom was 'as committed as I am. This is for real.'

However, whether he liked it or not, Tom's career was feeding too many mouths in Tinseltown for there to be any let up in his work commitments. Hollywood wanted its pound of flesh and personal happiness was not going to get in the way of making movies. Mimi herself took a rather dim view of those who live for the glare of publicity: 'I want to work but the pure concept of fame is not the point with me. Being famous is not all that great,' she insisted. There were obviously many fundamental differences between Tom and Mimi and they were only just beginning to surface.

Hollywood was hardly in a state of shock about Tom's decision to marry. His relationship with Mimi was perceived to be solid and gracious, with just an added touch of spice because of their age differences. Tom's fears about his image being damaged by marriage were rapidly discounted, especially since older women across the globe were delighted to see one of their number making such a handsome catch.

Mimi's magnetism was undoubted. 'There's a little something about her that appeals to an awful lot of men,' explained her old family friend, former San Francisco 49er quarterback John Brodie. 'Everybody did better whenever she was around them. Tom Cruise certainly did.'

Mimi was just as committed to the idea of a wedding, as she explained. 'Beforehand you don't think it's going to change things, but it does. There's just a deeper sense of responsibility and commitment and it's great.'

Friends of the couple recalled that they were 'heavily into each other almost to the point where the rest of the world did not exist'. Mimi admitted that she and her new young husband were 'very much mutual boosters'. She explained: 'We rely on each other to tell the truth. I guess we're very lucky and I think he's very talented and he thinks I'm talented.'

Shortly after the wedding, Paul Newman and his wife Joanne Woodward made up for not showing up at the ceremony by taking Tom and Mimi out for dinner at a trendy New York restaurant called Wilkinson's Seafood Cafe on York Avenue. *Cosmopolitan* even awarded Tom and Mimi their coveted 'Couple of the Month' award in late 1987.

Before their marriage, Tom and Mimi's relationship had been noted as one of the happiest in Tinseltown. By all accounts, no one ever heard them even raise their voices to each other. Mimi – with her ample bosom and penchant for not being afraid to show off her figure in a subtle sort of way – seemed to complement the conservative image of Tom. They were known as 'the perfect couple'.

However, slight cracks began to appear shortly after their wedding and these alleged tiffs were reported with glee in the US and British tabloids. Their first row concerned Tom's speedy driving. It was claimed that Mimi asked Paul

Newman to have a chat with him but no one could ever quite fathom if Newman actually talked to his young protégé or not.

When Tom luckily escaped serious injury after his Nissan 200SX hit a wall during the Sports Car Grand Prix at Ponoco International Raceway in Pennsylvania in August 1989, Mimi felt her nerves becoming frayed. Tom got out of the car himself and walked to an ambulance. He was taken to the infield hospital and released. Tom's only comment: 'I wanted to improve on my second place finish ... I was following a team-mate into turn one, and I lost the draft.'

Another major long-term problem for the couple was that Tom was planning to continue living in his recently aquired $3 million apartment on East 13th Street in New York, while Californian Mimi seemed intent on remaining in Los Angeles. In the first few months after the wedding they tried hard to see as much as possible of each other, but it wasn't easy.

Mimi did not particularly like New York as a place to live because she had been brought up in hotter climates. Tom's apartment – in one of the most sought-after blocks in the city – enjoyed fantastic views and celebrity neighbours, including Rolling Stone Keith Richards and Phil Collins. Tom even tried to make the place more homely by getting a highly paid interior decorator in to make some adjustments to the apartment, including the purchase of some $5,000 sofas which caused a major traffic jam in the narrow street outside when they had to be delivered by crane because they were too big to go in the elevator!

The couple laughed off constant claims in the tabloids that Tom was jealous of Mimi's love scenes and vice versa. Tom was consistently linked with every leading lady he starred alongside, but the couple managed to laugh off all the outrageous claims in a way that Tom seemed unable to do later in life. In Tom's Los Angeles office he even had a favourite absurdity framed and hung on the wall. The head-line read: 'WIFE JEALOUS'.

Mimi went off to play the steamy lead in *Someone to Watch Over Me*, directed by Ridley Scott, who had spent the best part of a year in London with Tom on *Legend*. Some of the sex scenes with co-star Tom Berenger were fairly explicit and there was some speculation that Cruise was upset by them.

After completing *Someone to Watch Over Me*, Mimi announced that she definitely still believed there was a lot more to life than making movies. 'I want to go through the whole Museum of Natural History and read everything. I love the gems and natural minerals exhibit and the whale. It always amazes me that something could be so big.' Mimi's focus was definitely not on the same objectives as Tom's

The couple did look as perfect as ever when they attended the premiere of *Ishtar*, starring Dustin Hoffman who had been slated to appear with Tom in his next project *Rain Man*. Mimi seemed to revel in the company of Tom's glamorous young Brat Pack pals, although Tom's friendship with Sean Penn had become a little cooler after his marriage to Madonna because Penn was now much more inaccessible.

There was also talk in Hollywood that Tom wanted to start a family with Mimi. At one stage, a friend of Tom's was quoted as saying the star had told him: 'I've always loved kids and Mimi is the one that I want to have them with.'

By the summer of 1988, reports started to circulate alleging that Mimi was having problems getting pregnant. *The Sunday People* in Britain claimed that Tom had dis-missed fertility experts called in to try to find a way of ensuring that Mimi became pregnant. The report alleged that Tom and Mimi had been keeping to a strict lovemaking schedule in order to pick the most fertile times of the month. The article signed off by quoting a friend as claiming that after Mimi failed to get pregnant, Tom had said: 'We'll leave it to God's will.'

That report was followed up almost a year later by one in the US tabloid *Globe*, which claimed that Mimi had been seeking advice from her best friend, actress Kirstie Alley, who was also having problems conceiving. The report alleged that Mimi and Kirstie had been 'giving each other a lot of moral support. They talk all the time about how badly they want a baby.'

However, the most significant allegation in that particular article was: 'Mimi told pals that Tom's sperm count was low.'

As fertility expert Dr David Hill explained: 'If the doctor finds that the man's sperm count is low, he will often recommend that the couple try timed intercourse – making love primarily during the woman's most fertile times – for at least six months.'

About a year after his marriage to Mimi, Tom made a fascinating comment about his career, which seemed to be an insight into his personal life as well. 'At times I look to see if I'm doing what I set out to do,' he explained. 'I'm always finding out new things about what's going on with a character. Making a movie is like a chess game. It's about constantly changing patterns, adapting to new things. It's not just black and white. Every day something happens and you think, "That's terrific, let's shift with this." '

A lot of Tom's friends wondered whether he was talking about love or work.

"Tom reminded me of those guys you see in boot-camp films, doing push-ups, and the sergeant is saying, "One more! One more!" And Tom is not only the guy doing the push-ups, he's also the guy saying, "One more!""

Dustin Hoffman

The bowling alley was crowded with families enjoying an American-style, classic Saturday night out. No one noticed the two shortish men aiming their bowls with deadly accuracy. They could have been father and son.

The two men were then joined by a family of four, including a clearly autistic child and his brother. They continued bowling. Still no one spotted them. Tom Cruise was out on a research field trip with Hollywood icon Dustin Hoffman.

The two actors were trying to gain some real-life experience for the characters they hoped to portray in *Rain Man*. For Tom, it was like a dream come true to find himself slated to appear opposite Hoffman. The *Rain Man* project appeared to be on the verge of production and he could not believe his good fortune in moving from the classy role in *The Color of Money* to an even more impressive part opposite a truly legendary name.

It seemed that Tom was on a creative roll following the acclaim he had received after the release of *The Color of Money*. Still only 24 years old, he had mapped out his future with great precision and had been casting around very carefully for the perfect next movie when the *Rain Man* project fell into his lap. Tom was absolutely determined not to take any retrograde steps in terms of his career. If that meant waiting months, even years, for the right sort of project to come along, then so be it.

When Tom's agent, the ever-loyal Paula Wagner, had earlier slipped her client a script of *Rain Man* that was circulating Hollywood, she already knew that it would appeal to him but her first approach to Hoffman's people got a polite rebuff because the star of such classics as *The Graduate* wanted comedian Bill Murray to co-star alongside him. Then Murray started making big demands and, within days, Tom and Hoffman had teamed up and the project seemed to be on the verge of being green-lighted.

Tom could not believe his luck. Only two years earlier he and Sean Penn had driven past Hoffman's Beverly Hills mansion and dared each other to go and knock on the door of their acting hero. In the end, neither had the courage to do it.

The stories about Hoffman were legendary. In Hollywood, everyone knew his reputation: Dustin Hoffman is a perfectionist; Dustin Hoffman demands absolute accuracy and won't proceed until he gets it; Dustin Hoffman even held up the shooting of *Marathon Man* for hours because the scene called for his character to jump out of bed and grab a flashlight and Dustin knew that his character wouldn't keep a flashlight by the bed ...

Dustin Hoffman represented the sort of perfectionist that Tom Cruise wanted to be. He felt they would be soul-mates even before they actually got to work together.

Then *Rain Man* got caught up in what is known as development hell – in other words, several versions of the screenplay were written and rewritten and numerous directors were attached at one time or another and it became clear that *Rain Man* was no nearer actual production than the first day it was considered.

What makes this all the more surprising is that among the cluster of directors involved was Steven Spielberg – the most powerful auteur in Hollywood and surely someone who could get a movie underway at the flick of a finger? Unfortunately, this was not actually the case. In movieland no project – whoever is involved – gets financial backing until a studio says 'yes' and, in the case of *Rain Main*, studio executives were having very big problems coming to terms with the subject matter: an autistic man's reunion with his criminally inclined brother. Hollywood just did not feel ready or able to cope with dealing with mental retardation.

A year had passed since Hollywood's most powerful talent agency, the awesome CAA, decreed that Dustin Hoffman, who had just starred in a miserable failure of a movie entitled *Ishtar*, should be teamed up with Tom. The notion of a Hoffman-Cruise movie sent Tinseltown into paroxysms of excitement – rapidly followed by total confusion. The age gap between the two stars was 28 years! How could they be believable as brothers? *Rain Man* was supposed to be a story about an idiot savant, not about a biological accident. The casting of Tom and Hoffman would require a massive restructuring, yet another rewrite ...

Under the auspices of Mike Ovitz and his most trusted foot soldiers, CAA completely disagreed. They argued that although Hollywood might be cognizant of the age gap, the great viewing public wouldn't even notice. The charisma of the actors would carry the day.

With the project back to swimming around in development hell, Tom decided to commit to a film called *Cocktail*. If ever it was true that every two steps forward require one step back, then this project was definitely the proof. While there is no reason why Tom should make his every film choice serious and dramatic, people inside Hollywood were rather puzzled as to why he picked a movie like *Cocktail*.

One theory is that Tom had waited around so long for *Rain Man* to be given the green light that he felt he needed some light relief. *Cocktail* could certainly never be classified as anything more.

The plot was simple: Tom played a Manhattan barman who falls in love with a wealthy woman (played by Elizabeth Shue) and the movie chronicled their relationship and the one between him and his mentor, played by Australian actor Bryan Brown. The result was a movie that's all flash and no substance.

Even before starting the shoot, Tom got a light hearted reminder from his old mentor and father figure Paul Newman not to take life too seriously. The veteran star sent Tom a six-pack of beer with a note attached that read: 'You're always working. I want you to sit down. I want you to take a weekend. I want you to drink all these beers.'

Tom thought long and hard about that note from Newman. He knew what the older actor was trying to tell him; slow down or you'll burn yourself out before you get into your thirties. A few years later Tom reflected: 'I've thought about that a lot. And I have slowed down. Some ...'

Tom did his usual thorough research on *Cocktail* but this time it was certainly a little more convivial than usual. For the best part of a month he hung around at some of New York's best known bars and was even spotted mixing drinks behind the bar at John Clancy's Seafood Restaurant before flying to LA to take bartending classes with Glendale barman John Bandy.

Tom's character in *Cocktail*, Brian Flanagan, was brash and flash, and Tom found himself defending his image during press junkets in the lead up to the movie's release. The public was getting the impression from *Cocktail* that Tom was a 'cocky bastard'. He was keen to pour scorn on that notion. 'I feel a responsibility to bring the truth to the character that I play. This is not Tom Cruise. This is Brian. But people often misinterpret it.'

Tom was even publicly criticised because his character jumped in and out of bed with a host of different women and never once wore a condom. He had a clear response:

'I don't think it's my job to educate people on safe sex. Do I have to wear a condom in my scenes on the screen? This is an R-rated film. People under 17 won't get in without their parents. This is the eighties. There is AIDS. There is alcoholism. People should be able to figure it out for themselves.

'Images of how people perceive you can't control your life, so I just do what I'm doing. I'm a working actor who feels fortunate to be where I am and to do what I've done.'

Tom continued to defend *Cocktail* fiercely but there was an underlying current of disappointment in his voice when he said: 'The film meant well, you know?' Then he went on to admit:

'I can't even sit here and say to you how many things I felt I did wrong or what happened, because we could sit here for three days and talk. It's painful as hell. You don't work less hard. I mean, I worked my butt off on that movie. It knocks you and you learn. But that's the thing. You've got to say, "Let's go, get off your butt and get out there and try it again." '

Behind the scenes, shooting in glamorous locations like Port Antonio, Jamaica turned into nightmare scenarios when four days' worth of shot film was found to be overexposed and had to be reshot. Tom was joined by Mimi in Jamaica for a few days and the rest of the cast and crew noted that the young actor hardly ever mixed with his colleagues off the set. Instead, he and Mimi would wander off along the beach for long walks away from the crowds.

One of the few good things about *Cocktail* was Tom's beautiful co-star Elizabeth Shue. A native of South Orange, New Jersey, just a stone's throw from Tom's old home at Glen Ridge, Elizabeth also came from a broken home but there the similarities ended. While enormously polite to one another, there was no offscreen friendship, although Tom was reported to be angry about a scene in which Elizabeth nearly knocked his teeth out during a fight. Tom got his own back a few days later when he dunked his co-star in the water during a scene and accidentally-on-purpose held her under for just a few moments too long.

The recently married Tom proved more than a handful in the sex symbol department during the making of the film. He was not keen on exposing his assets on the big screen. As director Roger Donaldson – a straight-talking New Zealander – admitted: 'Tom was very concerned about showing his ass.'

Tom was reluctant to perform a crucial love scene with Elizabeth Shue. Many believed his increased shyness had been caused by his marriage to Mimi Rogers. Others were convinced that Tom simply did not believe a star of his stature should be having to do gratuitous bedroom scenes.

'Love scenes make me nervous,' insisted Tom on the

set. 'It's very strange to get in bed with someone you don't really know. They're embarrassed and I'm kinda going, "You okay?" ' He then laughed: ' "Right then, let's do it." It's no fun at all. You have to be professional about it. You respect the other person's feelings. There's a line to cross. I don't do it and it's never been done to me. That's the way it is.'

Shue – a very attractive, bubbly blonde – had shot to fame in *Karate Kid*, a movie that did incredibly well at the box office despite having no stars in it and nothing more than a rather weak plot line. She tactfully remained silent about her steamy kissing scenes with Tom and even refused to comment on them when one tabloid incorrectly tried to suggest that Tom had a real-life romance with her.

Cocktail eventually proved an interesting testimony to the pulling power of Tom because it took more than $70 million at the box office after its release in July 1988, even though it was dubbed one of the worst movies of that year. One angry reviewer wrote damningly that Tom 'doesn't even try to act'. Highly respected TV critic and Chicago-based writer Roger Ebert wrote stingingly: 'This is the kind of movie that uses Cruise's materialism as a target all through the story, and then rewards him for it at the end. The more you think about what really happens in *Cocktail*, the more you realise how empty and fabricated it really is.'

Tom insisted that the mistakes he made during *Cocktail* would help his next performance. Typically, he was managing to turn a cinematic disaster into a learning experience.

When the *Rain Man* saga reconvened at the end of the *Cocktail* shoot, the latest director attached to the project was Steven Spielberg. However, instead of being overly impressed by Spielberg, Tom let it be known that while he was delighted to hear about the master helmsman's interest in the script, he was far more concerned about keeping Dustin Hoffman and himself attached to the project.

When Spielberg's interest also faded, Tom started genuinely to worry about whether it would ever actually get made. One day he phoned Hoffman in a virtual state of panic. Tom recalled: 'I said, "Listen, it doesn't look good but I wanna make this movie," and Hoffman said, "You wanna make this movie?" I said, "Yeah, I wanna make the goddamn movie." And he said, "Then we're gonna make the film. Hang tight, Cruise: We're gonna make this movie." '

Later, when told of Tom's account of what happened, Hoffman agreed with everything except he insisted that he never called Tom by his last name.

Then in stepped director Sydney Pollack (*Out of Africa*). He had already passed on the project once before because 'it had been around a long time and everybody was having problems with it'.

Initially, fellow director Barry Levinson was asked by super agent Mike Ovitz to help Pollack to try to knock the project into shape. As is surprisingly often the way in Tinseltown, Levinson did not mind helping out a rival director as he would no doubt be expected to return the favour some day.

By this stage, neither Tom nor Dustin Hoffman had even faced the reality that they might act together in a film, because neither of them believed the project would ever get off the ground.

Then Levinson – a quietly spoken man with shoulder-length, grey hair – got a call from Ovitz telling him Sydney Pollack had dropped out of *Rain Man* and would he like to do it? Levinson accepted and then found himself in a desperate scramble to rewrite the script before principal photography was scheduled to start just seven weeks later.

Before Levinson climbed on board, Dustin Hoffman had done extensive research into autism and he felt very committed to trying to portray an autistic correctly.

Levinson backed his actor all the way because he was con-vinced that Hoffman's character, Raymond Babbitt, would provide the main thrust of the film. Tom was more than happy to play second fiddle to Hoffman because he acknow-ledged that he was in the company of a true master of his art.

Levinson was no pushover either. The former writer had a formidable directorial reputation (*Tin Men, Good Morning Vietnam*) and while he liked everyone to suggest new ideas, he was not afraid of telling interfering actors where to get off – and he was in the company of two of the most notorious of that breed in modern Hollywood history. Explained Levinson:

> 'If an actor wants everything to be the way he wants it to be, then it's best to say, "Look, get your own fucking movie and do it yourself." But if you are working on collaboration, that's terrific, because if you are exchanging ideas you may find a better one that takes you to a higher level. That's what gives you adrenalin; it's what drives you and stimulates you.'

The director then cast beautiful Italian actress Valerie Golino as Tom's character, Charlie's, girlfriend and the movie got underway in Cincinnati. Within days, the attrac-tive brunette actress was experiencing Cruisemania at first hand. 'Once after Tom and I shot an outdoor scene in which we hold hands, a trembling girl came up to me and tried to kiss my hand because it had just been in Tom's. Things like that happened all the time with his fans. It was amazing.'

Valerie and Tom also became the subject of endless rumours of a love affair which – the notoriously inaccurate US tabloids predicted – was threatening to break up his marriage to Mimi Rogers. Nothing could have been further from the truth. There was no affair. In fact Valerie and Tom hardly mixed off the set.

Hoffman – known as a bit of a movie-set maniac – was full of praise for his young co-star. 'He's a demon,' Hoffman marvelled. 'He gets up early, he works out, he goes home early, he studies, he works out again at night ... and he always wanted to rehearse.'

Tom then got a few words in and it all started to sound a bit like a mutual admiration society. 'What you get from great actors like Newman and Hoffman is where to focus your energies and what to worry about and what not to worry about,' Tom even conceded, '... because as a young actor, you're worried about everything.'

Privately, Tom had to keep pinching himself because he could not quite believe that, in the space of one year, he had appeared in movies with both Newman and Hoffman. He was fairly concerned that Hoffman might prove too strong for him but, in the end he decided that he was 'excited enough just to be there – it wasn't important whether or not I won. I always took it from the point of view of the student.'

In 1984, long before the *Rain Man* project had got underway, Tom had been in a New York restaurant with his sister when they had spotted Hoffman across the crowded room. Eventually, the young actor plucked up enough courage to go over and tell Hoffman what a great admirer of his he was. Hoffman immediately insisted that Tom and his sister go and see him in a play that very evening and then come backstage afterwards. Tom was astonished because Hoffman knew precisely who he was.

While Tom and Hoffman might have sounded as if they were going to make the perfect match, others involved with *Rain Man* were not so sure, especially when it came to dealing with Hoffman. The production manager and the assistant director – both veterans of Hoffman's greatest triumph as the sex-swap actor *Tootsie* – told Levinson's producer Mark Johnson that Hoffman had been so difficult that they'd given him bad news or asked for favours only when he was in his full Dorothy Michaels drag; as a woman, they said, he was much nicer.

During shooting, the expected clash of egos between Tom and Hoffman never materialised. In fact, it simply did not exist. Explained Tom:

> 'Dustin was very supportive. 'I mean he's so shrewd, so intelligent. He's a consummate professional. He knew what was best for the film. He saw the limitations of his role and saw the whole picture. He had the over-view to see where the film should go, as if to say, "Look, we've got to set up who this guy is", because I kept saying, "Who am I. What is this guy about? What is going on?"''

Beneath Tom's slightly desperate-sounding words was an actor's genuine concern with his character. He was playing the smooth, car-dealer, yuppy brother to autistic Dustin and he knew he was going to have to battle to make his presence felt. He cleverly allowed Hoffman to become his mentor to a certain degree. He did not want to make the older actor feel inferior in any way – he also wanted to learn.

Hoffman was very receptive. He gushed about Tom: 'He's a moment-to-moment actor. He's there in the moment. He doesn't have any intellectual idea of what he wants to do – he's coming off the gut, and that makes him a pleasure to play ping-pong with.' Hoffman admitted that, by the end of *Rain Man*, the situations had completely reversed. 'Tom was as much directing me as I was directing him.'

Levinson was also full of praise for Tom's acting abilities

and insisted that his apparently inferior role was, in fact, the most essential element in the movie. 'I thought Tom Cruise did well because he had to drive the whole movie. He had to be on top of it the whole time because if he didn't the movie would lay down.'

The day after *Rain Man* wrapped, Tom headed east for a car race, even though he didn't really have time to test the car he'd be driving fully. During the race he lost control of his back end, spun out of control and his car ended up in a wall. Fortunately unhurt by his experience, Tom was fuming about headlines like 'Tom Cruise wrecks sports car' that followed his crash but he hardly had reason to be surprised.

Both Tom's and Dustin's performances in *Rain Man* were highly acclaimed. Hoffman was incredible as Raymond, developing a twitch of his head, a unique style of walking, an interesting choice of vocalisation and managing to give a terrific performance without the benefit of making eye contact with his co-stars. To an extent, it's almost as if he were acting his scenes by himself.

Tom simply overshadowed any of his previous performances. Under his gifted hand, Charlie is emotionally frozen on the surface but, just beneath, he's a weapon ready to fire – a bit like Tom Cruise in real life. The frustration and barely controlled anger he's feeling become a tangible thing for the audience. It's interesting that, through these feelings, he unwittingly begins to develop an understanding of his brother that might not have been possible at the outset.

Nobody in Hollywood thought *Rain Man* would make any money, not even director Levinson. 'I thought this would be a kind of offbeat piece, even if it did star Tom Cruise. On opening night I drove past one of the theatres and it was half full. So I thought it's going to do some business, but not do particularly well.'

The movie's backer, MGM/UA, was not a healthy

studio at the time so *Rain Man* only had one preview before release. The usual audience research was abandoned because their reaction to the film was so negative. The audience resented the fact that there was no happy ending in the film and many people were upset by Tom's character's cruelty to his brother. However, Levinson refused to pander to the audience and stuck firmly to his guns. 'I did not set out to make something that was going to be this great piece of mass entertainment.'

Former studio executive Peter Bart explained:

'The conventional wisdom on *Rain Man* was that it met none of the normal criteria of a "hot picture". *Rain Man* was not sexy. It wasn't especially comedic. Its perspective on humanity was rather dark. The Dustin Hoffman character was not redeemed or transformed into a "normal" person. Indeed, the only thing the picture had going for it was that it was superbly directed and performed. And it rang true.'

The analysts' dire predictions were wrong from the outset. *Rain Man* was not just a hit. It was a complete blockbuster. In its first 18 days the film registered a remarkable $42.4 million at the US box office. By the end of March 1988, five months after its release, receipts had soared to $155.7 million, thus overtaking *Rocky IV* as the highest grossing picture in the history of United Artists.

Rain Man came in under budget by $2.5 million (the original estimate was $30 million) and went on to gross an estimated $500 million worldwide. Once again, a movie featuring Tom Cruise was heavily nominated at the following year's Oscars and went on to win eight Academy Awards including Best Director for Levinson and Best Film. Once again, Tom was overlooked when Hoffman won Best Actor. He found it difficult to hide his disappointment but felt that, like all the knocks he had faced in life, this was just another learning experience and he would build on it and continue seeking out quality roles until he got what he deserved.

Movie expert Edward Gross said that Tom was perfectly entitled to feel disappointed.

'The feeling of teamwork between the two is obvious in the finished film, for they work together like one complete individual. Hoffman won the Academy Award and the lion's share of the credit for his excellent performance as Raymond. It's disconcerting, however, to see that Cruise was not equally lauded. In his hands, Charlie Babbitt is a flesh and blood human being who goes through a 180-degree transformation due to contact with the brother he never knew existed. Never again would anyone doubt his abilities as an actor.'

Los Angeles Times film critic Sheila Benson wrote: 'No one can argue that *Rain Man* is Cruise's quantum leap, or that it can be said unblushingly that he holds his own with the masterly Hoffman.'

Not everyone was so impressed by the film. New York's *Village Voice* insisted: '*Rain Man* is a small, sweet, unconvincing road movie that over inflates itself on the gaseous notion of a lovable autistic idiot savant "curing" his conventional, that is to say "normal", kid brother in the course of a week-long drive to California.'

In *New Yorker* the notorious Pauline Kael was even harder on the young star: 'And Cruise as a slimeball is just a sugarpuss in Italian tailoring. He doesn't even use his body in an expressive way. His performance here consists of not smiling too much – so as not to distract his fans from watching Hoffman. Cruise is an actor in the same sense that Robert Taylor was an actor. He's patented: his knowing that a camera is on him produces nothing but fraudulence.'

However, there were consolations for Tom. Not only did he make a whopping $5 million flat fee for *Rain Man*, he also made at least a further $5 million when the movie topped the $100 million mark because of a complex deal that meant he and Hoffman were making more cash from the movie than the backers, United Artists!

Tom was at least able to reflect in the movie's commercial glory.

'People asked after *Rain Man*, "How are you going to match the success of that picture?" I said, "I can't live my life by what is going to make $20 or $100 million. I don't know what is going to happen to my career. I am going to take a lot of risks and some of it is going to work and some of it is not going to work. Some of it will be trash and some of it, I hope, will be good. I make the decisions. I pick the scripts. I have only myself to blame if things don't work out. That is why I want to live my life. That is the way I set out to live it at the beginning.'

'I think he became middle-aged making this movie. I think he passed out of his youth truly into early middle age. He'll never be the same boy he was before. He knows too much now.'

Oliver Stone

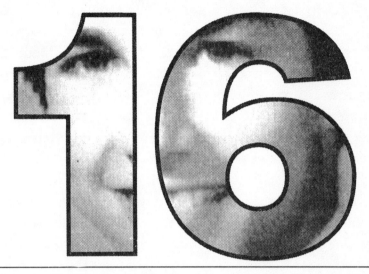

Like so many American kids of his generation, Tom Cruise came of age long after his country's defeat in the Vietnam War. Tet, My Lai, Cambodia, Kent State: to Tom they were just names, vague and confusing, void of any historial or emotional interest. The war was something that was not among his concerns or in his consciousness. Finding out what happened to America after the war, when thousands of Vietnam veterans came home crippled and in wheelchairs, was not high on his agenda. By his own admission, when it came to Vietnam, Tom was a complete innocent.

Then, one night in Manhattan in January 1988, he found himself having dinner with a charismatic man called Oliver Stone. Stone had been a United States Marine who was twice decorated in Vietnam but Tom only knew him as the brilliant director of movies like *Wall Street*, *Salvador* and the Oscar award-winning Vietnam film, *Platoon*. Tom listened intently as Stone told him about his next project, a

Vietnam movie even more ambitious than *Platoon*, a movie that, maybe, just maybe, could draw out the core of the Vietnam tragedy and make it a lasting testimony to peace for generations to come.

In vivid detail Stone described the elements that would be portrayed in his film, such as battlefield horrors and confusion, women and children mistakenly killed, the physical and psychological wounds inflicted on a nation that left many GIs so badly injured they would come home with shattered bodies that would stay that way for the rest of their lives. Then would come shots of the veteran hospitals where tens of thousands of soldiers suffered anguish after the rest of the country had turned its back on them. Then, Stone promised, he would focus in on how the war tore America apart at home – the politicians, the anti-war movement and how it attracted many of those very same GIs who had suffered so much for their country. That was the second war ... in their own backyard.

Tom was riveted and completely overawed by the wide-scape scenario being described by Oliver Stone, probably the single most influential moviemaker in Hollywood at the time. Then when Stone started to explain to the young actor that he intended to draw the essence of Vietnam through the true story of just one man, United States Marine Sgt Ron Kovic of Massapequa, Long Island, Tom tried not to look too overawed. It was starting to dawn on him that Stone was considering him for the role of Kovic.

To Stone, Kovic was the symbol of the Vietnam War. In his best-selling autobiography, the ex-Marine even described himself as a true Yankee Doodle Dandee. Born on 4 July American Independence Day, he grew up in a working class Roman Catholic family steeped in the virtues and traditions of God and country, community and flag. His heroes had been John Wayne and President John F.

Kennedy. When the call to fight for his country came, Kovic did not hesitate to take his place in the battle to stop the march of communism. He paid for his loyalty by being wounded in action and sent home in a wheelchair. Permanently crippled. Impotent.

As Ron's character says: 'I'll never feel the inside of a woman. I can feel the pressure of her body, but I'll never feel her skin against my chest. I'll never really. That whole thing. And the beauty of this woman, holding a naked woman for the first time and how incredible that is.'

Stone's project sounded like an intriguing subject and he had not yet even so much as suggested that Tom might like to consider the lead role. There were, explained the stern-faced director, one or two problems; to start with, he had not lined up an actor to play Kovic and, probably even more important, he had little or no actual money with which to finance the film. At this point, Tom would normally have stood up, said a gracious goodbye and departed through the restaurant door. However, he was sitting with no ordinary director; Oliver Stone was a legendary, hard-hitting, blunt-speaking moviemaker with a passion for subjects that often proved infectious. And Tom was already hooked.

Stone went on to explain that he had written a screen-play with his old friend Ron Kovic in the late-1970s. At that time they had lined up Al Pacino to play the lead but the money had fallen through at the last minute after rumours of creative discord between Pacino and Stone. Ron Kovic had been especially hard hit by the disappointment of not seeing his life story converted to the big screen. Stone's voice lowered to a virtual whisper as he asked Tom if he would like the part.

Tom nodded instantly. He was more than ready for a personal declaration of independence after a bellyful of highly commercial Hollywood movies. The biggest other project on the horizon was a sequel to *Top Gun* and he had promised himself he would never do that even if they paid him a hundred million dollars.

What Tom did not fully appreciate at the time of that dinner with Oliver Stone was that he was about to embark on his own frightening rite of passage, accompanied by two wartorn characters called Kovic and Stone. Tom's decision to go with Stone's project was probably the most important decision of his career. It was a done deal and, with his name and face attached to the project, Stone would get his funds to back the project. Not only did Tom enlist with Stone, he also agreed to defer his own fee until revenue started coming in. Stone had made the same arrangement in regard to his own fees. Another common bond was forged, bringing star and director even closer together. Stone explained:

'Our only concern was bringing the film to a certain level, to make it real. I always admired Tom as an actor. I had a feeling about him. And I had known Ron about ten years. When you put them together, you know.

'Both men are motivated by a desire to be the best, to be No.1. And they both had high self-esteem. In the 1960s, with Ron Kovic that took the form of joining the Marines. And, at the end of the day, I sensed with Tom a crack in his background, some kind of unhappiness, that he had seen some kind of trouble. And I thought that trouble could be helpful to him in dealing with the second part of Ron's life.'

Kovic's own involvement in the project was essential so it was only natural that Stone's next task was to take Tom to see this man, crippled and confined to a wheelchair, so that

Tom could understand the man he was going to bring to life on the screen, and so that he could also understand the thousands of other veterans who had come home in wheelchairs.

The meeting between Tom and Kovic was, by all accounts, a true eye opener. The two men forged a common bond immediately. 'It was very emotional. If it had been me, back in the fifties, back in the sixties, well, I understand that feeling of country, of wanting to do something good for people and your country,' enthused Tom.

Tom, Ron and Oliver Stone sat on the vet's bed at his modest home near Los Angeles and watched Kovic's home movies from his childhood. Kovic was understandably apprehensive. He had great doubts and fears about how the project would take shape but Tom soon convinced him otherwise.

Ron Kovic served as Tom's guide, confidant and advisor throughout the entire production of the movie Oliver Stone intended to make, entitled *Born on the Fourth of July*. Kovic became like a sort of modern-day Virgil leading Dante through the chambers of Hell, showing his young impersonator the pitfalls and correct way to walk. Tom accompanied Kovic to some veterans' hospitals where he saw at first hand some of the relics of the Vietnam War, destined to remain hospitalised for the remainder of their lives.

Tom became totally immersed in the world of paraplegics and began to discover some startling similarities between his own upbringing and that of Ron Kovic. Both men came from Catholic backgrounds, both men knew what hunger was, both men suffered from a lack of formal education. Tom became increasingly convinced that fate had landed him the lead role in Stone's megamovie. It made him all the more determined to make a success of the film.

Beneath the surface, Tom was nervous, excited and

unable to believe that such a major acting role had come his way. 'There was an element of great challenge, of great emotional commitment. But at the end of it, I didn't want Ron to say, "Oh man, I made a mistake, you shouldn't have played the role." '

Male bonding complete, next came two separate weeks in an army boot camp for Tom. Stone brought in a no-nonsense, straight-talking, former Marine captain named Dale Dye to take charge of Tom and a handful of other actors during their training. The first week was at a camp in the USA and this was followed by a trip to the Philippines, where the battle shots for the movie would eventually be shot.

Stone then decided that, in order to make Tom's role look entirely authentic, they would inject him with a special serum that would paralyse him for two days at a time. Tom – by this time completely and utterly swept up in the project – agreed to Stone's suggestion immediately. Anything that would add authenticity to his part was OK by him. It took a very worried movie insurance broker to point out that if something went wrong they would not pay up to replace Tom and start the film all over again. The serum plan was finally abandoned. 'The point is, he was willing to do it,' Stone later recalled.

Tom then spent weeks in a wheelchair alongside his new found friend Kovic. It was an enlightening experience, exhausting both mentally and physically. On one occasion he nearly got in a fight with a store owner who objected to him being in his shop in the wheelchair because it might mark the carpet.

When *Vanity Fair* journalist Jesse Kornbluth showed up for a prearranged interview with Tom, he thought the star had failed to show up until he noticed a thin man in a wheelchair wearing a baseball cap with a Southern

Methodist University insignia, cheap checked shirt and jeans. He had dark, insomnia smudges under his eyes and a week's growth of beard. Suddenly the man in the wheelchair rolled alongside Kornbluth. 'Hey, I guess it's working.' Tom Cruise had arrived for his interview.

The journalist was stunned and impressed as he walked alongside paralysed Tom through a busy shopping centre. Not once was Tom recognised by the many shoppers, many of whom were some of Tom's most typical fans. Then Tom saw a kid in a wheelchair. He could not have been more than nine and his wheelchair was definitely not something borrowed for a movie.

Tom approached him, rolling his wheels gently yet smoothly. 'Hey man, what's your name?'

The boy told him.

'Some shopping center, huh?' came Tom's reply.

The boy agreed.

'Where are you from?'

Tom had friends there. They talked about the Olympics, the restaurant where the boy and his family ate lunch.

'Well, you take care of yourself,' Tom said. He patted the boy's arm and moved on. There was a dead silence. Kornbluth then asked Tom if he felt torn by the fact that he could actually walk in real life, that he could just get up and walk away from that wheelchair.

Tom replied: 'Listen, you talk to people in wheelchairs. They don't want to see me in a chair and they don't want you to feel sorry for them. They work like hell to live and be alive; if they didn't want to be alive, they wouldn't be. But seeing a boy in a wheelchair like that ... it's not easy. It's not easy to go home and say, "Hey, I'm getting it." '

Born also starred William Dafoe as Kovic's paraplegic soulmate Charlie, Raymond Barry as his father, Caroline

Kava as his mother and Kyra Sedgwick as his teenage love, Donna. However, no amount of co-stars could get away from the fact that all the pent-up primal feelings throughout the movie were expressed through Tom.

Much of the shooting of *Born* remains a complete blur – the battle scenes; the wounding; the sense of shame and alienation Ron Kovic felt when he returned to the USA.

Oliver Stone kept to a strict shooting schedule that frequently involved 12- or 13-hour days, often shouting nothing other than 'Action' at the assembled actors, followed a few seconds later by 'Do it!'

Stone became quite irritated when Tom threw a few temper tantrums on the set. Tom's already legendary attention to detail involved challenging everything from a line in a script to the exact shading of make-up. Oliver Stone admitted that while Cruise always tried to be decent to the people he worked with, his drive for a controlling sense of excellence could get in the way.

The upside of all this was that Tom meant well; his desire for control was tempered by a need to get it right. Like Kovic, he took himself very seriously, and when characters like that get hot in a culture that's often frivolous or superficial, they can miss a beat. In Tom's case, it sometimes bogged him down in his own intensity. But if Tom came across as a bit serious, hey, life can be serious too. As Tom said, at least he could get up out of that wheelchair after each scene; Ron Kovic never could.

Tom found shooting Kovic's hospital scenes the toughest part of all. In real life, Kovic had spent four months strapped to a bed in a desperate bid to save his leg. Tom had to try to be that character and, deep inside, it really hurt.

Tom's biggest problem was that, as he tried to be Kovic, he started to feel the same notes of desperation, the same disillusionment, the same rage at the government for the way they treated all those injured vets.

Next came the most visually and psychologically uncomfortable scenes for the audience – Kovic's living hell as an impotent man. A scene in a Mexican whorehouse catering especially for crippled Vietnam veterans drove home the point with typical Oliver Stone bluntness. Once again, the settings were of filth and degradation but Kovic is trading that against the minute chance that he might be able to achieve sexual satisfaction. As Kovic, Tom is shown paralysed from the waist down, with catheters running out of his crotch, so lonely that he risks potential humiliation for a woman's touch.

As he explained later, Tom's found those scenes harrowing.

'The way I work best is to be totally relaxed. I don't pretend to be the character; I am the character. But you know what struck me? Intellectually, philosophically, you sit back and you go, "Well, I'm someone who doesn't feel that being masculine is in my, you know, crotch. There are many other elements to being a human being and a man." But there were moments when I read the script, when it just struck me, WHAACK! to the marrow. Hold it! The realisation of losing that ...

'Reading those scenes it was right there in my face: you're going to play this. The loss of manhood. The loss of one's ability to create on a physical level. It's not just being able to feel a woman, to be inside a woman, it's being able to create a family. To procreate is a very important aspect to life. And where does that take you, if you can't?'

Tom sounded as if he clearly understood every one of the

torn emotions that Ron Kovic suffered. In later years his own wish to be a father would cause no end of anguish, so perhaps those words have rung in his ears ever since.

In the key bedroom scene in the movie, Tom found himself completely unable to perform for the camera for the first time in his entire career. This time it was nothing to do with immodesty or fears that such a scene was gratuitous. He got up from the set and walked to Oliver Stone's side and muttered quietly: 'I'm just not there. It's just not working.'

Later he explained: 'I remember feeling a lot of anxiety actually. Going, "Why do I feel all this anxiety?".'

Looking sternly at his young star, Stone was unrepentant. His reply sounded like that of a battle commander: 'Look. You got it. Just don't think about it. Just do it, man, do it.' Then he shrieked: 'Action! Snap to it Mr Cruise!'

But still Tom could not do it. He went through the motions for a few moments before the cameras, then broke down in floods of tears, unable to contain himself for a moment longer. All the memories of his childhood, his father, the pain, the loneliness just came flooding back. 'I was crying and laughing a little, too. It was an absolute relief. Essentially, I just let go.'

What happened in that scene occurred over and over again as Tom drove himself to the edge of his abilities. All that cold, clinical focus that he had always referred to so keenly had gone out of the window. In its place was good old-fashioned emotion. It was this kind of intensity and commitment that brought Tom universal praise for the quality of his performance in *Born*.

Ron Kovic himself was reduced to tears on many occasions as he watched from the edge of the movie set. 'I'm extremely proud of his performance,' says Kovic. 'I truly believe he actually becomes me.'

Just before heading to the Philippines for the final stage of the *Born* shoot, Tom started to wonder if perhaps he had taken on too much with the strenuous part. Every night was punctuated by appalling nightmares in which he was being shot in the jungle. The terrifying reality of the dream helped Tom to take stock of what he was doing. One lesson it taught him was that he had to learn how to loosen up, to move 'in and out' of a role more comfortably so that it didn't dominate his life to an unhealthy degree.

On the last day of shooting, Kovic took the Bronze Star he had kept in a box by the side of his bed for 21 years and gave it to Tom as a lasting tribute to his performance. 'I told him it was for his heroic performance,' added Kovic. In truth, it was a gesture of thanks from the crippled ex-soldier. Somehow, through Tom's performance, Kovic had exorcised many of the demons that had haunted him since the day he was shot in Vietnam. As a celebration of that, he wanted the young actor – still only 26 years old – to have his last actual reminder of the war. In turn, Tom gave Ron a watch that the vet still wears to this day.

Oliver Stone also hailed Tom's performance as heroic. After shooting was completed, he told the star he felt indebted to him for standing by his project because it meant that Stone could keep his promise – to himself; to his friend Ron Kovic; to tens of thousands of fellow veterans who share the wounds of Vietnam. 'We wanted to show America, and Tom, and through Tom, Ron, being put in the wheelchair, losing their potency. We wanted to show America being forced to redefine its concept of heroism.'

Despite this, the picture backer's, Universal, fought a raging battle with Tom's publicists to prevent them from releasing still photos of Tom in a wheelchair, for fear of turning the audience off. The studio was concerned about whether the film would attract the folk who had flocked to see Tom in the past. The young star was privately furious at this interference because he genuinely believed that he did not have a stereotypical audience. It deeply offended him even to consider such a thought.

After *Born* was released, Tom was proclaimed by many critics as having deftly made the transformation from screen cutsey to serious dramatic actor. Oliver Stone summed it up when he said: 'He's not the simplistic cardboard figure many believe. He's very serious. Committed.' *Newsweek* movie critic David Ansen reckoned: 'Cruise has been very smart by taking risks.'

In the *New York Post*, David Edelston acclaimed the movie as 'powerful, bombastic and furiously uneven.' Movie writer Edward Gross reckoned: 'Tom Cruise's portrayal of Ron Kovic is proof positive that he is one of the most versatile actors working in Hollywood today; a presence that will undoubtedly leave others of his generation behind in his wake.'

The movie went on to gross $70 million at the US box office alone, an incredible achievement when one considers how uncommercial the subject matter was.

The best news of all to come out of the *Born* project, as far as Tom was concerned, was that he was nominated for a Best Actor Oscar for his astounding performance as Kovic. Maybe this time he would stand a real chance. Hollywood sneerers instantly started predicting that *Driving Miss Daisy*, a gentle and subtle tale of an old lady and her black chauffeur, would overtake *Born* in the race for Oscars. Many of the old guard inside Tinseltown still felt that Tom ought to suffer a few more years for his art before he would merit a seat at the top table.

However, Tom's millions of fans in the United States thought otherwise. In a poll conducted on the eve of the Oscars ceremony in March 1990, 39 per cent of *New York*

Daily News readers reckoned that Tom should get the Best Actor award. Some movie experts believed that Tom would get the statue because he had not even been nominated for *Rain Man* the previous year and the Academy 'wants to kiss and make up'.

Tom was nominated and attended the ceremony but had to forgo the Governor's Ball and other post-Awards galas to get back to the set of *Days of Thunder*, which was shooting at Daytona Beach. Universal transported him to Los Angeles by private jet and then flew him back to the location just a few hours after the end of the ceremony.

Tom did not win the Oscar that year but he seemed genuinely delighted when British actor Daniel Day Lewis got the award for Best Actor for his work in *My Left Foot*. Tom knew that one day his time would come – it was only a matter of time. Just as long as he remained focused it would happen ... eventually.

After the ceremony he said sportingly: 'It's exciting just getting nominated. That acknowledgement from my peers. It's also good for movies. I believe in the Oscars, because I feel it's good for what we do. It's tradition.' And he wanted a part of that tradition – badly. Tom was actually fairly over-awed just to be sitting in the audience for the Oscars along-side such luminaries as Anjelica Huston, Jessica Lange, Jessica Tandy and Morgan Freeman.

Then, out of the blue, came a story that rocked Tom more than anything ever published about him before. In a huge page-one spread, the *News of the World* tabloid in Britain claimed that Tom had been secretly rushed to a hospital in Paris because he was suffering from breast cancer. The report went on to infer that Tom's mother, Mary Lee, had confirmed that her son was seriously ill. The article dropped like a bombshell in Hollywood. Anything that even remotely suggested that the world's biggest box office attraction might be ill was big news in the movie capital. Soon everyone was saying, 'Have you heard about Tom Cruise?'

Meanwhile, Tom's personal publicist, Andrea Jaffe, was juggling hundreds of press inquiries from around the world following the *News of the World* 'revelations'. She insisted that Tom's mother never gave an interview to the British tabloid and went on to warn that Tom's lawyers were considering legal action. 'Believe me,' insisted Jaffe, 'he's fine.'

Claims that Tom was also receiving treatment for breast cancer at Los Angeles's Cedar Sinai Hospital were also discounted.

Subsequent articles claimed that Tom had simply been suffering from a heavy bout of flu, but the damage had already been done. Some believe the rumours were started when Tom – in London on a get-away-from-it-all holiday with Mimi – interrupted his peace and quiet to attend a premiere of *Rain Man* sporting a startling shaved head, which had been done for a crucial scene at the end of shooting *Born*.

Later, Tom seemed remarkably jocular about the rumours, even though they gathered momentum to include a claim that he had developed AIDS. Many Hollywood insiders believe that Tom's *Born on the Fourth of July* haircut was definitely responsible. 'Some bright spark added two and two together and decided he was dying,' explained one Tinseltown source.

Tom saw the AIDS rumours as yet more evidence of the media's attempt to undermine his career. He made a note of the circumstances behind the stories that circulated and promised himself that, as his stardom grew, so would his ability to silence the gossip mongers ...

'This isn't film making, it's war.'

Tom Cruise

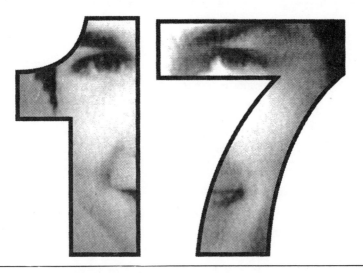

17

Tom's ever-increasing obsession with racing car competitions crystalised into his Hollywood persona towards the end of 1989. With megaproducers Don Simpson and Jerry Bruckheimer badgering him to commit to their sequel to *Top Gun*, Tom came up with the perfect solution – he decided his next motion picture should be the greatest car racing adventure ever filmed.

The idea of starring in a motor racing movie had been tucked neatly in the back of Tom's very focused mind ever since he drove his old friend Rick Hendrick's Winston Cup cars around Daytona – the most famous track in the world – three years earlier. After just a few laps of thrills and spills, Tom decided he had to make a movie about the profession.

He then quietly started his homework on the subject and carefully studied just about every race-car film ever made, including Paul Newman's own effort, entitled *Winning*, and a number of other even less auspicious flicks, like

Grand Prix, starring James Garner. Tom soon discovered that there had never been a truly great race-car film. He also could not have failed to notice that most of these movies were made after stars had expressed an interest in the subject and the films had then been built around their personalities. In other words, the drama had to be created out of nothing and that was always a bit of a problem.

'A lot of them didn't have a story, just the action. As a result, you felt separated from the movie,' explained Tom. 'I mean, I don't care how much machinery you have in a film. If I can't get involved with the characters, then for my money I'm not gonna enjoy it. I want the racing scenes to punctuate what's happening in the characters' lives.'

Tom wrote a brief outline and took it to Ned Tanen, a Paramount executive and fellow car freak. The studio then recruited screenwriter Donald Stewart to flesh out the young star's treatment. When a less-than-visionary script came back, Tanen and Tom took the idea to Simpson and Bruckheimer. It was an exact reverse of what happened with *Top Gun*. This time, the two savvy producers offered Tom all the advice and encouragement – they clearly saw the project as *Top Gun* on four wheels. The fact that there was not a decent script in sight did not bother them in the slightest. Don and Jerry could fix that easily!

Meanwhile, Tom was still explaining to all his friends and associates in Hollywood how he came to be so obsessed with starring in a race-car movie. They all listened eagerly, aware that this could be their meal ticket for the next year. 'I just became caught up with the people, their dedication to their profession and level of intensity,' an ever enthusiastic Tom told one Hollywood associate.

However, starting a new screenplay from the brief outline written with great care by Tom was not as easy as he thought it would be. Tom, Simpson and Bruckheimer hired Warran Skaaren (*Top Gun*, *Beetlejuice* and *Batman*) to write it. That was where the problems began. Tom, ever the perfectionist, forced the weary writer to produce dozens of drafts before he burned out and politely pulled away from the project.

Tom was feeling very frustrated by this stage. He actually thought that his idea was so strong that it would virtually write itself on the page but screenwriting is a severe test of patience; a bit like having a huge jigsaw puzzle with tens of thousands of pieces to put together. The notion that a writer could go home, sit down and knock out a perfect script is just not true. In reality, he goes home, writes a few pages, then rewrites them, then rewrites them and so on until he has achieved the basic shape of the story and then he goes back to the producer – in this case Tom – to be told, more often than not, to start again.

By the time Skaaren walked away from the race-car project – provisionally entitled 'Daytona' by this stage – Tom was starting to realise that a producer's role is not as easy as it seemed. He decided that he would try to land a really big name to mould his idea into a winning screenplay, so he went right to the top and hired Robert Towne, a legendary hellraiser and script writer of such classics as *Bonnie and Clyde*, *The Godfather* and *Chinatown*. You couldn't go much higher than that.

Tom was relieved and elated. He threw out Skaaren's original draft completely and got down to work with Towne. Within weeks, he was telling anyone who would listen: 'What's great about Bob Towne is that he just came in and understood the world. He focused on the piece. He liked these people. I remember after an hour – we had gone to a race track – he said, "I get it, Cruise. I know what you're talking about. This is fantastic." That was exciting.'

Naturally, Tom saw his project as more than just fast,

throbbing cars cutting in and out of beefcake shots of himself. 'It's manipulating a vehicle with tremendous power around a track. The level of competition is driver to driver. It's modern day gladiators. It's a war. There's a tremendous amount of dignity in the characters and in the people I've met just hanging around the circuit.'

Tom believed that racing cars was not that different from making movies. Both professions required complete and utter dedication, working sometimes 14 hours a day, seven days a week, often for ten months of the year. Just like on a film set, a family is created by this process and everyone goes through the ups and downs together. However, those close to Tom at the time say that he became so embroiled, even in the pre-production stages of the development of 'Daytona', that he might not have been quite focusing on the wood for the trees ...

Teaming up with Simpson and Bruckheimer, his old acquaintances from *Top Gun*, certainly made Tom feel more secure about the project's viability. He believed that, as long as the dynamic duo were running their side of things, then it would surely end up being a highly commercial project. When *Top Gun* director Tony Scott climbed on board, the word in Hollywood was that this was one movie that simply could not fail. Tom publicly declared that he liked to work with people he knew, although he was very careful not to give the impression that their partnership would last beyond that actual movie.

Don Simpson was well aware of the comparisons being made between this new project and the successful *Top Gun* and he didn't mind one bit. He knew that if Tom would not agree to do a *Top Gun* sequel, then this was the next best thing. Simpson also realised that making a movie about racing cars was going to be no easier than their previous outing with those mach-one pilots. He explained:

'In *Top Gun* we shot the ground story, then the sea story, then the air story. It was like shooting three separate movies. This time, we have dramatic scenes and then all the racing. And the racing is nearly impossible for us to predict or control. But we're going to take the image of stock car racing as most of the public perceive it and turn it around. We're going to show them how high tech and professional it really is.'

Jerry Bruckheimer insisted: 'I don't think there's ever been pressure to produce a big film. What we try to do is make effective films and films that we are real proud of. To satisfy myself, there's always pressure, creative pressure to do something different, unique.' Brave words ...

Apart from *Born on the Fourth of July*, which was a completely Oliver Stone-led operation, Tom had been allowed to have a large say in the casting of his previous three or four movies and in this project, now renamed *Days of Thunder*, he was going to use that clout to devastating effect. His initial insistence on casting Australian actress Nicole Kidman was eventually to change his life.

Veteran actor Robert Duvall was hired to play yet another father figure to Tom's character of Cole Trickle. Filming of *Days of Thunder* got underway in November 1989.

Within weeks, rumours were spreading around Hollywood that the project's actual production costs had soared way beyond the original estimate of $30 million. The studio backing the film had insisted that the movie be ready for an autumn 1990 release, which meant that director Tony Scott would have to edit the entire movie at an incredibly fast pace in order to complete on time. Every day new pressures were heaped on the producers and director.

Then there was Tom. He was starting to spot holes in the script that he had not noticed before shooting began. Bob Towne had to be on hand throughout the entire shoot to make last-minute revisions as Tom and Scott tried desperately to polish the script even further. The situation wasn't helped by the fact that few people on the set had realised that Tom was becoming completely diverted by his co-star Nicole Kidman. The pair only exchanged glances and smiles to start with but it was clearly building up into something much more serious.

In the middle of all this, Tom took a spin round the Charlotte Motor Speedway track in Carolina and set a new track record, averaging 166 mph. It was almost as if he was trying to prove he could do it for real as well as in the movies.

For much of the time, filming of *Days of Thunder* was hampered by foul weather conditions. Unexpected rainstorms and a severe freezing spell made racing scenes especially difficult to shoot.

In the middle of all this (January 1990) Tom made the cover of the prestigious *Time* magazine as a tribute to his extraordinary performance in *Born on the Fourth of July*. The background to the article provides a fascinating insight into how it can often help to have friends in high places. Over the years, Tom had built up quite a rapport with *Rolling Stone* owner Jann Wenner and, as a result, had received rather more than his fair share of coverage in the magazine, including an appearance on its cover at virtually the same time as the *Time* magazine piece was published.

Tom was so worried that he might offend Wenner by appearing on the cover of *Time* as well that he rang the publisher to explain the situation behind his decision. 'When Tom first told Jann about the cover, Jann was a little upset,' revealed a source.

Then, in an astonishing example of Cruise control at its mightiest, Universal Studios chairman Tom Pollock (the studio which backed *Born on the Fourth of July*) called Jann and appealed to his sense of friendship and the two men agreed that it would be OK for Tom to appear on the cover of *Time* magazine. Ironically – and some would say typically – Tom still managed to insist on the *Rolling Stone* article being penned by a writer he approved of.

Back on the *Days of Thunder* shoot, Tom, ever the focused one, came up with a novel solution to keep up with the ever-changing script. He taped pieces of the screenplay on to the car's dashboard, so that he could recite dialogue while zooming around the track. It was a dangerous habit which diverted his concentration on a number of occasions, not something to be recommended when doing 150 mph on one of the fastest race circuits in the world. Somehow, Tom avoided any serious crashes but there were numerous dented fenders.

Days of Thunder's backers, Paramount, sent teams of executives down to Daytona to make sure that Tom and his co-stars were not taking any unnecessary risks as their insurance policies did not allow the stars to get involved in the thick of the racing action. Secretly, Tom insisted on doing his own share of stunts because he wanted the movie to look as authentic as possible.

When Paramount decided to bring forward the US release of *Days of Thunder* to the 4 July holiday weekend of 1990, Tony Scott and his team of editors found themselves with just six weeks to complete post-production of the movie – a process that usually takes at least six months. It was even decided to shoot an extra love scene between Tom and Nicole Kidman in a thinly disguised attempt to cash in on the couple's real-life love affair.

Producers Bruckheimer and Simpson tried to avoid

talking to Scott towards the end of that day's extra shooting, following heated exchanges between the pair and their director. They simply did not have time left to allow the director to shoot any extra footage. Paramount were putting enormous pressure on the entire production because the film's escalating costs had convinced them to release it earlier than planned in order to get their huge investment back as fast as possible.

That extra day's shooting finally ended at four the following morning and Tom immediately threw himself into his role in the post-production process by visiting the editing room, cutting, looping dialogue and then taking care of TC Productions business during the evening. It was a gruelling schedule but Tom relished every minute of it, although, curiously, he did not wear a watch, which played havoc with his time keeping.

'It's exciting because it really puts you absolutely to the limit,' he explained. No wonder Simpson and Bruckheimer nicknamed Tom 'Laserhead' after finishing *Days of Thunder*. Tom had a simple explanation for his nickname. 'Because when I focus in on something I kinda tear it apart until I understand it. But it takes a laserhead to know a laserhead.'

In the end, *Days of Thunder* knew exactly which buttons to push to keep an audience as finely tuned as one of Tom's cars. Tony Scott's direction was as effective as ever in the circumstances but the film was missing a heart and soul. It seemed like a classic formula movie without any real punch and much of the blame was laid at the door of the screenplay. 'The biggest problem with the film are aspects of the screenplay. There's nothing wrong with pure escapism, but many parts of the story are so formula and so much like *Top Gun*, it's annoying,' wrote film critic Edward Gross.

Basically, too many cooks were involved in *Days of Thunder* and the script paid the ultimate price. Tom, Scott,

Simpson and Bruckheimer all wanted a say and for a writer of Bob Towne's calibre it was a nightmare. He allowed them all to have some input and the result was a hotch-potch of formula ideas.

There were also very strong rumours about the ever-escalating budget of the film. By the time of its release, estimates ranged in the $60–$70 million range, making it one of the most expensive movies ever made. Tom got a $10 million fee for his troubles.

The reviews were predictably appalling. 'It is one thing to market a film solely on the strength of its star. It's quite another to go ahead and make the film that way,' wrote the icy Janet Maslin, referring to Paramount's multi-million-dollar promotional campaign, launched weeks before the movie's premiere in a desperate attempt to cash in on Tom's so-called star appeal.

Tom even had to grit his teeth and be charming to the media as part of the push to promote *Days of Thunder*. Women writers were literally lined up to take it in turns to do a few laps with him on the Daytona circuit, all in the name of good publicity. Some of them were mightily disappointed. Wrote Jeanne Marie Laskas in *Life* magazine:

'He doesn't look like Tom Cruise. He's a lot smaller than Tom Cruise. Small hips, small shoulders, just plain little. I wonder how they made him look so big in the movies. I wonder why these movie people have lightened his hair and also permed it. It doesn't look good. It looks overdone, exhausted, as if to shout, "Just leave me alone already!" – a sentiment very much in keeping with the mood here today.'

Then followed a terrifying 180-mph tour of the circuit that

reduced Laskas to a virtual gibbering wreck as she became queasy and dizzy. After numerous pleas to return safely to the pits, Tom finally rolled to a halt with a grin on his face that was subtle evidence that he had just scored a major victory over the piranhas.

Movie critic Marilyn Moss wrote just as damningly: '*Days of Thunder* is a minor film with major pretensions, not to mention a major noise factor that barely masks what the story lacks in believability.'

Women reviewers seemed to find the film particularly unappealing. In the *Philadelphia Inquirer* Carrie Rickey wrote: 'Not only does *Days of Thunder* disappoint on the basic narrative level, it is also a peculiarly thrill-less action movie. Shot from the driver's point of view, the race sequences lose their novelty as swiftly as a video game.'

Soon everyone was on the bandwagon. In the *Los Angeles Times Days of Thunder* was described as a 'fake of a film'. The highly respected *Hollywood Reporter* dubbed it a 'very fast film by its nature with some story wobbles'. Last word goes to Henry Sheehan of the *Los Angeles Reader*: 'As soon as the screen is empty of speeding cars it is empty of their impact as well.'

In the middle of all this, Tom was highly embarrassed to be voted *People* magazine's Sexiest Man of the Year. Previous winners included Sean Connery, John F. Kennedy, Harry Hamlin, Mark Harmon and Mel Gibson.

Other problems for *Days of Thunder* occurred when the American Humane Society slammed into the moviemakers for allowing the slaughter of some innocent seagulls. Apparently, the unfortunate incident occurred when two cars were racing against each other on Daytona Beach and, in order to get a shot of the gulls scattering when the cars approached, members of the crew were ordered to scatter some food on the sand to attract the birds. Two gulls died, reported the society, after being hit by the approaching cars. The society concluded: 'Although the film crew was grossly negligent in the luring of the birds to achieve the desired effect, it is not felt that the intent to commit the injury was deliberate. But this accident could have been avoided.' As a result of the incident, *Days of Thunder* was rated 'marginal' by the society's movie review board.

Tom refused to concede that there had been problems and even talked in glowing terms about *Days of Thunder* being a so-called big picture and why he would continue to make them.

> 'My favourite thing is to go to a film opening night or opening weekend and sit there and have a group experience. I enjoy films that run the gamut ... I'm looking for what's going to have the greatest impact, what's going to communicate. But I look at everything. I just haven't found anything small that I felt was interesting enough for me to spend the time.
>
> 'When I'm making a film, it's a year out of my life, I mean, I've been working on *Days of Thunder* for a year and a half, really, and for a year straight of seven days a week. So you have to believe in what you're doing and love it, because there are sacrifices. When I do something, I have to feel 100 per cent committed.'

Days of Thunder went on to gross more than $80 million at the box office but it was still deemed to be a failure as the original costs of the movie would have swallowed up all of the profit. It also managed to make the 'worst movie of the year' lists in many publications.

Shortly after *Days of Thunder* wrapped, Tom was, by

his own admission, about 90 per cent committed to a highly controversial role as a drug-addicted undercover policeman in *Rush*, a movie based on the real-life memoirs of a Texan policewoman called Kim Wozencraft. His only dilemma about the part was that he had turned down the lead in *Bright Lights, Big City* and this was another movie that had a very ominous drug-taking content. Tom admitted that he was concerned about the project and told producer Richard Zanuck that he would make a commitment to it once he saw the finished script, which was being written by his *Days of Thunder* collaborator Robert Towne.

Eventually, Tom turned down the controversial role and it went to Julia Roberts's one-time beau Jason Patrick. Around this time, Tom also found himself being offered another off-the-wall part as *Edward Scissorhands* for Twentieth Century-Fox. *Batman* director Tim Burton was to helm the project which was described as a modern-day *Elephant Man* yarn. For some inexplicable reason, Tom pulled out of starring in the movie and that role went to teenage heart-throb Johnny Depp instead. Another role that never came to fruition was *The Curious Case of Benjamin Button* for Universal. The F. Scott Fitzgerald short story had been turned into a screenplay by writer Robin Swincoard and there was speculation that Steven Spielberg was slated to be director. Once again, this was a project that faded from sight for Tom. Then came the supposed pairing of Tom with Eddie Murphy for *Out West* with veteran Walter Hill at the helm. Again, Tom dropped out for no apparent reason. However, there would be plenty more offers. Tom knew he could well afford to wait for the perfect platform.

'You have to assume there are small-minded or nasty people out there. And for some reason it makes them feel better to think, "That little no-talent slut, she just looks for celebrities to date."'

Mimi Rogers

'My need to achieve was really great. It took its toll on the marriage.'

Tom Cruise

18

A few months before starting rehearsals for *Days of Thunder*, Tom went to a private screening of a small-budget, but highly acclaimed, Australian film called *Dead Calm*. The movie was directed with great skill by Australian Philip Noyce and starred New Zealander Sam Neill, one of the most accomplished actors ever to come out of the Southern Hemisphere.

However, it was Neill's co-star who caught Tom's eye. Nicole Kidman was just 20 years old when she played the part of the wife of naval officer Neill. The film centred around the story of a couple setting off on a yacht for a vacation following the tragic death of their child in a car crash. Somehow, despite Nicole's pre-Raphaelite shoulder-length red hair and porcelain features, she managed to be convincing as a housewife and all who saw her performance proclaimed her as a big star of tomorrow.

Tom was entranced as he watched *Dead Calm*, which

featured some harrowing scenes, including Nicole's rape by a man who breaks into their yacht, leaving her husband floating helplessly in the ocean. That girl, he decided, would be his co-star in *Days of Thunder*. So it was that Nicole Kidman landed the role of Dr Claire Lewicki and became Tom's love interest on, and eventually off, the big screen.

From the moment Tom met Nicole, during a casting session in the autumn of 1989, he knew that his marriage to Mimi Rogers would have to be sacrificed. Initially, the actor fought against falling in love with Nicole but every time he found himself alone with Mimi he could not put Nicole out of his mind. On a number of occasions during those difficult months in the latter half of 1989, he moved out of the couple's luxurious house in Brentwood, Los Angeles and went to stay with friends – only to move back in with Mimi after a few days away.

Mimi obviously realised that they were having marital problems but she genuinely felt they could talk it through. She made Tom attend marriage guidance counselling through the Scientologists. However, the few sessions the couple attended did nothing to improve the situation. Even a number of quiet dinners together in small Brentwood restaurants ended in temper tantrums all round. It was becoming clear to all of Tom and Mimi's friends and associates that the marriage was in deep trouble.

At first, Tom hid his true feelings about Nicole by claiming that the main reason for his marital problems was that he felt he had outgrown Mimi – even though she was at least six years older than him. He reportedly told one friend: 'I may be younger but it seems to me that she's the one who really has some growing to do.'

One of the friends Tom went to stay with was actor Emilio Estevez. The two stars had been friends since Tom first arrived in Hollywood. Tom even encouraged Emilio –

best man at his wedding to Mimi less than three years earlier – to console Mimi. He hoped that Emilio might be able to talk some sense into Mimi and either help to mend their broken marriage or – much more likely – suggest that she 'should just let it go'.

It all sounds terribly civilised, although the truth was that Tom felt riddled with guilt about Nicole, even though there is no suggestion that he began a physical relationship with her until later.

In early December, Mimi Rogers flew to Florida to be with Tom during the filming of *Days of Thunder*. She still hoped to save their marriage. Within hours of her arrival, Tom asked for a divorce and told the stunned actress: 'I'm with Nicole now.'

Mimi was completely shattered and took the first plane back to Los Angeles. She knew there was no point in trying to make it work. Tom had made up his mind – there was nothing left between them. The end had been sudden and clinical – a bit like a business deal that had gone wrong.

Later, Tom told writer James Greenberg that he considered his split from Mimi as

'no different from what other people go through. You've got to confront it and say, "Okay, where do you take it from here?" You handle it and take responsibility for what occurred and move on. It's as simple and not as simple as that. As years go by, it's not even something I think about; after a couple of years you go, "What were those issues?" I'm living now.'

Tom defended his decision to dump Mimi in favour of Nicole by telling Greenberg, 'It just seemed right. I think anyone who has met Nicole would understand. It was like nothing occurred before, and just because you get divorced doesn't mean that's it. I was ready, I was really excited.'

The actor was already blotting Mimi out of his mind like some bad dream.

Tom also told Greenberg: 'My divorce was something that had to be done.' He refused to acknowledge that his own parents' divorce made the split with Mimi even more difficult. 'I think anyone who has been through a divorce can't believe it's happening to them, whether you come from a divorced family or not.'

Mimi returned to Los Angeles stunned by Tom's request for a divorce. Within days his lawyers were in touch. They wanted to hammer out a deal that would make the split as painless (and non-controversial) as possible. The top secret negotiations meant that Mimi would end up with a fortune, including the house in Brentwood, West Los Angeles, leaving her wealthy enough never to have to work again. Conservative estimates put the entire settlement in the $10 million range.

A reported call by Paul Newman to Tom, advising him to reconsider ending his marriage, got the young actor thinking about whether he was right or wrong to split up with Mimi. Newman told him: 'Time heals all wounds. Joanne and I learned that a long time ago.' Tom was impressed that Paul Newman had found the time to talk to him but he did not think it was the right advice in the circumstances.

Just before Christmas 1989, Tom forgot his own marital problems and slipped quietly into a hospital in Fort Mill, South Carolina to give a boost to a ten-year-old girl waiting for a heart transplant. Little Brandi Mason could not believe her eyes when her idol walked in clutching a hat and shirt from *Days of Thunder* Tom autographed her pillowcase before visiting some of the other sick children in the hospital. It was a pleasant diversion after all the emotional upheaval.

On the *Days of Thunder* set, Tom and Nicole were very careful to keep their friendship out of everyone's sight. Tom did not want anything to upset his carefully laid plans for a smooth and satisfactory divorce from Mimi.

On New Year's Eve 1989–90, Tom splashed out $13,000 for a party for the rest of the cast and crew on location in Charlotte, North Carolina. Despite going through one of his regular teetotaller stages, Tom was still happy to pay for the bash as it was his way of saying 'thank you' to the *Days of Thunder* team for all their sterling efforts. Wearing a red cardigan over a simple white T-shirt and jeans, Tom shook lots of hands and talked with many people. Nicole Kidman kept her distance from Tom throughout the evening. That relationship would be kept under lock and key for a while longer. Tom did not want to appear to be rubbing in the fact that he had a new love.

'He was a very gracious host,' recalled *Days of Thunder* caterer Wanda Edwards. 'I saw him walk over to people and see if they were having a good time. He shakes with both hands, a real warm handshake.' The crowd that night mostly left him alone but when Tom stepped into a department store in Charlotte to do some shopping, the whole place erupted. Reported Edwards: 'I went in there about 15 minutes after he left and traffic had stopped moving and all the girls working there were out in the middle of the floor screaming.' Tom beat a hasty retreat.

There was a drastic, and unexpected, knock on effect from all this activity. Friends and colleagues on the set of *Days of Thunder* reported that Tom changed into a much more relaxed character after his friendship with Nicole began to blossom. He no longer felt the same level of intensity which had haunted his final few months of marriage. Nicole's motto was 'Life is for living'. She was about to re-educate Tom along those lines. Nicole was a refreshingly, unaffected, down-to-earth, typically Aussie girl with a spark and vitality for life which Tom had never encountered in Hollywood before.

By the beginning of January 1990, Tom still refused to admit publicly that his marriage to Mimi was in the process of being dismantled, despite the rumours flying around the *Days of Thunder* set. Back in Los Angeles, Mimi tried to get over the shock of Tom's request for a divorce by being seen out in public with Emilio Estevez. They were photographed by members of Hollywood's infamous paparazzi outside a nightclub and, according to one report, were seen holding hands at a pizza parlour called Damiano's. One so-called friend was quoted in a US tabloid as saying: 'Mimi thinks you have to fight fire with fire.' At that stage no official announcement had yet been made about the couple's split. No one realised that Mimi and Emilio's friendship had been sanctioned by Tom himself.

Estevez persuaded Mimi to fly to the *Days of Thunder* set to make one last appeal to Tom to save their marriage. Mimi held a teary-eyed meeting with Tom on 11 January at the Charlotte Hilton-University Place hotel, but Tom told her it was too late.

Tom's cousin and childhood friend William Mapother told one publication that the couple's joint membership of the Scientologists had partly led to the divorce situation. 'Cousellors for that religious group have told them that if they're unhappy together, they should divorce,' William was quoted as saying.

For once, the outrageous US tabloids seemed to have been one step ahead with the story. Before any news of the break-up had been officially released, *Globe* ran a piece that was splashed across an entire page, headlined 'Wife gives Cruise the boot'.

The story quoted a source close to Tom as saying: 'The marriage is in serious trouble. They're having big problems.'

However, the most intriguing aspect of the piece came in a claim that the couple felt under a lot of pressure to have a baby. It read: 'They've had no luck, but Tom is still desperate to have a child. He's almost fanatical about it.' *Globe* claimed that, during a discussion about parenthood in October 1989, 'things got out of hand and they got into a real screamfest. Mimi hit the roof and she yelled at Tom to pack his bags and get out of the house.' (Ironically, in August 1994 a delighted Mimi announced she was expecting her first child by longstanding boyfriend Chris. Interestingly, there were no references made to her struggle to get pregnant while married to Tom.)

References to Mimi being heartbroken about not getting pregnant may not be accurate but there is little doubt that the couple were feeling under intense pressure to start a family. There was even talk of Mimi seeking fertility treatment.

Just after that final meeting at the Charlotte Hilton-University Place Hotel, divorce papers were secretly filed in Los Angeles. Tom told friends it was the honourable way out of the relationship as he was starting to feel a certain amount of wanderlust and, rather than sneak around behind his wife's back, he would rather be completely honest with her.

The actual divorce papers were filed on 16 January, citing as petitioner 'Thomas Cruise' and the respondent as 'Miriam Cruise, aka Mimi Rogers Cruise'. The petition (No. WED 052576), signed personally by Tom on 12 January after his attorney had flown out specially to the *Days of Thunder* set in North Carolina, was for a dissolution of the marriage and gave as the date of actual separation 9 December 1989. It cited 'irreconcilable differences'.

The most interesting aspect of the very brief divorce papers filed at Los Angeles County's Superior Court of California is the fact that Tom requested confirmation of the couple's separate assets and obligations and a line had been typed on the form which read: 'All such assets and obligations of the parties have been confirmed by written agreement.' On the following page, under a section marked 'Property rights to be determined', his lawyer had typed 'in accordance with written agreement'. In other words, a deal had already been struck, Tom and his attorneys had managed to get Mimi's complete agreement on a split of possessions even before news of the separation was made public.

The following day, in a tersely worded statement, the couple said: 'While there have been positive aspects to our marriage, there were some issues which could not be resolved even after working on them for a period of time.'

Tom defended his decision not to admit earlier that his marriage was in trouble by saying: 'I felt that to compromise our privacy was to compromise a basic trust. I hope that can be understood.'

Rolling Stone were furious that Tom had sat through their earlier interview without admitting that his marriage was in trouble. Writer Trip Gabriel had even asked Tom point blank about his marriage problems. If this was a special relationship with a magazine, then goodness knows how many lies Tom would tell if he did not like the publication, they reasoned. Senior Editor Peter Travers complained: 'He sort of talked around the issues. We feel misled by what happened.'

Time magazine film critic Richard Corliss probably summed it up best when he said: 'His was an Academy Award-worthy performance. He gave it to all reporters. Every celebrity plays a game. Tom Cruise was giving one of his best performances by playing Tom Cruise.'

Tom was severely criticised in the media for the role he played in covering up the fact that his marriage to Mimi was in trouble. The prestigious *Newsweek* magazine even ran a piece on 29 January 1990, headlined: 'The great Tom Cruise cover-up'.

> 'Who said that the tabloids are always wrong and that serious magazines are always right? And furthermore, who ever said Tom Cruise always tells the truth? Case in point: last week's announcement that Cruise and his wife, actress Mimi Rogers, are getting a divorce. While such, shall we say, colourful publications as the Star have reported the couple's marital woes ad nauseam, Cruise charmed and fudged his way past the more respected magazines. In the January 11 Rolling Stone: "I couldn't imagine being without her or being alone." In the December 25 Time: "The most important thing for me is I want Mimi to be happy." On January 22 he told US magazine, "I just really enjoy our marriage." It should be pointed out that, in a joint statement issued last week, the unhappy couple noted that "there were some issues which could not be resolved even after working on them for a period of time." That period of time, presumably, covered the quotations in question, which Cruise later apologised for.'

The entire cover-up operation had misfired badly for Tom, who actually thought that his denials would be stored away and forgotten about.

Tom didn't realise that these public attacks on him were the result of what the media perceived to be a deception on his part. He saw nothing wrong with lying to the press for the sake of his own privacy but they seemed deeply offended that he should dare to do such a thing.

At the time Tom only agreed to one request for a media interview and that came from ten-year-old Sarah Lawing, who managed to scoop a chat with the star for her school newspaper. He allotted her five minutes and part of that time was taken up by Tom trying to help Sarah, from Long Creek, North Carolina, to operate her tape recorder. Perhaps unsurprisingly, Tom did not mention his split-up with Mimi and little Sarah commented afterwards: 'I was disappointed. I have on my tape that he was married.' But that did not ruin the little girl's day. She added: 'After he drove away, I just stood there thinking about what had happened that day. I'll never forget that day.' Tom must have been wondering why all his interviews could not be as pleasant as that one.

On 22 January, Tom faced the full might of the world's press at the annual Golden Globe Awards ceremony where he picked up a Best Actor trophy for *Born on the Fourth of July*. The young star tried desperately to avoid shouted questions as he left the festivities at the Beverly Hilton Hotel in Los Angeles. But when the press turned their attentions towards his mother Mary Lee he looked about ready to explode.

Mary Lee, however, was more than capable of looking after herself. 'It's a personal thing. I have nothing to add,' she told reporters with great professionalism and coolness.

The following month, Mimi – already resigned to becoming an ex-Mrs Tom Cruise – threw a birthday party celebration that was described as her 'coming-out party, of sorts'.

For months after the divorce papers were filed, Mimi found it difficult even to mention Tom's name. After all, she honestly believed that she had fallen in love with Tom all those years earlier when they first set eyes on each other at that dinner party hosted by mutual friends. She had thought their union would last forever. Now she had a lot of time on her hands and started to do some intense thinking about where the relationship went wrong. She even admitted to friends, in roundabout terms, how difficult her marriage to Tom had been, especially the fact that he was a successful actor.

She had the distinct impression Tom had become an object of such extreme attention that it had, inevitably, made him much more demanding to the people around him. Mimi came away from her marriage to Tom convinced that actors were definitely more emotionally immature than the rest of the world.

She had witnessed at first hand the coddling and cotton wool treatment and firmly believed it had contributed to the break-up. Mimi reckoned that success had hit Tom so suddenly that his entire world had turned upside down. Virtually overnight, he had become the focus of a tremendous amount of attention. Everybody wanted to be his best friend and nobody would dare to say no to him. Mimi felt that perhaps he had lost his footing because no one would criticise him. In many ways, she wished that his success had come more slowly, then he would have been able to learn along the way and make adjustments in order to work out what was real and what was an illusion.

Until just a few months before the break-up, Mimi genuinely believed that Tom was someone who was secure enough to open up emotionally. She saw him as very tender and caring, which was just the way she liked men to be. Eventually, however, she noticed that he developed a more compulsive, even a slightly obsessive, personality – and she found that very annoying. She had always loved Tom because he was not the kind of man who thought emotion was a sign of weakness but that attitude had changed enormously towards the end of their marriage as the cracks began to appear. Mimi – a strong independent spirit – found it difficult to cope with the changes.

The final evidence of that change came in the months after the separation, when Tom's people insisted on a complex set of rules and regulations that Mimi knew she had to obey. This was all part of the Tom Cruise machinery, now in charge of a carefully orchestrated damage control operation designed specifically to avoid Tom being embroiled in an unpleasant tit-for-tat divorce with Mimi.

Tom's team of image makers – lawyers, movie executives, agents – all wanted to preserve the wholesome image of their 'property'. The result was that Mimi was restricted to an oblique interview with *Hello!*, during which she had to pretend she was not talking about Tom when, in fact, the whole world knew she was.

Tom didn't really care that much for the media. At that time, one New York paper published a story claiming he had sent one of his two golden retrievers to an animal psychiatrist for therapy. That hardly earned his respect. 'People so easily – blindly – believe what they read. For example, I read the paper and see so many things about myself that are so untrue. When I started out, I'd think, "Those mother fuckers – I am going to go out and get every one of them!" ' he told one startled writer at the time.

As the weeks of 1990 turned to months, Tom and Nicole started to become a definite item, although most members of the cast and crew of *Days of Thunder* were still only aware of gossip about the couple. On the set, the couple were very careful not to be seen showing any signs of affection towards one another. After the film moved location to Daytona Beach, Florida, however, the couple dined out regularly at the Olive Garden restaurant, part of a nationwide chain, and shopped at Publix market for burgers and other cookout fare. Tom even took Nicole skydiving.

The ultimate proof of their blossoming affair came during their first simultaneous parachute jump. As they hurtled earthward at 110 mph – with instructors by their side – speed demon Tom swooped in and planted a kiss on Nicole's mouth ... their union was sealed. Before they left Florida, Tom bought four top-of-the-line skydiving rigs, two for himself and two for Nicole – total cost, a mere $10,000. What he did not reveal at the time was that he had been skydiving throughout the making of *Days of Thunder*, behind the backs of the film's insurers.

Tom managed to get himself stopped when driving at 66 mph in a 35-mph zone on 2 March in Darlington, North Carolina. Fearful of bad publicity if they dropped the charges, officials eventually fined him a paultry $125 after city judge Dan Causey reduced the charge to careless operation of a vehicle, which carried no point penalty.

Soon Tom and Nicole were appearing in public in Daytona Beach, hand in hand. It was very noticeable because Nicole is a good two inches taller than Tom. However, Tom was so completely besotted by Nicole that her height seemed irrelevant. Significantly, up until that point in his career, Tom had never once asked for built-up insteps, or any other false measures to avoid revealing his shortness.

Days of Thunder producer Jerry Bruckheimer also confirmed Tom's complete lack of sensitivity concerning his height – at a conservative guess definitely no more than five feet nine inches. 'It's not like dealing with Alan Ladd, where they had to stand him on apple boxes. With Tom we don't even toy with camera techniques.' True or false, Tom was proving to be the consummate pro on a film set.

Fellow-star Mel Gibson – another short character at just

over five foot eight inches – spent his early years constantly being made to look taller through a number of ingenious pieces of skulduggery which have been traditional in movie-land since the start of film making. He never forgot the time he appeared in a little known Australian movie with a six feet five inch co-star and the other guy ended up crouching on all fours for every close-up!

Tom and Nicole took a break from the bone-shattering shooting schedule of *Days of Thunder* and turned up at the 1990 Oscars hand in hand, the final public proclamation of their relationship. Tom's mother Mary Lee looked on proudly at her son and his new lover. Tom had given his mother three $10,000 hand-beaded designer gowns to choose from for the big event. That Easter, Tom even took Mary Lee, then aged 50, for a parachute jump with Nicole and planted a mid-air kiss on her as well as on his girlfriend!

By April 1990 – as the *Days of Thunder* team continued shooting highly complex racing scenes at Daytona Beach – Tom and Nicole were openly romancing each other. Tom's rented white BMW and Harley-Davidson motorbike were frequently parked outside the luxurious apartment leased for Nicole a mile from Tom's place on the exclusive Fly-In resort, complete with its own private runway in the backyard.

In keeping with Tom's unwillingness to strip for movies, he curtly refused to remove his underpants for a shower scene in *Days of Thunder*. Some Hollywood observers speculated that Tom's romance with Nicole was a likely influence on this decision.

Besides seeing Nicole, Tom also spent a lot of time in Florida with actor John Travolta. The two celebrities were both heavily committed members of the Church of Scientology and appeared to have a lot in common.

However, it was Tom's love affair with Nicole that dominated his life. He felt as if he had finally found true happiness.

'My agent is the only person who understands what I really want. And my wife. Other people just don't get it.'

Tom Cruise

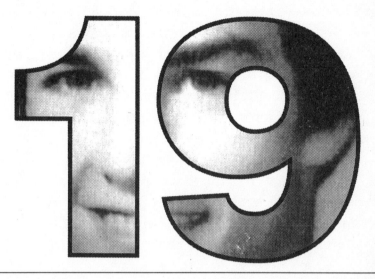

19

Nicole Kidman will probably loathe the notion but she really did start living a fairytale life from the moment she caught Tom Cruise's eye. She'll loathe it not only because it's a cliché but also because it betrays the true perspective of her life. Fantastic things may happen to and around her but, at heart, according to friends and family, she has remained unchanged from the bouncy little girl who grew up happy and secure in a big family in Sydney, Australia.

From the periphery, at least, the fairytale analogy is hard to ignore. For Nicole, time has done anything but stand still. The young actress had already made a reasonable name for herself in a handful of Australian mini-series and television shows before grabbing the lead in the movie *Dead Calm*, which opened up her world and led her into the arms of Tom.

Nicole left Australia in the autumn of 1989, amid goodbye tears from her mother, father and sisters ...

basically off on a wing and a prayer. She had absolutely no idea if her grandiose plan to make it as an actress in Hollywood would work. All her friends inside the Australian movie industry warned her that it would be tough and to expect it to take at least five years to get any decent parts.

However, Nicole wasn't in the least bit worried. She's the sort of girl whose spirit and vitality override any fears of the outside world. If it didn't work out, she thought to herself, then so be it. However, even her eternal optimism could never have foreseen the chance encounters that would lie ahead.

The key to Nicole's character lies in her safe, secure, happy background. It is the exact opposite of Tom Cruise's upbringing in that her family always remained together and they moved home about once in her entire childhood.

Tom had learned from his marriage to Mimi Rogers that two likes don't necessarily make a happy union inside wedlock. Even at the pinnacle of his career, there was an underlying current of insecurity in Tom's character. What he really needed was someone who could be outgoing, entertaining and loving but also capable of accepting him for what he was and providing the security net he so desperately craved.

Nicole's family consists of her father Dr Anthony Kidman, her mother Janelle and younger sister Antonia. Nicole was actually born in Honolulu while her father was a student at the University of Hawaii, and thus gained duel Australian-American citizenship which allowed her later to work in the United States unhindered by visa problems. The family eventually moved to Sydney's northern suburbs, the sort of area where just about any parents would be happy to bring up their children – rolling hills to the west, hundreds of miles of sandy beaches to the east and an atmosphere of safety that would be difficult to match anywhere else in the civilised world.

op left: Tom's grandfather. Thomas Cruise Mapother Jnr. in 1948.
op right: Tom's great-grandmother Mrs Thomas Cruise Mapother, then aged 80, at a azaar in Louisville in 1957.
ottom left: Tom's great-great-grandfather Dillon Mapother, who emigrated to ouisville from Ireland in the mid-1800s.
ottom right: The impressive eight-bedroom mansion near the centre of Louisville, here Tom's great-great-uncle Wible Mapother lived when he was one of the most owerful public figures in Kentucky.

Top left: Tom at the St Francis Seminary.

Top centre: Tom looking chubbier, and featuring a chipped tooth, in a photograph taken shortly after his parents separated when he was 12 years old.

Top right: Marian, one of Tom's two elder sisters.

Middle: Tom (second from right) dressing up for some improvised theatre at his home when he was just 11 years old.

Below: St Xavier's School, in Louisville, which Tom attended following his parents' divorce.

p left: Tom with mom Mary Lee at the 1990 Oscars.
p right: Tom's first ever girlfriend Laurie Hobbs, aged 15.
ntre right: An excerpt from Tom's first ever appearance in print in the Glen Ridge
:wspaper's report of a school wrestling match.
low: Tom in the Glen Ridge soccer team *(third from left, back row).*

Top left: Tom aged 15.
Top right: The house that Tom's mother Mary Lee rented in Louisville, when the actor was just 13 years old.
Centre: Tom in soccer action at the St Francis Seminary.
Bottom: The imposing St Francis Seminary as it looks today.

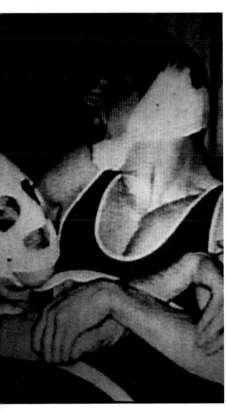

Top left: Tom had powerful good looks, even at the age of 13.
Top right: Tom aged 16.
Bottom left: Tom, aged 17, in action for the Glen Ridge wrestling team.
Bottom right: The beautiful mansion on Washington Avenue, Glen Ridge, New Jersey, where Tom moved with his sisters after his mother met Jack South.

Top left: Tom in a team photograph for the Glen Ridge wrestling team.
Top right: Tom aged 14 *(left, front row)* in the soccer team at the St. Francis Seminary.
Centre right: Tom in the basketball team at St Francis Seminary *(kneeling, left)*.
Bottom: The $400,000 house, in the most exclusive area of Louisville, where Tom's grandfather and grandmother on the Mapother side of his family lived until their deaths.

op left: Tom with classmate at Glen Ridge High.
op right: Tom's wrestling coach and confidante Angelo Corbo as he is today.
entre: The modest rented house on Cardwell Way, Louisville, where Tom befriended
eighbour Bill Lewis.
elow: The Mapother family plot at the Calvary Cemetery, in Louisville. Staff at the
emetery say that the star has rarely visited the graves where his father and grandfather
e buried.

Top left: Tom aged 16.
Top right: The scruffy apartment complex in Louisville where Tom's father Thomas Cruise Mapother III spent the last two years of his life.
Below: Tom in the Glen Ridge High soccer team.

By all accounts, Nicole knew precisely what she wanted out of life even at the ripe old age of nine. One former school friend recalled: 'When I was nine I went to her sister's birthday party. Nicole bossed us around and made us play games properly.'

Intriguingly, the young Nicole hated her now-famed curly locks and used to try to do everything to flatten them. Explained the friend: 'She used to wash her hair in this rose-water stuff and when she came to class it stank the whole room out. It smelt like rose toilet freshner, it was so strong. She insisted her hair was a perm. She hated her hair and slicked down the curls every morning.'

By the age of 13, Nicole had grown to be a gangly five feet ten inches tall and was frequently mistaken for someone in their late teens. Her talent was spotted so early on that she was recruited for her first starring role, in the mini-series *Vietnam*, while still attending North Sydney Girls High School.

Actor Patrick Phillips met and starred with Nicole in an episode of the Australian series *A Country Practice* when she was just 16. He recalled: 'Even then, I thought she was incredible. She just had this naturalness and loved the camera. A good personality, Nicole; she's something really special.'

It was at this time that another actor called Tom walked into Nicole's life – and caused rather a mini-controversy among her family because he was almost 20 years older than her. Tom Burlinson swept Nicole off her feet when they made a feature film together entitled *Windrider*. The couple had a passionate two-year affair which only ended when Tom began suggesting that they might like to make the union more permanent. Nicole felt she was too young and immediately departed.

Within weeks of arriving in America, she found herself

being chased by Hollywood's most infamous casanova Warren Beatty. The Oscar-winning actor and director met Nicole at a movie premiere and then repeatedly called her up asking her to go out for dinner with him. Nicole was never tempted, however, because Beatty was not her type. After meeting Tom Cruise, she claimed the entire Beatty episode was a piece of tabloid fiction but, in fact, following Beatty's attempt at seduction, she had openly talked about it to people she encountered in Australia. She felt a little embarrassed when the story leaked out in Hollywood following her marriage.

But there was no doubting Nicole's star quality. Back in early 1989, director Phil Noyce said: 'It is this ability to be both a man's woman and a woman's woman that makes her so extraordinary.' He made Nicole sound like a female version of Tom Cruise.

No one knows precisely when Nicole and Tom actually started dating but it seems likely that it was just before Christmas 1989, in the middle of the *Days of Thunder* gruelling schedule. At that same time, back in Australia, handsome actor Marcus Graham was sitting in his luxurious flat in Sydney, presuming that Nicole, then 22, would be flying home to continue their relationship – but she never came.

Marcus – hailed as Australia's newest sex symbol at the time – has the sort of looks that make women sigh – an unruly mop of jet black hair, strong eyebrows and an intense expression that could melt a female at 20 paces. In other words, he has the same sort of looks that skyrocketed Tom Cruise to the top of his profession.

In 1989, aged 26 and a former star of Australia's top rating soap *E-Street*, Marcus was establishing himself as a serious actor when Nicole announced her intention to fly to Los Angeles to seek her fame and fortune. The couple had been living together for some time before she announced her plans and, in fact, their relationship had been well documented in some of Australia's numerous teeny magazines. They were deemed to be the country's most glamorous young couple and very much in love.

Nic (as she likes to be called by all her family and friends) and Marcus had first met a year earlier when he was appearing in a play called *Heartbreak Kid*. The two bumped into each other in the foyer and it was, according to Marcus, love at first sight. Soon Nic and Marcus became an item in Sydney's closely knit acting circle and Marcus even watched admiringly as Nic's career took off. 'While I was really happy for Nic, I felt it magnified my own inadequacies,' reflects the young actor now.

Those insecurities – an actor's biggest enemy – arose with a vengeance when Nic phoned Marcus shortly after arriving in America to announce excitedly that she had been signed up by Sam Cohen, the legendary agent who has many famous clients, including Nic's heroine Meryl Streep. 'I thought, "That's great, I can't even get a bloody commercial!"' recalled Marcus. He continued: 'I really felt lousy and small but, instead of feeling envious, I turned the situation into a positive thing.'

Then Marcus said something that must surely provide an insight into what Tom Cruise saw in her that made her so special. 'An actor's most valuable tool is his confidence and Nicole, no matter where she was, would always give me lots of that.'

During that lonely Christmas of 1989, Marcus Graham started to find his separation from Nicole very difficult. 'She was not just my girl, she was also my best friend and I missed her terribly.'

Thousands of miles away, however, a much wealthier, more powerful version of Marcus Graham was wooing his

WENSLEY CLARKSON

lover – and his name was Tom Cruise. Despite virtually daily calls from Marcus to Nic, the young actor still had no idea of what was happening. In those final three months, Marcus's telephone bill came to a whopping $1300. He was still dreaming about working on a pet movie project with Nic and regretting the fact that she had turned down a chance for them to star together in a theatre version of *A Midsummer Night's Dream* to go off and do *Days of Thunder*.

Without doubt, Marcus felt a twinge of concern about his beautiful young girlfriend travelling so far to appear in a huge Hollywood blockbuster and that is no doubt why he made so many calls to Nicole. All along, however, he just presumed they would get back together. He had already planned a trip to a paradise island in the Pacific with Nicole, to relax and put their relationship back on track. It was not to be ...

The first confirmation of the break-up of their relationship came when Marcus saw television pictures of Tom and Nicole together at the 1990 Oscars ceremony in March that year. The young actor was gutted. He could not quite believe what he was seeing. He tried to call her but she would not take his calls. That was when he knew for certain it was all over ...

*   *   *

Nicole's parents took the massive surge of publicity surrounding their daughter's affair with Tom very much in their stride but they began to get irritated and took a leaf out of Tom's book when blatantly inaccurate reports started circulating.

According to Nicole's sister Antonia: 'When a radio station read out a piece from a newspaper which had Tom Cruise buying Nicole a $50,000 Corvette and a house, Mum demanded, and got, a retraction.'

Nicole's mother knew it was untrue because, through-out the early months of her affair with Tom, Nicole rang her mother on numerous occasions and, according to Antonia, 'she tells Mum everything'.

Nicole's family found being thrust under an inter-national spotlight rather irritating at times. Antonia recalled: 'In three different stores, I used my credit card which, naturally, has the Kidman name. Every time I was asked if I was related to Nicole. In the end I denied it, not because I don't love and feel proud of her, but because it's easier to pretend that I'm not her sister rather than face a barrage of questions.'

Within months of the relationship being revealed, Tom and Nicole were on their way to becoming one of the most famous couples in the world. Her father Anthony, a bio-chemist and stress-management book author, happily played the role of the most calming influence in the family. While her mother Janelle says that Nicole is prone to playing every-thing down, she did reveal that her elder daughter some-times fears that her mother will put her foot in it by being too sentimental.

Throughout those early, difficult days of Tom's romance with Nicole, the young actress called her mother every other day to keep her abreast of what was happen-ing. Nicole told her mother that Tom was an 'intense, energetic 27-year-old with a great sense of humour and a very nice way of throwing back his head when he laughs,' explained Janelle. She also added: 'He's got that American way of not doing things by halves. He works and plays full on.'

Janelle is always introduced to people by Nicole as 'my mother Janelle Kidman' after she decided it was 'ghastly' to be referred to as 'Nicole's mum'.

Others in Australia were not in the least bit surprised

that Nicole's career and love life took off after the release of *Dead Calm*. 'I remember promising Nicole that even if *Dead Calm* didn't make a dollar, it would make her an international film star,' recalled the movie's writer and co-producer Terry Hayes, longtime friend and mentor to Nicole.

Only a few months after their relationship went public, Tom delighted Nicole and his family and friends by splashing out almost $5 million on a secluded house set in an acre of ground in exclusive Pacific Palisades, just west of Los Angeles, one of the most expensive real estate areas in the world. Tom purchased the secluded, Colonial-style home with electric gates in the name of a trust to avoid news of the deal leaking out.

Built in the early 1940s, the two-storey house was newly refurbished and contained five bedrooms, five bathrooms and four fireplaces in an area of slightly more than 6,200 square feet. The home also included a dramatic spiral staircase, wood-panelled library, two-storey guest house, motor court, swimming pool, spa, and English garden.

Despite the house being immaculate, the couple hired an army of painters and carpenters to transform it into a palace. They added a movie theatre, billiard room and weight room as well as gold-plated bathroom fixtures and marble and mahogany fireplaces. There is also a free-form swimming pool with an eight-foot water slide at one end and a jacuzzi at the other.

The house seemed to be Tom's way of saying he was deadly serious about Nicole. Shortly after the purchase, he bought her a $200,000 diamond ring although they were not officially engaged until later.

This had followed the sort of wooing that would put any romantic lead actor to shame. Tom sent Nicole a dozen red roses every day for two weeks, then bought her a

$40,000 pair of diamond earrings. At one stage during his courtship, he even left a folded note on her pillow at their hotel in Los Angeles, saying: 'My darling Nicole, I chased you and chased you until you finally caught me. Now will you marry me?'

Nicole read the note as she got up and immediately rushed into the kitchen of their suite, flung her arms around Tom and said: 'I will, I will!'

More parachute diving followed, including a high flier at 25,000 feet with Tom and Nicole holding hands for the cameras.

With Tom and Nicole's relationship now definitely in the public domain, the couple made a very secretive visit to Sydney by private jet from Los Angeles, so that Tom could meet Nicole's parents. The actress even managed to fit in a brief visit to her ex-lover Marcus Graham's Sydney house, with Tom in tow. It was a remarkably tactless thing to do. A friend explained: 'She just wanted to see how Marcus was, but bringing Tom along was thoughtless.'

When the couple showed up at the door, a friend of Marcus's answered the door and told them the actor was not at home. In fact, he was in but could not face his former lover.

Marcus later reflected that his role in what was dubbed a love triangle by the tabloids truly tested his patience and sense of humour. Close friends said that, privately, Marcus was nursing a broken heart about the end of his relationship with Nicole. 'He was devastated by what happened. I think the worst aspect for him was that he ended up being one of the last people to find out that she was seeing Tom when he thought she was still his girlfriend,' said one of the actor's closest friends in Australia.

To rub salt in the wound, Marcus had to put up with being constantly referred to as 'Nicole's ex-boyfriend', a label that hurt him deeply. When Tom and Nicole flew in to Sydney, he found himself in the spotlight for all the wrong reasons. This time, his patience snapped and he told one friend angrily: 'It was a nightmare when Nicole brought Tom to Sydney. No one gives a thought to what I'm thinking or feeling. I'm sick of it. Actually Tom Cruise would make a great Daffy Duck. He's got the perfect teeth for it.'

Later, having regained his composure, Marcus insisted: 'I have nothing against Tom. When you are a public person, I know your private life is more interesting. Sure, people want to read about that stuff, but this sort of publicity gives no thought to what I'm thinking or feeling.'

Privately, Marcus was torn apart by the end of his relationship with Nicole.

During that hush-hush trip to Sydney, Tom and Nicole went with her parents to a well known Indian restaurant called the Maharani, in the Crow's Nest district of the city. Tom even joined in the spirit of the evening by drinking potent Indian beer, even though he had spent much of the previous five years as a teetotaller. They also went to the opera, met Nicole's old friend and mentor, producer/writer Terry Hayes, and even managed to help a member of the paparazzi when he tripped over a kerb while trying to take photos of the couple. It all seemed a million miles away from Hollywood.

There was another reason behind Nicole's visit to her homeland. She was missing her family terribly, even though her mother had visited her at least three times in the first year she was in moviedom. Nicole admitted to Australian writer Susan Duncan: 'The hardest part is the loneliness. It can get very lonely so far from home.' Often, Nicole's mother would send her daughter a 'care package' from home, containing newspapers, magazines and jars of Vegemite.

There was another downside to this fairytale for the young Australian actress; Nicole sometimes found that things with Tom were happening so fast she could barely cope. Frequently, she would wake up in the middle of the night and wander around the streets, just walking until she felt she had calmed down. She felt a little scared of what was happening. 'It's scary. That's why I can't place a lot of emphasis on it. I mean, you can be hot one day and not the next. One moment you're on the "in" list and the next you're "out".'

On their return to Los Angeles, Tom took Nicole for a weekend to the desert at Palm Springs, to learn how to ride motorbikes in the sand-dunes, and then whisked her off to the Bahamas for a couple of weeks of complete rest. The couple went scuba diving and, for the first time in their relationship, actually started to get to know each other properly.

Every now and again Nicole would pinch herself just to make sure it was all still really happening. 'I still feel, "Gosh, I really shouldn't be here." I get insecure. I ring my mum. There is never a time when I don't think the role I'm playing is going to be the last I'll ever be offered. Then I ring my mum again.'

For Tom, being with Nicole was obviously the best thing that had ever happened to him. Sometimes it seemed as if he could not keep his hands off her! When the couple went to an afternoon performance at a New York theatre, they started hugging and kissing the moment they got to their seats on the front row of the balcony. When the lights dimmed, a sudden scream pierced the theatre, followed by a thud as an elderly woman collapsed in the orchestra pit. Tom immediately vaulted the balcony railing, jumped down to the floor below and was the first person to reach the stricken woman. 'Call 911!' he yelled out as he comforted

WENSLEY CLARKSON

the old lady. An ambulance arrived within minutes and the woman was taken away. Meanwhile, Tom returned to his seat and proceeded to start kissing and cuddling with Nicole.

*   *   *

On 18 December 1990, Nicole's parents and sister slipped discreetly out of Australia for a Christmas break in the United States. Six days later they and only seven other guests – including Tom's mother, Mary Lee, and his three sisters – attended Tom and Nicole's wedding in the ski resort of Aspen, Colorado. The couple had been secretly planning the marriage for about a month.

However, the wedding nearly did not go ahead when Tom was arrested for speeding by a disbelieving Colorado marshall Norman Squire, who thought Tom was lying when he announced: 'Hi, I'm Tom Cruise and I'm getting married.'

The cop shot back: 'Sure you are, and I'm Mary Queen of Scots.' Tom wasn't carrying any means of identification so the lawman told him: 'Take off your hat if you're really him.' It was only then that Marshall Squire believed his celebrity suspect and allowed Tom to continue on his way back for the wedding.

On the morning of 24 December, the stately log house was filled with fragrant flower arrangements, including a willow arbor laced with white lilies and red roses. As the sun began to set, Nicole, wearing a white silk gown with a long train, joined Tom, dressed in a black tuxedo, for the start of the 30-minute ceremony, conducted by a civil celebrant.

With younger sister Antonia standing by as her brides-maid, Nicole peered down at her shorter husband-to-be to exchange their self-written marriage vows. According to Australian actress Deborra-Lee Furness, who was among the guests, 'Both Tom and Nicole, as well as their families, had tears in their eyes.'

It was all in great contrast to Tom's earlier marriage to Mimi Rogers when both bride and groom had worn jeans and bare feet.

Nicole was given only four days off from filming her latest movie *Billy Bathgate* with Tom's *Rain Man* co-star Dustin Hoffman, for the couple to have a mini honeymoon, although Tom had sent bouquets of flowers to the set in a small town in North Carolina virtually every day in the lead up to the wedding.

The following day – Christmas Day – Nicole rang the rest of her family back in Australia to tell them the news. Tom even came on the line to wish his new family 'Happy Christmas'. 'Nicole was very happy when she called. She said all the normal things that brides say,' reported her aunt, Linda Fawcett.

The day after Christmas, Nicole called a Sydney radio journalist called Peter Ford to tell him the big news. 'She was blissfully happy. They are very much in love and Nicole was ecstatic when she called,' explained Ford.

By May of 1991, Nicole's parents had become even more active about pursuing inaccurate reports concerning their daughter and her husband. The worst example was when an Australian magazine claimed that Tom had attacked and bruised his wife during an incident on the set of her movie, *Billy Bathgate*. The article, headlined 'Nicole – Were Those Bruises Cruise's?' stunned Dr and Mrs Kidman and they immediately filed a complaint with Australia's Press Council, claiming that the story was not presented fairly, did not respect their daughter's privacy and was harmfully inaccurate. The complaint was upheld and the magazine was ordered to print an apology and a retraction. It seemed that Tom's anti-press attitudes were clearly becoming infectious.

The following month rumours that the couple were expecting a baby reached almost epidemic proportions. The *Daily Mail* in Britain kicked off the stories by publishing a front page article claiming that Tom was 'bursting with pride' at the news. Newspapers even alleged that Tom had ordered his new bride to take a fertility test before they actually got married. Tom was also quoted as saying: 'It's a miracle. She's pregnant and I did it. I'm going to be a dad. I can't wait to hold my first-born in my arms.' Nicole's father was reportedly refusing to confirm the claims, which eventually turned out to be completely false.

No one knows if a sudden, and highly secretive, trip to a Los Angeles hospital in October 1991 was in any way linked to Nicole's alleged 'pregnancy' but her admittance to St John's Hospital and Health Centre in Santa Monica, just a few miles from Tom and Nicole's luxurious home in Pacific Palisades, certainly appeared to be dramatic. She was booked into the hospital under a false name after suffering from 'stomach pains'.

Nicole had fallen ill two weeks earlier during the reshooting of certain scenes in *Billy Bathgate* in New York. She immediately underwent tests in New York and then flew to Los Angeles for surgery, described as 'minor abdominal surgery to remove scar tissue that was causing her pain', one source at the hospital revealed. It is not known whether Tom was with Nicole at the time.

Soon after getting out of hospital, Nicole jetted off to see her family and friends back in Sydney, without Tom, who stayed behind in Los Angeles after falling from a tree while gardening in their Pacific Palisades home. Tom fractured a rib and broke the little finger of his left hand during the fall and Nicole had to drive him to hospital where he was fitted with an elastic chest brace to protect his rib and a sling for his arm.

The visit to Sydney was pronounced a private trip by Nicole's publicists and they insisted that she would not carry out any public engagements. Since her marriage to Tom, she had become the most famous actress in Australia and everyone wanted to meet her, however briefly.

Nicole actually weakened and brought some Christmas cheer plus gifts to sick youngsters at the Camperdown Children's Hospital in Sydney. She chatted with teenagers and spoke warmly about Tom during the one-hour visit. She promised the assembled crowd she would be back in Australia with Tom the following February.

Nicole had two special reasons for visiting that particular hospital; her mother Janelle had, at one time, worked there as a nurse and she also felt a special affinity for children which was rapidly manifesting itself into a genuine urge to be a parent.

Back in Los Angeles, Tom kept tabs on his pretty young wife by calling her every day without fail. He started to notice that, after a few days, Nicole's Australian accent had kicked right back into gear. He told her not to lose it 'because it is one of the things about me he really loves,' said Nicole later.

However, there was another side to being Mrs Tom Cruise, as Nicole complained during that trip to Australia. 'There is an intense interest in my personal life and I've spent a lot of time building up a career and my first love is acting. When you meet someone – a high profile person – and you fall in love with them, you don't have any choice. You're suddenly thrown into the limelight.'

Nicole was particularly upset by reports in some US publications which suggested that she had got some of her work because Tom had campaigned for her. At one stage, rumours circulating Hollywood cruelly suggested that Tom had persuaded Nicole to agree to marriage and a family in exchange for some sort of contract guaranteeing her lead roles in half a dozen movies. It was a nonsensical suggestion of course, but it hurt the actress deeply. 'As Tom says, "There are a lot of actors around with girlfriends who are actresses who aren't working",' she told one writer. 'I'm not blowing my own trumpet here, but it makes me irritated because you never get the part unless you come up with the goods. Studios have millions of dollars riding on these movies and they're not going to go, "Let's please Tom and put Nicole in this movie." It just doesn't work that way.'

Although Nicole had fought hard to maintain her own identity, she admitted that the media attention on her marriage sometimes became a heavy burden. 'I have trouble because I'm very honest and if someone asks me a question, I'll usually answer it.'

Her attitude towards the press was refreshingly straight-forward compared with Tom's rather duplicitous feelings. 'It's like a game and we treat it like a game. We haven't had people lurking in the bushes yet. Occasionally we get people following us, but Tom is a very good driver so we can usually get away.'

Then, in an interesting reference to the couple's future plans to have children, she added: 'When I have children, I don't want my children splashed across the cover of magazines and I don't want them put into the spotlight like that.'

Nicole continued to deny the never-ending rumours of her pregnancy. Unlike Tom, she insisted on handling the media's constant inquiries head on with a complete and utter denial rather than a 'no comment' which she believed simply fuelled the speculation. Beneath the public façade she and Tom were getting increasingly anxious to start a family. Seeing friends like Dustin Hoffman and Paul Newman – both happily married with children – had convinced them that it should be sooner rather than later.

One of the more intriguing aspects of Tom and Nicole's marriage was that Nicole openly admitted to friends that her husband bought most of her clothes for her and she rarely went with him to choose them! 'He just sees something he likes and brings it home to surprise me,' she told one acquaintance.

It was almost as if Tom was moulding his young bride into exactly what he wanted, although Nicole was hardly complaining. Tom would often buy outfits from the best designers, like Karl Lagerfeld, and thought nothing of spending $10,000 on a dress for his wife. Another gift from Tom was a bright red Mercedes sports car which cost a cool $100,000 plus $10,000 a year for insurance!

Amid all this talk of children, the broody Nicole was presented with a lovable labrador puppy by Tom. It seemed to be wedded bliss. Life inside the palatial mansion in the Palisades did sound rather impersonal, however. Nicole told one friend that Tom, who had started smoking the occasional huge cigar, had taken to listening to Bruce Springsteen on his state-of-the-art stereo system while sitting alone in a room in the house that had been designated as 'his' den. Meanwhile, Nicole spent a lot of her time in different parts of the vast mansion.

None the less, everywhere Tom went in public, he couldn't wait to tell the world what a wonderful wife Nicole was. At the prestigious American Cinema Award ceremony in Los Angeles in early January 1991, he accepted an award and then proceeded to announce that Nicole had been 'a great source of support … I thank her from my heart'.

When he told the disappointed audience that Nicole was unable to attend, Sean Connery, who had presented the award, jokingly put his arm around Cruise and proclaimed: 'I like them a little younger.'

To all the world, Tom and Nicole seemed like the perfect couple but they had their problems just like everyone else.

'I'm much more relaxed now than I used to be. I was much more intense and driven. I had to live all my life today as opposed to just relaxing and trusting that I'm going to be here tomorrow.'

Tom Cruise

20

Tom was feeling a touch uncomfortable, lying there stark naked with his eyes closed, even if there was a bowl protecting his modesty from a young lady. She could not, of course, resist a peek followed by a smirk, which the camera caught but Tom didn't. 'What did she do?' he yelled, sitting bolt upright in the bed. Tom hates to be left out.

The lady playing peekaboo was his brand-new wife Nicole Kidman and the couple were acting out a scene from *Far and Away*, an epic tale of an Irish labourer who hooks up with a spirited landowner's daughter to travel in turn-of-the-century America. Hundreds of millions of people were expected to watch the film when it was released and it was not just Tom's smile but what was underneath that bowl which was expected to bring the punters in.

By all accounts, Tom spent most of the making of *Far and Away*, during the first half of 1991, telling anyone who would listen of his love for Nicole. On and off the set the couple seemed to be forever smooching and kissing. Even director Ron Howard admitted it was a bit of a worry:

'There was a lot of kissing going on – all day long. There really was a honeymoon glow. For while they never consummate their love in the movie, it was easy for them to draw upon the awe and mesmerising attraction that was in their recent memory. Tom would look at her sometimes and say: "Isn't she beautiful". Or he'd have his shirt off and be boxing and she'd come by and exclaim: "What a chest!"'

Propman Derek Wallace said that every time director Howard called 'action' the couple would be kissing passionately in some corner or other. 'Finally, one of the drivers threatened to throw a bucket of cold water over them. I've never seen a couple so close or so ecstatically happy,' explained Wallace. Tom would even bring his wife constant cups of coffee, to keep out the cold, and regularly bullied her to keep a thick sweater on at all times.

Tom explained that he just could not help himself. 'I love being with her 24 hours a day. She is both my wife and my best friend. The perfect day with Nicole would be when we don't get up in the morning, a room-service day. I'll leave the rest for interpretation.'

What he did not mention was that he and Nicole would regularly disappear into their personalised luxury trailer for hours at a time, no doubt to 'reassure' each other of their mutual love and respect.

Since meeting Tom, Nicole had perfected a mid-Pacific drawl, despite her insistence that Tom preferred her Aussie accent. For *Far and Away* she had to be Irish-American. She perfected it with ease after the pair hired a couple of locals to hang out with. However, Tom continued to have a 'divil of a time' mastering the lingo. In the end, he had to sit down with dialect coach Sean O'Casey in an effort to get it right. Most who've seen the film say he still managed to get it badly wrong.

However, nothing could deter Nicole from her passion for Tom. She seemed as full of love for him as he was for her. 'There's a light about him. When he laughs, his eyes crinkle up, he throws his head back; it's contagious and you've gotta laugh too. He's this powerhouse, he sort of fills the room – the energy coming out is amazing.'

In a specially arranged television interview with Oprah Winfrey, just before the shooting of *Far and Away* commenced, the couple giggled and hugged like school sweethearts when the TV hostess asked them if they did everything as a couple. 'Yes,' replied Tom. 'We like being together 24 hours a day.'

It certainly sounded as if Tom had returned to his favoured, mutual appreciation society mode when talking about Nicole but there was another motive behind his gushing words; he really wanted to avoid the sort of problems that were caused by the long separations during his first marriage, and that was why *Far and Away* seemed the ideal project for the couple to embark on.

The added bonus was that Nicole was as determined to start a family as Tom. She even told one writer that she wanted 'at least three children' with the added proviso that they be brought up in Australia 'to keep their feet on the ground'.

The *Far and Away* shoot took place in Montana and Ireland, an area steeped in the history of Tom's ancestral family, the Mapothers. The actor, by now approaching his twenty-ninth birthday, also hoped that the luck of the Irish would rub off on him and Nicole following the dismal failure of *Days of Thunder*.

Tom even had to learn how to ride a horse and managed to master the art after only four lessons. He proudly claimed that he fell off only one time throughout the entire filming. Nicole, already an accomplished rider, had no problems whatsoever. During subsequent filming, a note of rivalry built up between husband and wife with Tom desperately trying to ride faster than his wife on certain occasions.

Things got off to a bad start in Montana after a spectacular wagon-race sequence turned to mayhem when 1,000 extras and stunt riders, plus hundreds of horses, mules and wagons, hurtled across a desolate plain. According to crew members, a cannon shot, plus noise from a helicopter filming overhead, spooked the animals before the race and out-of-control wagons broke up, hurling animals under the wheels. Several animals were hurt and one horse was so badly injured it had to be destroyed.

However, at least Tom and Nicole had their wondrous dressing room-trailer to retire to when things got too hectic. The vehicle was a sort of belated wedding present for Nicole. Valued at $750,000, it came complete with marble floors and was said to be five feet longer than any other star's trailer in Hollywood. The ultimate status symbol, no doubt.

After wrapping in Montana, the film moved to Dublin and things really started to go wrong. To start with, Tom was warned that he and Nicole, by now probably the most famous couple in the western world, were likely would-be victims of a terrorist attack by loyalists from Northern Ireland who were desperate to upset the so-called peace talks that were in progress between Britain and Eire at the time. Tom was shaken by the warning and reluctantly agreed to have three bodyguards shadow him and Nicole throughout their stay in the Emerald Isle.

'Tom was very worried by the threats. He took them very seriously and it certainly made the couple feel a little isolated at times,' explained one Irish member of the crew.

The three armed minders included two former members of the SAS. Two years later one of them, Barry Croft, was arrested for drug offences after claiming that Thai gangsters had put out a contract on him. Croft had a habit of carrying a Magnum around with him all the time.

Tom had realised that he could take no chances while in Ireland. Within days he started to feel like a prisoner in his own hotel suite – he was just grateful to have Nicole with him. Tom and Nicole settled comfortably into a vast honeymoon suite at the Westbury Hotel. Every morning, like clockwork, they would appear on the set by chauffeur driven car at 10 a.m.

Later they moved to Dublin's Berkeley Court Hotel and stayed in the penthouse suite, complete with a marble kitchen, peach bedroom, jacuzzi-equipped bathroom and a view of Dublin Bay. They played a daily round of squash, their favourite game, at Dublin's Riverside Racquet and Fitness Club.

The couple, complete with their army of bodyguards, even shopped for Irish linen at a small Dublin shop, where Tom bought two queen-sized virgin-fleece mattress pads. They then attended a play at the city's famous Abbey Theatre. During their stay in Dublin they also entertained friends like Sean Penn and actor Billy Baldwin, Nicole's parents and Tom's mother, Mary Lee.

Tom's friendship with Sean Penn is fairly unique because he is the only member of the so-called Brat Pack of the early 1980s to whom Tom remained close. For a while during Penn's troublesome marriage to Madonna the two actors saw little of each other but once Penn set up home with beautiful blonde actress Robyn Wright, the two stars became good friends again. Wright was involved in a smaller-budget version of *Far and Away* called *The Playboys* so the two couples had lots of stories to swap about their experiences in Ireland.

Halfway through their stay in Dublin, Tom and Nicole sneaked off to Paris for a romantic weekend away from the movie set – and those bodyguards. The couple strolled hand in hand near the Louvre, stopping occasionally for a completely spontaneous embrace. Then they headed back to their $500-a-night suite at the famous Hotel Bristol. A chauffeur-driven Rolls-Royce was at their disposal throughout the trip.

After ten weeks' non-stop filming in and around Dublin, Nicole, Tom and their entourage of minders moved to a rented cottage in the beautiful west-coast town of Dingle, County Kerry. There filming centred on a farmyard set, built on a blustery cliff top near the tiny village of Ventry.

While Irish eyes might have been smiling on them up until then, their luck soon changed fast. Only weeks before their arrival in the town, three teenage boys had plunged to their deaths close to where the movie was set. Then filming was halted when Tom nearly took a tumble over the same cliff.

He was trying to lead a donkey across the farmyard in one scene and lost control of it. He panicked and, as he moved away, he slipped and started to fall down the slope. It was particularly frightening because it was the exact same spot where those poor boys had died.

Two crewmen on the movie then had a lucky escape when their helicopter was hit by a freak 50-foot wave as they were taking low aerial shots of the ocean. The chopper crashed but, amazingly, both pilot and cameraman escaped unhurt, although a $1 million camera sank to the bottom of the sea.

Tom and Nicole were seldom seen during their stay on the west coast. However, their landlord, Swiss lawyer Dr Albert Schumacher, did play the piano for them at several sing-songs that lasted until 2 a.m. at the little cottage.

But relations between the couple and their landlord soured after only six days when Schumacher claimed that he was roughed up by one of Tom's bodyguards after he complained about the heavies wearing wet clothes and shoes in the house. 'I tried speaking to the chief bodyguard but he took no notice,' explained Dr Schumacher. 'So I spoke to Tom but, as I was talking to him, the bodyguards came over and lifted me up. They dragged me about 40 yards and kicked me for ten minutes.'

Schumacher demanded a written apology from the star but Tom refused so Schumacher ordered the Cruise party out of his house. Tom, who was fed up with the good doctor by this stage, was more than happy to set up a new base five miles along the coast. Shortly after this, Nicole flew home in a private jet after her part in the movie was completed.

Following Nicole's departure, Tom headed straight for the local pub, Paidi O Se, to spend an hour patching things up with the locals who had heard about the fracas with Dr Schumacher. This time the actor's bodyguards kept a low profile, while casually dressed Tom rubbed shoulders with the villagers, signed autographs and posed for photographs.

Barman David Connor even noticed that Tom had developed a taste for the black stuff but he pointed out that the star never drank a whole pint of Guinness – only halves.

Tom was the laughing stock of the crew on *Far and Away* because he sprinted to the toilet between takes in order to set a good example. 'He seemed to think that by doing so, we would realise how important it is not to delay a shoot,' said one member of the crew. Many of the crew laughed behind Tom's back because they could not believe that anyone would take their work that seriously.

However, the film's producer, Brian Grazer, a true Hollywood player, did not see the funny side of it at all. He explained in a deadpan tone: 'If Tom Cruise can run from his trailer to the set or run to the bathroom, it sets a tone for everyone. They realised how serious he was about bringing this movie in on time.' Some of the Gods on the set certainly thought otherwise.

Other, more dangerous, pursuits on the movie included a bare-knuckle boxing sequence that got fairly ferocious at one stage.

Although the bare-knuckle fight scenes were choreographed, Tom still got quite seriously injured during an incident when the stunt boxers tried to make a scene look 'too real'. Suddenly, Nicole, who was watching on the sidelines, screamed out to stop the action because she feared Tom was about to get seriously hurt. She then pulled director Ron Howard aside and talked to him at length before being convinced that the action was a vital ingredient of the film. Tom and Nicole were both frequently thrown from their horses during some of the tricky land rush scenes.

After *Far and Away* was completed, there were strong rumours that Tom had forced the movie's producers to cast Nicole in the leading female role. The couple became hyper-sensitive to such suggestions and, during pre-release publicity interviews with the media, insisted on being interviewed separately to make their point.

One publicist working on the film said emphatically: 'They're separate people, with separate careers.' Besides that, 30 pages of studio-produced publicity material did not even mention the fact they were married!

The publicity work that accompanied *Far and Away* was exhausting for both Tom and Nicole. At one stage he had to speak to 150 newspaper, magazine and television journalists over a two-day period and the one question on everyone's lips was: 'Is Nicole pregnant?'

Even more ludicrous than the pregnancy rumour,

however, was one little titbit about Tom having allegedly had liposuction on his bottom. According to one disreputable source, Tom wanted to look good from the back for some of his scenes in *Far and Away*, even though there were no nude scenes in the film. Tom's publicist Pat Kingsley flatly denied the rumour.

Far and Away was released virtually simultaneously in many countries around the world, so Tom and Nicole embarked on a gruelling round-the-world promotional trip. In May 1992, they went to the Cannes Film Festival, where the film was featured, then on to London for the royal premiere, followed by Japan for the opening of the picture there. The main feature of the film – besides starring Tom and Nicole – was that it had been shot on 65 mm film, which gave it a widescope appearance when shown in cinemas. This was supposed to help to capture the essence of the Oklahoma gold rush of 1889 and the rolling hills of Ireland but audiences were not impressed.

The reviews of *Far and Away* were mixed, to say the least. In the *New York Daily News* Kathleen Carroll described the movie as containing 'surprisingly little passion or electricity in this boisterous period love story.' In the *New York Times* Caryn James wrote: 'This film is as much an epic event as sitting at home watching television.'

In Britain, the reaction to the film was no better. '*Far and Away* proves you can lay out a fortune on a film and end up having a film fit only for laying out,' wrote the *Daily Mirror* critic.

However, the normally hyper-critical Julie Salamon was kinder when she wrote in the *Wall Street Journal*: 'Odd as it seems for a film built on such a grand scale, sweet is the operative word here, and that's not meant as an insult.'

The movie's other big problem was that it had been

slated as Universal's big blockbuster for the summer of 1992, against *Lethal Weapon III* and *Batman II*. The other two films fared much better.

Far and Away proved a disappointment at the box office because it did not take the expected $100 million-plus in the United States. Tom, who had been paid a whopping $12 million for his role, took the film's failure philosophically. As usual, he looked on it as a learning experience and the definite lesson was that, after two attempts, appearing in movies with Nicole maybe wasn't such a viable idea. The couple agreed to go their separate ways professionally. It had been a bold experiment while it lasted but they really had to get on with their own acting from now on.

'I keep telling people not to say a movie is going to make $200 million because you're setting yourself up to take a fall. You can't predict,' Tom told anyone who would listen.

Hollywood insiders refused to slam Tom's performance in the film, blaming the script instead. 'Tom Cruise didn't bomb. The movie bombed. If someone came to me now with a Tom Cruise project and a good script, would I want it? You bet I would!' said one Hollywood producer.

One Tinseltown agent explained the reasons behind the film's failure: 'This is a minor lull in a very strong career. *Far and Away* was too weighty for a summer movie, too ambitious, and selling it as a Tom Cruise picture was a mistake by Universal.'

Libby Gelman-Waxner – a *nom de plume* for a very well-known screenwriter in Hollywood – wrote in 'her' *Premiere* magazine column: '*Far and Away* proves once and for all that Americans are right to avoid historical subjects. Tom, you're adorable, but your dental work is circa 1992, if you ask me.'

When the movie was shown at the Cannes Film Festival in May 1992, the audience hooted and groaned and it was dubbed a cliché-ridden epic.

Tom also faced some flack about his reported fee of $12 million for *Far and Away*. In a prerecorded interview with American TV's *Entertainment Tonight*, Tom insisted that Hollywood would not pay him that kind of money if they did not think he was worth it.

As if to drive home the point that he was really a rather modest kind of guy, Tom's involvement with environmental groups had led to him driving around Los Angeles in an electric car, in marked contrast to his black Acura NSX which can top 160 mph and was usually left in the garage except for special occasions. Tom was growing increasingly sensitive to criticism about his lifestyle and was determined to show he could be an example for America's youth. His strategy was carefully mapped out. As always, he knew exactly where he was going.

'Honour is a very important thing in my life. I got that in the family, in terms of being true to yourself and standing by your own truth. That doesn't mean I'm always perfect.'

Tom Cruise

21

It was a clear, chilly night, the kind of early autumn evening on which your breath comes out in little puffs of vapour. Groups of teenagers clogged the patio of a restaurant across the street from the movie crew. But they were not ordering a thing; they were just waiting.

Suddenly a Chevy approached, pulled up to the kerb and Tom Cruise popped out, strode less than ten paces to a news-stand and bought a magazine while exchanging a few words with a man standing on the sidewalk.

'Cut!' screamed the assistant director. That 50 seconds of screen time had taken hours and hours to shoot and the crowds watching from across the street gasped with excitement. They had caught a glimpse of their hero, Tom Cruise, in the flesh.

In a trailer a few hundred yards away was Jack Nicholson but none of the hundreds of fans was there to see him. They all wanted to see Tom, their hero, the good guy who always wins in the end.

The scene was a brief, albeit important, one from Tom's next movie *A Few Good Men*, but it proved beyond any shadow of a doubt that he had arrived as the world's number one box office attraction. Alongside Tom in *A Few Good Men* was a glittering array of other big Hollywood names, including Nicholson, Demi Moore, Keifer Sutherland, Kevin Pollack and Kevin Bacon – all overshadowed by Tom.

A Few Good Men was adapted from Aaron Sorkin's acclaimed stage play which took some of America's big cities by storm in the early-1990s. The military court-room drama about a pair of Marines accused of murder was not just expected to do well. It had to, because all of the major stars were being paid huge salaries.

On the first day of rehearsals, the cast of *A Few Good Men* gathered around a table for a first read-through of the script. 'Normally in those situations', explained director Rob Reiner, 'actors are just marking themselves because they haven't yet found all the colours of their characters.'

However, Jack Nicholson came in with a full-blown performance that shook everyone in the room. Everyone, that is, except Tom. He said nothing and did not respond. All the other actors noticed, but said nothing. As Reiner explained: 'It was like the young titan and the old titan going at each other.'

Tom's attitude towards Nicholson was much cooler than it had been with people like Hoffman, Newman and Duvall. He was now 30 years old and a much more accomplished actor. There were to be no more 'yes, sirs' and 'no, sirs'. In front of the older star, Tom even mastered a superb Jack Nicholson impersonation that had everyone – including the old maestro himself – in stitches.

In interviews during the run-up to the release of the movie, Tom was full of praise for Nicholson but it was different from the deferential tone he had used about other, older male stars. 'Nicholson's a legend and he's very unpretentious. He knows acting and he loves acting. He was really generous off-camera when I was working. He was right there,' said Tom.

Beside his huge fee, Tom also received a number of incredible perks during the filming of *A Few Good Men*. He had the biggest trailer on the set, which featured phones, faxes, a TV and a jacuzzi; he had two chauffeurs on 24-hour standby and a luxury jet with full security in case he had to rush back to Los Angeles at a moment's notice; plus his own personal make-up and hairdresser.

Tom's part in *A Few Good Men*, as a callow young lawyer forced to defend two soldiers during a disciplinary action, had many shades of familiarity about it. To start with, the character had to emerge from the legend created by his highly successful late father and, secondly, he was playing a lawyer, a career that many previous Mapothers, including Tom's uncle and grandfather, had been very successful in, back in Louisville, Kentucky.

The theme of fathers and sons had been played out over and over again in Tom's previous work. In fact, the issue of manhood had become a very common thread. As his *Days of Thunder* co-star Robert Duvall commented: 'Tom's father wasn't around. I guess he grew up having to prove something on his own. I'm sure it's something of a catalyst. It drives you farther into new areas. To prove some things.'

Certainly Tom's role as Lieutenant Daniel Kaffee in *A Few Good Men* called for more mastery of the English language than any of his previous roles and mastering complex dialogue was not easy for the actor, considering his past battles with dyslexia. Co-star Kevin Bacon become friendly with Tom after the two actors found they both had problems reading their lines. They even started rehearsing each other while being made up before each day's shoot because some of the dialogue was so legally complicated that it was very difficult to remember. 'It was completely foreign to me and, to a certain extent, to him,' explained Bacon. 'It was exhausting, but fun. That's why you act.'

Director Rob Reiner believed Tom's part as Kaffee was the biggest challenge he ever had as an actor. 'He went to work, studied the terminology. He really steeped himself in it,' commented Reiner.

The most significant aspect of the movie was that all the traditional Tom Cruise ingredients were thrown to the wind. As director Reiner explained: 'The character is really a bigger stretch than anything he'd ever done. There were no scenes when he could turn on the charm. There was no romance in the film.'

Even Tom, who usually never conceded that any aspect of his work was difficult, agreed. 'You can always tell when someone on screen doesn't understand what they're saying. I understood everything I was saying. You have to get it right. Like anything, you have to get it right.'

Screenwriter Aaron Sorkin, who became close to Tom during the making of the film, recalled: 'He really had the instincts. The non-wise ass moments, the non-glib moments. There's not a lot of pyrotechnics. For a lot of other actors, it could be a rude awakening, but not Tom.'

Those on the set said that Tom behaved as immaculately as ever but there was an inner battle going on all the time that no one was aware of. Tom was desperately trying to make his own voice sound more authoritative, stronger, more forceful. In the past, some film industry experts had pronounced Tom's voice to be 'thin and high pitched', and said it did not aid his performance and might well have hindered his chances of an Oscar.

Tom saw *A Few Good Men* as an opportunity to

improve on that problem because his character had to hold his own against older, more experienced men in a court-room setting. It was not easy by any means.

Tom even called on advice from Robert Duvall who seemed to have replaced Paul Newman as a father figure in his life at that time. In Christmas 1991, Tom gave the veteran Oscar-winning star a $20,000 show jumping horse as a gift. Some saw it as a thank you to Duvall for helping Tom and Nicole to seal their love for one another during the shooting of *Days of Thunder*.

Later Duvall said, with just a hint of paternal pride: 'He's got his own world. He may have a small entourage, but mostly it's his wife, Nicole. They hibernate with certain friends and associates. She's quieter than he is. I hope it lasts because it's tough.'

Duvall insisted: 'He's very open hearted on a certain level. And he's the most genuine and most accessible of that whole group of young actors.'

Probably the single most controversial aspect of *A Few Good Men* was the astronomical fees paid to the three principal actors. Tom was on a reported $12.5 million; Jack Nicholson was paid $5 million for just ten days' work; Demi Moore was on a cool $3 million, Keifer Sutherland got a relatively modest $1 million; Bacon ended up with $750,000. Tom's deal put him firmly at the top of the best-paid actors' league and sparked a furore in the press about overpaid Hollywood stars and directors because *A Few Good Men* would have cost less than half its $41 million budget if it had not been for the huge sums paid out to those actors.

Some accused the stars' agents of taking advantage of the power vacuum at the studios where certain films were being green-lighted only on condition that a specific star became attached. The actual film seemed to be taking second place to the celebrity content. Others in Tinseltown argued that only a tiny per cent of a film's profits was ever returned to the star under the so-called points system which was supposed to provide an actor with a bonus system if his or her movie was a big box office success.

'No one will complain if Disney make half a billion dollars because it's a company,' explained movie analyst Jim Logsdon. 'But people will complain about an actor making $15 to $20 million as a person.'

Increasingly, the studios were putting pressure on stars to share the financial burden of certain projects in order to avoid situations where star involvement got an otherwise bad movie off the ground, which then still lost huge amount of money.

Perhaps the ultimate evidence that Tom had truly become Hollywood's number-one star came when Disney chairman Jeffrey Katzenberg was shown preliminary drawings for his up-and-coming cartoon movie *Aladdin*. Katzenberg complained bitterly about the low hunk content of the appearance of the Aladdin character. He was convinced that, as it was drawn, it would not attract enough older children. The Disney chief ordered his artists to make the character look more like Tom Cruise! The Disney team of experts immediately bought dozens of photographs of Tom, pinned them up in their production offices and promptly converted the previously weedy Aladdin into a Cruise lookalike. The result was a cartoon character who definitely resembles Tom and also proved to have his box office magnetism, because *Aladdin* went on to become the biggest grossing cartoon of all time.

One incident that slightly soured the atmosphere on the set of *A Few Good Men* occurred during the filming of the climactic courtroom scene in which Jack Nicholson's character lunges at Tom from the witness stand and has to be restrained by two Marine guards. While being made up between takes, a real Marine, who had been cast as one of the guards, joked to the make-up artists to take it easy, he didn't want to be 'prettier' than Tom. Overhearing the remark, Tom barked angrily at the young Marine, 'What do you mean by that?'

'I don't want to be a pretty boy like you,' the Marine joked.

'Yeah, then you'd have to get a real job,' Tom told the $17,000-a-year Marine.

It was an uncharacteristic slip of the tongue by Tom and indicated that perhaps his attitude towards people was not so perfect after all.

Apart from that flare-up, the production itself was remarkably trouble-free considering the number of fragile egos on display. Tom and Nicholson exchanged sickly sweet compliments about each other, much to the annoyance of petulant Demi Moore who reportedly threw a few 'temper tantrums' because she felt ignored when Tom and Nicholson were both on set.

Later Demi said sportingly of Tom: 'He's very smart about himself. He knows his strengths and his weaknesses and he's not afraid to expose them to get what he needs.' Behind the polite words, however, Demi Moore was definitely feeling a little neglected.

The relationship between the characters played by Tom and Demi was, except for a few longing looks, essentially non-romantic. The actress even admitted that her agent was wondering: 'Isn't there at least going to be a kiss?'

However, Tom was saving all his passion for real-life wife Nicole, who turned up on the set in Boston and spent much of the time smooching with him in a corner between takes. The couple sneaked off one night to watch a video version of Tom's screen début Endless Love, in which he had a brief walk-on part. Tom doubled up with embarrassment as Nicole laughed and then told him she thought he was really sexy in it.

Tom also proved that there was another side to his work-obsessed persona when he paid for all of his co-stars to fly to Las Vegas in his private Lear jet for dinner and an evening of gambling. Tom even arranged for a private salon at the Mirage Hotel and casino where everyone could play blackjack. Demi's outspoken husband Bruce Willis won more than $10,000 and there was a minor crowd control crisis when Willis, Demi Moore and Tom decided they wanted to play the slot machines in the main casino.

A Few Good Men co-star Kevin Pollack explained: 'I really enjoyed hanging out with Tom. It gave me a chance to see how the other one per cent live.'

A Few Good Men got mixed reviews but proved that there is nothing to beat the sheer pulling power of stars by taking in more than $100 million at the US box office. *Vogue* magazine described the movie as being filled with 'a great deal of young and not so young and pretty much middle aged talent.'

Meanwhile, Tom's loyalty to his immediate family and friends was becoming increasingly apparent. A few years earlier his close friend and cousin, William Mapother, had joined Tom's TC Productions company and now eldest sister Lee Anne came on board as Tom's main assistant. The actor believed that he could trust his close family and friends much more than the rest of Hollywood. After leasing the ultimate status symbol, a Gulf-stream jet, he decided to shell out a reported $15 million for the plane.

The success of *A Good Few Men* was yet another lesson for Tom. He knew that the time was approaching when he would have to take a vast creative leap into a role that no one would expect him to take. It might not be his next film or the one after that, but sooner or later he had to find something that would shock and amaze his fans and prove once and for all that he was an actor capable of anything.

When one writer asked him if he could play a junkie or a gay character without damaging his career, Tom answered: 'What do you mean by "could I"? Like, who would stop me?'

'If I read a character that had some value and he was gay or a drug addict – and it had some payoff – then you do it. Right now those kind of things are available to me but have I read any great scripts where I wanted to do it? I can say right now, "No, I haven't". That doesn't mean that in the future I'm not open to doing it if I fine it.'

Tom's ability to look to the future was always apparent and he always had one eye on something completely different.

'Guys want to be like him and girls want to be with him.'

Jerry Bruckheimer

22

Counteracting all the high-tech effects movies of the summer of 1993 came the action pyrotechnics of Paramount Pictures *The Firm*, based on John Grisham's best-selling suspense novel and starring Tom with veteran actor Gene Hackman.

Besides being a great page-turner, Grisham's book was a parable of greed in the money-loving 1980s. To bite the golden apple, it reminded us, was to risk poison. This was also a decade that had given birth to the career of Tom Cruise.

He and Hackman played two members of a Memphis firm which just happens to represent the Mafia. Tom was Mitch McDeere, a new recruit lured into the partnership under honourable pretences; Hackman portrayed Avery Tolar, the veteran lawyer who becomes his mentor.

The film's dynamic ensemble also included Jeanne Tripplehorn (the other woman in *Basic Instinct*) as Mitch's sceptical but strong-willed wife, Abby; Ed Harris as FBI agent Wayne Tarrance, who tries to force Mitch to hand over evidence against his employers; Wilfred Brimely as William Devasher, the gritty head of security for the firm; and Gary Busey in a small, but smarmy, role as an ex-con lawyer who tries to help Mitch while he can. A cameo by Holly Hunter was also much acclaimed after the movie's release and eventually helped to earn her an Oscar nomination.

However, it was *The Firm*'s director, Sydney Pollack who drew the most intense respect from Tom and his co-stars. Pollack's movies had earned 43 Academy Award nominations, including four for Best Picture, and he had personally been nominated three times, winning once for the 1985 Best Picture *Out of Africa*.

The much talked about pairing of Tom and Hackman seemed destined to initiate yet another father-son relationship between the younger star and the more established veteran performer. However, Tom was now older and wiser and, just as with Jack Nicholson in *A Few Good Men*, he was no longer prepared to defer to his more senior colleagues.

This change of attitude towards his elders resulted in a new problem that is also an old problem. In fact, it's as old as the hills of Hollywood. Halfway through the movie's back-breaking post-production schedule, reports in the Hollywood trade press suggested that Hackman was furious to discover that his name was not above the title of *The Firm* alongside that of Tom. Sources in *Daily Variety* suggested that Hackman, having just won a Best Supporting Oscar for his brilliant work in the Clint Eastwood-directed Western *Unforgiven*, felt that he should get due credit in his next movie, *The Firm*. However, Paramount insisted that only Tom's name should be above the title because they believed his name could draw big crowds. Hackman was begged to agree but in the end his agents insisted that his name was dropped completely from the credits

Insiders said Hackman was 'dismayed' to be put in such an awkward position but Tom had it in writing that his face and name would dominate posters, billboards and printed advertisements for *The Firm*. Paramount tried to pacify Hackman by claiming that if both stars' names and faces dominated the film's publicity material, people might think it was a buddy-buddy movie rather than a thriller but Hackman didn't buy that and he demanded that all references to him be removed. No one knows how slighted Gene Hackman felt but the message was loud and clear: Tom Cruise is the most powerful movie star on the planet and what he says goes!

There was another ego at stake besides that of the two starring actors. *The Firm* had been devised and written as a million-selling novel by former Memphis lawyer John Grisham. In the early 1990s it became virtually impossible to enter any bookshop without seeing a Grisham book and Tom had first set eyes on this one after one of the crew members on *Far and Away* had sent him a copy.

The rise of Grisham had been almost as phenomenal as that of Tom Cruise yet he had written only four novels, *A Time To Kill*, *The Firm*, *The Pelican Brief* and *The Client* – all within five years. *The Firm* had even been sold as a movie to Paramount on the strength of a one-sentence pitch by Grisham's agent. Not one word had been written, yet he landed a $600,000 deal for the movie rights. So while Tom and Hackman each burnt the boards on the acting side, the question on more people's lips was: 'Where's Grisham?' No one knows if this slight diversion away from the movie's main players had any effect on their performance – probably not – but for the first time in his professional life Tom was actually competing for coverage with a non-actor.

Filming *The Firm* in Memphis, in November 1992, Tom seemed more relaxed than he had been in years. One night he paid an entire dinner tab for some college kids who sang his *Top Gun* song 'You've Lost That Loving Feelin'' at a restaurant. The star also donated $15,000 to a local children's hospital.

The Firm's presence in Memphis was a big event for the city where the blues were born. Much of the shooting took place in tranquil, tree-lined roads in the suburbs. The locals got used to being woken at 5 a.m. as crew members wrestled with the contrivances of film making, from catering vans, lighting and sound equipment to the details of props and costumes.

In Tuckahoe Lane, where Tom's character Mitch lived, neighbours stood on their front lawns, craning for a glimpse of Tom and his attractive co-star Jeanne Tripplehorn. Often there early in his leather bomber jacket, vest and white T-shirt Tom even managed to shake a few hands.

After four wet months in freezing cold Memphis, the cast and crew of *The Firm* headed for the sunshine of the Cayman Islands. 'The mood in the cabin became religious – like a revival meeting,' said Jeanne Tripplehorn echoing everyone else's sentiments at the time.

The Firm soon became the talk of the islands. Rumours spread about the shoot taking place on deserted beaches and hundreds of locals would show up at some picturesque spot only to discover the gossip was false. Often the most exciting event was the daily visit of the turtles who swim in to be fed their breakfast doggie biscuits by the residents along the shoreline. Local tourist officials believed that all three island – Grand Cayman, Cayman Brac and Little Cayman – would finally be put on the tourist map by *The Firm*.

In actual fact, offshore banking and diving drew the characters in the movie to the Caymans. In real life, the actors considered the location a 'real perk'. Gene Hackman got himself a diving certificate especially for the movie and he and Cruise dived at a picturesque bay called Orange Canyon. Going down to depths of around 100 feet, they proclaimed that the sights beneath the surface were 'spectacular'. Neither actor used a stand-in for any of the film's diving scenes. There was a little friendly macho rivalry between the two stars. To some it seemed somewhat more intense.

Tripplehorn chased barracuda as she snorkelled in her free time, but none of the actors was permitted to get a tan because they still had two more weeks of filming the office scenes back in Los Angeles.

The atmosphere on the Caymans was much more relaxed and by the end of that part of the shoot, crew members were begging Tripplehorn to fluff lines so that they could stay longer. Gene Hackman even announced he loved the place so much he was considering buying a property on the paradise island.

Then in stepped a beautiful young brunette actress called Karina Lombard, from Venice Beach, California. The starlet had been cast to play a prostitute who seduces Tom in a sizzling sex scene on the beach. However, she was bitterly rude about her famous co-star after their love scenes together.

Because she was a mere nobody playing a small role, no one paid her much attention and that grated with the 24-year-old actress. When the director yelled 'Cut!' she complained: 'There were like 50 people rushing to clean him up and I'm standing there full of sand, and nobody comes to help me … I thought, "Ewww!" 'Lombard provoked that same sort of reaction herself when she made an astonishing public attack on Tom's wife Nicole, criticising her for hanging around during the filming of that love scene.

Even more revealing, the young actress claimed that Nicole had flown into the Caymans on the same flight as her and caught the same flight back to Los Angeles after her role was wrapped. If this was true, it seemed an extraordinarily over-jealous way to behave on the part of Nicole, but then she and Tom are both very possessive people so perhaps it was not so surprising.

Lombard summed it up by saying: 'She [Nicole] was on the set the whole time watching, watching, watching. Everyone stared at me like I had come, I'd see, I'd conquer.'

Later, after a few calls from 'people in Hollywood', she hurriedly issued a 'clarification' of what her remarks really meant, saying, 'Nicole was absolutely not spying on me!' but then Lombard, who was put under ridiculous pressure not to talk following her original outburst, went back on the warpath, exclaiming that Tom was 'whisked away by his beloved' after each take. 'I was there to do a job,' added Lombard, who lambasted any suggestion that she was a starlet on the make by rightly pointing out that she was happily married to actor/playwright Anthony Crane at the time. Meanwhile Nicole Kidman was quoted in the press as saying that her husband's attractive co-star was 'very rude'.

Others speculated that Lombard was simply trying to generate publicity by her outbursts but friends of the actress hotly denied it and insisted that the attractive actress was simply very serious about her work. 'She's terrifically passionate about her work,' explained friend Martine Beswicke. 'There's a wonderful naivety about her.'

Certainly Lombard's background did not suggest that she was of the cashing-in-on-a-non-scandal bimbo variety. Born in Tahiti, daughter of a banking heir and an Indian medicine woman, she was brought up for much of her life in Barcelona.

It makes her comments about *The Firm* all the more

interesting. 'When I think about *The Firm* shoot, it hurts. I was quite lonely.' The young actress felt that she had been neglected by nervous production people fearful that Tom might think she was throwing herself at him. Actually, the reverse was true. Tom never even gave her a second thought but the army of advisors who surrounded his every move were second-guessing a situation they feared might arise, especially since everyone knew that Nicole and Tom were still behaving like honeymooners most of the time.

Reports in some of the US tabloids claimed that Tom had personally insisted that Karina be banned from *The Firm*'s publicity rounds just before the film's release. Show-business reporters pointed out that there were no photographs available of the sexy beach scene with Tom and claimed that he had insisted Paramount did not release them in the usual press-packs that go out to help to promote movies.

Months later, Karina got some subtle revenge when she was asked whom she preferred kissing, Tom or another co-star, hunky Brad Pitt (who went on to appear in *Interview with a Vampire* with Tom). She said: 'They are both great kissers, but since I got along more with Brad I would have to say he was the best. We were kissing a lot longer. There's a lot more heat and I really respect him.'

In the book of *The Firm*, Tom's character Mitch has his fling on the beach but does not tell his wife about it. In the movie version, Tom confesses all to his wife. No one will say exactly who suggested the change but there was talk that Tom contributed towards the script changes.

Jeanne Tripplehorn was allowed to comment about Tom as she played his wife in *The Firm*. The most frequently asked question was 'What is it like kissing Tom Cruise?'

'Well, he's got some very nice lips, I enjoyed it,' came her giggly reply. At least someone enjoyed kissing Tom!

Then Tripplehorn – in common with just about every other person ever asked a professional opinion of Tom – added: 'He's a very committed, very focused actor. It's a very unnatural thing for actors, just the situation that two people are in, especially when you're either married or engaged.'

Tom was married and Tripplehorn was engaged to American TV star Ben Stiller. She found her love scenes with Tom especially hard for that reason. 'You have your private life and those you love, and then you're thrown into this very unnatural situation. But you want it to work, and hopefully you find something to enjoy about it.'

Reviews of *The Firm* were fairly good. In the *Los Angeles Times* respected critic Kenneth Turan hailed the acting as 'quietly effective' but saved much of his praise for veteran director Sidney Pollack. 'He has not only taken the risk of letting his film run the two and a half hours needed to include relevant characterisation, he has demonstrated how emotional shading and subtlety can be worked into big-ticket items.'

In Britain, the *Daily Mirror* was not so full of praise: 'Cruise fans may be satisfied by their boy's angst-ridden heroics. The rest of us will have to wait for *The Fugitive* for the real thing.' The paper described the movie as a 'tedious tale' and accused it of not being a real thriller in the traditional sense.

The *Los Angeles Weekly* wrote: 'It's no disgrace that, having held his own with the likes of Newman, Hoffman and Nicholson, he's met his match in Hackman. Cruise is the weakest thing in *The Firm*.'

Tom did get some praise from *The Hollywood Reporter*, whose reviewer Duane Byrge wrote: 'As the tenacious young lawyer, Cruise brilliantly embodies the character's ambitious resolve.'

Some Hollywood observers began to wonder if the

enormous success of *The Firm* and *A Few Good Men* in tremendously similar roles argued against the notion that Tom possessed some mystical and durable popularity. In both films, Tom played a glib, cocky legal eagle who's just graduated from Harvard Law School and audiences flocked to see him. Would moviegoers have reacted with similar enthusiasm had the Cruise characters been associated with less prestigious academic institutions? What if he avoided the legal profession altogether?

Tom, well aware of what was being said about the similarities of the two roles, was already carefully looking around for something completely different but he couldn't help smiling as *The Firm* toppled Steven Spielberg's epic *Jurassic Park* from the number one box office slot in the United States. The movie made an astounding $100 million within 23 days of release in the States.

"We expected this to be a big movie, but no way did we anticipate this kind of box office result so quickly", said a delighted Paramount President Barry London. Only *Jurassic Park* (9 days) *Batman* (10 days) *Batman Returns* (11 days) *Terminator 2: Judgement Day* (16 days) and *Indiana Jones and the Last Crusade* (19 days) achieved the $100 million milestone faster.

Tom surprised the crew on *The Firm* by presenting them all with glass paperweights containing a miniature replica of the movie's poster. There were some rumblings about a bottle of booze or a production bomber jacket being a whole lot more useful.

The crew's grumblings were not quietened when news spread that Tom, director Sydney Pollack and producer Scott Rudin had each been given a $100,000 Mercedes 500SL as a personal thank you when *The Firm* topped the $100 million mark at the US box office. Ironically, the movie's backer, Paramount, had to fork out a further

$50,000 to each of the three after it was discovered that they would have to pay that in tax on their perks. There were also mutterings as to why novelist John Grisham did not get one, especially as it was reported in the spring of 1994 that Tom was planning to play the lead in a screen adaptation of Grisham's latest blockbuster, called *The Chamber*. Paramount paid the writer $3.5 million for the film rights before he had written the first word of the book!

Back in Memphis, a pair of underpants left by accident in Tom's rented house were sold in a charity auction for $200 as if to compound the fact that Tom was the most-sought after male in the universe.

*　　*　　*

After *The Firm* wrapped, anxious Paramount executives started trawling around desperately for another project for Tom, aware that the movie was going to be a huge hit. They wanted to get Tom into something else as quickly as possible, so as to cash in on that success. The only thing they could find that seemed of any interest to Tom was a screen adaptation of *Mission: Impossible*, the TV series that ran on CBS and in Britain from 1966–73. Actor Peter Graves starred in the show and became its trademark across the world. He played the head of a secret government agency called the Impossible Missions Force but, as such, he was principally the conduit for interaction among an espionage group.

At Paramount writers were busily reworking the script so that Tom could be the main spy. They were painfully aware that if Tom gave the project the thumbs down it could self-destruct in five seconds. A year later, in early 1994, rumours of Tom's involvement resurfaced following the phenomenal success of *The Fugitive*, another project that started life as a TV series.

On the *Forbes* magazine's list of the highest paid entertainers in the United States, Tom came in at number sixteen, one million dollars above Arnold Schwarzenegger, with a fortune estimated to be in the region of $35 million, although he is probably worth at least $10 million more than that.

In July 1992, Tom further expanded his Cruise control by setting up a new production company with his agent Paula Wagner from CAA. Wagner, who had loyally and expertly represented Tom for 11 years, became his producing partner and the pair were now in such a strong position, thanks to Tom's immense pulling power at the box office, that they decided to take their time before attaching the company to any of the big studios. This made a lot of sense as it would allow Tom to pick and choose the projects he wanted to do rather than having the studios dictate to him.

In a carefully worded statement, Tom said: 'For some time I have wanted to create a film company that would give me the opportunity to develop and work on a wider range of films – some of which I would act in or direct, and others which I would produce. I wanted to find the right partner to make it work and, as Paula and I talked about it, it became clear to both of us that we ought to do it together.'

Tom also wanted to ensure that his company had enough muscle to give him the freedom to direct if and when he decided it was time to make that most significant step of all. He knew that helming a picture was a whole different ballgame from acting and he was determined to take his time and start with something modest.

Wagner, a former New York actress and playwright, had become one of Tom's closest friends. With her husband, CAA motion picture department head Rick Nicita, she was a regular visitor to the Cruise household in Pacific Palisades.

Significantly, CAA mogul Mike Ovitz – one of the two most powerful men in Hollywood – stepped up his links with Tom after Paula left his company, and CAA continued to handle the superstar. Ovitz and his president, Ron Meyer, even issued a joint statement to the Tinseltown daily bible, *Variety*, about Tom's link-up with Wagner: 'Their relationship has developed into what we know will be a very successful partnership. As their friends and agents, we look forward to working with them and their new company for many years to come.'

In the launch announcement, Wagner also made a point of stating that Nicole Kidman was not involved in any way with the newly formed company.

A few weeks after that initial announcement, Tom and Wagner announced that they had signed an exclusive multi-picture deal with Paramount Pictures, completely contradicting the pair's intention to pick and chose whatever projects they liked. Hollywood insiders pointed to Tom's close working relationship with Paramount chief Stanley Jaffe, who gave Tom his first big chance when he was producer of *Taps*.

Meanwhile, Tom and Nicole continued to prove to the world that they were as heavily in love as ever. For Christmas 1992, Nicole contacted the International Star Registry in Ingelside, Illinois, and paid $45 to name a star for Tom in the Hercules constellation. ISR representative Elaine Stolpe explained that Nicole named the star Forever Tom. The moniker is not recognised by scientists, but for anyone with a telescope the co-ordinates are: right ascension – 16 hr, 55 min, 48 sec; declination – 47 degrees, 39 min.

Around this time Tom took his environmentally friendly electric car with him to an interview with a journalist from *Rolling Stone* and ended up having a race up Sunset Boulevard with the writer!

Another movie project that Tom was allegedly attached to was Paramount's big screen adaptation of Ira Levin's best-selling *Sliver*. The actor was rumoured to be set to get his biggest ever paycheck of $20 million, but eventually the deal fell through because Tom did not like the erotic content of the film which centres around the sexual activities of residents in a New York apartment block. If Tom had taken the role he would have ended up cast alongside Hollywood's so-called sexiest actress Sharon Stone, but he was looking for something to really get his teeth into ... and it was lurking just around the corner.

*'Man's wars, his revolutions,
his suffering, all stem from his lack
of data on the mind and man.'*

L. Ron Hubbard

23

Scientology is an applied religious philosophy. Its goal is to bring an individual to an understanding of himself and his life as a spiritual being and in relationship to the universe as a whole.

Scientology provides mankind the means to attain a comprehensive understanding of the human spirit and to achieve the traditional religious goals of spiritual enlightenment and salvation. This spiritual path is the result of almost 50 years of extensive research by the Founder of the Scientology religion, L. Ron Hubbard. The millions of Scientologists and others who benefit from L. Ron Hubbard's discoveries regard him with great respect and admiration.

This is the official description of the Church of Scientology which appeared in a full page advertisement taken out in *The Times* on 28 May 1994. It cost more than £20,000 and came out just a few weeks after Richard Gere and Cindy Crawford took out a similarly sized advertisement in the same publication to announce to the world that they were not gay. The Scientologists had decided it was time to tell the world that the United States Internal Revenue Service had finally recognized them as a charity.

* * *

It's not clear exactly when Tom Cruise began to call himself a Scientologist. In 1989, a Church of Scientology publication included Tom Mapother (the Cruise part of his name was left out deliberately) and his cousin William Mapother on a list of people who had just completed basic Scientology courses.

In fact, Tom was first introduced to the church after he married Mimi Rogers, whose father was an early member of Scientology. Tom and Mimi even attended marriage-counselling sessions at the church when their relationship started to crumble in the summer of 1989.

As a petite 15-year-old schoolgirl, Mimi was already a hugely committed member of the church. She insisted that she was never converted to Scientology.

'Rather, that philosophy was simply part of my upbringing. And I think it was an excellent system of belief to grow up with because Scientology offers an extremely pragmatic method for taking spiritual concerns and breaking them down into everyday applications.

'Scientology is controversial because it doesn't deal with traditional concepts of God and people are always threatened by anything that veers away from the accepted norm. However, I've never been disenchanted with Scientology because the basic philosophic tenets I grew up with have proven to be sound.'

The reason behind Tom's conversion might have been just as simple as the fact that he craved belonging. Movie critic and screenwriter Michael Medved reckons that artists and entertainers need 'a community, a tribe, a place where they can fit in'. He also explained: 'Part of being in the arts has to do with rejecting whatever the conventional wisdom is.'

Beverly Hills psychologist Dr Eugene Landy, who has treated some of Hollywood's most famous names, explained: 'Religion is just one of those things celebrities turn to.' The need for structure in every life, but especially in a celebrity's, declared Dr Landy, is 'one of the basics of all basics.'

The Church of Scientology itself has always insisted that it was not concerned about the number of famous people who have joined its ranks in recent years, but there is no doubt that celebrities such as Tom do serve a useful purpose. But Scientology is in all likelihood the only religion that offers a church set aside exclusively for artists and professionals.

That church, called the Celebrity Centre, is quite understandably located in Hollywood. The church claims it was originally established to fulfill the demands of artists and other professionals in Hollywood to provide a quiet place for them to receive religious services without the disruption celebrity sometimes inspires. That desire for privacy meshed well with Scientology founder Hubbard's belief that artists were important to the well-being of a society. 'A culture is only as great as its dreams,' he wrote, 'and its dreams are dreamed by artists.'

Hubbard – a larger than life figure – was no stranger to controversy himself. Widely known as a popular fiction author before developing Scientology, it was the publication of his book *Dianetics, the Modern Science of Mental Health*, in 1950 that thrust him onto the world stage. As with so many famous people, it is difficult to sort the fiction from fact, and the stories surrounding Hubbard's life are as varied as the sources from which they come.

What is clear is that Hubbard was a man of many facets – a writer, an explorer, a photographer, a musician, an aviator and a philosopher. To those who follow his teachings and to many other scholars (as the Scientologists are quick to point out), he is considered a genius, and yet there are many who have targeted him for exceptionally harsh criticism.

The Scientologists provide voluminous documentation to refute the allegations levelled against Hubbard and it does appear from the documents uncovered by the Scientologists using the liberal Freedom of Information Act in the United States that a concerted campaign to destroy his reputation began just weeks after the publication of *Dianetics*. The medical and mental health fields accused him of being a charlatan, yet *Dianetics* became enormously popular all across the United States even as the negative press was running.

Hubbard's writings on the subject of Scientology are vast – hundreds of books and lectures describe the principles and rules of Scientology. Out of these vast writings, the Scientologists often quote Hubbard in an effort to explain the man. One widely published quote gives a glimpse of his vision of himself and his fellow Scientologists:

'This work does not represent a revolt. All it represents is the hope that Man again can find his own feet, can find himself – in a very confused, mechanistic society – and can recover to himself some of the happiness, some of the sincerity, some of the love and kindness with which he was created, and if Man can do this and if we can help in any way to accomplish this, then all the years of my life and all the years of yours will have been well paid for, and none of us will have lived in vain.'

Perhaps Hubbard's involvement in the arts has made his teachings particularly attractive to other artists. It certainly is no secret that Scientology has become the 'religion of the stars.'

Yet, at the same time, Hubbard and the Scientologists have battled governments around the world for years. Scientology was banned in Australia in the 1960s, and foreign Scientologists were banned from entering Britain to study later in that decade. But ultimately the Scientologists – who follow Hubbard's teachings to the letter, writings which cover an astonishing array of subjects as diverse as principles of Scientology practice and how to deal with governments – prevailed in each case. The Australian government lifted the ban on Scientology with an apology, and the Home Office rescinded the ban on the entry of Scientologists into the United Kingdom.

The Scientologists have earned a reputation for being relentless. They just don't take 'no' for an answer. They fought the Internal Revenue Service in the United States for decades both in the media and in the courts. Ultimately the Scientologists got what they wanted when the IRS recognized them as a non-profit religion, operated exclusively for religious and charitable purposes.

Hubbard's philosophy with its emphasis on the

individual achieving his own spiritual fulfilment through an understanding of himself and his objectives in life, seems to be a good match for Tom's purposeful approach to his life and his work.

It wasn't until the mid-1970s conversion of *Saturday Night Fever* star John Travolta that Hollywood began to sit up and take notice of the Scientologists. In 1990, the actor and his wife Kelly Preston even insisted that the birth of their son Jett should be held in complete silence following church teaching that this helped to safeguard the well-being of both mother and child.

Kirstie Alley – Travolta's co-star in the phenomenally successful *Look Who's Talking* series of movies – also joined the Scientologists. Other famous members include jazz pianist Chick Corea, actress Karen Black, opera star Julia Migenes, Priscilla Presley and her daughter Lisa Marie Presley; actresses Anne Archer and Juliette Lewis; singers Isaac Hayes and Maxine Nightingale; Nancy Cartwright, the voice of TV's Bart Simpson. Even one-time pop star and now United States Congressman Sonny Bono – former husband of Cher – who wrote a poem for the Scientologists: 'I'm on the first step to the stairway to infinity . . . and now I feel the force of something new surrounding me . . .'

The list of celebrity Scientologists goes on and on – performers, writers, directors, producers, and so forth. But there can be little doubt that Tom is the biggest name of all. With Tom, the church has become a heavyweight player, more likely to influence others in Scientology's efforts to achieve its lofty aims laid out by Hubbard:

'A civilisation without insanity, without criminals and without war, where the able can prosper and honest beings can have rights, and where man is free to rise to greater heights.'

Many Hollywood observers say that Tom's renowned focus and intensity have become especially apparent since his involvement in Scientology.

> 'Essentially it's enabled me – it's just helped me to become more me. It gives me certain tools to utilize to be the person I want to be and explore the areas I want to explore as an artist.'

Tom has always insisted that his religious choices were an entirely personal matter and his legal advisors frequently react very strongly to any references to his involvement in the Church of Scientology. He is known by the initials 'TC' to everyone inside the church.

Tom has reached a high level in the religion's controversial auditing programme and there is little doubt that his religion plays a regular role in both his work and home life.

On one hand, the church insists it does not cash in on the big name members, but the Scientologists call one of their many in-house magazines *Celebrity* and its star disciples happily appear to endorse the church's 'message'.

Scientology is based on a concept that involves exorcising 'the painful experiences of your life' which interfere with rational thought. That is achieved through a spiritual counselling process called 'auditing' which the Scientologists describe this way:

> 'It is a very unique form of personal counselling which helps an individual look at his own existence and improves his ability to confront what he is and where he is. The goal of auditing is to restore being-ness and ability. This is accomplished by 1) helping the individual rid himself of any disabilities and 2) increasing individual abilities.'

'Auditors' often employ a device called an 'E-meter' – a device that measures changes in a person's state of mind. Scientology has never been accused of being like any other religion, and the use of the E-meter is just one of those differences that has stirred up controversy as it is often described as something akin to a lie-detector, a characterisation the Scientologists strenuously object to and for which they provide technical analysis from electronics experts as refutation. Yet, as unorthodox as it may seem, Scientology, at its essence, is all about gaining control of one's self and one's environment. As someone who certainly suffered from his share of emotional upheaval as a child and then grew into a controlling sort of person, the church offered an ideal base for Tom.

Tom rarely refers directly to the church – which has millions of members around the world and centres in more than 70 countries – but in the summer of 1992 he did tell writer James Greenberg of his anger over the bad press the church regularly receives.

'The articles you've read have come from an absolute point of mystery and knowing. They talk about how religion dictates people's lives; it's the reverse of that. It doesn't dictate anything. The whole thing is not something that's directed towards dictating; it's actually directed toward conceptual thinking and independent ideas.

'It [Scientology] works for me. It's helped me be more me and do the things I want to do. I can't tell anybody what their path to enlightenment is. It's your own adventure. The whole thing is about self-discovery and deciding on your own what is real and true for you. It's not like Scientology wants a war with anyone. But it wants to get information out to people so they will be able to decide for themselves what they want.'

That theme – the very personal nature of Scientology to each Scientologist is one that Tom often repeats, as he did not long ago in *Vanity Fair* magazine.

'It's a very personal thing. Truly this is how I feel about it. People come up to me and ask me, "So what is Scientology?" I say, "Hey, if you want to know about it, then read a book about it and see what it means to you." It's curious to me why people want to fixate on it. It has certainly helped me. Very much so. It has helped my spiritual life. I enjoy it. But people try to create this whole thing about how Scientology is controlling my money and my career.'

On the set of *A Few Good Men*, Tom insisted that his assistant Michael Doven be called his 'communicator' by all members of the crew. Doven – a Tom lookalike – wore the star's 'bat utility belt', complete with a cellular phone and water bottle.

The basic *Dictionary of Dianetics and Scientology* describes a communicator as 'the person who keeps an executive's communication lines (body, dispatch, intercom and phone) moving or controlled. The communicator helps an executive free his or her time for essential income-earning actions, rest or recreation and prolongs the term of appointment of the executive by safeguarding against overload.'

Other members of Tom's personal staff have been encouraged to join the church. His secretary has been listed in the church's in-house *Celebrity* magazine as having completed at least one Scientology course.

Tom's sensitivity towards the publication of such information has sparked some unpleasant communication between his PR woman Pat Kingsley and a number of magazines in the United States. Before *Los Angeles* magazine published an article entitled 'No More Mr Nice Guy', writer Rod Lurie could only put certain points to Tom if he did it through Pat Kingsley.

After requesting an answer to the whole question of Tom encouraging his staff to join the Scientologists, the actor snarled back (through Kingsley, naturally): 'I don't ask any employee or prospective employee what his or her religion is. Isn't that against the law? If not, why not?'

Nicole Kidman was introduced to the church through her husband who even admitted to Lurie that she 'learned Scientology from me and then investigated for herself.'

In 1992, Tom sparked an angry response from the Dyslexia Foundation of America when he was quoted as saying that Scientology had helped him to cure his dyslexia problems.

The foundation was angry that Tom's statement implied that dyslexia could be cured as easily as a common cold. Executive vice president of the foundation Joyce Bulifant accused Tom of 'spreading misinformation'. She added: 'It would be nice if he understood the disease better.'

After this public outburst, Tom contacted Hollywood columnists Marilyn Beck and Stacy Jenel Smith to insist:

'I was diagnosed as dyslexic a long time ago, took remedial reading courses all through school. Then I was given The Basic Study Manual, written by L. Ron Hubbard. I started applying its principles, began reading faster, and that convinced me I had never been dyslexic.'

It also seemed that the church has caused some friction between Tom and *Top Gun/Days of Thunder* producer Don Simpson.

Simpson was quoted in the media concerning the use of a sound recording system developed by the Scientologists called Clearsound. Tom had been very impressed when he first heard the system in use at the church's film studio, and he wanted it used in his own movies.

Simpson – who reportedly had earlier been involved with Scientology himself – allegedly had a falling out with Tom and the Scientologists.

However, in early 1994 Simpson refused to get drawn any further into the furore concerning his membership in the Church of Scientology and ignored three faxed messages and a number of telephone inquiries to his office on the Disney lot in Los Angeles, where he is now producing.

When *Los Angeles* writer Rod Lurie tried to press Tom (through Pat Kingsley) about the Simpson situation, the star simply said: 'Don Simpson's relationship to Scientology is his business, just as my relationship to Scientology is my business.'

Simpson himself then sent a letter claiming to have been misquoted, stating 'I bear no animosity or ill-will toward the tech of Scientology or any individuals presently involved.' He had his attorneys send a letter threatening legal action to *Los Angeles* magazine demanding a retraction of the quotes attributed to him. Apparently Don Simpson did not want any upset with Tom Cruise and the Scientologists.

There seems little doubt that Tom's own aversion to the media has been fuelled by the Church of Scientology's basic mistrust of the press. A fair portrait is what the church claims is all they ask for, and that's hardly surprising. The

Scientologists have long contended that a controversy-thirsty media has latched onto the unsubstantiated claims of a handful of discontented former members and given those allegations disproportionate prominence in relation to what the church says is the true story.

But the church insists that it is not in any way obsessed with countering 'negative' publicity about the organisation. However, founder L. Ron Hubbard, who died in January 1986, did produce a so-called 'Code of Honour' for Scientologists which clearly states: 'Do not give or receive communication unless you yourself desire it.'

The use of the controversial Clearsound system was a continuing situation throughout all of Tom's films after *Days of Thunder* in 1990. Film makers who have used the system claim that, while they are often impressed with the results, it still has enough kinks to make its use questionable.

Tom did succeed in getting director Ron Howard to use the system on *Far and Away*. On *A Few Good Men*, director Rob Reiner used both Clearsound and a standard sound machine. A similar situation occurred on *The Firm*.

However, while news of Tom's demands about Clearsound have swept Hollywood, in fairness, it should be pointed out that many people have missed the point entirely. Tom seems genuinely to believe that his weakest point – his voice – can be improved by using Clearsound. As one movieland observer pointed out:

'Every actor in the world has a duty to himself to make sure that the best possible image of himself is projected on the screen. If Tom had elected to use some new system from a traditional source the whole fuss would have died down years ago. Unfortunately, because it is linked with the

Scientologists, some people are not entirely happy about it.'

Therein lies the basic problem about Tom's links with the Scientologists, for the Church upholds what some call an 'eccentric' belief in past lives, has a unique form of personal counselling, and uses the term 'wogs' to describe non-Scientologists.

Members, however, swear that Scientology rids them of their troublesome mental baggage, sharpens their focus and enables them to be free from unnecessary distractions and to be in complete control of their own destiny. To members, their religion is a personalised commitment and an individual journey. As Tom said,

'I can't tell anyone what their path to enlighten-ment is. It's their own adventure. But for me, Scientology is about self-discovery and deciding on my own what is real and true. I know people say that as a religion it dictates. But for me it's the reverse of that. I don't think it dictates anything. I believe it's directed towards conceptual thinking and independent ideas.'

By all accounts, Tom has progressed up the ladder of the church's unusually titled 'courses'. Take 'The Student Hat' course as a classic example. It features a section called 'word clearing', a simple technique to make sure you never skip over a word you don't understand. Many believe that Tom's difficulty during press interviews, when he was some-times branded as a 'bad interview', was overcome thanks to that particular course.

Despite Tom's involvement and that of dozens of other Hollywood types, the church was the target of a very one-sided story on Scientology in *Time* magazine in 1991. Many observers decried its lack of objectivity and the apparent bias of the reporter. The Scientologists sued not only *Time* and its writer, but also a number of sources quoted in the magazine, as well as the religion's own former public relations firm and *Reader's Digest*, who reprinted the article. The Church has prevailed in five of their suits so far, collecting sizeable settlements.

A year earlier, the very serious-minded *Los Angeles Times* published a six-part series on the church which was highly critical, though like most other observers, it noted that the church was continuing to grow at a rapid rate, a contradiction that is not easily explained. The Scientologists reacted in their characteristic fashion – by sending the *Los Angeles Times'* lawyers a 39-page letter of complaint and by renting dozens of billboards all around Los Angeles which quoted the favourable observations of the *Times* reporters like film reviews, featured the *Times'* logo, and virtually created endorsements of the church on billboards and buses everywhere.

There can be little doubt that the church is quick to respond to allegations it finds to be untrue or unfounded. The *Time* cover story is a prime example. Within days of the magazine's publication the church broadly circulated a pamphlet disputing with documentation *Time's* charges on a point by point basis and was poised to launch what would become perhaps the largest, most ambitious series of full-page national newspaper advertisements in US history, all directed to discrediting statements made in *Time* and furnishing the national audience with positive information about the church and its founder.

Scientology is often labelled litigious. There have been

literally hundreds of other writs issued over the years, against and by the Scientologists.

The Scientologists say the vast majority of legal suits came from people who tried to get rich by suing the church. Not an uncommon occurence in a country where lawsuits are filed by plaintiffs seeking millions, using attorneys who are paid by a cut of the winnings should they succeed, and who are paid nothing if they lose, a system which is designed to proliferate such suits, not just against the Church of Scientology but against anyone perceived to have a lot of money.

In the early 1980s, Scientology was engaged in court battles across the United States, but according to the Scientologists, since the IRS exemption confirmed their right to religious freedom under the United States Con-stitution's First Amendment, there is practically no litigation remaining.

There were two huge judgements awarded to church opponents a decade or so ago, but these were overturned. Ultimately the church survived that era, though it gained a reputation among lawyers in the United States for tough litigation tactics. One prominent Los Angeles attorney reportedly refused to enter a case against them by say-ing, 'Life's too short to litigate against the Church of Scientology.'

* * *

The most common entry into Scientology is through Dianetics, a mental 'science' formulated by L. Ron Hubbard and introduced to the world through his book *Dianetics: The Modern Science of Mental Health*. The book has sold in huge numbers since its release in the 1950s.

The church itself has its biggest base in California, with

a group of tall, powder-blue offices on famous Sunset Boulevard and Berendo Street in East Hollywood, just a few miles from Tom's main home in Pacific Palisades. There is also the ten-storey L. Ron Hubbard Life Exhibition building on Hollywood Boulevard by the junction with Cahuenga. Swarms of Scientology staff officers – dressed in naval-style uniforms complete with ribbons and epaulettes – and students pour in and out of all the buildings every day.

Nearby is the Celebrity Centre, an aesthetic wonder based in what used to be the Manor Hotel, a magnificent seven-storey, turreted mansion built in 1927 in the style of a seventeenth-century chateau. During Hollywood's Golden Days it was a luxury pit stop for the likes of Clark Gable, Humphrey Bogart and Errol Flynn and its suites offer a magnificent view of the city.

It is here where the famous – and many not so famous – receive their religious services in a peaceful, manor-like setting. The Celebrity Centre offers the whole panoply of Scientology courses, but also features seminars such as 'How to Make It as a TV Writer', 'Artists Revitalisation Workshop' and 'Success in the Music Industry'. Each Sunday there are talent nights with an open mike providing sin-free karaoke sessions for members.

As one visitor explained: 'There are hundreds of artists that take courses at the Celebrity Centre. They all claim in the most glowing terms that Scientology has helped them both spiritually and in pursuit of their careers.'

A large gold bust of founder Hubbard perches at the side of the stage in the Celebrity Centre's small theatre, and church staff members often exhort the faithful by proclaiming: 'Go out and raise the tone scale of this planet.'

The Scientologists also have a 550 acre property located in Gilman Hot Springs, about 70 miles east of Los Angeles.

It houses film studios and audio production facilities that are used to make films that explain the principles of Scientology auditing, as well as the radio and television programmes that are among the church's best known promotional efforts.

Gilman Hot Springs is also a retreat where Scientology services are provided and where, after his divorce from Mimi, Tom tended to go to receive his religious services.

Visitors to the camp in those days say that Tom and Scientology's highest official David Miscavige were obviously well acquainted with one another.

Tom uses the same bungalow when he visits the complex, one in a series that are kept available for visitors and professional actors and film-makers that travel to the property to work on the church's films. Tom has never appeared in one of the church's in-house films, nor has any of the other big-name Scientology celebrities.

At Gilman Hot Springs, Tom has full use of the facilities provided for the staff, including the swimming pool, gym, sports fields and dining rooms. Tom and Nicole always arrive at Gilman Hot Springs – known as 'Gold' to the Scientologists – by private helicopter.

The Gilman facility reflects a substantial effort made by the Scientologists to rejuvenate an area that had fallen into disuse. Before the war it was as big a resort as Palm Springs, 40 miles to the east.

The basecamp – about one mile wide and six miles long – features carefully manicured grounds and a man-made lake with a single yacht bobbing on the water. A specially sculpted waterfall flows serenely at the edge of the lake. The centre also features a golf course, soccer pitch, basketball courts and a softball field, which are used by the staff and members of the local community. Walkways for pedestrians and lanes for motor-bikes link a series of buildings on the site.

Staff are dressed in blue trousers, light blue shirts and ties. More senior officers dress in more formal, naval-style attire. I noticed one statuesque blonde clipping along in three-inch heels, looking terribly officious in her full naval officer-style regalia. Security guards wear brown, but none are armed. Every entrance has electronically operated fencing. The main entrance – the one used by the public for weekly tours of the centre – is reminiscent of the entrance to a film studio. In fact, with the guard booth at the entrance, the fences and conducted tours, they go to great pains to make this just like the other studios in Southern California.

In April 1994 when I joined one such tour, the Scientologists were constructing yet another new building intended as a sound studio to go along with the existing movie and sound studios. Security personnel on motor cycles were constantly visible as we walked around the property.

There is even a clipper-shaped building on the edge of the basecamp, which looks like a ship moored at the edge of the desert with the rugged San Jacinto mountains as a backdrop. Apart from a variety of uses the Scientologists put it to, the ship is used for a weekly radio broadcast on a local station of community interest news.

All in all, 'Gold' is a unique place, where Tom and other celebrities are reportedly well looked after when they visit the facility.

* * *

Nicole Kidman claimed she was into Scientology even before she met Tom, despite what he has said publicly, although it was reported that she was upset by the number of members present at the couple's wedding in Telluride on Christmas Eve 1990.

At a dinner party given in Tom and Nicole's honour after their wedding, Tom sat next to CAA superagent Michael Ovitz, often called the most powerful man in Hollywood. On his other side was Miscavige. Nearby were two full tables of Scientologists. According to one report, the Scientologists around Tom were 'like they always are – very direct, very attentive, very protective – hovering over Tom. And shaking a lot of hands.'

Tom's relationship with David Miscavige is the subject of much discussion in Hollywood. Miscavige is described as the head of the church.

Miscavige also flew out to the location where Tom was filming *Far and Away* to help the star to celebrate Nicole's birthday at her invitation, as well as spending time together at the organization's basecamp at Gilman Hot Springs.

Before filming of *Far and Away* began, screenwriter Bob Dolman attended a story meeting with director Ron Howard at the basecamp. He was flown in a private helicopter from Los Angeles. Dolman says it was made very obvious that Tom and Miscavige are very good friends. Tom agrees, and he said so publicly:

> 'Dave Miscavige is a good friend of mine and while we both wish we could see each other more often, due to my schedule and his we rarely ever see each other . . . We are friends.'

The Church is not without its critics. Some are former members who have left the religion with one degree of bitterness or another. Others were introduced to Scientology, but did not stay around for very long. Most of their laments are reminiscent of people who grew unhappy with their religions – any religion – over the course of time.

Some former members claim that they are almost afraid to speak out publicly about life with the Scientologists. They say that their hesitation arises from the fact that Scientology is not characteristically a 'turn-the-other-cheek' religion.

The media, too, sometimes feels intimidated by the church and its lawyers. After a lengthy article by John H. Richardson appeared in *Premiere*, lawyers representing the Scientologists sent dozens of letters complaining about the story he had written.

Ultimately, *Premiere* ran a two-page response penned by Miscavige himself. It was an unusual concession for any magazine to make, and it is an illustration of just how forceful the Scientologists are in getting the media to correct false statements about the church.

Richardson – a highly respected investigative reporter – spent almost two years researching the article. 'It seemed like a lot to take. It was a huge, overwhelming thing.'

His initial request to Tom's PR woman, Pat Kingsley, to interview the star left him with the impression the actor was going to co-operate. 'Then when I contacted Pat Kingsley with whom I believed this agreement had been made, she acted as if she had never heard of it and said no. "Why would he want to co-operate with such a story?" I was a little surprised and said I would get back to her when I had my fact-checking questions ready and she said I hope you will,' explained Richardson.

Then Pat Kingsley contacted Richardson and said Tom had got the questions he had submitted and he would like to respond, but then made an extraordinary demand.

'We had to agree that I gave her my questions verbally over the telephone and she wrote them down and she said I would have to print both the questions and the answers as they came.

'It seemed very high-handed of her but we were eager to get Cruise's response.

'I wanted to get him on the record any way I could so we decided this was a good thing. I did feel very blind-sided by the whole thing because he was responding to fact-checking questions just as if they were bad reporting questions that he would deem to answer. I though it was very disingenuous of him.'

In the end, Richardson never actually met Tom because the entire operation was performed through Pat Kingsley.

Richardson was full of praise for Kingsley's skills as a public relations person:

'She is a very good publicist. Her line to everyone who asks her anything about this question [Scientology] is that it is not American to question someone's religion, which is ludicrous. Religious freedom does not mean that suddenly freedom of the press stops. Pat was just giving statements. It is her job.'

Richardson said he was definitely under the impression that Tom Cruise is extremely involved with the Scientologists. 'He is definitely a member and, from everything that I was able to determine, very close to Miscavige and very active from a day-to-day level in Scientology.'

Tom admitted to *Premiere*: 'I have gained a lot from Scientology. I know how I can help people from my own personal involvement and study of the subject.' But the actor refused even to refer to the *Premiere* article as an interview because he only agreed to the questions being asked through Kingsley as a form of 'fact checking'.

The magazine even had to present Tom's reaction in a position laid out separately in the middle of the main article, under an apt headline entitled 'Cruise Control' and with a letter to the editor from Pat Kingsley which stated:

> 'I got Tom Cruise to answer the questions and I offer them to you on one condition. The condition is that you use the questions exactly as they were asked and use the answers exactly as they were given. We have agreed that if any changes are contemplated by *Premiere* we can then withdraw all the material and nothing can be printed without our specific approval. With that in mind I send these sheets on to you and would appreciate hearing from you once you have an opportunity to look at them.'

One experienced Hollywood show business writer described the conditions as 'the most outrageous attempt at editorial control ever attempted by an actor', but *Premiere* decided to accept the conditions anyway and most of Tom's replies were fairly dull. However he did state:

> 'I have no idea why my religion, or anybody's, would be the subject of an article in *Premiere* and that is why I have refused to participate in any interview. I make movies. And when *Premiere* wants to talk about movies I make, I have been and will continue to be willing to discuss such at length.

'Not one of these questions has anything to do with that . . . The Church of Scientology doesn't run my life or career. By being asked to answer these questions I'm perceived as having to defend my religion or Church and by having to deny accusations a false impression is created. This is not what freedom of religion is about . . . I should not be subjected to an inquiry . . . Likewise, my Church shouldn't be subjected to press disparagement because I'm a member. My work speaks for itself . . . and as far as *Premiere* is concerned that should be the end of the matter.'

Premiere writer Richardson believes that the attraction of the Scientologists for people like Tom Cruise is intriguing.

'I think Scientology is very effective in persuading its members that there are things said about them that are false. I think for whatever reasons Scientology seems to be a way of thinking that helps you get confidence and helps you overcome your doubts more so even than most religions.

'It is well suited to the kind of temperaments that many actors have. There are a lot of strange experimental things in Los Angeles and I think it is a combination of things; the receptivity of people and the arts to new ideas combined with the specific character of Scientology combined with the way that once you become involved in Scientology it becomes a world filled with people who think a certain way. It is a total experience.

'The question is why are the Scientologists so interested in Hollywood? Why do they have the celebrity centre? I find that a little unusual for a religious organisation.'

After publication of the *Premiere* article, the magazine was flooded with letters from Scientologists insisting that they had been deeply offended by the tone of the article and the church even paid out tens of thousands of dollars to publish a 16-page booklet denouncing the piece, entitled: 'Premiere Propaganda'.

The magazine published the Scientologists' response to the article, after spokeswoman Leisa Goodman claimed that: '*Premiere*'s reporter was not interested in writing a fair story on the church. Instead he went out of his way to seek individuals who he could use as a vehicle for his animus against Scientology.'

The church believed the magazine's decision to publish their lengthy reply came about because when they were 'confronted with their appalling use of journalistic ethics, *Premiere* magazine was forced to realise that the church was due a far fuller response than a mere letter to the editor.'

Even journalists who have written about Tom's involvement in Scientology are very sensitive about talking publicly about their articles. John Richardson – who wrote that sizeable piece in *Premiere* magazine – insisted that his lawyer read every one of the quotes used in this book because he feared the Scientologists might pursue him legally. 'This is a legally dangerous area. I know that reporters do not like this but can you run these quotes by my lawyer before you run this?' he said.

One tabloid journalist who dared to write in depth about Tom's relationship with the Church was approached by a private eye pretending to be a fellow reporter trying to find out the sources used for the article. The Scientologists later openly admitted hiring the private eye because they wanted to find out who was selling information about the church and various celebrity members to the tabloid press, following a number of articles about Scientology artists that quoted unnamed 'inside sources'.

The Scientologists go to great lengths to protect the privacy of their members and refuse to provide any information about their activities in pursuing Scientology. They publicise their charitable contributions on behalf of the church-sponsored drug, education and community service programmes, but remain extremely tight-lipped when it come to just what anyone is doing in their Scientology auditing or studies.

Other Hollywood players have also fallen victim to the Scientologists' sensitivity about unwanted publicity. *Lethal Weapon* director Richard Donner – one of the best liked figures in movieland – faced the religion's damage control tactics after he produced a film called *Delirious* with the late John Candy. In the movie, the actress Emma Samms comments on Candy's power over her by saying: 'It's like I don't have a will of my own. Do you think he's a Scientologist?'

Donner and *Delirious* director Tom Mankiewicz received an onslaught of letters protesting about the joke. Strongly worded phone calls followed. The two film makers then decided to cut the joke out of the film before it was released.

One Hollywood star who reportedly entered the church and then left abruptly was *Thirtysomething* star Peter Horton. His introduction to the church came through acting classes, and Emilio Estevez reportedly had a similar experience.

Scientology leaders claim that the organisation's continuing bad press often comes from psychiatrists who are angry that the church exposes their 'barbaric methods'. They cite their fight against psychiatry and drug abuse as evidence of the beneficial side of the religion. 'We're helping celebrities,' said one official. 'We service them – to be more capable, to be more ethical, to be more able . . . Scientology celebrities are successful, and they're not messed up! They're not messed up!'

Little clues of the teachings of the Scientologists occasionally slip out in press interviews given by Tom. In an article in *Entertainment Weekly*, he said:

> 'I look at certain people that aren't doing well and say, "Well, who's around him? Do they want to see this person do well?" And often I might find one person that really doesn't want to see this guy succeed.'

However, most of the time he is very defensive about his Scientology membership. 'He feels he has been misunderstood,' explained writer Stephanie Mansfield, who met Tom for an interview with GQ magazine. That attitude also came through in Tom's responses to *Premiere*'s questions, particularly about his relationship with Scientology officials.

> 'I know the inference as I have seen it in other articles. The problem is it's wrong. This line of questioning shows a lack of interest in learning what the Church of Scientology represents. I know more about Scientology and the church and its staff than any reporter I've ever met or whose articles I have read. I know the good work they do. I shouldn't be subjected to an enquiry on my religion. Likewise, my church shouldn't be subjected to press disparagement because I'm a member.'

Yet an entirely different perspective on Tom's involvement in Scientology came from *A Few Good Men* director Rob Reiner, who was quoted by Mansfield in her GQ article:

> 'Look, I don't know anything about Scientology, but if Scientology means you're the way Tom Cruise is, then everyone should be a Scientologist. He cares, and he works his butt off.'

Whatever else Tom does in his career, the spectre of the Scientologists will always be close by.

'Ask not what your country can do for you:
ask what you can do for your country.'

JFK

24

When Ronald Reagan was elected President of the United States, he proved what many had suspected for a long time; that if your face fitted then the ultimate American dream could come true. Reagan forged such an indelible link between Hollywood and Washington that he opened up the political floodgates to prove that anyone handsome and presentable could become the world's most powerful leader.

When Bill Clinton took over at the White House, ties between the showbiz glitterati and politics seemed to get even closer, with two Hollywood producers acting as the new President's closest advisors and a host of other show-business 'link-ups'.

So when Tom said, recently: 'I do believe in the American dream. I think we're in trouble right now, there's no question about it. This country needs a boost,' it was deemed to be significant in Hollywood terms.

Tom Cruise has never openly said that he harbours

ambitions one day to become President of the United States, but many inside moviedom believe he will eventually turn his back on Hollywood to pursue the ultimate job. He is young enough to spend at least another ten years at the top of his profession – Reagan did not even think seriously about entering politics full time until he was well into his forties. It has to be said, of course, that Tom's political beliefs are a million miles away from the Reagan philosophy and that of many of his relatives back in Louisville, Kentucky.

Tom has some very strong opinions about his home country and where things have gone wrong. Over the past few years, he has let it be known that he is 'very concerned' about the future development of the United States. Friends have urged him to make his opinions more loudly heard and he is starting to realise that when he speaks on any subject people are prepared to sit up and take notice.

Tom even saw a deep political message behind the relatively light *Risky Business*, which makes him sound as if politics are never far from his mind.

'It's about today's capitalistic society. Do the means justify the ends? Do you want to help people, or do you just want to make money? Joel is questioning all of that. So am I. Today the thinking of people is so linear and non-creative. It's all about money. Unfortunately, we need something like Vietnam to force people to deal with political issues. I'm not saying I'm some erudite political figure – but it bothers me. At least I'm asking the question. The movie is Joel's exploration of society, how he gets sucked into this wild capitalistic ride.'

It was very heavy stuff considering Tom had only just hit his twenties at the time.

Like every other aspect of his life, Tom has quietly and carefully started to learn more about politics, social issues, even foreign affairs. If he did take the leap it would not be a Clint Eastwood-style stab at being mayor of a small town, it would be the real thing.

One Hollywood associate claims it is an open secret in California that Tom is looking beyond just being a movie star. 'He has healthy political aspirations. There is no doubt about it,' said the source.

During an interview with writer Jeanne Marie Laskas, Tom was asked about his obsession to be best:

'You know, that's a very small idea. That's too narrow a stake. The bigger one is: What can I do for myself, what can I do for the world, what can I do to make myself better, what-do-I-want-to-do? That's what's important. Not complaining. It's done, it's over. Now it's time to flourish and prosper. People can complain about things and there's always things to complain about, but the joy in life is solving problems. You know, I remember thinking when I was growing up, I was like, "Oh, I won't have any problems when I grow up." And I used to fight these problems, oh these terrible problems, and all of a sudden I realised, "Hold it! I love problems!"

'That's what I look at. That's what I think about. You work like hell and you solve problems. You know what made this country great, that-is-what-made-this-country-great! I mean, look at this country; it's built on democracy by these renegade rebels. I mean: who the hell thought? Look at this now! Look at this! Look! That's what's important, that, you know, it's time to flourish and prosper.'

Almost ten years after the success of *Top Gun* there is little doubt that the movie's aspiring right-wing, gung-ho ideals are far removed from Tom's real political opinions. If there is ever a sequel made of the movie, it will almost certainly be a much more sensitive, issue-led project.

Tom said: 'Some people felt that *Top Gun* was a right-wing film to promote the navy. And a lot of kids loved it. But I want the kids to know that's not the way war is – that *Top Gun* was just an amusement-park ride.'

The flip side to *Top Gun* was *Born on the Fourth of July*, a movie with the profound message that war is a waste of human life and effort. It seems that during the making of that movie, the beliefs of director Oliver Stone rubbed off on Tom to a certain degree. Stone – a passionate anti-war convert following his own experiences in Vietnam – indirectly had a great influence on Tom. The young actor carefully absorbed many of the relatively left-wing opinions that flew around the set on *Born* and chose to follow the aspects that appealed to him.

Tom saw *Born* as a film that started in an era when there was a real sense of flag and country and loyalty to the Pledge of Allegiance. He referred to it as a time of 'blind commitment' to the government of the time. In an interview in January 1990, he told *Playboy* magazine that Americans 'had no business' being in Vietnam. 'The country [USA] became impotent and embarrassed.'

Born on the Fourth of July was definitely a turning point in Tom's political beliefs. As he told *Playboy*:

'I heard the other day that President Bush said that we should forget about Vietnam and move on into a new era. No! Let's never forget Vietnam! Never! The second we forget Vietnam, we are going to make the same mistake again. That's an important

lesson. History shows that we always forget. We
didn't pay attention to the French; let's remember
Vietnam and become better because of it. Let's not
send our men to fight in a poor peasant country for
no reason. It meant nothing to us. It had no value.
It only killed off a generation of young men.'

Fortunately, Tom still believed in the American dream but
he recognised that it was in trouble and needed a big boost.

Around the same time as his encounters with Ron Kovic
and Oliver Stone on *Born on the Fourth of July*, Tom became
heavily involved in fighting the destruction of the rain forests
in Brazil. Soon, like any good politician, Tom was referring
to that particular situation. He told *Playboy*:

'You have to bring Brazil in and have it become
part of the team. You can't point a finger at Brazil
and say, "Why the fuck are you letting everybody
take – how many football fields is it a day? – of the
rain forests?" I want to understand it more. I want
to see it. I want to make sure there is air to breathe
when my children are my age. It's one of the most
important issues that this world has to face right
now.'

Trips to Brazil with Mimi followed Tom's initial burst of
interest. By the early 1990s, however, the subject matter
seemed to have been replaced by a keener involvement in
issues closer to home.

In Hollywood, close friends and associates were noticing
Tom's increasing interest in politics. All of them recognised
that the actor had what it takes to make the leap to Washington and they have all quietly encouraged him ever since.

Tom's own political hero in recent years has been one-time Californian Governor Jerry Brown, a left-of-centre liberal Democrat who masterminded a controversial tax programme to help the poor and needy throughout the state when he tried to win the Democratic presidential nomination that eventually went to Bill Clinton. Tom is full of admiration for Brown because he is known as a blunt, honest speaker prepared to attack any political friend or foe if he disagrees with a certain policy.

'Tom sees himself in that Jerry Brown mould,' says one Hollywood observer. 'He is interested in the under-dog, the guy in the street who is battling against all the elements just like he and his mom and sisters had to do when they were together.'

Tom told writer James Greenberg: 'He [Brown] attacks the press, he attacks Clinton, he attacks Bush, he attacks big business. He says whatever is on his mind because no one's telling him what to do.'

Tom is particularly concerned with the future for the children of America and he told Greenberg: 'I look at the young faces in schools and it's so important to keep them dreaming, to educate them and give them purpose and responsibility.'

Tom has been careful not to squander his fortune. He could easily live the rest of his life very comfortably without ever working again. This is not to suggest that he has in any way lost the will to act. Nothing could be further from the truth. As a meticulous planner, however, he is definitely looking to the future.

Some cynics might suggest that any such plan would be a non-starter because Nicole is Australian and that would prove unacceptable to the public. This is nonsense as she was born in Hawaii and has always retained dual American-Australian nationality. Friends say her American accent is becoming more distinct now and it is virtually impossible to tell her apart from the locals in her Pacific Palisades neighbourhood.

Tom was among the celebrities who jetted into Little Rock, Arkansas for the huge party given to celebrate Bill Clinton's win in the US presidential race. Although there were a lot of things about Clinton that Tom did not agree with, he certainly felt they were on the same side. Some saw Tom's presence as simply yet more evidence of his eventual intentions. In his own classic way, he was learning, observing, taking in the atmosphere in preparation for what might turn out to be the biggest role of his entire life.

In 1993, Tom started to take a much closer interest in politics in New York, where he still considered he had his strongest ties. He observed the mayor's election campaign in November 1993 with great interest and even nailed his flag firmly to the Democrat mast by holding a number of highly confidential meetings with the then mayor David Dinkins. Tom is known to have been sourly disappointed when right-wing Republican Rudy Guillano eventually won the election in November 1993.

*   *   *

One of the other reasons why Tom may gradually begin to pursue his political ambitions is that his long-held desire to direct movies came to fruition in 1993 and by all accounts it was a very low key affair considering his status as the world's most famous movie star.

Tom had always been convinced that moviemaking was primarily a director's medium and that was why so many actors like Kevin Costner, Mel Gibson and, to a lesser extent, Arnold Schwarzenegger had tried their hand at directing with very differing results.

'A director has to have a vision ... that he has great taste in performance, the ability to tell a story, and that he is going to create interesting characters in telling that story and use those characters to tell the story,' reckoned Tom.

With these strong opinions in mind, Tom helmed an episode of *Fallen Angels*, a series of half-hour *films noir* co-produced by Tom's *The Firm* director Sydney Pollack. Although there was no doubting that Tom held his own in the impressive field of *Fallen Angels* directors – who included Steven Soderbergh, Jonathan Kaplan, Phil Joanou and fellow actor-turned-director novice Tom Hanks – his episode did not exactly set Hollywood ablaze.

Tom picked *The Frightening Frammies* – described as a 'first class story' – penned by classic crime writer Jim Thompson. Series producer William Hornberg explained: 'Tom loved the main character, this hapless con-artist. And it's a love story between two people who are always conning each other and who end up wary but together – he liked that.'

Having cast Peter Gallagher and Nancy Travis, Tom put a call through to Isabella Rossellini and asked her if she wanted to play the *femme fatale*. Rossellini – whose first name inspired Tom and Nicole to call their daughter Isabella – was incredibly flattered and immediately accepted.

Producer Hornberg admitted, rather surprisingly, that Tom was 'a little self-conscious' during filming of the short film. 'You know, "Here I am, the star, giving you your directions," but he went into it with the appropriate sense of humour.'

Tom proved a little terse on the set, barking at actors to repeat their lines if he thought they got them wrong. Rossellini insisted later: 'I don't think I could take it from another director because I would feel diminished. But because he was an actor, I could take it from him. I felt he was on my side.'

One of Tom's biggest problems was adjusting to the sort of penny pinching required on a $700,000 budget as opposed to the $30 million variety he was more used to. The schedule only allowed for a six-day shoot. Insiders on the set said that Tom found it quite a strain and eventually went into 'blitzkrieg mode' in a desperate bid to get the film completed in time.

Tom worked for scale on *Frightening Frammies*, which meant he received a fee of approximately $70,000. Articles published at the time of the actual shoot suggested that Tom had acquitted himself adequately but the actor knew that all these comments were worthless until the actual film was completed and out on the *Showtime* cable channel in September 1993.

The *New York Daily News* proclaimed the film to be 'full of twists and turns, yet Cruise leaves room for his actors to add their own touches – and his eye for composing scenes, while never too showy, demonstrates a feel for, as well as an appreciation of, the classic film noir techniques.'

Tom later admitted that he had found the entire directing experience far from easy and voiced his delight at having chosen a relatively simple début project as opposed to directing something as heavyweight as *The Firm*, which had briefly been suggested to him.

The summer of 1993 was definitely a time of consolidation for Tom. He not only learned to relax a little – thanks mainly to Nicole and their adopted baby daughter Isabella – he also began to socialise more in Hollywood. One weekend he and former basketball star Magic Johnson rounded up some pals for a friendly game of softball at Palisades High School, near the Cruise mansion. Tom played second base for one team; Magic pitched for the other. Cruise's team beat Magic's, 12–11 as Nicole watched from the sideline.

When Tom accepted the Actor of the Decade award at

the twenty-ninth annual Chicago International Film Festival, it marked yet another significant step for the still relatively young star. Previous winners included such luminaries as Orson Welles, François Truffaut, Sophia Loren, Oliver Stone and Jack Lemmon.

Co-host of the awards, Londoner John Russell Taylor commented that Tom represented 'the great American hero of his generation, in a league with such screen idols as Gary Cooper, James Stewart and Tyrone Power'. Clips from many of Tom's previous films were shown and a host of celebrities paid tribute to Tom, together with some telegrams from other big names like Jack Nicholson and Paramount chief Sherry Lansing.

Nicole's standing as a star in her own right took another turn when she hosted the American comedy show *Saturday Night Live*. At home, Tom played house father with true relish. While Nicole was rehearsing one day, he took Isabella, then aged ten months, with his sister Lee Anne to see the Big Apple Circus in the grounds of Manhattan's Lincoln Center.

Paparazzi lensmen popped up everywhere within minutes of Tom's arrival and then Isabella threw a tantrum and Tom could do nothing to stop her crying, so he and his sister beat a hasty retreat.

Nicole's obvious contentment at home with Tom and baby Isabella tended to be regularly disrupted by her unfortunate inability to sleep well at night. Often, Tom would stir in the early hours to find his young wife sitting downstairs watching television. On such occasions, the couple would play a round of backgammon before returning to bed. Beneath that bubbly exterior, Nicole was obviously a bundle of nerves.

The couple often found themselves so busy that they paid a professional wardrobe designer called Kate Harrington to go and buy them clothes in New York if they got stuck in Los Angeles because of some project or other. Harrington met the Cruises through her work for famous photographer-to-the-stars Herb Ritts, who the couple usually insist takes their pictures for any publicity. On at least three occasions in 1993, Kate was paid $1,000 a day to fly from California to New York to go on a shopping spree on behalf of her multi-millionaire clients Tom and Nicole. 'Sometimes she would spend as much as $20,000 on a few clothes for the couple without batting an eyelid,' explained one close associate. Often Tom would reject half the clothes Harrington brought back but no one seemed worried about the enormous waste of money.

In January 1994, Tom was approached by his old friend Harold Becker – who directed him in *Taps* and Nicole in *Malice* – to consider a role that might well help to fuel his involvement in politics. *City Hall* is described as a network-type drama set in city government. Bo Goldman – who wrote the Oscar-winning *Scent of a Woman* with Al Pacino – penned the script. Hollywood observers expect that Tom's fee for this project could top $20 million, putting him in a league of his own when it comes to per-picture deals.

There seemed to be no stopping Tom – only in his early thirties, married to a beautiful wife and the father of a young child. On the surface, his life seemed to be perfect but the star was still fighting demons of self-doubt that would continue to drive him further and faster than any other actor in Hollywood history.

'A lie can travel halfway around the world while the truth is putting on its shoes.'

Mark Twain

25

Once upon a time in Hollywood, everybody told lies. With so much valuable product to shield from public attention, the studio bosses wanted it that way; and the stars were happy when whoppers were told on their behalf. So the scandals came and went more or less unnoticed. When one of Jean Harlow's husbands was murdered, MGM's chief of police simply sealed off the lot until the studio press agents were ready with their version of what had happened.

Meanwhile, as Nathanael West demonstrated in his classic 1939 novel *The Day of the Locust*, the tabloid reality of Los Angeles (lynchings, murder, sex crimes, explosions, car wrecks, love nests, fires, etc.) kept the crowd in the front row busy. Nobody expected to be told the truth about their idols.

When the stars went freelance in the sixties, everyone expected things to change. They didn't. Instead, Hollywood became an even more secretive place where the value of privacy and wealth predominates and comfortable lies are told easily.

'It's a joke being here. If I was in Detroit, I'd be able to find out about cars; if I was in New York, I'd know about the mob, or about money. But in Hollywood you just can't find out anything about the stars,' said one Tinseltown reporter.

If Tom Cruise had his way, that's how it would stay forever. The actor has become increasingly sensitive to any publicity he receives. That means that 'authorised interviews' are about all anyone can get with the most famous box office star on the globe. Such interviews involve Tom making himself available to the media in the run-up to a film, usually in a plush hotel suite or his publicist's office. For many journalists who have interviewed Tom over the past ten years, such antechambers have become synonymous with bowing to the star's demands. In other words they feel the system is humiliating.

Interviews can only be arranged through Tom's personal PR Pat Kingsley, a woman who believes that publicity people should choose magazine covers, not editors. Tom has never denied that he looks on journalists as obstacles or liabilities and he carefully scrutinises every single writer's credentials before giving anyone an audience.

The restrictive contracts that Kingsley now demands every journalist should sign before allowing them to interview Tom have caused a lot of bitterness and resentment. Writers who break the rules have been denied access to Tom and banned from subsequent press conferences or movie junkets. Newspapers and magazines that have published hostile copy have been admonished by Kingsley on Tom's behalf.

The Cruise control system kicked in with the press junket for *Far and Away* in 1992. Typically, print, radio and

TV people are flown to a hotel, usually at the film company's expense, where they meet the stars at tables of about ten reporters each, asking innocuous questions like: 'How was it to work with your wife?'

This time, however, Tom and Nicole demanded that most reporters sign contracts stipulating which publications these stories would appear in and when they would run. The contract also stated that anything Tom said could only be used in conjunction with *Far and Away* and could not be mentioned in regard to any other Cruise article or project. In other words, the content of the interviews would be the sole property of Tom.

At the Cannes Film Festival in May 1992, two journalists were escorted out of a press conference after refusing to sign similar agreements with Tom's PR people

At another junket for *A Few Good Men*, in November 1992, the same old contracts were pulled out for journalists to sign. Tom's ever-faithful PR woman Pat Kingsley approached Columbia about printing the contracts on their letter-headed notepaper but the studio refused. This time when reporters flew in for the gathering Tom was nowhere in sight. Instead, most journalists found a letter awaiting him or her at their seats, explaining that he had had to leave town early to be on the set of *The Firm*. Tom ended the note saying: 'I look forward to the opportunity to speak with you again in the future.' Really?

The same situation occurred just before the release of *The Firm*, although Tom did do some American television interviews but only after most journalists had, once again, signed a contract which, this time, also stipulated that his interview could only be used during the cinema release of *The Firm*.

Even when Tom does give the very occasional public statement he tends to look irritated, especially when the questioners come around to his looks or religious beliefs. His replies are usually abrupt and short and his body language soon makes it clear if he does not like the tone of a certain question.

Examples of Tom's obsessive quest for secrecy are wide ranging. On the set for the shooting of *Far and Away*, extras were cautioned against talking to the stars. Tom and Nicole spent much of their time holed up in their customised Bluebird mobile home, complete with king-sized bed and satellite TV.

When the Cruises rented a five-bed, six-bath, 7,500 square foot wooden house at the end of a private dirt road while filming in Montana for *Far and Away*, the owner Mike Overstreet, his wife Linda and 15-year-old daughter Shara temporarily moved into a nearby apartment, telling friends they were having the house redecorated. The written agreement with Tom's people had stipulated that any news of Tom's stay at the house would, in effect, make the contract null and void.

There was also the most incredible amount of small print in all of Tom's movie deal contracts, which completely restricted photography of him – even if it was for personal use. During *Far and Away*, Tom and Nicole posed for a cast picture with a hundred-odd extras, with promises that each would get a copy. Then they were 'unable' to authorise its release. 'It left a real bitter taste in everyone's mouth,' said one crew member.

Even Jeff Bayers – Tom's best friend from his days in Louisville – had been carefully briefed by the ever-self-protective star about not helping writers who contact him about their friendship.

'I don't feel comfortable talking about Tommy unless I get his permission. I really don't want to give much detail until I get Tommy's permission,' explained Jeff Bayers nervously.

He also insisted that Tom Cruise had made him promise not to hand over any of his photos of the two of them together when they were kids in Kentucky. 'He has asked me not to hand any out. He is concerned with his image,' added Jeff ominously.

Mr Jarratt, the father of Tom's wrestling captain at school in Glen Ridge, proudly took hundreds of photographs of the team in action and would often appear a few days after a match to offer the other team members copies of the pictures. Years later, after Tom's career had taken off, his wrestling coach Angelo Corbo went to the Jarratts to try to find some old photos. He was told that he could not have any because a representative of Tom Cruise had contacted them and requested that Mr Jarratt did not distribute the photographs. It seems that the star's obsession with privacy even reaches back as far as his days as an innocent high school pupil.

'I wish I'd got my hands on some of the shower-room photos, then I'd be a millionaire by now,' joked Corbo. Letters to Tom's agent from his old team-mates have gone unanswered. His old acquaintances in Glen Ridge are not surprised, just a little disappointed that he did not take the time to reply.

Tom became very agitated when he encountered author Larry Wolfe Horwitz, who was about to publish a book entitled '*New York Star Walks*' featuring stars' addresses and where 'they hung out'. The actor bumped into Horwitz at the famous Russian Tea Rooms in New York, and told the writer: 'I'm not too excited by the idea.' Tom then proceeded to tell the author horror stories about stargazers and nut cases who have loitered near his vast apartment on 13th Street in the past. It obviously grated with Tom that anyone would actually publish the full address of one of his homes.

During the couple's holiday in Italy in July 1993, Tom

exploded at a group of local photographers after Nicole fell over a step carrying Isabella while trying to avoid having their photograph taken at an airport. Journalists present claimed that Tom made a lunge for the lensman and screamed four letter words at him. 'He was really furious, swearing and jabbing his finger in my face,' explained the photographer afterwards. 'He was incredibly menacing because he blamed his wife's fall on me. But in fact she fell because she simply did not see the step.'

Tom returned to the cameraman an hour later and tried to apologise for his actions but the photographer insisted that he was considering legal action against the star.

Respected showbusiness reporter Stephanie Mansfield interviewed Tom for GQ magazine's December 1992 issue in an article headlined 'Tom Cruise From The Neck Up'. The first stage of the interview went off without incident but when Tom had further contact with Mansfield to answer a few post-interview questions, the warmth and camaraderie of that first meeting were replaced by white-hot anger because Tom had discovered that the writer had dared to call one of his old girlfriends from Glen Ridge High School. Further questions about his family and details of his parents' divorce brought an angry response: 'That's really nobody's business.' Then he snapped at Mansfield: 'We're supposed to be discussing a movie,' referring to *A Few Good Men* which was about to be released at the time. Finally, before hanging up on Mansfield, Tom added bitterly: 'Whatever you want to say is what you've got to say.'

Then Tom called back. 'Look, I just would have appreciated it if you had told me,' he said, his voice still edgy and tinged with condescension. 'It doesn't matter what these people say about me – people I knew for a very short time in high school. They knew me, but not really. I didn't go to that place and disclose my innermost feelings. The people who knew me were my sisters.'

'Well then,' asked Mansfield. 'How about I talk to them?'

'You wanna talk to my sisters? No! They don't want to do interviews! They're not interested in it.'

Tom proclaimed to a somewhat surprised Stephanie Mansfield that her attempts to interview these people from his past were akin to 'a covert operation. It's just, like, rude. It's just a courtesy to tell me first. That's just common decency. It's not a matter of doing it. It's just a courtesy.'

Behind the magazine article lay a complex web of Hollywood pressure which was exerted specifically on Stephanie Mansfield because she had dared to look into Tom's background. Within hours of that second interview, Mansfield says she got a call from Tom's PR woman Pat Kingsley. 'She made a veiled threat that she knew my career was going well and Tom was going to be around for a long time,' explained Mansfield.

> 'I am certain I am not Pat Kingsley's favorite inter-viewer at this point. I think that she has to under-stand that as a reporter you are doing your job and she has to respect that but she has her job to do too which is to protect him.
>
> 'It was all kind of silly. I think he felt some-how that his privacy had been invaded.'

Mansfield believes that Tom did not like the fact that, 'It was out of his control. Most people would have laughed about it but he seemed extremely angry.'

Despite the row, Mansfield still says, begrudgingly: 'I sort of liked him. He's a kid. Not too bright. He is not very educated but he is an OK guy I guess.'

Mansfield's original interview had been at the plush Bel Air Hotel in Los Angeles, and Cruise had, at that stage, been charming and congenial. She has her own theories as to why Tom turned nasty during the second interview.

> 'He is very young and this is his life. A lot of other people had a life before acting but Cruise never did. He was very successful at a very young age and this is his life.
>
> 'He is not spontaneous. You can see the wheels turning almost robotically when he is asked a question. I think he is very wary of the press. That's the control. He has to protect that image because it is all he's got.'

In retrospect, Mansfield believes that she would have achieved a more satisfying, revealing portrait of Tom if she had insisted he conduct the interview driving 'or doing something. It would have been more revealing.'

She says Tom is 'very manipulative. He knows what he wants. He has a a switch-on smile. Tom Cruise created himself. Tom Cruise is a creation, so he naturally would be upset if people looked into his background. I remember feeling it was forced and carefully practised.'

Mansfield thinks it is a shame that Tom is so over-protective. 'He is a wonderful actor. He was wonderful in *Born on the Fourth of July*.' On her overview of the bust-up with Tom, she explained:

> 'Celebrities have always had a need for control, but it's worse now than ever I think. In the case with this piece, I think Tom is very conscious of his image, his press, and when he thought even for a minute that he lost control, he freaked. The whole situation, which was very unpleasant for all parties involved, made me feel that Tom Cruise

really invented himself and was worried that I was going to reveal something. I felt sad for him, ultimately. It was a very sad experience.'

Reporter Roger Fristoe, who has worked on the *Louisville Courier Journal* for more than 15 years, had an even tougher time when he tried to put together a piece on the town's local boy made good. The article was to be a follow-up to a story he wrote in 1983, when he interviewed Tom on the telephone before publicity agents advised Tom to stop giving such off-the-cuff interviews.

'It was like a steel curtain had dropped. Everything seemed fairly favorable when I first tried to do the follow-up piece. We wanted to do a cover story on our magazine that would elaborate on what I had originally written and be a more in-depth piece.'

Andrea Jaffe was Tom's PR woman at the time and at first she assured Fristoe that an interview could be arranged. She even told Fristoe she would be back in touch with a date for a meeting.

'I waited and waited for the call to confirm this but it never came,' explained Fristoe. Then *Top Gun* came along and Tom leapt into the superstardom bracket and Andrea Jaffe stopped returning Fristoe's calls.

'So I wrote her a letter. I kept pursuing it but started getting these very frosty letters in return. It would be something from her assistant that would say: "Ms Jaffe is aware of your interest in her client Tom Cruise and will get in touch with you when she feels it is appropriate" or something like that. But she never did. I kept a file in the hope that some day it would work out, but in the end I gave up,' explained Fristoe.

Another, even more innocent, victim of the protective publicity shield that surrounds Tom was retired grandfather

Warder Harrison. The Louisville-based, former real-estate broker was trying to put together a history of Kentucky and all its famous residents in 1990, so he wrote a letter to Tom's then agent Paula Wagner at CAA in Los Angeles, asking if he could mention Tom's name in the book. It was an act of courtesy on the part of Harrison.

The letter he got back from the megapowerful agents at CAA shook the pensioner. A brief, curse note advised Harrison that 'Mr Cruise is unwilling to consent to your request. He has always been very protective of the use of his name, likeness or personal information and will take whatever steps are available to maintain his privacy.'

Harrison was astounded by what was a complete over-reaction to a simple request to mention Tom's name in a history book! Afraid of the big guns at CAA, Harrison dropped the matter entirely.

Then, almost two years ago, he saw Tom and Nicole on the *Oprah Winfrey Show* and felt obliged to try again with another request to use Tom in his book, which had still not been published. As a professional genealogist who was at one time commissioned by the Sons of the American Revolution to work on the genealogy of President Reagan, he felt that perhaps they would look kindly on his letter asking them to reconsider their earlier decision. Harrison's only request to Tom's agent was for a current photograph to use in the book.

The reply, dated 29 May 1992, sounded even more sinister. This time one Lawrence Kopeiken wrote back on behalf of Tom's agent Paula Wagner and publicist Pat Kingsley. He stated: 'Mr Cruise has not changed his mind regarding this project ... Mr Cruise will take whatever steps are available to maintain his privacy.'

'I did not understand it. If anything, I was going to embellish his image. I was saying what a fine gentlemen he was and what kind of bloodline he came from. It was harmless stuff,' explained Harrison.

Harrison said the letters from CAA 'had a threatening undertone to them. They said they will take any steps to stop me. Are they going to hang me, shoot me or what? I was not writing anything derogatory about him. It seemed so strange. Tom Cruise is something else.'

Tom himself genuinely believes his attitude is just part of the job. He said: 'I think people who say I'm a control freak haven't worked with me. I expect a lot. I have very high standards, as do the people I work with. It's not a matter of control, it's a matter of contributing to the picture.'

Tom's 'controlling' influence over press interviews was only the tip of the Cruise iceberg, it seems.

Besides his problems with Gene Hackman's agents over top billing in *The Firm*, Tom also demanded veto power over advertisements for all his movies after *Top Gun* because he was annoyed that a lookalike was used to promote the home video version of *Top Gun*. Studio insiders say that Tom's contracts for each movie role he undertakes now grant him 'more control over the entire production than anyone has ever seen'. However, it must be said that Tom and *Rain Man* co-star Dustin Hoffman did make an exception to that rule when they allowed a Buick advertisement to run before the video version of *Rain Man* on condition that a portion of the fee for the commercial was donated to the Autism Society of America.

Tom's sensitivity to revealing any secretive aspects of his life can be summed up by a comment he made to one writer: 'There are no secrets. Sometimes you walk along a beach, looking for a piece of sand. Sometimes it's right in front of you. You don't have to dig. The sand is the sand – do you know what I'm saying?'

*   *   *

Just four miles from Tom's secluded home in the hills over-looking Pacific Palisades, his former wife Mimi Rogers was finding that life without the world's most famous movie star had certain distinct advantages.

The beautiful actress had, as they say, slipped gracefully into the background following the break-up and divorce from Tom. In fact, that 18-month period was more like the lull before a storm.

Mimi had been deeply hurt by some of the rumours flying around Hollywood about her and Tom and why their marriage fell apart. Ludicrous gossips claimed that he was gay and she was a lesbian. Others spoke of a sexless marriage between two people who were never suited in the first place. In actual fact, Tom and Mimi had genuinely loved each other for the first two years of their relationship. Then they gradually discovered they had opposing priorities.

By the beginning of 1993, Tom must have been think-ing that his first marriage was well and truly in the shadows and destined to stay there forever. Within weeks of the separation in January 1990, Mimi had been given a sizeable house in Brentwood, a wealthy LA suburb which separates Bel Air from Pacific Palisades, plus a rumoured multi million dollar settlement.

Mimi turned down dozens of lucrative offers to tell all about her marriage to Tom, partly because she did not want to air her dirty linen in public and also because, as part of the divorce settlement, she had made certain 'agreements' about not talking about her former husband.

In one brief reference to her successor, Nicole Kidman, Mimi said she felt sorry for the young Australian actress: 'All of a sudden her name is never mentioned without his. No matter what the article is, it's "Tom Cruise's wife, Nicole

Kidman." That is it! You're never again mentioned without that name and that's hard. I am waiting for the moment when I don't have to talk about that fucking name any more. I've had it welded on to mine for years now.'

That was the full extent of Mimi's references to any personal aspect of her marriage to Tom. She did not feel she could complain about the marriage because she had truly loved Tom until the association with him became too much to handle. She felt genuinely sorry for Nicole because she was now having to take the heat much more than Mimi ever did. She knew what a burden that could be and could not help feeling relieved herself. All Mimi now wanted was for that Cruise tag to disappear completely.

So, when Tom picked up an issue of *Playboy* magazine in March 1993, he must have got quite a surprise. Spread across the page, in glorious technicolour, was his former wife with nothing on other than a sequined bathing cap and a pair of stilettos. Other photographs inside the seven-page spread revealed Mimi to be a very well-built, sexually active woman approaching her forties but still as proud of her body as ever. One particularly erotic shot showed her grasping her own breasts as her nipples protruded through a skimpy, white, see-through vest.

For good measure, there was also a still photo taken from *The Rapture*, a highly controversial, recently released movie about a sexually promiscuous woman, showing Mimi being caressed by another woman and a man at the same time. Suddenly, Mimi had come of age. No longer Mrs Tom Cruise, she was making her mark on Hollywood in her own sweet way.

The photos in the *Playboy* spread were only the tip of the iceberg. The interview, conducted by respected writer Michael Angeli, went on to mention the rumour mongers who claimed that Tom and Mimi divorced because she liked to go out and party and he preferred to stay at home. 'Is that the story?' Mimi questioned Angeli. 'That I was bored with that child and threw him over, chewed him up and spit him out? Shall we let that be the story? Because here's the real story. Tom was seriously thinking of becoming a monk. At least for that period of time, it looked as though marriage wouldn't fit into his overall spiritual need. And he thought he had to be celibate to maintain the purity of his instrument. Therefore it became obvious that we had to split.'

It was sensational stuff from Mimi after a silence of almost three years. There was more to come.

Angeli then asked pointedly: 'What about your instrument?'

'Oh, my instrument needed tuning,' purred Mimi. Then she went on to say: 'Finances aside, divorce just sucks. I thought as part of my settlement I would get my age back.'

Mimi even tackled the rumours about her being a lesbian by explaining the gossip had started because she used to go out to bars with her best friend actress Kirstie Alley and they would get drunk and flirt with each other. Mimi talked freely about men's 'dicks' and having threesomes and how men's penises look silly on screen.

The article must have infuriated Tom but behind it lay Mimi's frustration at what she perceived to have been a time in her life when she completely lost her own identity. She was simply Mrs Tom Cruise and she did not like it one bit. The fact that she received in the region of $200,000 for the photo spread and interview was almost irrelevant.

'It can be frustrating to have your work kind of passed over as being irrelevant. And that's what happened to a certain extent,' she insisted.

Mimi said she agreed to the controversial article and photographs because 'I am a big fan of nudity and art'.

After the *Playboy* interview hit the news-stands, Mimi

frantically tried to withdraw the clear implication of her quotes that Tom was not keen on making love during their brief marriage. She appeared on US television to say that her claims in *Playboy* were merely a joke. Behind the scenes, some were saying that Tom's powerful Hollywood associates had 'suggested' to Mimi that it might be rather a good idea if she retracted her controversial comments.

Mimi told host Jay Leno on the *Tonight Show*: 'I came up with what I thought was a ridiculous story about how we split up because Tom was thinking of becoming a monk and needed to be celibate. I was kidding. It was a joke.'

Mimi even took the trouble to write to *Playboy* to suggest that her remarks were 'totally playful and completely in jest'. *Playboy* said they stood by the article entirely. Mimi had been given a clear message by Tom's lawyers that the confidentiality clauses in her divorce settlement should be strictly adhered to.

The articles in *Playboy* had another infuriating knock-on effect as far as Tom Cruise Inc. was concerned; newspapers around the world picked up on the story and put their own spin on Mimi's words with the result that dozens of highly personalised articles appeared talking about 'celibate Tom' and interpreting Mimi's quotes as meaning that the world's number one sex symbol was not interested in sex. It was great tabloid fodder and very hurtful to Tom.

Mimi Rogers's decision to answer back to some of the rumours concerning her sexuality coincided with increasingly strong gossip about Tom being gay. A homosexual magazine in New York, called *Outlines*, printed this plea to Tom and other celebrities it claimed were closet gays: 'Come out of the closet! By publicly identifying yourself as a lesbian or gay man, you can change the course of history and create a positive image of who we are.'

The campaign was rightly vilified. Even the tabloids

refused to try to substantiate the magazine's claims because they simply did not believe there was an ounce of truth in them. The vicious campaign backfired in the end because it became clear that most of the celebrities accused of being gay – Oscar winner Jodie Foster was labelled a lesbian – were simply the victims of gossip-mongers. The group had no evidence to back their claims and other homosexual groups condemned the entire exercise as pointless and very hurtful. Many observers believe that it put the entire homosexual issue back at least five years because all it did was convince the 'straights' of Middle America that homosexuals were, in some strange way, less reliable and nastier than the rest of us.

In Hollywood, however, the campaign did have the effect of fuelling the gossip to a certain degree and ridiculous, dangerously inaccurate rumours about Tom being gay continued to fly around. Things came to a head in late 1993 when writer Stephen Rebello asked Nicole Kidman if her husband was gay during an interview for *Movieline* magazine.

Kidman, smart enough not to bristle at the suggestion, replied: 'Really? Well, ummmm, he's not gay to my knowledge. You'll have to ask him that question.' Earlier in the interview she had described Tom as 'the best lover I've ever had. He's a very sexual guy.'

As if to reiterate the point, the couple requested tickets for a theatre production of Terrence McNally's *Lips Together, Teeth Apart*, in New York, and made it clear that they didn't want the press or anyone else tipped off. Then the two lovers proceeded to kiss and cuddle and whisper sweet nothings in each other's ears throughout the performance. 'Anyone sitting behind them had a hard time watching the play,' said one theatregoer.

Actor John Stockwell – a one-time close friend of Tom's from their days together in *Top Gun* and *Losin' It* – reiterated that his old pal was definitely not gay. Referring to his numerous nights out on the town in Los Angeles with Tom, Stockwell insisted: 'He is definitely not gay as we were in situations where it would have been clearly evident.'

Stockwell has his own theories as to why so many Hollywood stars are frequently accused of being homosexual. 'Everyone who is attractive is now projected as they must be gay. It is ridiculous. Especially those in the gay community. They want them to be gay. In some way it makes them acceptable.'

Every now and again the couple continued to pop up in public with an ever-so-loving display of matrimonial bliss. On Easter Sunday 1993, they astonished moviegoers at the Century City Mall in West Los Angeles by queuing up for the reduced-price afternoon matinee of *This Boy's Life*, starring Robert De Niro and Ellen Barkin. After splashing out the princely sum of $3.75 for their bargain cinema tickets, they proceeded to sit near the front and share a huge bucket of popcorn. Tom had his head on Nicole's shoulder and she had her arm around him the entire time.

'It was almost as if they wanted to make sure everyone saw them,' commented one person who sat near them. Whether Tom and Nicole's public displays of affection were a determined effort to tell the world they were very happily married or just a spontaneous gesture, no one will ever know.

Just before Christmas 1993, Tom turned down an extraordinary $2 million offer from a Swiss businessman who wanted the star to spend two hours at his daughter's twenty-first birthday party.

One highly unlikely movie role that Tom was linked with was *The Saint*. According to Hollywood observers, the actor was approached by controversial producer Bob Evans – one-time husband of Ali McGraw – and asked if he would star in the movie version of the sixties British TV series that made Roger Moore famous.

Some of the tabloids had a lot of fun running photographs of six feet two inch Roger up against five feet nine inch Tom, accompanied by articles that suggested he was too short for the role. In fact, Tom's height never came into question because he turned down the role.

Other parts that seem more likely to materialise for Tom include the lead role in *Criminal Conversation*, based on a novel by Evan Hunter, who wrote movies such as *The Blackboard Jungle*, *Strangers When We Meet* and *Mister Buddwing*.

Meanwhile, Nicole's career was going from strength to strength. In late 1993 she completed her part as the heroine in Jane (*The Piano*) Campion's film of the classic Henry James period piece *The Portrait of a Lady*.

However, her role as Tom's wife was definitely proving rather more demanding. Nicole came face to face with her predecessor Mimi Rogers when they bumped into each other outside the Hollywood premiere of the Australian film *Strictly Ballroom*. Nicole had arrived first in a black stretch limousine which was followed, literally seconds later, by Mimi in her own car. Tom was not at the premiere. Witnesses said the two Mrs Cruises glared momentarily at each other and then walked off in opposite directions.

Nicole was then stopped and asked to pose for photographers outside the premiere while Mimi gave TV interviews just a few feet away. At no time did either woman acknowledge the other.

At one stage, Tom was toying with the idea of starring in a remake of William Wyler's great film version of *The*

Heiress. However, on seeing the performances by Mont-
gomery Clift and Olivia de Havilland in the original version,
Tom wisely backed off. Another role he considered in late
1993 was the leading part in *The Chinese Lady*, an original
screenplay about a young man investigating a murder in
Illinois. Siren Productions was the company behind the
project, which had the victim's ghost reappearing to help to
solve the homicide.

At the 1994 Oscar ceremony, Tom presented his old
mentor Paul Newman with the Jean Hersholt Humanitarian
Award. The two men embraced warmly and it was clear to
the hundreds of millions of people watching the ceremony
across the world that Tom and Paul had kept up a very warm
and touching friendship since the shooting of *The Color of
Money* eight years earlier. Tom rounded off the evening by
smooching with Nicole – who was wearing a $5,000 black
dress from Valentino – at the after-show event held at
Morton's restaurant in Beverly Hills. Sporting a few days'
growth of beard for his part in *Interview with the Vampire*,
Tom seemed relaxed and happily planted a kiss on his wife's
neck for the cameras.

Tom also proved he did have a sense of humour when
he put on a bra and red stilettos over his clothes to collect
the Man of the Year award from Harvard University's Hasty
Pudding theatrical group. Tom put on the heels after jokes
about his reputation for not wanting to share a stage with
anyone taller. He was then given a bra with a Harvard
insignia on each cup. Tom insisted after the ceremony that
the awards had 'nothing to do with the fact I just played two
Harvard grads' in *The Firm* and *A Few Good Men*.

On the property front, Tom was carefully and quietly
expanding his empire. With the apartment in New York
worth approximately $5 million and the $15 million house
in Pacific Palisades, he decided that it was time the couple

purchased a 'country home'. They had fallen in love with Telluride, Colorado when they got married there on Christmas Eve 1990, so it was not that much of a surprise when they bought a 77-acre estate in the same town just two years later, for a reported $2.5 million. Locals were told that, within weeks of the purchase, Tom had architects planning the construction of a vast mansion and two guest houses on the estate, which is next door to a spread owned by Sly Stallone.

About six months later, in a secretive property transaction, Tom is also believed to have bought a vast ranch in New South Wales, Australia, although this has never been officially confirmed. The reports were refuelled when, at an awards ceremony in early 1994, Tom let slip that he and Nicole were looking for a play to do together in Australia. For once in her life, Nicole gave her husband a scornful look and reprimanded him when he blurted it out. She put her foot down. 'You told the press!' she scolded.

'Sorry, honey,' he replied sheepishly.

Over the years, Nicole had made no secret of how much she has missed Australia and buying a bolt-hole down under seemed a sensible way of giving her an opportunity to fly back there whenever she wanted to see her mother, father and sister, which seems to be at least three times a year.

After the disappointing box office performance of *Far and Away*, Tom and Nicole sensibly decided to pursue their own individual movie projects. For some strange reason, the public did not appear to like watching the couple together on the big screen. The real-life chemistry that obviously existed between them did not really translate. Many Hollywood observers speculated that Tom's tens of millions of female fans did not like seeing him alongside the woman who, in reality, had him to herself.

Both Tom and Nicole burst into fits of giggles when

they read reports in some of the tabloids claiming that they had agreed to play Prince Andrew and Fergie in a movie about the royal couple's trials and tribulations. It seemed that the rumours got going when some bright spark worked out that Nicole and Fergie were both redheads so that made the actress top contender for the role.

However, while they laughed off reports of playing royalty on the big screen, Tom and Nicole were fast gaining a reputation as Hollywood's newly crowned king and queen. In San Francisco, Tom spent $3,000 a night staying in a luxurious hotel suite – and still insisted on providing his own sheets!

In France in September 1993, Tom left Nicole and Isabella in Paris and flew by private helicopter to Deauville for the annual film festival where he was guest of honour. The trip was only scheduled to last ten hours but an entire floor of the five-star Regency Hotel was cordoned off for his use.

A large crowd of French fans gathered outside the town's casino where the 31-year-old star was expected for a press conference. Most were disappointed because Tom was hidden behind a wall of beefy minders as he made the mere 50-yard journey from the hotel to the casino limousine.

As Hollywood's most glamorous couple, it was therefore not surprising when Tom helped to raise $50,000 for an AIDS benefit by planting an autographed kiss on a piece of cardboard. Lathered in lipstick, Tom's imprint brought in a price approaching $1,000.

Tom was even ranked number 18 in the *Entertainment Weekly* magazine's top '100 in Hollywood' list for 1994. Leaping from a previous year's ranking of number 31, the magazine claimed his power and influence inside Tinseltown had been considerably increased thanks to the success of *The Firm* and *A Few Good Men*.

Besides agreeing not to appear together on the big screen, Nicole started to let it be known through her agents at CAA that she was interested in some meatier roles, especially since husband Tom had also begun changing direction with *Interview with the Vampire*. In early 1994, she beat Meg Ryan to the part of a sociopathic housewife who hires her teenage boyfriend to kill her husband in *To Die For*, to be directed by Gus Van Sant, the controversial character behind such films as the drug-riddled *My Private Idaho* and *Drugstore Cowboy*.

On the personal front, without realising it, Tom managed to avoid meeting America's most controversial so-called shock-jock Howard Stern, whose radio show is listened to by at least 20 million people every morning. The fearsome Stern admitted that even he felt too uncomfortable to approach Tom when he visited the Monkey Bar in Los Angeles, because he was always making fun of his squeaky-clean image on his radio show.

One role that Tom might live to regret turning down was the lead in brilliant young director Quentin Tarantino's award-winning *Pulp Fiction*. The movie won the Best Film category at the Cannes Film Festival in May 1994, after John Travolta revived his career by stepping into the part, first offered to Tom, of a charismatic hitman hooked on heroin.

The time had come for Tom to sit back and take stock of his career. Perhaps there would be opportunities in fresh pastures that lay ahead.

'Hollywood can keep the Oscars.
The only reward I want is a baby.'

Tom Cruise

26

To the outside world, Tom and Nicole seemed like the world's most perfect couple. They shared good looks, success and their fair share of good fortune, or so it seemed. However, there was one aspect of their marriage that was putting them both under immense strain: their desperation to have a child.

In the months leading up to their marriage on Christmas Eve 1990, it was even claimed that Tom had persuaded Nicole to have fertility tests to ensure that she was capable of motherhood. If so, presumably the results were positive.

The first two years following the wedding seemed like an extended honeymoon for the couple. To all their friends and family it was apparent that their love was growing by the day. They took romantic holidays in faraway places and were frequently seen smooching in cinemas and shopping malls in West Los Angeles. It all seemed as if the fairytale romance was set to last for ever and ever.

Tom even commissioned interior decorators – who had already completely redesigned the couple's palatial home in Pacific Palisades – to build a nursery for the children they intended to have as quickly as possible.

In private, however, away from the public appearances and the snatched paparazzi shots, Tom and Nicole were fighting a lonely battle to become parents. For Tom, it was the second time he had faced the stark reality of not being able to become a father. During his marriage to Mimi Rogers, the couple had reportedly had dozens of fertility tests and spent tens of thousands of dollars on specialist advice as to how Mimi could become pregnant.

Said Tom shortly after the break-up with Mimi: 'I have cried tears of frustration over the past year. I would love to have kids. I would turn down an Oscar to see my boy at a baseball game or my girl at a song recital.'

During a visit to London for the royal premiere of *Far and Away*, in the summer of 1992, Tom and Nicole were seen purchasing baby clothes at the Laura Ashley store in the King's Road, Chelsea.

Almost every week a new rumour surfaced about Nicole being pregnant and the constant speculation was starting to get the couple down. In 1992, Nicole's publicist Nancy Seltzer demanded a retraction from *Parade* magazine in America for claiming Nicole was about to give birth. They had spent the best part of two years ignoring the stories but the gossip was starting to make them feel uncomfortable about not being parents.

By the end of 1992, Tom and Nicole were becoming increasingly frustrated. The tests had proved positive and yet Nicole was not pregnant. Why? Tom once again sought out top medical advice. It was gently pointed out to him that some couples have to wait a lot longer than two years. It's just the way it goes.

But that wasn't good enough for Tom. He had steadily gained complete and utter control of his business and personal life but here was something that he could not influence. After ten years of getting more or less what he wanted, mother nature was standing in his way. In any case, he had turned 30 and had already told many friends that he had no intention of being an elderly father.

In early December 1992, the couple felt they could wait no longer and filed papers for adoption in Palm Beach, Florida, one of the few states where a biological mother can't change her mind and try to regain custody after giving a child up for adoption. The paperwork stipulated that they were waiting for a baby from either a 'broking' company, a childrens' home or even through a privately reached financial agreement with the natural mother. The adoption process was shrouded in mystery, with claims that some of Tom's associates in the Scientologists were involved.

Under local laws, Tom and Nicole were required to be residents of Palm Beach. This was no problem. Tom had owned a magnificent, luxury condominium in the area for a number of years and his parents had lived there for quite a while.

Ironically when the news of their plans leaked out it simply reignited speculation about Tom's own fertility. People were well aware of his problems with Mimi and now, after a relationship of just 30 months, some were citing the couple's failure to have a child as the reason behind their attempt to adopt.

'Their adoption announcement is the first formal admission that there may be a problem,' said writer Jane Warren. 'Either Mimi and Nicole both had trouble conceiving, or Tom has a problem – the filing of adoption papers seem to point to Tom.'

Warren claimed that Tom and Nicole became

incredibly jealous when Hollywood's other king and queen, Bruce Willis and Demi Moore, started churning out babies following her much hyped naked and pregnant cover on *Vanity Fair*.

Tom was incensed by the hundreds of stories sparked by the news of the intended adoption. For a few days, in classic PR style, his publicity woman Pat Kingsley steadfastly denied that the papers even existed. Then, at the end of December, when it became clear that the press hounds would not be deterred, Tom ordered his Palm Beach lawyer Weston Sigmund to withdraw the adoption papers. He insisted to friends that stories of jealousy and the clinical manipulation of the adoption system were far from the truth. One claim, that Nicole did not want to be bothered with a nine-month pregnancy because it would get in the way of her movie career, was discounted as nonsense.

In fact, Tom and Nicole could have continued trying for a lot longer. They simply recognised that their desperation for a child might lead to problems in their own relationship. In any case, adoption was becoming all the rage in Hollywood, with people like Kirstie Alley and Michelle Pfeiffer heading the long list of celebrities who had arranged to take delivery of a child.

Tom's decision to order the adoption papers to be withdrawn was a heartbreaking one for the couple but they were angry that the papers' existence had been made public by the Palm Beach records office. Tom's lawyers complained of a blatant breach of confidence and told Chief Circuit Judge Daniel T.K. Hurley that Tom and Nicole had suffered an irreparable invasion of privacy and were robbed of an opportunity to become parents. In fact, Tom and Nicole actually instructed their lawyers secretly to continue the adoption process.

At first, representatives of the couple tried to strike

a deal with a surrogate mother in Florida but that plan was abandoned when it was pointed out that the identification of the real parent would be certain to leak out because the scandal-hungry US tabloids would pay a king's ransom for such information. There were also genuine fears that the couple could become blackmail victims if someone decided to threaten to release the information if Tom did not pay over a fortune.

Tom was discovering that being the world's hottest box office movie star certainly had its drawbacks but all these obstacles made the couple realise that they both held a deep-set desire to give an unwanted child the sort of life most of us can only dream about. Tom's team of laywers and advisors suggested that adopting – rather than surrogacy – would be a much more sensitive way of handling the no-baby issue.

'In my marriage to Nicole, I have learned to be sensitive to someone else's feelings, that life isn't all about me. When you're married, "me" has to become "us",' Tom told one acquaintance at the time.

Nicole deliberately left a very carefully laid trail of confusion over the entire baby issue by insisting publicly that she was not ready to start a family. 'There is plenty of time for that later. Tom and I have only just settled into each other's ways,' she said in the summer of 1992. 'We both realise that we are too selfish in our marriage and our careers to worry about the responsibilities that parenthood brings.'

Nicole was understandably concerned about her career. It had just started to get going and she was being offered movie roles without Tom, which proved to a sometimes cynical Hollywood that she could carry a film without her famous husband. After *Days of Thunder* and *Far and Away*, some had said that Nicole could only get decent parts if Tom came along for the ride as well.

Tom actually felt indebted to Nicole for making him happier than at any other time in his life but he, more than her, felt the need to make it a complete family. All the heartbreak and anguish caused by the break up of his own first marriage and that of his parents had made him even more determined.

There was an added pressure on Nicole. All the constant speculation over whether she was pregnant was putting her under some very awkward pressure. She explained: 'It's true. People do that. One woman walked up to me recently and said loudly to her friend: "Of course she's pregnant – look at that little belly." ' She then added a comment that must have brought a wry smile to the face of her predecessor, Mimi Rogers: ' I'm never sure whether people are interested in me because I'm a movie star or because I'm married to Tom.'

There lay the couple's dilemma; Nicole wanted to pursue her career to prove she was an actress in her own right, while Tom was more concerned with making sure she got pregnant. In the end, they reached a compromise and visited an adoption agency in Palm Beach, Florida.

The adoption was formalised in the second week of January 1993, and the couple became parents to a nine-pound girl whom they decided to call Isabella Jane Kidman Cruise. The child's married mother already had two children but she was so poor that she could not afford to look after a third.

From the set of *The Firm* in Memphis, Tom rushed to the hospital in Miami where the baby was born, while Nicole flew in from Los Angeles. Both were shaking with nerves as they looked down at the baby for the first time while she lay asleep in a cot. Nicole leaned down and gently picked the baby up, tears welling in her eyes. Then she held her close. Tom looked on in awe. This was going to be the biggest test of character he had ever faced.

As far as Tom was concerned, the baby represented the final chapter in his long and sometimes painful search for happiness and contentment. To her credit, Nicole fully appreciated what an enormous responsibility a child would mean to them. While she was undoubtedly determined to continue her career, she knew that the baby would need a considerable amount of loving care and attention. Far from being daunted by parenthood, Nicole was supremely confident that she could handle every aspect of bringing up a child in safe and pleasant surroundings.

It was even claimed that the baby's birth was carried out in complete silence after a request from Tom to the child's real mother because Scientologists believe in complete silence at birth. Before taking delivery of Isabella, Tom and Nicole added a nanny and a nurse to their permanent staff back in Pacific Palisades. The strangest rumour of all concerned the candid photographs of the couple with their baby which appeared in the notorious *National Enquirer* tabloid. The pictures looked as if they had been taken by a paparazzo armed with a telephoto lense but claims were afterwards made that Tom and Nicole helped set up the shoot in exchange for a share of the worldwide sales of the shots, which would add up to several hundred thousand dollars.

That is patent nonsense as Tom hardly needs the money! However, rumours that the photos were taken in exchange for the cameraman agreeing to lay off Tom, Nicole and Isabella in the future sound more likely. Intriguingly, the *Enquirer* seemed to have some impeccable sources as far as all of Tom's efforts to become a father were concerned. The magazine even revealed Tom's alleged fertility problems with Mimi Rogers three years earlier and spoke with great authority when discussing all aspects of the star's desperation to be a father, although it also has to be pointed out that the *Enquirer* did announce Nicole was pregnant in July

1991, with a headline that screamed: Tom Cruise fertility ordeal over at last ... "She's pregnant and I did it"' – all of which turned out to be completely untrue.

As if to contradict the entire *Enquirer* situation, Tom's lawyers answered the rumours in March 1993, by requesting an injunction to prevent an Australian magazine from running photographs of baby Isabella. The couple feared that the pictures might be seen by the birth mother, who apparently remained unaware of the adoptive parents' identities. 'Isabella doesn't have to be public, too. We want to do everything we can to make her life as normal as possible, like our childhoods,' insisted Nicole.

Within a week of the adoption, Tom was moved to speak about the joys of parenthood while at the Golden Globe awards ceremony in Los Angeles. 'Becoming a father is the greatest thing that has ever happened to me. I have longed for a child for so long. Now that I have little Isabella, I look at her and thank God every day for giving me such a precious gift. I adore her to death and I hope I will love and protect her to my dying day – I am ecstatically happy.'

Tom even insisted: 'Isabella comes before everything – career, films, business, everything. The baby and Nicole are the most important things in my life. Becoming a father makes you realise what it is all about.'

Nicole was just as overwhelmed and poured out her feelings to one associate:

'We chose to call the baby Isabella not because it has any family connections but simply because we both love the name.

'She has turned our world upside down. We thought we had everything, but having a child makes you put everything into perspective. I cannot even begin to describe the change that has come over Tom. I always knew he would be a loving father, but seeing him with our little girl makes me pinch myself.'

The first night little Isabella came home to the house in Pacific Palisades, Tom even got up in the middle of the night to feed her. Friends said that he seemed to 'loosen up' and become a much warmer person after the couple adopted their baby. Having the child made Tom reflect even more on his own childhood and the lessons he had learned from that sometimes painful experience.

Isabella seemed to be the icing on the cake for Tom and Nicole. At the Golden Globes awards ceremony the couple could barely keep their hands off each other as they spoke to journalists. They stroked each other, touched hair and kissed tenderly. They also held hands constantly.

Nicole – barely recognisable after straighting her normally curly red hair and dying it blonde for her latest movie role, even admitted that the couple had been trying to conceive 'for so long that we are making the most of Isabella now'.

Before Isabella came on to the scene, Tom was asked by respected American writer Stephen Rebello what trait of his he hoped his children would not inherit from him. The reply was typical serious pre-fatherhood Tom: 'I guess, physically, one thing is my bone-straight hair. It's something that terrifies hairdressers. I hate it when it gets in my eyes.'

Within weeks of baby Isabella arriving at her new home, Nicole was starting rehearsals for her starring part alongside Michael Keaton in *My Life* with a shooting scheduled for Los Angeles and Chicago. Some observers pointed out that if she had got pregnant that particular role would have had to be sacrificed.

Nicole was particularly attracted to the role offered in

My Life because it was a poignant drama about a young woman who is expecting her first child and then discovers her husband has cancer. She relished the prospect of playing a pregnant person on film and insisted to everyone she met that she and Tom would definitely be having children of their own eventually.

By the time *The Firm* toppled *Jurassic Park* at the top of US box office ratings in July 1993, Isabella was seven months old and Tom, despite a back-breaking schedule, insisted that neither he nor Nicole were going to be absentee parents. 'Nic and I were never going to have a child and disappear off to work every day to leave her with a nanny. I mean, what kind of way is that to treat a child?' Admirable words spoken with utter intent no doubt. However, when a multi-million-dollar movie rests on your performance it does not exactly leave much time for a home life, although it has to be said that, during the late spring and most of the summer of 1993, Tom made a remarkable effort to be with baby Isabella whenever possible. The couple adored getting up early and taking the baby out in a three-wheeled pram while jogging along behind it. There were even rumours that Tom and Nicole had decided to adopt a second baby because they so enjoyed parenthood. These turned out to be false, having been fuelled by the couple's open admission to friends that they still hoped to have children of their own and the fact that they had to appear in a Florida courthouse in July 1993 to finalise the January adoption of Isabella.

One of the most unlikely public appearances by Tom, Nicole and baby Isabella came when the threesome visited the well-known British pub, the King's Head, in Santa Monica, California, just five miles from their home in Pacific Palisades. Locals could not believe their eyes when the couple walked in and ordered a plate of bangers and mash each. (The pub is the favourite drinking spot for more than a dozen British tabloid journalists based in the LA area.)

'Talk about walking into the enemy camp. We could not believe it when he came in and sat down. Maybe nobody told Tom that the King's Head is Santa Monica's equivalent of Fleet Street-by-the-sea,' said one veteran tabloid reporter.

Meanwhile, Nicole seemed to be working non-stop. Tom flew from Los Angeles to Boston every other weekend to see her and Isabella while she was making *Malice* with handsome Alec Baldwin. In the *Star* tabloid one report claimed that Tom showed up unannounced on the set of the movie to watch some of his wife's passionate clinches being filmed for one scene and then declared: 'Some of those kissing scenes are a little too strong – and a little too long!' The article went on to insist that Tom also added: 'A kiss shouldn't take a minute and a half – ten seconds is more like it!' Apparently, Alec Baldwin snapped back: 'Sorry, but Kim (his girlfriend Kim Basinger) is away for five days.'

Malice was directed by Harold Becker – the same helmsman who gave Tom his chance in *Taps* all those years earlier. Reviews of the film were mediocre, but Nicole's acting skills were given some praise. *Movieline* described it as 'a wicked thriller that dances on the grave of the ordinary murder mystery'. Nicole was, said the magazine, 'unsuspecting, but push her in the wrong direction and you get a Nicole Kidman never seen on screen before: ruthless, confrontational and angry as hell'.

Tom managed to persuade Nicole to take enough time off to fly to Australia to show Isabella off to all Nicole's relatives. Tom even sneaked in a few visits to some of the finest properties in the Sydney area as he secretly contemplated buying a place down under. The high point of the trip – which coincided with the 40th Sydney Film Festival – was a three-hour voyage in Sydney Harbour with some of Nicole's family on board a yacht called the *Sea Gypsy*.

Tom and Nicole took turns to hold baby Isabella and enjoyed a tasty lunch from a hamper as the baby's nanny stayed out of sight in a cabin. Nicole even took the time and trouble to dab some sun tan lotion on the child to ensure that she did not get burnt.

In August 1993, Tom told *Hello!* magazine that he had actually started to learn how to relax, thanks to Nicole and Isabella. 'For a long time before I met Nicole, I always put my career ahead of everything. Now we do everything together. Nic just makes it feel fun to be around her. The littlest things she'll do will get to me. 'She'll say, "Oh, a little tense today? The world's treating you a little rough." When she does that you realise things aren't so terrible.'

In August 1993, Tom discovered that taking one's family on holiday can prove a little tiresome if you happen to be one of the world's most famous people. The happy threesome hired a yacht and went cruising off the Mediterranean island of Sardinia. The local paparazzi became so intrusive that Tom begged local police to help him to deter the lensmen.

The police proved so vigorous in their pursuit of the dozens of photographers that a few days later Tom hired one of them as the family bodyguard for the rest of the holiday at a cost of $1,500. The incidents with the paparazzi reminded Tom how risky it was to not always have body-guards, especially in Europe where terrorism seemed more of a problem. The couple had been proud of the fact that they tried to get out into the real world as often as possible as was proved by their appearances in LA shopping malls and restaurants on a frequent basis.

In London, during the making of *Interview with the Vampire*, Tom even hired a top doctor to 'babysit' baby daughter Isabella in case she got ill. The couple recruited senior registrar Jane Deal from the paediatric ward at St

Mary's Hospital, Paddington to make sure that instant medical attention was on hand if Isabella fell ill. Tom paid Jane $200 an hour plus a weekly retainer of $700.

Various opportunistic people jumped on the Cruise baby bandwagon. Florida gubernatorial candidate Anthony Martin threatened to sue Tom and his Hollywood attorney Bertram Fields for $50 million after claiming that Fields, according to court papers, 'disseminated false and defamatory information' about Martin following the politician's statements questioning the legality of whether Tom, a Californian resident, could adopt a baby in Florida.

In September 1993, Martin alleged that Tom's adoption amounted to nothing more than 'baby selling' and he suggested, according to court papers, that the adoption 'may amount to *de facto* child kidnapping'. Martin said: 'I am going to have a sheriff ready to serve Cruise with papers if he sets foot in Florida.'

Martin launched his legal battle against Tom and Fields after claiming that Fields threatened him with 'ten years of litigation' if Martin did not drop his investigation into the legality of Tom's adoption. Martin said Fields 'threatened him legally and every other way possible', to the very implication of a 'physical threat'.

Fields refused to comment on Martin's complaint but admitted: 'I did say if he libelled my client I would sue him.' Martin, 46, was labelled an independently wealthy man who simply criss-crossed the country filing lawsuits, demanding investigations and calling press conferences.

Tom and Nicole's decision to become parents had brought with it a number of unforeseen problems.

'For vampires, physical love culminates and is satisfied in one thing, the kill.'

Vampire Louis in *Interview with the Vampire*

27

After completing *The Firm*, Tom realised that his career had reached a watershed. At only 31 his roles seemed predestined, his salary stuck in the $15 million-a-picture range and his movies virtually guaranteed to deliver a huge opening box office weekend. However, Tom actually feared that the parts he had so far been playing to perfection might be wearing a little thin.

Hundreds of millions of moviegoers across the globe still adored the routine: pushy kid matures to manhood over the course of a 90-minute movie (applause and roll credits, please). That familiar wink, smile and expression of mild bewilderment had become his calling card.

Tom wanted to be stretched further. He wanted to go beyond the expected roles of a megastar and venture into unknown territory. So far, he had not put a foot wrong.

However, at the urging of Hollywood's two most awesome powerbrokers – CAA chief Mike Ovitz and record company boss/movie producer David Geffen – Tom decided to enter that highly dangerous movie terrain called character depiction. The project his two mentors encouraged him to take on was to prove the most controversial move of his entire career.

Interview with the Vampire was first published as a novel in 1976 and gained cult status as probably the greatest vampire book to come along since Bram Stoker's *Dracula*. Author Anne Rice updated her version for a morally ambiguous age and the result was that Rice's vampire was not just evil incarnate, he was burdened with a conscience that haunted his every waking hour.

That was precisely what happened to Tom after he was offered the role of Rice's chief vampire, Lestat. He found himself haunted by the controversy surrounding his decision to take the part and was plunged into self-doubt – not helped by the fact that the character he had agreed to play was known to millions of Rice fans as tall, blond, European and androgynous.

Even more significant than that, Tom's part meant he would be playing a villain for the first time in his life – a sallow mass murderer, an after-hours fiend who sinks his teeth into every man, woman and child he meets.

Tom insisted publicly that he was not in the least bit concerned that what Oliver Stone so rightly called his 'Wheaties-box image' would clash with his ability to play the vampire Lestat. 'I just couldn't resist the role. Besides, he's not a bad guy, he just has villainous aspects to him. From his point of view, he's right. He's really a terribly lonely character.'

In many ways, Tom could have been describing himself, apart from the 'villainous aspects'. In fact, he wanted to be badder. He wanted to show audiences that he was capable of a much wider range of human emotions.

The role of Lestat will stretch him to breaking point. Lestat is an amoral, solitary supervampire who voyages through time and space feasting on flesh. In *Interview*, he coldly turns Louis, played by up-and-coming Robert Redford lookalike Brad Pitt, into a vampire because he likes the company and is envious of Louis's impressive home. Later, still bored and lonely, Lestat persuades Louis to 'adopt' a five-year-old girl and turns her into a vampire as well.

Tom first heard of the *Interview* project when David Geffen contacted him in December 1992, while Tom was vacationing in Australia with Nicole. Geffen – the king of Hollywood's so-called velvet mafia – had gained billionaire status after the megasale of Geffen Records a few years earlier. His influence on Tom went way back to the successes of *Risky Business*, the movie that helped to launch Tom's career more than any other film. Geffen had backed the movie financially and played the main producer's role. Tom had never forgotten how supportive Geffen had been and had kept in touch with him throughout the following ten years.

Geffen became increasingly influential in Tom's career moves in the late-1980s. He looked on Tom as a star whom he had helped to steer to the top and the two men had a special affinity for each other, fuelled by Tom's eternal gratitude to Geffen for helping him to land that all-important part in *Risky Business*.

When Geffen told Tom about *Interview*, he immediately took notice and, as he later admitted, 'got very excited'. Tom told Geffen – an immaculately turned out man in his early fifties – that he had read *Interview* when he was a teenager and loved it. (For a kid with dyslexia, Anne Rice's novel must have taken a hell of a long time to read!)

By the time Geffen and Tom had ended that phone

conversation, Tom was convinced that Lestat was going to be his next role. It was a decision that would turn into the most controversial, headline-hitting storm to hit Hollywood in 1993.

Tom immediately called his production company in Los Angeles and asked them to get hold of every one of Anne Rice's novels. On his return to California, he began the first stage of his homework for the role. He 'busted ass' reading every one of her books and tried to come to terms with the decadent lifestyle of the eighteenth-century French aristocrat-turned-vampire Lestat. Then he took piano lessons from teacher Margie Balter, who was recommended to Tom by Holly Hunter, his co-star in *The Firm* who got Best Actress Oscar in March 1994 for her portrayal of a dumb woman in *The Piano*. Margie's comment on her new pupil was not that surprising. 'He's very smart and very focused.'

Tom travelled to Paris to cruise round museums. He visited Versailles to get the feel of the period furniture and fashions. He also went on his most stringent-ever diet and exercise regimen in order to lose 12 pounds to take on Lestat's gaunt physique. Then he streaked his hair blond, had his eyebrows flecked with gold and parted his newly grown locks in the centre – the transformation was underway.

What Tom did not expect when he told David Geffen he wanted the role, was the frequent and unflattering attacks made against him by a furious Anne Rice, who believed that Geffen and the movie's director, Irishman Neil Jordan, had committed a cardinal sin by casting the all-American hero in the part of her most sick and twisted vampire. She was incensed.

Rice publicly lashed out at Tom for being too short. She said his voice was too high and complained bitterly to the *Los Angeles Times* that Tom was no more her Lestat 'than

Edward G. Robinson is Rhett Butler'. Rice – who looks herself a little like a coiffured Morticia Addams – stirred up such an angry response to Tom's casting as Lestat that protesters would turn up at her book-signings across America with placards reading 'No Tom Cruise! No Tom Cruise! No Tom Cruise!' Dozens of petitions were raised calling for a boycott of the movie.

Spurred on by her readers, Rice, aged 52, embarked on a one-woman crusade to embarrass Tom, the movie studio backers Warner Brothers and David Geffen. To cheering crowds at her public appearances, Rice cursed Tom for allegedly butchering her script, sanitising the sexual content to accommodate his so-called clean-cut image and perpetrating one of the worst examples of bad casting in Hollywood history. Addressing an audience of one thousand on Halloween Night 1993, she said: 'I wanted to call David Geffen and say, "How the hell could you do this?"'

Rice's fans vented their outrage in classic terms: 'Tom Cruise is the man you take home to Momma. Lestat is the man you don't want Momma to know about,' said one. Then came: 'Cruise is a nice American boy not an evil European.'

Some Hollywood regulars compared the miscasting of Tom in *Interview with the Vampire* with such classic movie mistakes as Clark Gable's stab at Irish nationalist Charles Parnell in *Parnell*, and Spencer Tracey in *Dr Jekyll and Mr Hyde*.

What all these so-called experts failed to realise was that Tom's image was being decanted into the role because the movie's main backers, Warner Brothers, actually required his beaming charisma to defuse a potentially repellent portrayal and draw customers to the ticket booth.

Tom was gutted by the fury of the reaction against him. Normally carefully shielded from the press by his overprotective and highly professional PR woman Pat Kingsley, he had been caught completely offguard by Anne Rice's wrath. 'When it first hit, it really hurt my feelings, to be candid about it,' he admitted. 'Her venom hurt.'

What really shook Tom was when he started to get calls from Hollywood friends and acquaintances asking him what was going on. Tom claimed: 'Nobody could see what the big deal was.' Tom had initially hoped to meet and consult Anne Rice just like he had Ron Kovic for *Born on the Fourth of July*. That was now obviously completely out of the question. 'You don't usually start a movie with someone not wanting you to do it. That's unusual,' said Tom.

America's best known gossip columnist Liz Smith – always a stout defender of Tom even when she had been the last to be told of his wedding to Mimi Rogers years earlier – wrote in her widely read column that she was 'disappointed' with Anne Rice for attacking the casting of Tom as Lestat. 'You'd think that stretching oneself artistically was some sort of crime!'

Smith continued: 'Tom Cruise is an actor – a good actor – and he will undoubtedly approach his role as the vampire Lestat with as much commitment as he has devoted to his other projects. This is exciting and daring movie making; the most exciting thing, actually, to have happened in Hollywood in ages.' According to many Tinseltown insiders, Liz Smith frequently gets calls from stars' agents 'suggesting' that she might like to place certain items in her column.

Even Paula Wagner leapt to his defence. 'None of this is new. After *Taps* people were convinced Tom was a brilliant young character actor. At first, no one would even see him for *Risky Business*. People had much the same reaction when Tom was cast as Ron Kovic. Two years later he received an Academy Award nomination.'

Tom's Hollywood friends and associates were rallying behind their favourite star and countering Anne Rice's 'trouble-making' stance over his casting with great defiance. Reading between the lines, they were telling the author that she had no chance of changing things and they proved that he did have the backing of Hollywood for the role of Lestat.

The other player involved in the *Interview* controversy was CAA boss Mike Ovitz – the single most influential agent in Hollywood history and the man who had helped steer Tom's career in recent years. He was so disturbed by the public reaction against his number one client that he issued a statement: '*Interview with the Vampire* will stand on its own intrinsic quality, which, given the talented people involved, will likely be very high.'

However, others inside Tinseltown genuinely feared that Anne Rice's very public campaign to smear the movie version of her book might seriously damaged the $50 million film before it is even completed. Many Hollywood observers began dubbing the movie everything from 'Cruise's Coffin' to 'Geffen's Grave' to 'Fangs a Lot'. Industry publications began to predict that it could be one of the biggest bombs of all time.

Then there was talk of a curse on the entire project, further fuelled by the untimely death of actor River Phoenix just a few days before he was due to join the cast in the role of a young reporter. The 22-year-old actor died after consuming a cocktail of drugs at a Hollywood nightclub owned by fellow star Johnny Depp. Christian Slater stepped into Phoenix's role.

Just days after filming began on the project, a number of death threats were made against Tom. Security was stepped up and a secret tunnel constructed between Tom's trailer and the film set so that he could walk to work without being exposed to any of Anne Rice's overzealous fans who might, it was feared, take a pop at him in retaliation against his casting.

Behind the scenes, David Geffen – ever the protector of his carefully nurtured project and his favourite star Tom Cruise – was starting to feel very bitter about Anne Rice's campaign against the movie. 'Anne is a difficult woman at best, and what her motives are remains somewhat beyond me,' he said. 'But for her to attack this movie for her own self-importance, when she has been paid $2 million [in rights] and stands to make a lot more money selling her books, is just capricious. It lacks kindness. It lacks discretion. And it lacks professionalism.'

David Geffen was certainly no hypocrite in the discretion stakes and his professionalism is renowned, but 'kindness' from a man reckoned to be the wealthiest individual in Hollywood does sound rather hollow.

Behind Tom's casting lay a complex web of Hollywood power-playing that provides interesting evidence that he was by no means first choice for the role of Lestat. Initially, Geffen had – with Anne Rice's blessing – pursued Daniel Day-Lewis to star as the ultimate vampire. He kept them waiting for six months before turning down the role on the basis that it was yet another costume drama. Rice pushed for John Malcovich, having already conceded that the actor on whom she had originally based the character of Lestat – chunky Guinness ad star Rutger Hauer – was perhaps too long in the tooth at the age of 49. Another name mentioned was Jeremy Irons.

Then in stepped Irish director Neil Jordan, fresh from his extraordinary success with *The Crying Game*. He pronounced Rice's suggestions as too old and clichéd. Then Tom's name came into the frame. No one knows if it was Jordan or Geffen who actually chose him. Although the decision for such creative aspects of a movie is usually left to the director, in Hollywood, where a star's name can make or break a film, it is often the powerbrokers like Geffen who actually decide.

Anyhow, Jordan defended the decision by insisting: 'Sometimes when you go the opposite way from what people expect, you get the best results. Every casting choice is a leap and, if it works, it's because the actor makes it fit his own skin.'

Casting aside, the most extraordinary aspect behind Tom's decision to star in *Interview* is the blatantly perverted, downright kinky aspects of the movie. In the book, there are scenes of Lestat and a five-year-old girl cuddling in a manner which can only be described as paedophilic.

David Geffen insists that Tom did not demand any changes to the script's sexually explicit ingredients, which also include homosexuality on the part of Lestat. If this is the case, it would be the first time since the disastrous *Losin' It* that Tom had not interfered with a script.

'He has not had any input into this script whatsoever,' says Geffen angrily. The megarich producer then hit out at the rumours that Tom was concerned about the film's gay elements, by stating, very significantly, 'Any homophobia being alleged against Tom is an outrage and a bald-faced lie.'

Tom confessed: 'There's a lot of biting going on. It is a very erotic picture. The hard part is learning to bite someone in a different way each time. Each kill has to tell the story of that relationship.'

Director Jordan tried to elicit some sympathy for Tom by pointing out that, for him, 'there is a huge amount on the line – money, reputation, everything.'

The other fascinating aspect to the *Interview* saga is that if the movie is a runaway success then, for the first time in his career, Tom will almost definitely play Lestat again in a sequel.

On the shoot itself, a procession of beautiful young actresss were recruited to play the parts of some of Lestat's victims. Anouk Fontaine was given a juicy role on the strength of a single press photo of her. The 19-year-old brunette from Barnes, West London gushed: 'When I'm down on the set I'm totally in awe of what's going on. I have to keep running back into my room.'

Another recruit to *Interview* was British model Sarah Stockbridge. The beautiful blonde 27 year old landed the part after years of modelling some of the most outrageous fashions of cult designer Vivienne Westwood. Young Irish actress Susan Lynch was similarly cast, as the numbers of beautiful young women being recruited for the movie increased by the day.

On 15 October 1993, Tom was awarded the Actor of the Decade prize at the Chicago International Film Festival. Looking very gaunt and blond, Tom asserted: 'I'm terribly excited to be working with the cast.' He was still concerned about the way things were going. 'I hope to prove a lot of people wrong.'

The casting of handsome Brad Pitt, aged 25, as Tom's co-star in the 'good guy' role of Louis, sparked further reports of problems on the set of *Interview*. Observers were claiming that Tom was obsessed with how much better look-ing Pitt was – and how much taller at five feet eleven inches. Rumours flew around that Tom had three-inch insteps built into his shoes to make him look taller. Tom's ever loyal publicity guru Pat Kingsley insisted that was not the case and that the high heels on Tom's boots were simply in keep-ing with the fashion of the period in which the film is set.

Pitt – who is definitely currently on a Hollywood roll – said: 'People are gunning for us. So what? The way I see it, I'm going to give some good performances and probably some bad performances, but I'm going to try my hardest on every one. I can't see there's much else I can do or should do. I also try to ignore the controversy and hype.'

In fact, Pitt had nothing whatsoever to lose by being

cast opposite Tom. Having him on the picture would take the pressure off his shoulders and put it on to Tom's. Pitt was also savvy enough to know that Tom's name on the titles could add tens of millions to the box office taking and that would mean a fatter fee for the young actor.

At one stage, Tom insisted that the movie's producers hire an 'eyebrow person' to make sure that his vampire-look, gold-flecked brows were carefully maintained. Reports from the set claimed that director Jordan was, by this stage, 'sitting back and watching the whole scene looking miserable and uncomfortable'.

A report by British showbiz columnist Baz Bamigboye in the *Daily Mail* insisted that Tom was attending 'dailies' – where the previous day's footage is screened for the movie's executives – every day with director Jordan and often suggesting that some scenes be reshot. Bamigboye claimed that Tom was 'uptight all the time' and constantly displaying jealousy and nerves because his co-star Pitt steals nearly every scene.

British producer Stephen Woolley – a one-time London cinema usher – insisted that director Jordan was perfectly happy with the way things were going.

During filming at the haunted Oak Alley Plantation in New Orleans, staff members were forced to sign agreements not to speak to anyone, including their own family members, about the cast and crew's presence. Rumours circulating Hollywood claimed that even David Geffen's own employees had been persuaded to sign similar contracts.

In Louisiana, Tom and Nicole rented a palatial, three-storey, antebellum, Greek-revival mansion on Audubon Place in the distinctly upmarket Garden District of New Orleans – just a few miles from Anne Rice's own gothic palace. Perhaps not surprisingly, the two did not meet.

Besides his customary early morning jogging, Tom

occasionally played soccer with neighbourhood kids inside the gated, guarded community of just 30 houses. He took baby Isabella out in her three-wheeled pram, specially adapted so that Tom could jog as he pushed it.

In the middle of all this, Daniel Day-Lewis gallantly tried to cool the controversy over Tom's casting by saying: 'I find it upsetting. These people are trying to make a film as well as they possibly can with the choices there are. It's absolutely horrendous to me that they're having to deal with my name thrown in the mix.'

Rutger Hauer – Rice's original choice for Lestat – was less diplomatic: 'I can't quite see Tom Cruise as Lestat. But it's not the first time that someone got a part that I would have been much better for.'

Precious few photos of Tom in his vampire look were revealed to the media during the movie's actual production but the paparazzi did manage to snatch a few shots which showed the star with sunken eyes, a long wig and heavy white make-up. Some said he rather resembled an early Alice Cooper.

During filming in London, Tom and Nicole rented 42 Chester Terrace a Regency gatehouse leading into Regent's Park. Early risers spotted him jogging through the park at 4 a.m., wearing a waterproof, hooded top, President Clinton-style gloves and tracksuit bottoms. Sometimes, usually when it was a little warmer, Nicole would take her turn on the streets of London with her trainer in tow. After the couple vacated it, the property was put up for sale for one and a half million pounds.

Despite rumours to the contrary, Tom and director Jordan became very good friends during the shooting of *Interview*. The intense Irishman – who had astonished Hollywood with the success of *The Crying Game* – had visited Hollywood before during the late 1980s and found it distinctly not to his liking. This time around, he decided to play Tinseltown at its own game.

On New Year's Eve 1993, Tom and Nicole flew back to their beloved Dublin, where they had enjoyed so many romantic nights together during the making of *Far and Away*, to attend Jordan's private New Year's Eve party at the director's home in Dalkey, just outside the city. The couple joined in some classic Irish folk dancing and Tom was even said to have supped half a pint of Guinness.

While in Ireland, Tom and Nicole checked out a few properties in the area with a possible view to buying a place in the Emerald Isle. Maybe Tom was planning to abdicate his Hollywod crown if *Interview* ended up being a disaster.

'The whole star process can be destructive. The pressure is unbelievable. There's pressure to get to the top and to stay on top. There's fear of losing stardom. People who go into this business often just look at the rewards. They don't realise what they're getting into.'

Beverly Hills clinical psychologist Dr Eugene Landy

Epilogue

Tom Cruise probably doesn't look back at his young, gauche, arrogant, nakedly ambitious self with the ache of longing that he always imagined he would feel when he reached his thirties. On the contrary, he should feel a great sense of relief that his hyperactive twenties are over. If the thirties are the end of your youth, then good riddance. They also mark the beginning of that true adulthood promised to every 21 year old.

'Youth is overrated,' said one Hollywood starlet. For Tom, his thirties meant waving goodbye to a troublesome first marriage, the occasional love affair with unsuitable ladies and an addiction to the highs when things were going well, without any care or consideration for the abject misery of the lows.

Tom's twenties coincided with the 1980s. In that ten-year span, achievement was the name of the game but even that was not enough; with every attainment there were bonus points for each year that stood between him and the big three-O. The term 'young film star' ceased to mean an actor under the age of 45 and applied to Tom and his fellow Brat Packers, all under 25.

Like everyone else in his generation, Tom undoubtably had a long list of things he wanted to achieve by the age of 30, but when his birthday – 3 July 1992 – came and went, he realised that it had nothing to do with lowering his expectations. It was just that he started to appreciate that there was no value in being the most successful movie star on the planet for his age. You're either brilliant or you're not. The irony is that once Tom freed himself from the pressure of his own expectations, he actually kicked his career into a new gear.

The trials and troubles of Tom's twenties were, in a sense, a necessary evil, a rite of passage in the journey towards self-knowledge. A lot of Tom's confidence grew as he got older because he felt a huge relief at having survived and then thrived in Hollywood. He had come through a lot of emotional and personal problems unscathed. He had gained a new sense of purpose in life. Tom finally discovered his own values because he had tested them out in his twenties. That meant making decisions became even easier.

There is also a commonly held belief that Tom's looks will adjust to his thirties. He has already started to adopt a more lived-in appearance and, in his latest movie, *Interview with the Vampire*, he looks positively old at certain stages! Tom has obviously reacted to the end of his trademark good looks and kid next door appearance by taking on meatier, more mature roles, unlike the matinee idols of yesteryear who held on to their youth for far too long and ultimately paid the price of failure.

Tom has even adopted a grunge-style look for the nineties which defies his tuxedo image and sends a sharp message to his fans that his materialistic ideals have been left behind in the 1980s. His fee might have leapt up to the $20 million mark but he wants the world to know he is a regular sort of guy who cares about people.

However, one of the disadvantages for Tom of reaching his thirties is that he might actually be expected to reveal more of his inner self. Many TV chat shows have an unwritten rule to avoid featuring celebrities under the age of 30 because younger people simply don't have enough to talk about. Now those same programmes, and in turn their audiences, will start to expect Tom to 'come out' and prove he has attained new maturity. It remains to be seen if this notoriously private star will actually bow to the pressure.

Perversely, it seems that it's only as time goes by that Tom will truly learn to relax, to realise that there is no hurry to achieve fresh goals in his life. When he actually manages to do so, a new character may well emerge, a character with the true charm and relaxed demeanour of one of those old-time stars upon whom he has modelled himself so carefully.

Then, and only then, will he be crowned the real king of Hollywood...

Source and Chapter Notes

The following chapter notes give a general view of the sources who helped in the preparation of *Tom Cruise – Unauthorised* but they are by no means all-inclusive. The author has respected the wishes of many interview subjects to remain anonymous and, accordingly, has not named them here or elsewhere in the text.

Prologue and Chapter 1

Letters: Betram Fields, May 2, 1994; Blake Publishing, May 3, 1994; Interviews with Roger Fristoe, Nov 11, 1993; Jeff Bayers, Nov 10, 1993; Caroline Mapother, Nov 7, 1993; Dillon Mapother, April 3, 1994. Articles: *Los Angeles* magazine, Oct, 1993; GQ magazine, Dec, 1992; *LA Weekly*, July 2, 1993; *Time*, Aug 26, 1991; *US* magazine, Jan, 1993; *People* magazine, June 8, 1992; *Playboy*, Jan, 1990; US magazine, Oct, 1991; *Vanity Fair*, Jan, 1989; *Washington Post*, Aug 30, 1983; *Louisville Courier-Journal*, Mar 31, 1983; freelance article by Marilyn Beck, Nov 5, 1983; *Louisville Courier-Journal*, Dec 22, 1957; *Courier-Journal*, June, 19, 1948; *Courier-Journal* April 1, 1969; *Courier-Journal* Jan 9, 1973; Sept 25, 1954; July 1, 1954; Oct 21, 1951; Sept 29, 1951; Sept 5, 1951; March 5, 1945; Aug 16, 1978;

Oct 16, 1972; June 2, 1967; Jan 11, 1967; Jan 4, 1985; Feb 22, 1987; Feb 25, 1926; May 8, 1926; May 9, 1926; Feb 15, 1926; Feb 9, 1926; Jan 10, 1926; Feb 4, 1926; Oct 25, 1925; Feb 9, 1922; July 29, 1923; Oct 24, 1926; Mar 18, 1921; April 6, 1921; Feb 14, 1926; Feb 6, 1926; April 13, 1939; Mar 26, 1936; June 20, 1937; April 12, 1938; Aug 21, 1983; Dec 7, 1986; Jan 6, 1990; Aug 7, 1988; 'A Town Called Louisville' by Joe Creason, *Courier-Journal* Nov 7, 1993.

Chapter 2
Interviews with Father Aldric Heidlage, Father Hilarian Kistner, Nov 11, 1993; Roger Fristoe, Nov 11, 1993; Jeff Bayers, Nov 10, 1993; Caroline Mapother, Nov 7, 1993; Dillon Mapother April 3, 1994; Bill Lewis, Nov 11, 1993; confidential source, Nov 9, 1993. Articles: *Sunday Magazine* Sept 12, 1993; *Sunday Mirror*, Dec 8, 1990; *People*, summer, 1991; *Interview Magazine*, May, 1986; *Washington Post*, Aug 30, 1983; *New York Post*, May 1, 1990; *LA Times*, May 25, 1986; *Rolling Stone*, June 19, 1986; *Courier-Journal*, Mar 31, 1983; *Courier Journal*, April 2, 1950.

Chapters 3 and 4
Interviews with Roger Fristoe, Nov 11, 1993; Jeff Bayers, Nov 10, 1993; Caroline Mapother, Nov 7, 1993; Dillon Mapother April 3, 1994; Bill Lewis, Nov 11, 1993; confidential source, Nov 9, 1993. Articles: *Glen Ridge Paper*, Dec 14, 1978; September 10, 1978; August 31, 1978; March 29, 1979; Feb 2, 1979; Mar 1, 1979; Jan 25, 1979; Jan 18, 1979; Dec 6, 1979; Oct 25, 1979; Oct 11, 1979; Sept 20, 1979; Sept 13, 1979; Sept 6, 1979; July 12, 1979; June 19, 1980; June 12, 1980; *Star*, Sept 6, 1992; April 24, 1980; April 3, 1980; Feb 7, 1980; Jan 31, 1980; Jan 24, 1980; Jan 3, 1980; Jan 3, 1980; July 24, 1980; July 3, 1980; June 14, 1980; *LA Times*, Dec 12, 1993; *Seventeen Magazine*, Feb, 1984; *Current Biography*, April, 1987; *NY Post*, Mar 27, 1992; *Star*, May 15, 1990; *National Enquirer*, Sept 11, 1990; *Sunday Mirror*, Dec 8, 1990; *NY Post*, June 26, 1989; *Sunday Magazine*, Dec 9, 1993; *Cincinnati Examiner*, Nov 13, 1993; *Rolling Stone*, May 28, 1992; *Vanity Fair*, Jan, 1989; *US* magazine, June 30, 1986; *Globe*, Sept 4, 1990; *Daily Mirror*, July 25, 1992; *Ladies Home Journal*, April, 1987; *Santa Monica Evening Outlook*, July 29, 1988; *US* magazine, June 30, 1986.

Chapter 5

Interviews: Angelo Corbo, Nov 4, 1993; Articles: *Hollywood Reporter* Aug 27, 1988; *Village Voice*, July 12, 1988; *Movieline*, Nov 7, 1986; *US* magazine, Aug 18, 1981; *National Enquirer*, Dec 15, 1981; *Globe*, July 21, 1981; *Sanata Monica Evening Outlook*, July 29, 1988; *New York Post*, Nov 21, 1981; *Sunday Mirror*, Dec 27, 1990; *NY Daily News*, Oct 16, 1983; *Broadway Ballyhoo*, July 27, 1981; *LA Times* Aug 9, 1991; *LA Herald Examiner*, June 6, 1981; *Film Journal*, July 20, 1981; *Hollywood Reporter*, Aug 20, 1981; *Hollywood Soundtrade*, July 29, 1981; *New York Times* July 17, 1981.

Chapter 6

Interviews: Jeff Bayers, Nov 11, 1993; Roger Fristoe, Nov 11, 1993; confidential source, Nov 9, 1993. Articles: *Time Magazine*, Dec 14, 1981; *Village Voice*, Dec 9, 1981; *Motion Picture Product Digest*, Dec 16, 1981; *NY Post*, Jan 31, 1982; *Village Voice*, Jan 20, 1982; *Horizon*, March, 1982; *The Film Journal*, Dec 21, 1981; *LA Herald-Examiner*, Dec 20, 1981; Academy of Motion Picture Library, Twentieth Century press release, Dec, 1981; Pennsylvania Dept of Commerce Press Release, Dec, 1981; *NY Daily News*, Nov 22, 1981; *LA Times*, June 14, 1981; *Variety*, May 26, 1981; *Variety*, May 28, 1981; *Variety*, May 21, 1981; *Variety*, June 23, 1980; *Interview* magazine, May, 1986; *Washington Post*, Aug 30, 1983; *Rolling Stone*, June 19, 1986; *US* magazine, July, 1992.

Chapters 7 and 8

Interviews: confidential source, Mar 27, 1994; Mario Modelino, Jan 14, 1994; John Stockwell, Mar 31, 1994; Henry Darrow, Mar 30, 1994; Kale Brown, Jan 14, 1994; confidential source, Apr 1, 1994; Articles; *NY Daily News* Nov 21, 1981; *NY Post*, Oct 24, 1983; *NY Daily Post* May 17, 1985; *NY Daily News*, Oct 16, 1983; *Sunday Mirror*, Dec 27, 1990; *Variety*, June 23, 1980; *Variety*, May 21, 1980; *Village Voice*, April 5, 1983; *Time* magazine, April 4, 1983; *Hollywood Reporter*, Mar 23, 1983; *Sixteen* magazine, March, 1983; *Village Voice*, April 5, 1983; *Rolling Stone*, Aug 11, 1990; *Evening Standard*, May 13, 1982; *New York Post*, Aug 11, 1984; *Interview* magazine, May, 1986; *Moviegoer*, Dec, 1985.

Chapters 9 and 10

Interviews: Roger Fristoe, Nov 11, 1993; John Stockwell, Mar 31, 1994; confidential source, May 2, 1994; confidential source, Nov 26, 1993. Articles; *Hollywood Reporter* Nov 4, 1983; *People* magazine, Nov 7, 1983; *Newsweek*, Aug 29, 1983; *USA Today*, Aug 8, 1983; *Current Biography*, April 1987; *NY Daily News*, Aug 5, 1983; *NY Post*, July 28, 1983; *Variety Daily*, May 20, 1982; *Playboy* Jan, 1990; *US* magazine, Aug 8, 1988; *US* magazine, June 30, 1986; *NY Daily News*, Sept 24, 1986; *Daily News*, Oct 21, 1986; *Star*, June 24, 1986; *Interview* magazine, May, 1986; *Cosmopolitan*, Jan, 1984; *Hollywood Reporter*, Feb 12, 1990; *Playboy* Jan, 1990; *Los Angeles* magazine, Oct, 1993; *Globe*, Oct 2, 1990; *NY Daily News*, Oct 18, 1983; *NY Post* Jan 21, 1986; *NY Post*, Feb 17, 1985; *NY Post*, Jan 7, 1984; *Newark Star-Ledger*, Aug 28, 1983; *NY Post*, Oct 13, 1986; *Star*, Aug 3, 1993; *Totally Uninhibited* by Lawrence J. Quirk, Morrow NY 1991.

Chapters 11 and 12

Interviews: Roger Fristoe, Nov 8, 1993; Bill Ellison, Nov 12, 1993; confidential source, Nov 9, 1993; Caroline Mapother, Nov 7, 1993; Dillon Mapother, Mar 31, 1994; John Stockwell, Mar 31, 1994; confidential source, Mar 26, 1994. Articles: *USA Today*, June 30, 1984; *LA Daily News*, June 27, 1984; *NY Daily News*, Oct 16, 1983, *Cosmopolitan* March, 1984; *Current Biography*, April, 1987; *Rolling Stone*, Sept 15, 1983; *Life*, Jan, 1987; *LA Times*, Aug 31, 1983; *Variety*, May 25, 1987; *LA Herald Examiner*, Oct 22, 1983; *NY Daily News*, Oct 17, 1983; *New York Daily News*, Sept 15, 1983; *Newsweek*, Aug 29, 1983; *USA Today*, Oct 16, 1983; *US* magazine, Aug 8, 1988; *LA Daily News*, May 13, 1986; *New York Daily News*, June 12, 1985; *NY Post*, May 27, 1986; *News*, May 5, 1986, *New York Daily News*, May 26, 1986; *NY Post*, May 8, 1986; *NY Post*, May 12, 1987; *LA Times*, Dec 15, 1993; *Moviegoer*, Dec, 1985; *Variety*, May 16, 1985; *Newsweek*, June 9, 1986; *Star* magazine, June 10, 1986; *People* magazine, June 2, 1986; *People*, Dec 22, 1986; *NY Daily News*, June 24, 1985; *LA Herald Examiner*, Oct 14, 1985; *USA Today*, May 14, 1986; *LA Times*, May 25, 1986; *LA Times*, April 21, 1985; *LA Herald Examiner*, Aug 25, 1985; *Variety*, Apr 3, 1985; *Movieline* magazine, Jan, 1993.

Chapters 13 and 14

Interview: confidential source, Apr 4, 1994. Articles: *Variety*, May 25, 1987; *Newsweek*, May 25, 1987; *LA Times*, May 13, 1987; *People* magazine, July 11, 1986; *Variety*, Oct 10, 1986; *US* magazine, Oct, 1991; *Santa Monica Evening Outlook*, July 29, 1988; *US* magazine, June 30, 1986; *Variety*, Jan 22, 1990; *Newsweek*, Aug 29, 1983; *LA Herald Examiner*, Oct 21, 1987; *Cosmopolitan*, Nov, 1987; *LA Herald Examiner*, Dec 3, 1988; *Newsweek*, Jan 29, 1990; *LA Herald Examiner*, May 26, 1987; *LA Herald Examiner*, Oct 24, 1985; *LA Times*, May 3, 1992; *LA Daily News*, Sept 14, 1993; *LA Times*, Aug 16, 1992; *Chicago Tribune*, Oct 25, 1990; *New York Daily News*, Oct 26, 1990; *Daily News*, Mar 2, 1989; *Daily News*, Oct 22, 1990; *LA Times*, June 29, 1990; *USA Today*, Apr 16, 1987; *NY Post*, Aug 24, 1987; *Globe*, Sept 5, 1989; *Sunday People*, May 29, 1988; *US* magazine, July, 1992; *Star* magazine, Oct 16, 1990; *The Daily Telegraph* magazine, July 18, 1992.

Chapter 15

Articles: *New York Post*, May 27, 1986; *Post*, July 27, 1988; *Christian Science Monitor*, July 29, 1988; *New York Daily News*, July 24, 1988; *Associated Press*, Feb 20, 1992; *L.A. Herald-Examiner*, Oct 21, 1987; *Louisville Courier-Journal*, Aug 7, 1988; *People* magazine, May 30, 1988; *NY Post*, Nov 26, 1987; *Variety*, May 13, 1987; *GQ*, December, 1988; *Newsweek*, Jan 16, 1989; *Louisville Press Telegram*, Dec 16, 1988; *L.A. Times*, Dec 16, 1988; *The Movie Magazine*, June, 1985; *Toronto Sun*, Dec 9, 1988; *L.A. Herald-Examiner* Dec 27, 1988; *L.A. Herald-Examiner*, Oct 15, 1987; *New York Post*, Apr 6, 1986; *Post*, May 5, 1988; *Post*, July 24, 1986; *Post*, Jan 24, 1988; *L.A. Herald-Examiner*, Dec 3, 1988; *Playboy*, Jan, 1990.

Chapter 16

Articles: *Ottawa Citizen*, May 22, 1992; *NY Post*, Mar 29, 1989; *NY News* Apr 29, 1989; *New York Times*, Dec 17, 1989; *US* magazine, Jan 22, 1990; *Rolling Stone*, Jan 11, 1990; *NY Times*, June 3, 1988; *LA Times*, Aug 7, 1988; *NY Times*, Dec 17, 1989; *Vanity Fair*, Jan, 1990; *Time*, Dec 25, 1989; *The Times*, Feb 21, 1990; *Variety*, Dec 23, 1991; *UCLA Daily Bruin*, May 11, 1990; *LA Herald Examiner*, Mar 5, 1989; *LA Herald Examiner*, Mar 29, 1989; *NY Daily News*, Mar 21, 1990; *Daily News*, Feb 20, 1990; *Time* magazine, Jan 22,

WENSLEY

1990; *Time Out* magazine, Mar 1, 1989; *Star*, Mar 20, 1990; *NY Daily News*, Dec 2, 1989; *Daily News*, Feb 20, 1990; *Daily News*, Mar 25, 1989; *NY Times*, Dec 17, 1989; *Daily News*, Mar 25, 1990; *NY Post*, Feb 4, 1988; *Post*, Dec 20, 1989; *USA Today*, Mar 26, 1990; *Globe*, Oct 31, 1989.

Chapters 17 and 18

Articles: *People* magazine, June 9, 1986; *NY Daily News*, Oct 27, 1989; *Daily News*, Feb 15, 1990; *Daily News*, Feb 14, 1990; *New York Time*, June 27, 1990; *Daily News*, Feb 22, 1990; *Daily News*, Jan 3, 1990; *Daily News*, Jan 22, 1990; *Daily News*, July 1, 1990; *Daily News*, Aug 21, 1989; *Daily News*, Oct 20, 1989; *Daily News*, Jan 17, 1990; *NY Post*, Jan 21, 1990; *Car and Driver* magazine, Oct, 1990; *Daily News*, June 6, 1989; *Daily News*, Jan 17, 1990; *Daily News*, Apr 12, 1990; *New York Post*, Oct 31, 1989; *LA Times*, Mar 15, 1990; *Globe*, Oct 31, 1989; *Daily News*, Mar 15, 1990; *Globe*, Sept 5, 1989; *Life Magazine*, June, 1990; *Hollywood Reporter*, Feb 12, 1990; *People* magazine, Feb 12, 1990; *Daily News*, Mar 15, 1990; *Orlando Sentinel*, Jan 23, 1990; *LA Times*, July 17, 1990; *Star*, Jan 30, 1990; *Star*, Feb 6, 1990; *National Enquirer*, Feb 6, 1990; *Star*, March 6, 1990; *USA Today*, Jan 17, 1990; *Star*, Jan 9, 1990; *LA Times*, July 10, 1990; *Star*, July 17, 1990; *USA Today*, June 26, 1990; *LA Daily News*, June 28, 1990; *New York* magazine, Jan 8, 1990; *Press-telegraph*, Apr 23, 1989; *NY Daily News*, Aug 29, 1989; *Hollywood Reporter*, July 16, 1990; *Hollywood Reporter*, May 18, 1990; *LA Times*, Jan 21, 1990; *People* magazine, July 23, 1990; *Hello!* July 1990; *People* magazine, Feb 19, 1990; *Vanity Fair*, July, 1988; *LA Times*, Jan 17, 1990; *Time* magazine, July 13, 1987; *US* magazine, Aug 8, 1990; *Long Beach Times*, June 29, 1990; *Box Office* magazine, July, 1990; *Time* magazine, July 16, 1990; *LA Reader*, June 29, 1990; *Hollywood Reporter*, June 27, 1990; *LA Times*, July 7, 1990; *LA Times*, Sept 17, 1989; *Hollywood Reporter*, Oct, 1989; *LB Press Telegram*, Feb 15, 1990; *People*, April 2, 1990; *Variety*, Feb 15, 1990; *US* magazine, Dec 26, 1988; *Rolling Stone*, July 12, 1990; *National Enquirer*, Jan 30, 1990; *Screen International*, June 30, 1990; *LA Times*, July 10, 1990; *Variety*, May 7, 1990; *LA Times*, July 6, 1990; *Screen International*, Nov 18, 1989; *Screen International*, Mar 10, 1990; *LA Times*, Dec 25, 1989; *New York*, June 25, 1990; *US* magazine, July, 1992; *Newsweek*, Jan 29, 1990; *Vanity Fair*, Jan, 1989.

Chapter 19

Interviews: Tim Burstall, April 7, 1993, confidential source, April 10, 1993, Scott Murray, April 8, 1993, confidential source, April 8, 1994. Articles: *Woman's Day*, Jan 22, 1990; *Woman's Day*, May 22, 1990; *Sunday Telegraph*, June 10, 1990; *New Idea*, July 14, 1990; *TV Week*, Sept 8, 1990; *Sydney Morning Herald*, Aug 30, 1990; Sept 11, 1990; *Woman's Day*, Sept 25, 1990; *Sydney Morning Herald*, Sept 3, 1990; *Sunday Telegraph*, Dec 8, 1991; *Telegraph Mirror*, June 13, 1991; *Woman's Day*, March 19, 1991; *Telegraph Mirror*, Dec 27, 1990; *Sydney Morning Herald*, Nov 13, 1990; *Daily Mirror*, Oct 5, 1990; *Telegraph Mirror*, Mar 6, 1991; May 1, 1991; *Morning Herald*, May 1, 1991; *Telegraph Mirror*, June 24, 1991; *Sunday Telegraph*, Oct 20, 1991; *Sunday Telegraph*, Nov 3, 1991; Dec 4, 1991; Dec 5, 1991; Dec 7, 1991; Dec 5, 1991; *TV Week*, Dec 14, 1991; *New Idea*, Dec 28, 1991; *Telegraph*, Aug 24, 1990; *TV Week*, Aug 25, 1990; *Sunday Telegraph*, Aug 26, 1990; *Morning Herald*, Aug 30, 1990; *Women's Weekly*, September, 1990; *Daily Telegraph*, Aug 15, 1990; *Daily Mirror*, Aug 15, 1990; *Daily Telegraph*, Aug 11, 1990; *Daily Mirror*, July 13, 1990; *Sunday Telegraph*, April 8, 1990; *TV Week*, Apr 14, 1990; *Telegraph*, May 10, 1989; *Australian* magazine, Mar 11, 1989; *Daily Mirror*, June 19, 1989; June 24, 1988; *Sun Telegraph*, May 15, 1988; May 3, 1987; July 16, 1986; *Daily Mirror*, Feb 24, 1987; *LA Times*, Sept 9, 1990; *Star*, October 23, 1990; *NY Daily News*, June 15, 1990; *Vanity Fair*, July, 1990; *National Enquirer*, July 17, 1990; *People* magazine, Jan 14, 1991; *Woman's Day*, Dec 24, 1991; *NY Daily News*, Sept 14, 1990; Jan 8, 1989; *NY Post*, Dec 24, 1990; Oct 3, 1990; June 25, 1990; *NY Daily News Sept 4, 1990; Nov 7, 1990; Sept 14, 1990; Daily Mirror*, Sept 22, 1988; *Telegraph*, Nov 18, 1987; *Australian*, Dec 1, 1986; *Australian*, Mar 11, 1989; *US* magazine, Aug 8, 1988; *Playboy*, Jan, 1990.

Chapter 20

Interviews: Nick Williamson, April 7, 1994; confidential source, Feb 15, 1994; Finbarr Nowlan, Dec 21, 1993. Articles: *NY Daily News*, June 15, 1992; *Daily Star*, August, 1992; *LA Weekly*, May 29, 1992; *Variety*, May 11, 1992; *New Yorker*, June 1, 1992; *Village View*, May 22, 1992; *Wall Street Journal*, May 21, 1992; *USA Today*, May 22, 1992; *Hello!* Sept 9, 1991; *Hollywood* reporter craft series, 1992; *Daily Mirror*, April 10, 1992; *People* magazine special, Spring, 1992;

People magazine, June 8, 1992; *People* magazine, Mar 8, 1992; *Toronto Star*, May 22, 1992; *NY Daily News*, Feb 14, 1992; *Daily News*, Mar 18, 1991; *NY Times*, May 22, 1992; *NY Daily News*, May 21, 1992; *Daily News*, May 8, 1992; July 22, 1992; *Daily News*, May 22, 1992; Nov 14, 1992; May 1, 1992; *USA Today*, Aug 22, 1991; *NY Post*, May 13, 1992; *Daily News*, May 17, 1991; *NY Post*, Feb 9, 1991; *NY Daily News*, May 21, 1992; *LA Daily News*, Aug 8, 1991; *People* magazine, Aug 3, 1992; *LA Life*, May 8, 1992; *RTE Guide*, Sept 6, 1991; *Irish Independent*, Aug 17, 1991; *Irish Press*, May 29, 1991; *The Sun*, July 20, 1992; *Toronto Star*, Aug 11, 1992; *Daily Express*, Aug 7, 1992; *You* magazine, July 5, 1992; *Sunday* magazine, Jan 19, 1992; *Sunday Mirror Magazine*, July 19, 1992; *NY Post*, Mar 22, 1991; *US* magazine, July, 1992.

Chapter 21
Interview: Stephanie Mansfield, April 4, 1994. Articles: *US* magazine, Jan, 1993; *GQ* magazine, December, 1992; *NY Daily News*, Aug 1, 1991; *NY Daily News*, Nov 19, 1992; *Daily News*, Jan 2, 1992; *Daily News*, Mar 28, 1991; Nov 5, 1991; Dec 7, 1992; *Venice Magazine*, Dec, 1992; *NY Post*, Jan 18, 1991; *Vogue*, Jan, 1993; *LA Times*, Jan 11, 1992; *People* magazine, Apr 5, 1992; *Washington Times*, Oct 3, 1991; *Los Angeles* magazine, Oct, 1993; *Screen International*, Nov 5, 1993.

Chapter 22
Interviews: confidential source, Nov 20, 1993. Articles: *Dramalogue*, July 15, 1993; *LA Times*, May 12, 1993; *The Independent*, Sept 10, 1993; *Dallas Morning News*, Jan 21, 1993; *New York Daily News*, Feb 26, 1993; *The People*, Nov 7, 1993; *Daily Mirror*, April 20, 1993; *Star*, Sept 3, 1993; *Daily Mail*, Aug 28, 1993; *Memphis BJ*, July 5, 1993; July 22, 1992; Nov 10, 1992; *The Commercial*, Nov 10, 1992; Sept 16, 1992; July 24, 1993; *St Petersburg Times*, Oct 21, 1992; *Star*, Dec 15, 1992; Dec 22, 1992; *National Enquirer*, May 4, 1993; *Star*, Sept 7, 1993; *The Independent*, Sept 11, 1993; *LA Times*, June 27, 1993; *New York Post*, June 15, 1993; *USA Today*, Feb 26, 1992; *People* magazine, July 26, 1993; *NY Post*, Apr 6, 1993; *NY Daily News*, July 29, 1993; *Today*, June 26, 1993; *Daily Mirror*, July 29, 1993; *Newsweek*, Apr 26, 1993; *People* magazine, July 12, 1993; *Variety*, July 12, 1993; *Variety*, June 28, 1993; *LA Times*, June 30,

1993; *Variety*, June 24, 1993; *Conde Nast Traveler*, July 1993; *LA Times*, June 29, 1990; *Variety*, July 19, 1992; July 14, 1992; *Hollywood Reporter*, Sept 16, 1991; *LA Life*, Apr 15, 1992; *Rolling Stone*, Mar 28, 1992; *LA Weekly*, July 2, 1993.

Chapter 23

Interviews: Stephanie Mansfield, April 4, 1994; John Richardson, April 5, 1994; confidential security source, April 2, 1994; confidential source, Mar 31, 1994; confidential source, May 28, 1994. Articles: *Los Angeles* magazine, September, 1980; *LA Daily News*, July 28, 1992; *NY Daily News*, May 25, 1990; *NY Post*, Aug 7, 1993; *NY Post*, Mar 25, 1992; *NY Daily News*, Jan 12, 1993; *Daily News*, Feb 14, 1992; *NY Times*, July 23, 1986; *Los Angeles* magazine, Nov, 1993; *LA Times*, Oct 17, 1993; *Time* magazine, May 6, 1991; *LA Times*, June 25, 1990; *People* magazine, Aug 24, 1978; *People* magazine, June 3, 1985; *Village Voice*, Dec 19, 1991; *New York* magazine, May 20, 1991; *Daily Mirror*, Aug 26, 1993; *Hollywood Reporter*, Aug 6, 1993; *Los Angeles* magazine, Jan, 1994; *Spy* magazine, April, 1992; *LA Daily News*, Sept 16, 1992; *NY Post*, Nov 28, 1992; *Star* magazine, July 31, 1990; *LA Daily News*, July 23, 1992; Aug 11, 1993; *NY Daily News*, Oct 3, 1993; *NY Post*, Sept 23, 1993; *LA Daily News*, July 23, 1992; *NY Post*, Sept 23, 1993; *NY Daily News*, Sept 23, 1993; *Sunday Times*, Nov 8, 1987; *Daily Mail*, Sept 25, 1987; *Village Voice*, Nov 12, 1991; *Daily Express*, Aug 7, 1992; *Premiere* magazine, Sept, 1993; *LA Times*, June 25, 1990; *California* magazine, June, 1991; *Los Angeles* magazine, Oct, 1993; *The Times*, May 28, 1994; *Celebrity* magazine, issue 275, issue 274; *US* magazine, July, 1992; *LA Times*, Oct 6, 1991.

Chapter 24

Interviews: Stephanie Mansfield, April 4, 1994; confidential source, Feb 9, 1994; confidential source, Dec 10, 1993; confidential source, April 2, 1994. Articles: *New York Daily News*, Sept 3, 1993; *Hollywood Reporter*, Sept 13, 1993; *NY Daily News*, Sept 3, 1993; *LA Daily News*, May 6, 1993; *Premiere* magazine, Aug, 1993; *Variety*, Jan 20, 1994; *New York* magazine, Jan 24, 1994; *Hollywood Reporter*, Jan 3, 1994; *Variety*, Dec 13, 1993; *Variety*, Jan 3, 1994; *LA Daily News*, Feb 14, 1994; *New York* magazine, Dec 6, 1993; *LA*

Times, Mar 22, 1994; *Evening Standard*, Dec 30, 1993; *The People*, Dec 12, 1993; *Daily Mirror*, Mar 10, 1994; *Hollywood Reporter*, Oct 29, 1993; *People* magazine, Dec 6, 1993; *Variety*, Feb 22, 1993; *Hollywood Reporter*, Oct 21, 1993; *People* magazine, Jan 11, 1993; *Variety*, Sept 23, 1993; *People* magazine, Aug 30, 1993; *Parade* magazine, Sept 12, 1993; *US* magazine, July, 1992; *Playboy*, Jan, 1990; *Interview* magazine, May, 1986.

Chapter 25

Interviews: Stephanie Mansfield, April 4, 1994; confidential source, April 2, 1994; Roger Fristoe, Nov 11, 1993; John Stockwell, Mar 31, 1994; Warder Harrison, Nov 11, 1993. Articles: *LA Times*, Oct 1, 1993; *Globe*, Aug 10, 1993; *Hollywood Reporter*, May 5, 1992; *LA Life*, Aug 10, 1993; *Variety*, June 23, 1993; *Hollywood Reporter*, Sept 13, 1993; *New York Daily News*, Oct 22, 1993; *Daily News*, Jan 13, 1992; *Daily News*, Mar 11, 1992; *New York Live*, Aug 8, 1993; *Daily News*, Apr 9, 1993; *Entertainment Weekly*, Jan 14, 1994; *Daily Express*, Sept 11, 1993; *New York Post*, Sept 3, 1993; *Entertainment Weekly*, Nov 26, 1993; *New York Daily News*, Nov 4, 1992; *The People*, Jan 16, 1994; *NY Daily News*, Sept 2, 1993; *Daily News*, May 19, 1992; *Daily News*, Nov 30, 1992; *Daily News*, Apr 15, 1992; *Daily News*, Apr 29, 1992; *Daily Mirror*, Nov 3, 1992; *NY Daily News*, Dec 3, 1992; *People* magazine, Apr 26, 1993; *NY Daily News*, Aug 13, 1993; *Daily Express*, Jan 7, 1994; *Time Out*, July 15, 1992; *The Sunday Times*, Apr 10, 1994; *LA Times*, July 22, 1988; *Daily Mail*, Feb 24, 1994; *Daily Express*, Aug 17, 1993; *Movieline*, Apr 1994; *Daily Mirror*, Jan 19, 1994; *The People*, Nov 28, 1993; *Today*, Nov 11, 1993; *The People*, Jan 2, 1994; *The Times*, July 19, 1993; *LA Times*, Aug 16, 1992; *Playboy*, March, 1993; *Evening Standard*, Mar 3, 1993; *NY Post*, Feb 15, 1992; *Globe* magazine, Nov 20, 1990.

Chapter 26

Interviews: confidential source, May 10, 1994; confidential source, Mar 31, 1994. Articles: *Redbook*, Nov, 1993; *Variety*, Feb 18, 1993; *Globe*, Aug 10, 1993; *Daily Express*, Oct 23, 1993; *National Enquirer*, Jan 15, 1991; *Globe*, July 16, 1992; *LA Life*, Aug 14, 1991; *National Enquirer*, Dec 22, 1992; *USA Today*, Feb 26, 1992; *USA Today*, Jan 14, 1992; *New York Daily News*, Aug 8, 1991; *USA Today*, Dec 12, 1992; *National Enquirer*, Aug 31, 1993; *New York Post*, Dec 8, 1992;

LA Times, July 28, 1993; *Woman's Own*, Sept 13, 1993; *New York Post*, Dec 8, 1992; *NY Daily News*, Jan 25, 1993; *Daily News*, Dec 14, 1992; *Daily News*, June 21, 1993; *Daily News*, Feb 3, 1993; *Daily News*, Aug 22, 1993; *Daily News*, Sept 29, 1993; *Daily News*, Aug 9, 1991; *Daily News*, Oct 22, 1993; *Daily Star*, Dec 29, 1992; *National Enquirer*, Feb 4, 1992; *USA Today*, Jan 14, 1992; *The Sun*, Jan 25, 1993; *Daily Express*, Dec 24, 1992; *People*, Apr 26, 1993; *Star* magazine, Nov 17, 1992; *USA Today*, Oct 23, 1992.

Chapter 27
Interviews: James Cowan, Mar 20, 1994; Anthony Clare, Jan 30, 1994; Joseph Bennett, May 5, 1994. Articles: *Daily Mail*, Dec 13, 1993; *USA Today*, July 15, 1993; *USA Today*, Aug 20, 1993; *LA Times*, Aug 26, 1993; *LA Times*, July 15, 1993; *Daily Mail*, Nov 19, 1993; *LA Times*, July 19, 1993; *Variety*, July 14, 1993; *St Louis Post-Dispatch*, Sept 7, 1993; *Daily Telegraph*, Oct 16, 1993; *Entertainment Weekly*, Oct 22, 1993; *Movieline*, Jan, 1994; *Globe*, Jan 18, 1994; *Variety*, July 14, 1993; *LA Times*, July 15, 1993; *Today*, Nov 22, 1993; *LA Times*, Aug 22, 1993; *Today*, Dec 13, 1993; *Entertainment Weekly*, Oct 22, 1993; *Daily Mirror*, Sept 27, 1993; *The People*, Oct 31, 1993; *Evening Standard*, Feb 16, 1994; *Daily Mirror*, Sept 13, 1993; *You* magazine, Mar 20, 1994; *Sky Magazine*, March, 1994; *Esquire*, Mar, 1994; *The Independent*, Sept 15, 1993.

Filmography

Endless Love (1981) Director: Franco Zeffirelli. Producer Dyson Lovell. Screenplay: Scott Spencer. Photography: David Watkin. Editor: Michael J. Sheridan. Music: Jonathan Tunick. Released by: Polygram. Cast: Brooke Shields, Martin Hewitt, Shirley Knight, Don Murray, Richard Kiley, Tom Cruise.
Fee: NA
US Box Office: NA

Taps (1982) Director: Harold Becker. Producers: Stanley R. Jaffe, Howard B. Jaffe. Screenplay: Darryl Ponicsan and Robert Mark Kamen. Photography: Owen Roizman. Editor: Maury Winetrobe. Music: Maurice Jarre. Released by: Twentieth Century-Fox. Cast: George C. Scott, Timothy Hutton, Sean Penn, Tom Cruise, Brendan Ward, John P. Navin.
Fee: $70,000
US Box Office: $20.5 million

Losin 'It (1983) Director: Curtis Hanson. Producers: Bryan Gindoff and Hannah Hampstead. Screenplay: B.W.L.Norton. Photography: Cami Dempsy Taylor. Editor: Richard Halsey. Released by: Embassy Pictures. Cast: Tom Cruise, Jackie Earle Haley, John Stockwell, Shelley Long, Henry Darrow.
Fee: $100,000
US Box Office: NA

The Outsiders (1983) Director: Francis Ford Coppola. Producers: Fred Roos, Gray Frederickson. Screenplay: Kathleen Knutsen Rowell from a book by S.F. Hinton. Photography: Stephen H. Burum. Editor: Anne Goursaud. Music: Carmine Coppola. Released by: Warner Brothers. Cast: Matt Dillon, Emilio Estevez, Rob Lowe, C. Thomas Howell, Tom Cruise, Patrick Swayze, Ralph Macchio, Diane Lane.
Fee: $30,000
US Box office: $26 million

Risky Business (1983) Written and directed by: Paul Brickman. Producers: Steve Tisch and Jon Avnet. Photography: Reynaldo Villalobo and Bruce Surtees. Editor: Richard Chew. Music: Tangerine Dream. Released by Geffen Films. Cast: Tom Cruise, Rebecca DeMornay, Joe Pantoliano, Richard Masur, Bronson Pinchot, Curtis Armstrong.
Fee: $200,000
US Box Office: $63 million

All The Right Moves (1983) Director: Michael Chapman. Producer: Stephen Deutsch. Screenplay: Michael Kane. Photography: Jan De Bont. Editor: David Garfield. Music: David Campbell. Cast: Tom Cruise, Craig T. Nelson, Lea Thompson, Christopher Penn, Gary Graham.
Fee: $200,000
US Box Office: $20 million

Legend (1985) Director: Ridley Scott. Producer: Arnon Mildan. Screenplay: William Hjortssers. Photography: Alex Thompson. Editor: Terry Rawlings. Music: Tangerine Dream. Cast: Tom Cruise, Tim Curry, Mia Sara, Annbelle Lanyon, David Bennent, Alice Playten, Billy Barty.
Fee: $500,000
US Box Office: $15.5 million

Top Gun (1986) Director: Tony Scott. Producers: Don Simpson and Jerry Bruckheimer. Screenplay: Jim Cash and Jack Epps, Jr. Photography: Jeffrey Kimball. Editor: Billy Weber and Chris Lebetzan. Music: Harold Faltermeyer. Released by Paramount. Cast: Tom Cruise, Kelly McGillis, Anthony Edwards, Val Kilmer, Rick Rossovich, Tom Skerrit, Michael Ironside.
Fee: $2 million
US Box Office: $177 million

The Color of Money (1987) Director: Martin Scorsese. Producers: Irving Axelrad and Barbara De Fina. Screenplay: Richard Price based on a novel by Walter Trevis. Photography: Michael Ballhaus. Editor: Thelma Schoonmaker. Music: Robbie Robertson. Cast: Paul Newman, Tom Cruise, Elizabeth Mastrantonio, Helen Shaver, John Turtorro, Billy Cobbs, Forest Whittaker.
Fee: $2 million
US Box Office: $52 million

Cocktail (1988) Director: Roger Donaldson. Producers: Ted Field and Robert W. Cort. Screenplay: Heywood Gould, from his own book. Photography: Dean Semler. Editor: Neil Trank. Music: J. Peter Robinson. Released by: Touchstone Pictures. Cast: Tom Cruise, Bryan Brown, Elizabeth Shue, Lawrence Luckinbill, Ron Dean.
Fee: $4 million
US Box Office: $78 million

Rain Main (1988) Director: Barry Levinson. Producer: Mark Johnson. Screenplay: Barry Morrow and Ronald Bass. Photography: John Seale. Editor: Stu Linder. Music: Hans Zimmer. Released by United Artists. Cast: Dustin Hoffman, Tom Cruise, Valerie Golina, Jerry Molen, Jack Murdock, Michael D. Roberts, Ralph Seymour, Lucinda Jenney, Bonnie Hunt, Kim Robillard, Beth Grant.
Fee: $5 million (plus profit points)
US Box Office: $173 million

Born on the Fourth of July (1989) Director: Oliver Stone. Producers: A. Kitman Ho and Oliver Stone. Screenplay: Oliver Stone and Ron Kovic. Photography: Robert Richardson. Editor: David Brenner, Music: John Williams. Cast: Tom Cruise, Bryan Larkin, Raymond J. Barry, Caroline Kava, Josh Evans.
Fee: Approximately $1 million (profit points only)
US Box Office: $70 million

Days of Thunder (1990) Director: Tony Scott. Producers: Don Simpson and Jerry Bruckheimer. Screenplay: Robert Towne. Editor: Billy Weber. Released by: Paramount. Cast: Tom Cruise, Nicole Kidman, Robert Duvall, Randy Quaid.
Fee: $10 million
US BOx Office: $83 million

Far and Away (1991) Director: Ron Howard. Producers: Brian Grazer and Ron Howard. Screenplay by: Bob Dolman. Photography: Mikael Saloman. Editors: Michael Hill, Daniel Hanley. Music: John Williams. Released by: Universal. Cast: Tom Cruise, Nicole Kidman, Thomas Gibson, Barbara Babcock, Robert Prosky, Colin Meaney, Eileen Pollack, Michelle Johnson.
Fee: $12 million
US Box Office: $59 million

A Few Good Men (1992) Directed by Rob Reiner. Screenplay: Aaron Sorkin. Released by: Columbia Pictures. Cast: Tom Cruise, Jack Nicholson, Demi Moore, J.T. Walsh, Kevin Pollack, Kevin Bacon.
Fee: $12.5 million
US Box Office: $102 million

The Firm (1993) Director: Sidney Pollack. Producers: Scott Rudin, John Davis. Screenplay: David Rabe, Robert Towne and David Rayfiel. Photography: John Seale. Editors: William Steinkamp, Frederic Steinkamp. Music: David Grusin. Released by: Paramount. Cast: Tom Cruise, Gene Hackman, Jeanne Tripplehorn, Ed Harris, Wilford Brimley, Gary Busey, Holly Hunter, Tobin Bell.
Fee: $15 million
US Box Office: $155 million

The Frightening Frammies (1993) Director: Tom Cruise. Producer: William Hornberg. Screenplay: Jim Thompson. Released by: Showtime. Cast: Isabella Rossellini, Nancy Travis, Peter Gallagher.
Fee: $70,000
US Box Office: Cable television only.

Interview with the Vampire (1994) Director: Neil Jordan. Producer: Stephen Woolley. Screenplay: Neil Jordan, based on a book by Anne Rice. Released by Warner Brothers. Cast: Tom Cruise, Brad Pitt, Antonio Banderas, Stephen Rea, Christian Slater, Miranda Richardson.
Fee: $15 million
US Box Office: NA

Index

INDEX